T0214272

Communications in Computer and Information Science 1055

Commenced Publication in 2007
Founding and Former Series Editors:
Phoebe Chen, Alfredo Cuzzocrea, Xiaoyong Du, Orhun Kara, Ting Liu,
Krishna M. Sivalingam, Dominik Ślęzak, Takashi Washio, Xiaokang Yang,
and Junsong Yuan

Editorial Board Members

Simone Diniz Junqueira Barbosa ⓘD
Pontifical Catholic University of Rio de Janeiro (PUC-Rio),
Rio de Janeiro, Brazil

Joaquim Filipe ⓘD
Polytechnic Institute of Setúbal, Setúbal, Portugal

Ashish Ghosh
Indian Statistical Institute, Kolkata, India

Igor Kotenko ⓘD
St. Petersburg Institute for Informatics and Automation of the Russian
Academy of Sciences, St. Petersburg, Russia

Lizhu Zhou
Tsinghua University, Beijing, China

More information about this series at http://www.springer.com/series/7899

Sergey V. Ablameyko · Viktor V. Krasnoproshin ·
Maryna M. Lukashevich (Eds.)

Pattern Recognition and Information Processing

14th International Conference, PRIP 2019
Minsk, Belarus, May 21–23, 2019
Revised Selected Papers

 Springer

Editors
Sergey V. Ablameyko
Belarusian State University
Minsk, Belarus

Viktor V. Krasnoproshin
Belarusian State University
Minsk, Belarus

Maryna M. Lukashevich
Belarusian State University of Informatics
and Radioelectronics
Minsk, Belarus

ISSN 1865-0929   ISSN 1865-0937 (electronic)
Communications in Computer and Information Science
ISBN 978-3-030-35429-9   ISBN 978-3-030-35430-5   (eBook)
https://doi.org/10.1007/978-3-030-35430-5

This Springer imprint is published by the registered company Springer Nature Switzerland AG
The registered company address is: Gewerbestrasse 11, 6330 Cham, Switzerland

Preface

This book contains papers that have been presented at 14th International conference on Pattern Recognition and Information Processing (PRIP 2019).

The PRIP conference series is always held in Minsk, Belarus, and has a long history. It started in 1991 as the First USSR All-Union Conference on Pattern Recognition and Image Analysis. This first conference was held in October 1991, and more than 200 researchers participated in the conference. In December 1992, after the collapse of the USSR, the Belarusian Association for Image Analysis and Recognition (BAIAR) was founded and in March 1993 the International Association of Pattern Recognition (IAPR) officially accepted BAIAR as a national representative of Belarus in IAPR. Since then, the PRIP conference series has been held every two-three consecutive years. The conference in 2019 was the 14th conference in this series.

Nowadays, the PRIP conference series is well-known and well-recognized. Information about PRIP is included in all major home pages on computer vision and pattern recognition. Conference proceedings are cited in INSPEC – the main world database of publications.

PRIP is held in cooperation with other scientific establishments. PRIP 2019, as in previous conferences, was endorsed by IAPR.

120 papers were submitted to PRIP 2019 from 22 countries (289 authors). All submitted papers were reviewed by Program Committee members together with referees. As a result, 98 papers were selected for inclusion in the PRIP 2019 scientific program.

PRIP 2019 was held at the Belarusian State University of Informatics and Radioelectronics, the leading IT-Belarusian university, during May 21–23, 2019.

PRIP 2019 was made up of two categories of sessions: a plenary and a regular one. At plenary sessions, presentations were made by three invited speakers. All of the sessions were held in a single track and participants had enough time for hot discussions after each presentation.

The PRIP 2019 proceedings present new results in the area of pattern recognition and image processing and its applications.

Proceedings of PRIP conferences are regularly published by conference organizers. This year, a collection of selected papers, among those accepted to the program of the PRIP conference, were published in Springer's *Communications in Computer and Information Science* (CCIS) series.

This book includes the best papers from the conference selected by the PRIP Program Committee. These papers have been extended by their authors and the papers have been reviewed again.

The book is divided into three parts. The first part contains plenary (invited) lectures of famous scientists. The second part contains theoretical papers in the area of pattern recognition and image analysis. The third part includes applied papers that are devoted to applications of image and information processing in industry, medicine, video-surveillance, and other areas.

The book is aimed towards researchers working in pattern recognition and image analysis, as well as knowledge processing and knowledge-based decision support system.

April 2019

Sergey Ablameyko
Viktor V. Krasnoproshin
Maryna Lukashevich

Organization

The International Conference on Pattern Recognition and Information Processing (PRIP) was hosted by the Belarusian State University of Informatics and Radioelectronics in cooperation with the Belarusian State University, the United Institute of Informatics Problems of the National Academy of Sciences of Belarus, and the Belarusian Association for Image Analysis and Recognition.

Honorary Chairman

Vadim Bogush, Belarus

Chairman of the Conference

Valery Prytkov, Belarus

Vice-chairmen of the Conference

Alexander Tuzikov, Belarus
Sergey Ablameyko, Belarus

International Program Committee

Alexander Doudkin, Belarus
Alexey Petrovsky, Russia
Anatoly Sachenko, Ukraine
Andrzej Dziech, Poland
Angelo Marcelli, Italy
Elena Zaitseva, Slovakia
Gabriella Sanniti di Baja, Italy
Gunilla Borgefors, Sweden
Hubert Roth, Germany
Igor Gurevich, Russia
Ingela Nystrom, Sweden
Janusz Zalewsky, USA
Jean-Jacques Mariage, France
Kurosh Madani, France
Luigi Gallo, Italy
Maria Frucci, Italy

Mikhail Tatur, Belarus
Qiangfu Zhao, Japan
Robert Hiromoto, USA
Seiichi Uchida, Japan
Slobodan Ribaric, Croatia
Stanislav Sedukhin, Japan
Svetlana Yanushkevich, Canada
Valery Starovoitov, Belarus
Viktor Krasnoproshin, Belarus
Vincenzo Piuri, Italy
Vladimir Golenkov, Belarus
Vladimir Red'ko, Russia
Vlarimir Golovko, Belarus
Ye Shiping, China
Yuriy Kharin, Belarus
Yuriy Zhuravlev, Russia

Additional Reviewers

Maryna Lukashevich, Belarus
Vladimir Obraztsov, Belarus
Valery Prytkov, Belarus
Boris Nikulshin, Belarus
Dmitry Pertsau, Belarus
Alexander Tuzikov, Belarus
Sergey Ablameyko, Belarus
Vitaly Levashenko, Slovakia
Vladimir Shmerko, Canada

Alexander Dorogov, Russia
Alexander Vasilyev, Russia
Kolokolov Yury, Russia
Dvoenko Sergey, Russia
Valery Pisarenko, Ukraine
Jan Owsinski, Poland
Tadeusx Pawlowski, Poland
Vissia Herman, Netherlands
Volodymyr Turchenko, Ukraine

Local Organizing Committee

Maryna Lukashevich
   (Chairman), Belarus
Boris Nikulshin, Belarus
Eugene Sasin, Belarus
Natalia Iskra, Belarus
Sidarovich Aliaksandra, Belarus
Dziana Kupryianova, Belarus

Dzmitry Adzinets, Belarus
Anton Tratsiakou, Belarus
Ulyana Kiklevich, Belarus
Dmitry Pertsau, Belarus
Vladimir Obraztsov, Belarus
Valeria Makeeva, Belarus
Igor Frolov, Belarus

In Collaboration with

International Associations for Pattern Recognition
Netcracker Technology
ISsoft Solutions

Contents

Information Processing and Applications

Summarizing Lecture (Plenary Papers)

Recent Progress in Computer-Vision-Based Human Activity Recognition and Related Areas

Gerhard Rigoll$^{(\boxtimes)}$

Institute for Human-Machine Communication, TU Munich, Munich, Germany
rigoll@tum.de
http://www.mmk.ei.tum.de

Abstract. This paper presents some more recent developments in the research area of human activity recognition. In many cases, human activity recognition can be achieved with the support of body sensors that deliver information about the motion of a person or about acceleration and position. Such data can contribute substantially to the accuracy of the results, however wearing extra equipment is not a very popular practice for most human users and therefore camera-based methods are mostly preferred in today's systems, which is also a result of the tremendous progress achieved in recent years in pattern recognition and machine learning. Therefore, also this paper concentrates on camera-based methods for human activity recognition. Activity recognition has a large variety of sub-research areas and has many exciting application areas, such as e.g. interaction in smart spaces, surveillance, human-robot interaction or automatic analysis of interest, emotions and human traits.

Keywords: Computer Vision · Machine learning · Activity recognition · Gesture recognition · Gait recognition · Object tracking

1 Introduction

In the area of Computer Vision and Pattern Recognition, tremendous progress has been observed in recent years. It is quite obvious, that this is strongly related to the recent success of advanced machine learning methods, especially in the area of Deep Learning. Human activity recognition is nowadays mainly realized with camera-based methods, because the use of sensors for e.g. motion capture is typically coming with additional restrictions concerning comfort and mobility and is therefore less popular for humans. Therefore, human activity recognition has become a research area which is very closely connected to Computer Vision and Pattern Recognition. It is therefore not surprising that also advanced machine learning techniques play a constantly increasing role for human activity recognition. In this presentation, the major sub-areas for human activity recognition are investigated, namely:

- person tracking
- posture tracking
- gesture recognition
- action recognition
- gait recognition

S. V. Ablameyko et al. (Eds.): PRIP 2019, CCIS 1055, pp. 3–7, 2019.
https://doi.org/10.1007/978-3-030-35430-5_1

where special emphasis is given to the description of the transition from the use of traditional pattern recognition approaches, such as e.g. Hidden-Markov Models (HMMs) towards novel machine learning paradigms, especially the use of Deep Learning methods.

2   Person Tracking

In this research area one could observe a transition from single person tracking to multiple person tracking and even crowd tracking during the last approx. 20 years. There is also an observed development of the major employed algorithms over those years: The first successful person tracking systems were often based on a classical Kaman-Filter (KF) approach, where the motion model was realized by the system equation of the KF and the measurement equation included the position information obtained from the captured image of the camera. Then for many years, this method has been substituted by the very popular Particle-Filter (PF) approach, where the sampling of the camera image and the weighting of the particles were the major components for computing the bounding box of a tracked human and the motion model was mainly implemented in the generation of the new particles. One of the major reasons, why the PF approach has been partially replaced by other methods is the fact that the PF as well as the KF approach are somewhat difficult to apply for tracking a large number of people at the same time. Nowadays, approaches for multi-camera multi-person tracking are employed, that are mainly based on "tracking-by-detection", where a state-of-the-art detector localizes in one image frame a potentially huge number of persons and these detections are linked across frames which the help of a data-association approach where a possible trajectory for each object is hypothesized leading to a tracking hypergraph and trajectories for many individuals are computed with a flow graph approach based on this hypergraph. It has turned out that this is a very powerful approach which can also elegantly integrate the use of multiple cameras which are helpful to resolve occlusions by delivering detections of objects from different view-points. But even here, many challenges remain unsolved, such as e.g. handling occlusions, false alarms or person re-identification of objects which are e.g. crossing each other and where ID-switches might occur. This is nowadays the occasion where deep learning methods are also helpful to tackle these problems. In the paper presentation there will be shown examples where feedforward and recurrent deep neural networks are employed to e.g. compute the appearance similarity between detections or predict the motion of objects crossing each other.

3   Gesture Recognition

This research area has also a long tradition, reaching back to the early 1990s. Many of the first developed successful gesture recognition systems from that early generation were based on the popular dynamic pattern recognition principles that were already available at that time, of which the Hidden-Markov-Models (HMMs) where likely the most popular and powerful ones, since they were especially developed for highly dynamic patterns in areas like speech and handwriting recognition. HMMs were subsequently and successfully transferred to the task of dynamic gesture recognition, where each gesture is modeled by a multi-state HMM and a sequence of observations is computed from the frames of the captured video sequence. The paper presentation will introduce some more recent approaches that are replacing the traditional HMM approach and are again heavily based on machine learning techniques. Surprisingly, even "static" feedforward deep neural networks are nowadays yielding high recognition rates for dynamic gesture recognition tasks, by fusing static pixel information and dynamic motion information, e.g. obtained from improved optical flow computation methods, where sliding window techniques can be used to compensate for the missing dynamic time-modeling component of classical convolutional neural networks (CNNs). Also, neural network architectures can be employed here that are more suited for the dynamic nature of gesture patterns, such as e.g. LSTM neural networks.

4 Action Recognition

Action recognition is somewhat similar to gesture recognition, where one of the most significant differences is the fact that in gesture recognition, different classes are mostly characterized by also distinct motion patterns for each class, where the object in the video sequence is usually the same (i.e. the hand or arm). In contrast, different action classes could be characterized by the same motion pattern but by the occurrence of different objects in the video (e.g. playing tennis vs. playing baseball). Additionally, the number of possible classes can be much larger because the number of possible hand gestures is rather small in comparison with general human actions that can occur in daily situations and environments as e.g. living, cooking or sports. Therefore, action recognition can be considered as the more difficult and challenging pattern recognition task. It also means that the classifier in this case needs to process motion information as well as the information about objects or even colors in the video sequence. It is therefore important to find out which dynamic and static information needs to be extracted from each video frame and how these data streams can be optimally combined. Since neural networks were even in their early generation well-known for effective feature fusion/combination due to the trainable synaptic weighting of these different information sources, it is not amazing that also here, deep neural networks have been already applied very successfully, similar to the previously mentioned area of gesture recognition. The presentation will show possibilities to represent the static and the motion information in a compact way to the input layer of neural networks, because the presentation of pure pixel information can lead to serious data handling problems in case of videos with a standard frame rate.

5 Gait Recognition

Finally, the area of gait recognition shall be considered in this overview, because the gait of a person certainly belongs to its human activity and can represent additional valuable information about the identity of a person, which can be even acquired by camera sensors from longer distances with low resolution in a non-invasive manner that does not require any cooperation of the investigated individual. Gait recognition is a relatively specialized research area which was not yet very popular 20 or more years ago, which makes a certain difference to other mentioned image processing areas, such as tracking or gesture. Nevertheless, the progress in this field so far has already let to very promising results and demonstrated gait as a very informative special "modality" for biometrics, especially in combination with other biometric approaches, such as e.g. face or appearance recognition. Since also gait recognition can be considered as a classical dynamical pattern recognition task, some recent novel approaches have been concentrating on the question, how traditional classification schemes can be replaced by actual machine learning techniques and how the dynamic pattern information can be best incorporated into the classification task. The presentation will introduce a 3D-convolutional deep learning approach to this task and will explain the architecture of the employed 3D-CNNs for that purpose, along with the progress and improvements of the experimental results obtained with this novel approach.

6 Conclusion

This paper describes some of the most recent developments in human activity recognition. It demonstrates also the large variety of this research area, which is underpinned by the existence of many sub-research areas which all represent popular and active research domains in the computer vision area. One can observe in all these sub-areas a similarly strong trend from the use of classical stochastic modeling techniques for dynamic patterns (such e.g. Hidden Markov Models) to more state-of-the-art machine learning techniques, mostly represented by deep learning approaches today.

Acknowledgement. The research methods and themes presented in this paper have been mainly resulting from research contributions of many members from the Institute for Human-Machine Communication at TU Munich during recent years. The author would like to thank these persons cordially for their contributions and efforts, especially to Ma. Babaee, M. Babaee and O. Köpüklü.

References

1. Babaee, M., You, Y., Rigoll, G.: Combined segmentation, reconstruction, and tracking of multiple targets in multi-view video sequences. J. Comput. Vis. Image Underst. (CVIU) **154**, 166–181 (2017)
2. Babaee, M., You, Y., Rigoll, G.: Pixel level tracking of multiple targets in crowded environments. In: International Workshop on Crowd Understanding in conjunction with European Conference on Computer Vision (ECCV) (2016)
3. Köpüklü, O., Köse, N., Rigoll, G.: Motion fused frames: data level fusion strategy for hand gesture recognition. In: Proceedings of the IEEE Conference on Computer Vision and Pattern Recognition (CVPR) Workshops, pp. 2216–2224 (2018)

4. Köse, N., Babaee, M., Rigoll, G.: Multi-view human activity recognition using motion frequency. In: Proceedings of the International Conference on Image Processing (ICIP), article 1871-1917 (2017)
5. Lehment, N., Kaiser, M., Rigoll, G.: Using segmented 3D point clouds for accurate likelihood approximation in human pose tracking. Int. J. Comput. Vis., 1–16 (2012)
6. Babaee, Ma., Li, Z., Rigoll, G.: Occlusion handling in tracking multiple people using RNN. In: Proceedings of the 25th IEEE International Conference on Image Processing (ICIP), pp. 2715–2719 (2018)
7. Babaee, Ma., Babaee, M., Rigoll, G.: Joint tracking and gait recognition of multiple people in video. In: Proceedings of the International Conference on Image Processing (ICIP) (2017)
8. Babaee, Ma., Li, L., Rigoll, G.: Gait recognition from incomplete gait cycle. In: Proceedings of the 25th IEEE International Conference on Image Processing (ICIP), pp. 768–772 (2018)

Robots' Vision Humanization Through Machine-Learning Based Artificial Visual Attention

Kurosh Madani[(✉)]

Université Paris-Est, Signals, Images, and Intelligent Systems Laboratory
(LISSI/EA 3956), University Paris Est Creteil (UPEC), Senart-FB Institute
of Technology, Avenue Pierre Point, 77127 Lieusaint, France
madani@u-pe.fr

Abstract. If the main challenge of robotics during the industrial air of 19th century has consisted of automating repetitive tasks and the sophistication of these machines through digitization of these robots throughout the 20th century, the challenge of robotics in the current century will be to make cohabit humans and robots in the same living space. However, robots would not succeed in seamlessly integrate the humans' universe without developing the ability of perceiving similarly to humans the environment that they are supposed to share with them. In such a context, fitting the skills of the natural vision is an appealing perspective for autonomous robotics dealing with and prospecting Human-Robot interaction. The main goal of the present article is to debate the plausibility and the reality of humanizing the robots behavior focusing the perception of the surrounding environment. An implementation of the developed concept on a real humanoid robot nourishes the presented results and the related discussions.

Keywords: Autonomous robot · Artificial visual attention · Salient objects' extraction · Real-time · Implementation

1 Introduction

If the main challenge of robotics during the 19th century has consisted of automating repetitive tasks, and then, sophistication of these machines through digitization (computerization) of these robots throughout the 20th century, the challenge of robotics in the current century will be to make robots cohabit with humans, to share with them the "life space", cooperating and evolving with them within complex environments. An example of application is assistance or personal companion robots witnessing nowadays a great increase of interest.

However, robots would not succeed in seamlessly integrate the humans' universe without developing an ability of perceiving similarly to humans the environment that they are supposed to share with them. Thus, fitting the skills of the natural vision is an appealing perspective for autonomous robotics applications dealing with visual perception of the surrounding environment where robots and humans are asked for mutually evolve, cooperate and interacte. For example, emphasizing the importance of exploitation of robot's motion-related sensory information (as those relating the robot's

© Springer Nature Switzerland AG 2019
S. V. Ablameyko et al. (Eds.): PRIP 2019, CCIS 1055, pp. 8–19, 2019.
https://doi.org/10.1007/978-3-030-35430-5_2

head rotations and translations) in achieving efficient visual stabilization, authors of [1] address the problem of ocular compensatory behaviors' generation for a robot with moving eyes. Another original example of application is given in [2] where authors deal with a robot offering guided tours at the Archaeological Museum of Agrigento (Italy).

In this context, a foremost and necessary skill for accosting the agility of the natural vision relates the "saliency detection". In fact, by means of their "natural visual saliency detection", humans can intuitively, reflexively and promptly detect and extract relevant items in diverse situations, in quite strongly degraded conditions and within complex environments. Adjacent to human's cognitive (i.e. knowledge-based) exploration cleverness, this primary reflexive skill contributes to the efficiency of human's visual attention in detecting relevant items of complex environment in which he evolves. Another leading and requisite ability for reaching humans' visual suppleness relates the visual-attention making them to focus specific items of a scenery and guiding their actions accordingly to primacy of visual events stimulating their interest. Thus, a system endeavoring to approach the natural vision's dexterity has to be able to detect visually-salient items of its surrounding and to develop a selective visual awareness of the backdrop in which it evolves.

Visual saliency is described as a perceptual quality that makes a region of image stand out relative to its surroundings and to capture attention of the observer [3]. Although there exist biologically based computational approaches to visual saliency, most of the existing works do not claim to be biologically plausible: instead, they use purely computational techniques to achieve the goal. One of the first works using visual saliency in image processing has been published by Itti, Koch and Niebur [4]. Authors use a biologically plausible approach based on a center-surround contrast calculation using "Difference of Gaussians". Published more recently, other common techniques of visual saliency calculation include graph-based random walk [5], center-surround feature distances [6], multi-scale contrast, center-surround histogram and color spatial distribution or features of color and luminance [7]. A less common approach is described in [8]. It uses content-sensitive hyper-graph representation and partitioning instead of using traditional features and parameters commonly considered in images. Finally, in our recent works, we have investigated an intelligent autonomous salient vision system for humanoid robots' autonomous knowledge acquisition ([9] and [10] as well as a powerful segmentation approach taking advantage from RGB representation in spherical coordinates [11].

Concerning the appealing area of the human's attention modelling, and especially human visual attention modelling, it has benefited from a substantial gain of interest over last decade because of its potential for various domains of applications. The related wealthy scientific literature gathers numerous works highlighting an intense research activity in this field. In their work Borji and Itti made an overview of the human attention modelling dilemma and established a taxonomy of subtasks in this field, differentiating more than 60 different models into 28 subsets of methods [12]. Some of these subsets depend (at least partially) on detection of salient objects in scene [13–15]. Other subsets deal with detecting (or defining) the most interesting spots in scene, which may or may not be a part of the most salient object of this scene [15–17]. Finally, a number of reported models covers, transversally, both object detection and eye fixation prediction problems: as for example, the approach described in [18]. In the same way, our recent works relating the artificial visual-attention based detection and recognition of complex, deformed and multi-shaped objects [19, 20] cover "interesting items' detection" and "complex objects' detection" linking some similarity with human eye-fixation prediction.

Motivated by the progressive humanization of robots and the challenge of autonomous assistive robotics, the main goal of the present key-note paper is to highlight the SYANPSE research division's (of LISSI EA 3956 laboratory) investigations relating human-like robot-vision system developed by the team: a hybrid approach combining human-inspired vision, Machine-Learning paradigms and visual saliency detection techniques.

The paper is organized as follows: Sect. 2 is devoted to basis of statistically driven saliency detection. It reminds our previous works on statistically driven saliency detection in order to make understandable the notion of "Visual Attention Map" and describes the idea of the introduced AVA and the related parameters. Section 3 presents a dual analysis of analogy between "salient object detection" and human's issued "eye-fixation" cognitive mechanism. The Sect. 4 introduces the Artificial Visual Attention and its link with the saliency-detection process and related parameters. The Sect. 5 presents the concept and the groundwork of the Artificial Visual-Attention-based autonomous robot-vision. Finally, Sect. 6 concludes the paper sketching further perspectives of the presented work.

2   Visual Saliency Detection

The notion of visual saliency detection relates the saliency maps highlighting relevant items or stuffs of the image. Referring to our previous works [10, 11, 22], two kinds of saliency maps, representing two different saliency levels, contribute to make out the saliency detection: "Global Saliency Map" (GSM) and "Local Saliency Map" (LSM). Let us suppose the image I_{YCC}, represented by its pixels $I_{YCC}(x)$, in YCrCb color space, where $x \in N^2$ denotes 2D-pixel position. Let $I_Y(x)$, $I_{Cr}(x)$ and $I_{Cb}(x)$ be the colors values in channels Y, Cr and Cb, respectively. Similarly, let $I_{RGB}(x)$ be the same image in RGB color space and $I_R(x)$, $I_G(x)$ and $I_B(x)$ be its colors values in channels R, G and B, respectively. Finally, let $\overline{I_Y}$, $\overline{I_{Cr}}$ and $\overline{I_{Cb}}$ be median values for each channel throughout the whole image.

The GSM, the constituents of which are denoted $M_G(x)$, handles overall sway of items' visual relevance dealing with their overall contrast within the image. GSM is resulted from non-linear fusion of two elementary maps denoted $M_Y(x)$ and $M_{CrCb}(x)$, relating luminance and chromaticity separately. Equations (1), (2) and (3) detail the calculation of each elementary map as well as the resulting GSM.

$$M_Y(x) = \left\| \overline{I_Y} - I_Y(x) \right\| \tag{1}$$

$$M_{CrCb}(x) = \sqrt{\left(\overline{I_{Cr}} - I_{Cr}(x) \right)^2 + \left(\overline{I_{Cb}} - I_{Cb}(x) \right)^2} \tag{2}$$

$$M_G(x) = \frac{1}{1 - e^{-C(x)}} M_{CrCb}(x) + \left(1 - \frac{1}{1 - e^{-C(x)}}\right) M_Y(x) \qquad (3)$$

$C(x)$ is a coefficient which depends on saturation of each pixel in RGB color space expressed.

While LSM, the constituents of which are denoted $M_L(x)$, conveys persnickety bends of those items coping with their local center-surround contrast in the considered image [9–11, 22]. Involving statistical properties of two centered windows (over each pixel) sliding alongside whole the image, LSM is also obtained from a nonlinear fusion of two statistical-properties-based maps relating luminance and chromaticity of the image. Let $P(x)$ be a sliding window of size P, centered over a pixel located at position x, and let $Q(x)$ be another surrounding area around the same pixel of size Q, with $Q - P = p^2$. Let consider the "center-histogram" $H_C(x)$ as a histogram of pixels' intensities in window $P(x)$ with $h_C(x, k)$ representing the value of kth bin of this histogram. Let consider the "surrounding-histogram" $H_S(x)$ as a histogram of pixels' intensities in the surrounding window $Q(x)$ with $h_S(x, k)$ representing its kth bin's value. Let define the "center-surround feature" $d_{ch}(x)$ as a sum of differences between normalized center and surrounding histograms over all 256 histograms' bins computed for each channel "ch" ($ch \in \{Y, Cr, Cb\}$). Figure 1 gives the main idea of centered windows sliding alongside an image of size $m \times n$.

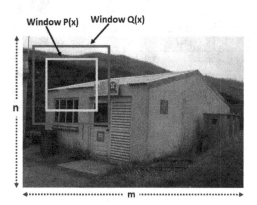

Fig. 1. Idea of centered windows sliding alongside an image of size $m \times n$.

Equation (4) details the computation of the so-called "center-surround feature", where $|H_C(x)|$ and $|H_S(x)|$ represent sums over all histogram bins. Concerning pixels near the image's borders, the areas $P(x)$ and $Q(x)$ are limited to the image itself (e.g. not exceeding the image's borders). The LSM, resulting from a nonlinear fusion of the so-called center-surround features, is obtained accordingly to the Eq. (5), where the coefficient $C_\mu(x)$ represents the average color saturation over the window $P(x)$, computed as average of saturations $C(x)$.

$$d_{ch}(x) = \sum_{k=1}^{256} \left| \frac{h_C(x, k)}{|H_C(x)|} - \frac{h_S(x, k)}{|H_S(x)|} \right| \tag{4}$$

$$M_L(x) = \frac{1}{1 - e^{-C_\mu(x)}} \, d_Y(x) + \left(1 - \frac{1}{1 - e^{-C_\mu(x)}} \right) Max\left(d_{Cr}(x), d_{Cb}(x) \right) \tag{5}$$

The computation of the Saliency Map (SM), the constituents of which are denoted $M_f(x)$, results from a conditional fusion of the so-called GSM and LSM using the Eq. (6). Figure 2 shows an example of GSM, LSM and SM saliency maps computed using the input image (a) and Fig. 3 shows an example of saliency map and the extracted salient objects from the image.

$$M_f(x) = \begin{cases} M_L(x) & if \ M_L(x) > M_G(x) \\ \sqrt{M_G(x)\,M_L(x)} & otherwise \end{cases} \tag{6}$$

Fig. 2. Examples of GSM (b), LSM (c) and Saliency Map (d) obtained from the let-side input image (a).

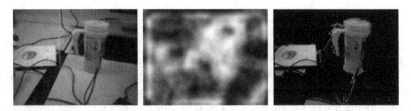

Fig. 3. Examples of saliency map and the salient object's extraction obtained from domestic objects' recognition.

3   Analogy Between "Visual Saliency Detection" and "Eye-Fixation" Tasks

The goal in the "eye-fixation" paradigm is modelling the human eye-fixation (supposed linking human visual attention) when watching a scene (namely an image). The paradigm provides appealing and potent source of inspiration linking "human-like" visual skills. Actually, taking into account that the human eye-fixation mechanism tends following what may be considered by the human as being relevant in visually perceived information, one may establish some similarity between the robot's artificial vision and human's natural vision, then exploit this likeness in order to make machine-vision come closer to human-like vision. Let's consider the "eye-fixation map" as an image that pixels' intensities represent the eye-fixation probability (interpretable as being some kind of pixels' visual-attractiveness-degree). Assimilating the eye-fixation map to such an image, one can define a *relevant-region* (or an *object* attracting the human's visual attention) as an item represented by a set of contiguous pixels (of the eye-fixation map) highlighted by relative probabilities (or intensities) higher than some threshold T. In other words, a map of such relevant-regions can be obtained by applying an arbitrary threshold to an eye-fixation map. On the other hand and in the same way, a relevant-region of such an image could also be seen, from the saliency detection point of view, as a salient object (or salient region) versus the rest of the image considered as background. Figure 4 gives an example of eye-fixation-map (EFM), (obtained from experimental acquisition involving a group of various humans watching the left-side input image projected to each of them) and two threshold-based images including computed relevant-region obtained accordingly to the two thresholds (T = 10 and T = 50) applied to eye-fixation-map.

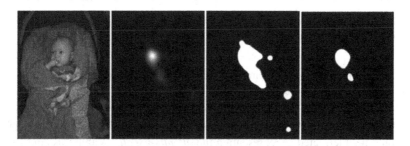

Fig. 4. Examples of eye-fixation-map and two threshold-based relevant-region computed by applying two thresholds T = 10 and T = 50 to eye-fixation-map, respectively.

On the other hand, according to Kienzle et al. [17], a center-surround feature based algorithm can be used for eye-fixation prediction tasks. Thus, by considering the "saliency map" as a map which shows a distribution of image's pixels' likelihood to match up pieces of images' items that may draw human's attention, one can make the reverse analogy by interpreting a saliency map as a kind of *machine's visual attention indicator*. Equating the final saliency map to an EFSM, the following question can be formulated: "how similar are the final saliency map and the human's eye-fixation behavior?" In other words, could the salient objects' detection algorithm fit human-like visual attention?

Before answering this pertinent question, let introduce the concept of Artificial Visual Attention.

4 Idea of Artificial Visual Attention

Linking the notion of LSM, the concept idea of *Artificial Visual Attention* (AVA) keeps to the idea of the *Visual Attentiveness Parameter* (VAP): an idiosyncratic interpretation of a control-parameter p involved in LSM's computation (respecting the condition mentioned in Sect. 2: $Q - P = p^2$). Flooding back to the parameter p, this parameter sways the average grain of the detected salient items. In other words, small values of p direct the saliency detection process toward highlighting details or small items, while larger values of this parameter push the saliency detection process stressing bulky items of the image [20–22]. Figure 5 depicts an example of the p parameter's influence on saliency grain from an input image (left-side) considering large value for p (middle) and small value for p (right), respectively.

Fig. 5. Examples of effect of the p parameter on saliency grain: input image (left), large value for p (middle) and small value for p (right).

To interpret the chore of the parameter p, Q may be seen as a fraction of the image and be expressed as $Q = \alpha \cdot n \cdot m$ where $0 \leq \alpha \leq 1$. α may be interpreted as the parameter linking the visual attention's perimeter. Within such statements, we can consider the ratio $\gamma = \frac{P}{Q}$ (with $0 \leq \gamma \leq 1$) taking to mean the visual-attention grain, which could be interpreted as representing the *attention scale*. Within this context, the area p^2, corresponding to the surrounding part between the two of the windows Q and P (e.g. $Q - P$, which is also a fraction of the same input image, could be expressed as $p^2 = \alpha(1 - \gamma)nm$ leading to expel the parameter p as a function of γ, α and the image's size as shows the Eq. (7).

$$p = \sqrt{\alpha(1 - \gamma)nm} \tag{7}$$

Therefore, p could be interpreted as the parameter relating the "visual attentiveness scale" of the system (e.g. the parameter controlling the system's visual attentiveness), depending on one hand on the considered "visual attention's perimeter" Q (involved through α) and on the other hand on "visual-attention grain" $\frac{P}{Q}$ (involved through γ). In other words, we identify the parameter p as a key-parameter controlling a kind of the system's "artificial visual attentiveness" (or system's "*Artificial Visual Attention*"). An appealing way of handling the choice of the p control parameter is to set it proportionally to the processed image's size (e.g. as proportional to number of image's pixels $n \cdot m$). Let denote by λ ($\lambda \geq 1$) the coefficient expressing the above-mentioned proportionality, i.e. $p = \frac{m \cdot n}{\lambda}$. In this case, linking on the one hand the visual attention's perimeter (i.e. the parameter p) and on the other hand the images size (i.e. the entire visual field), λ could be seen as VAP controlling a kind of artificial visual attention of the system and be linked to "visual attention's perimeter" (i.e. α) and "visual-attention grain" (i.e. γ) through the Eq. (8).

$$\lambda = \sqrt{\frac{nm}{\alpha(1 - \gamma)}} \tag{8}$$

5 Machine-Learning Based Human-like Robot-Vision

The answer to the question formulated at the end of the third section of the paper could now be articulated through the incorporation of the human eye-fixation mechanism within the process of visual saliency detection by means of a Machine-Learning procedure: namely, a *Genetic Algorithm* (GA). In fact, the primary action and thus the main outcome of the saliency detection algorithm is to detect and to isolate the potential salient items without any linkage to human's way of focusing objects in a landscape or to the human-like visual attention. In contrast with the aforementioned chain, although based on saliency detection concept, the incorporation through a GA-based Machine-Learning evolutionary training process the investigated concept and issued human-like robot-vision approach get underway the integration of human-like visual attention by launching an eyes-fixation mechanism based tuning of the saliency detection process. This is done through a Genetic Algorithm (GA) based evolutionary process shoving the saliency detection toward the human-like eyes-fixation behavior.

Taking into account what has been mentioned above, it is pertinent to emphasize that the investigated system admits two operational modes: the "tuning mode", acting as some kind of learning process, and the "operating mode" carrying out the so-called *Visual Attention Map* (VAP) once the system's parameters have appropriately been tuned. Except the GA-based Tuning Process, all other units composing the system contribute to both of above-mentioned operational modes of the system. While, the unit dedicated to GA-based Tuning Process is a central unit which operates only in "tuning mode" adapting (i.e. tuning) parameters of LSM, "Fusion Final Map", "Recognition-Extraction" units and other modulles of the investigated robot-vision system in order to make the system acquiring (i.e. fitting) "human-like" gazing skill. Thus, the artificial visual attention is constructed through learning (i.e. acquired knowledge) and experience involving humans. In other words, it makes the "final saliency map" more human-like leading to "visual attention map". As for the eye-fixation-map, the regions of highest brightness in visual-attention-map (issued from the recognition process) may be interpreted and considered as regions (or items) attracting the robot's artificial visual attention. Figure 6 an example of artificial visual-attention-map obtained from the input image representing a baby face where the red points represent the region of highest intensity and which correspond to the regions that attracted the robot's visual attention. The next image of the figure gives the eye-fixation map issued from experimental record of humans' gazing the same input image.

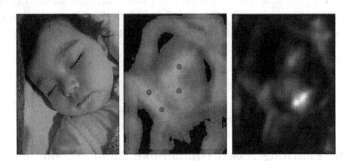

Fig. 6. Examples of "Artificial Visual-Attention-Map (middle) obtained from the input image (left) where the red points represent the region of highest intensity and corresponding to the regions that attracted the robot's visual attention. The right-side map gives the eye-fixation map issued from experimental record of humans' gazing, watching the same input image effect. (Color figure online)

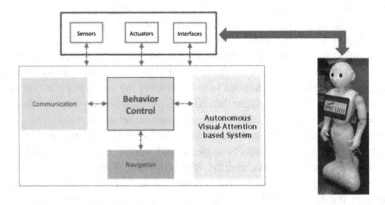

Fig. 7. Implementation diagram of the "Artificial Visual-Attention based robot vision system.

The investigated concept and the issued human-like robot-vision system have been implemented using a humanoid robot: namely, the Pepper Robot. The robot's vision system has been tuned in order to acquire the human-like way of gazing. This has been performed by showing to the robot a set of images (projected on a screen) for which were available the corresponding eye-fixation maps issued from humans gazing the same set of images. Figure 7 gives the implementation diagram of the system. Figure 8 depicts the experimental setup of robot's tuning and Fig. 9 gives examples of results obtained from the robot gazing either the learned projected images or unknown (not learned) projected images.

Fig. 8. Experimental setup of robot's tuning.

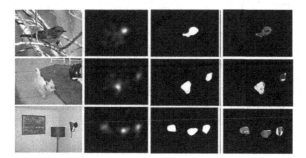

Fig. 9. Example of results obtained from the robot gazing either the learned projected images or unknown (not learned) projected images. From left to right: projected image (1st column), humans' issued eye-fixation-map (2nd column), the artificial visual-attention area stimulating the robot's attention (3rd column) and the extracted items (objects) of high visual attention by the robot (4th column).

6 Conclusion

On the one hand, the statistical nature of the proposed model relating images' statistical properties through the center-surround-based saliency detection, and on the other hand its GA-based parameters tuning affords pretty competency for detecting improved visual saliency detection in complex daily landscapes. The aforementioned basements proffer also a comprehensive and solid theoretical background of the investigated concepts.

Beside these appealing points, the dual analysis of analogy between "salient object detection" and "eye-fixation" tasks shows the fitness of the proposed concepts and the issued artificial attention based robot-vision system with human's eye-fixation behavior, emerging some kind of human-like visual skill of the proposed robot-vision system. This sets up a suitable skill for human-like artificial vision, opening the lane toward human-like robots' vision, proffering them kind of artificial visual attention and contributing to humanization of robots in the future.

References

1. Panerai, F., Metta, G., Sandini, G.: Learning visual stabilization reflexes in robots with moving eyes. Neurocomputing **48**(1–4), 323–337 (2002)
2. Chella, A., Macaluso, I.: The perception loop in CiceRobot, a museum guide robot. Neurocomputing **72**(4–6), 760–766 (2009)
3. Achanta, R., Hemami, S., Estrada, F., Susstrunk, S.: Frequency-tuned salient region detection. In: Proceedings of IEEE International Conference on Computer Vision and Pattern Recognition, Miami, Florida, USA, pp. 1597–1604 (2009)
4. Itti, L., Koch, C., Niebur, E.: A model of saliency-based visual attention for rapid scene analysis. IEEE Trans. Pattern Anal. Mach. Intel **20**, 1254–1259 (1998)
5. Harel, J., Koch, C., Perona, P.: Graph-based visual saliency. In: Advances in Neural Information Processing Systems, vol. 19, pp. 545–552 (2007). ISBN: 9780262195683
6. Achanta, R., Estrada, F., Wils, P., Susstrunk, S.: Salient region detection and segmentation. In: Proceedings of International Conference on Computer Vision Systems. LNCS, vol. 5008, pp. 66–75. Springer, Heidelberg (2008)
7. Liu, T., Yuan, Z., Sun, J., Wang, J., Zheng, N., Tang, X., Shum, H.-Y.: Learning to detect a salient object. IEEE Trans. Pattern Anal. Mach. Intell. **33**(2), 353–367 (2001)
8. Liang, Z., Chi, Z., Fu, H., Feng, D.: Salient object detection using content-sensitive hypergraph representation and partitioning. Pattern Rec. **45**(11), 3886–3901 (2012)
9. Ramik, D. M., Sabourin, C., Madani, K.: Hybrid salient object extraction approach with automatic estimation of visual attention scale. In: Proceedings of IEEE SITIS, Dijon, France, pp. 438–445 (2011)
10. Ramik, D.M., Sabourin, C., Moreno, R., Madani, K.: A machine learning based intelligent vision system for autonomous object detection and recognition. J. Appl. Intell. **40**(2), 358–375 (2014)
11. Moreno, R., Ramik, D.M., Graña, M., Madani, K.: Image segmentation on the spherical coordinate representation of the RGB color space. IET Image Proc. **6**(9), 1275–1283 (2012)
12. Borji, A., Itti, L.: State-of-the-Art in visual attention modeling. IEEE Trans. Pattern Anal. Mach. Intell. **35**(1), 185–207 (2013)
13. Navalpakkam, V., Itti L.: An integrated model of top-down and bottom-up attention for optimizing detection speed. In: Proceedings of IEEE CVPR, vol. II, New York, NJ, USA, pp. 2049–2056 (2006)
14. Holzbach, A., Cheng, G.: A scalable and efficient method for salient region detection using sampled template collation. In: Proceedings of IEEE ICIP, Paris, France, pp. 1110–1114 (2014)
15. Koehler, K., Guo, F., Zhang, S., Eckstein, M.P.: What do saliency models predict? J. Vis. **14**(3), 1–27 (2014)
16. Rajashekar, U., Vander Linde, I., Bovik, A.C., Cormack, L.K.: GAFFE: a gaze- attentive fixation finding engine. IEEE Trans. Image Process. **17**(4), 564–573 (2008)

17. Kadir, T., Brady, M.: Saliency, scale and image description. J. Vis. **45**(2), 83–105 (2011)
18. Kienzle, W., Franz, M.O., Schölkopf, B., Wichmann, F.A.: Center-surround patterns emerge as optimal predictors for human saccade targets. J. Vis. **9**, 1–15 (2009)
19. Zhang, J., Sclaroff, S.: Saliency detection: a boolean map approach. In: Proceedings of IEEE ICCV, Sydney, Australia, pp. 153–160 (2013)
20. Madani, K., Kachurka, V., Sabourin, C., Amarger, V., Golovko, V., Rossi, L.: A human-like visual-attention-based artificial vision system for wildland firefighting assistance. J. Appl. Intell. **48**(8), 2157–2179 (2018)
21. Madani, K., Kachurka, V., Sabourin, C., Golovko, V.: A soft-computing-based approach to artificial visual attention using human eye-fixation paradigm: toward a human-like skill in robot vision. Soft. Comput. (2018). https://doi.org/10.1007/s00500-017-2931-x
22. Ramik, D.M.: Contribution to complex visual information processing and autonomous knowledge extraction: application to autonomous robotics. Ph.D. dissertation, University Paris-Est, 2012, Pub. No. 2012PEST1100

Reliability Analysis Based
on Incompletely Specified Data

Elena Zaitseva$^{(\boxtimes)}$ iD, Vitaly Levashenko iD, and Peter Sedlacek iD

Faculty of Management Science and Informatics, University of Žilina, Žilina, Slovakia
{Elena.Zaitseva,Vitaly.Levashenko,Peter.Sedlacek}@fri.uniza.sk

Abstract. In this paper new algorithm for the reliability analysis of system is considered. The reliability analysis consists of 2 essential steps - creation of mathematical model and quantitative analysis. The system mathematical model is constructed depending on the specifics of analysis and properties of the investigated system. In this paper the mathematical model in form of the structure function of non-coherent Multi-State System (MSS) is considered. The non-coherent system is specific group of systems in context of reliability analysis for which for system component degradation does not always lead to a degradation or failure of the system. MSS is mathematical model that allows analyzing of some (not only two) states/performance levels of system reliability. The structure function is type of mathematical model, that express dependency between system behavior and behavior of its components. Structure function can be represented in different forms, for example, as minimal cuts/paths, fault tree, reliability bloc diagrams. One of them used in this paper is Multi-Valued Decision Diagram (MDD). MDD is typical used for representation of data of large dimension. Created mathematical model is then used for quantitative analysis. This analysis includes calculus of different system characteristics such as availability/unavailability and other indices and measures. New methods for the creating of structure function in form of MDD and calculation of some indices for quantitative analysis is proposed in the paper. Important advantage of this method is possibility to use for MDD construction based on incompletely specified data and analysis of non-coherent MSS. Usage of the method is demonstrated on biker crashes survival evaluation.

Keywords: Reliability analysis · Multi-valued decision diagrams · Non-coherent systems · Incompletely specified data · Structure importance

1 Introduction

Reliability analysis is one of system characteristics, that has to be taken into account as failures (system breakdown) can have fatal consequences. Important

This work was supported by the project VEGA 1/0354/17 and the Slovak Research and Development Agency under the contract No. SK-SRB-18-0002.

© Springer Nature Switzerland AG 2019
S. V. Ablameyko et al. (Eds.): PRIP 2019, CCIS 1055, pp. 20–32, 2019.
https://doi.org/10.1007/978-3-030-35430-5_3

step in the system reliability is constructing of mathematical model of system [3, 19, 35]. The system mathematical model is constructed depending on the specifics of system analysis and properties of the investigated system. Depending on number of system performance levels, mathematical models can be divided into two types depending on the detail of the analysis [19]. The first of them is Binary-state systems. This model can be used to analyse system behaviour on two performance levels - system is working or system fails. This model is effectively used to analyse system failures. The other type of systems are Multi-State Systems (MSS). Using this model, we can analyse system behavior on more than two performance levels. This is used to analyse gradual degradation of system performance, however this model is more complex to analyse as binary-state.

Except system type based on number of states, there are different mathematical models depending on mathematical methods used to analyse this system. One of these mathematical methods is Boolean algebra [9]. In this case, structure function is used as mathematical model. Structure function clearly maps system components performance level to system performance [25, 33]. Advantages of using structure function as mathematical model are for example uniform approach to analyse system using Boolean or multiple-valued logic [33]. However in case of real systems, structure function can have large dimension. Therefore it is necessary to represent it in efficient way, such as Multi-Valued Decision Diagram (MDD) [22]. MDD is graphical orthogonal and canonical form for representation of logical function of large dimension. Usage of these diagrams for MSS structure function was considered in [2, 31].

In order to create structure function, full information about system behavior is required. The problem is, in many real systems, there is lack of such information [3, 32]. Therefore different methods have been developed for reliability evaluation based on incompletely specified data, for example, graph databases based methods [8, 27] or datamining based methods [26, 32]. In case of the use of datamining based methods the structure function is interpreted as classification structure that should be created based on incompletely specified [32]. In this paper methods of datamining, specifically decision trees will be used in order to handle this problem [1, 5, 20, 26]. In this case the structure function is represented in form of decision tree that is transformed into MDD [22].

Created mathematical model in form of MDD is in next step of reliability analysis used to calculate system reliability indices and measures, such as availability [13, 35], importance measures [14], minimal cuts and paths set [15] etc. These characteristics can be divided into two types - topological and probabilistic. Topological analysis does not require information about state probabilities and can be used to analyse system behavior based on its topology. Typical example of this characteristic is structure importance [11]. The probabilistic analysis takes into account also probabilities of individual component performance. Typical example of probabilistic importance measure can be Birnbaum's importance. In most of investigations reliability indices and measures are considered for coherent system. But there are special group of non-coherent systems in reliability analysis. The degradation of some of components in such systems does not always lead to a degradation or failure of the system. This fact causes specific in reliability analysis of these system because the structure function of such system is not monotone. There are some investigations for analysis of non-coherent Binary-state systems [4, 10, 34], but the evaluation of MSS non-coherent systems is not investigated sufficient. In this paper the initial investigation for non-coherent MSS is considered based on calculation of Important measures.

Organization of this paper is following. Section 2 contains detailed information about used mathematical model - structure function together with its representation in form of multi-valued decision diagram. Section 3 contains description of system characteristics and their calculus and calculus of structure importance for multi-state non-coherent systems. These methods are used in Sect. 4 to analyse Bike crashes dataset and finally Sect. 5 concludes previous methods together with plans for next work.

2   Reliability Analysis

Reliability analysis of system consist of 2 essential steps:

1. Creation of mathematical model
2. Quantitative analysis - i.e. calculation of system characteristics and different types of reliability indices. In this paper importance measures will be used, with focus on topological analysis.

There are different mathematical models in reliability analysis. The creation of the mathematical model is caused by system properties and specifics of reliability analysis. For any mathematical model is defined:

- number of system states
- type of mathematical model.

The number of system states or system performance levels is caused by analysis detail. There are two groups of mathematical models:

- Binary-State System (BSS) is modelled in two performance levels - i.e. system is either working or not. This approach is used, if system is binary-state from its nature [6, 16], or we are analysing consequences of system failure [35].
- Multi-State System (MSS) is modelled in more than two performance levels. This approach allows us to describe gradual degradation of system performance from fully working to fully broken [18, 19, 25].

MSS allows the system analysis in more detail but computational complexity of this analysis increases and special methods and algorithms should be developed for quantitative analysis of MSS. The methods of quantitative analysis of MSS and other system associate with the types of mathematical model. The types correlates with background methods used in quantitative analysis. As a rule stochastic methods, methods of Boolean logic or algebra logic are used as background methods in reliability analysis [3]. The type of mathematical model correlated with algebra logic in reliability analysis is named structure function. This mathematical model can be used for representation of system of any topological complexity. It has favorable rules for the construction. But the computational complexity of the structure function analysis increases depending on this function dimensional. The development of special methods and algorithm for the structure function analysis allows creating effective approaches for reliability analysis of system.

2.1   Structure Function

Dependency between system performance and performance of system components can be expressed using Structure Function. It can be defined as following [11]:

$$\phi(x_1, x_2, ..., x_n) = \phi(\boldsymbol{x}) : \{0, 1, ..., m_1 - 1\} \times \{0, 1, ..., m_2 - 1\}$$
$$\times ... \times \{0, 1, ..., m_n - 1\} \rightarrow \{0, 1, ..., m - 1\} \tag{1}$$

where x_i is i-th system component state, $i \in \{1, 2, ..., n\}$, m is number of system performance levels and m_i is number of states of component i. In case $m = m_i = 2$ system is Binary-state (BSS).

Structure function can be used in topological analysis of system. But in case probabilistic analysis is required, we need to know not only structure function, but also state probabilities of individual system components. The i-th component state probabilities will be denoted as following [11,30]:

$$p_{i1} = \Pr\{x_i = 1\}, ...,$$
$$p_{i,j} = \Pr\{x_i = j\}, \tag{2}$$
$$q_i = \Pr\{x_i = 0\}$$

Depending on system behavior, systems can be divided into two types - **coherent** and **non-coherent**. In non-coherent systems there are cases, when degradation of system component leads to increase of system performance level. This is not possible for coherent systems. From structure function point of view according to [11] system is coherent, if system meets 2 conditions:

1. Structure function is non-decreasing - This condition implies, that improving of state of any component does not degrade the performance of system and vice versa.
2. Each system component is relevant - System component is relevant, if there exists at least one case in that the state of component dictates the state of the system.

If at least one of these conditions are not met, the system is non-coherent. Majority of technical systems are coherent in general. Examples of non-coherent systems can be systems including human factor. Case study presented in this paper is also non-coherent system.

The main problem with traditional methods in reliability analysis is the fact, we need all information about system behaviour to create mathematical model.

In many real systems, there is lack of such information, i.e. we either don't know all system components or we don't know system behavior based on these components behavior in some cases [3]. The other problem can be ambiguous data. This can be caused by many factors, for example inaccuracy of measurement [26].

This problem can be handled in different ways, for example usage of graph databases [8,27]. In this paper, we will be used methods of datamining to create decision trees [1,5,20]. This tree will be then reduced into multi-valued decision diagrams using reduction rules described in [21,24,28].

2.2 Multi-valued Decision Diagram

Structure function can be represented in multiple ways such as truth table, reliability block diagram, fault tree, etc. One, effective representation of structure function is Multi-valued Decision Diagram (MDD). According to publications [21,23], MDD is rooted acyclic graph that meets two conditions:

1. graph is canonical - the representation is unique for a particular variable ordering
2. graph is compact - any other graph representation contains more nodes.

There are two type of nodes in MDD - sink and non-sink. Sink nodes, labeled by numbers from 0 to $m - 1$, express system performance levels. There are exactly one sink node for each system state. Non-sink nodes represents system components. Node representing component x_i has exactly m_i outgoing edges expressed state of representing component.

Thanks to fact, MDD is orthogonal form of Structure Function [22], it can be used for the probabilistic analysis. In this case this graph is edge-weighted. Weight of j-th outgoing edge of node representing component x_i is equal to probability $p_{i,j}$, that component x_i is in state j.

3   Quantitative Analysis

Created mathematical model can be in the next step used to calculate system characteristics such as availability and unavailability.

Availability and Unavailability. Availability $A^{\geq j}$ can be defined as probability system is at least in j-th performance level. Unavailability can be defined similarly - i.e. probability system performance level is lower than j [18,19,25]:

$$A^{\geq j}(\boldsymbol{p}) = Pr\{\phi(\boldsymbol{x}) \geq j\},$$
$$U^{\geq j}(\boldsymbol{p}) = Pr\{\phi(\boldsymbol{x}) < j\}, \tag{3}$$
$$U^{\geq j}(\boldsymbol{p}) = 1 - A^{\geq j}(\boldsymbol{p})$$

These are characteristics of whole system but give us no information about how system performance in influenced by performance of its components.

For this purpose importance measures has to be calculated. There are 2 types of importance measures - topological and probabilistic. This paper will focus on topological analysis, therefore structure importance will be used.

3.1   Structure Importance

Structure importance can be used to express influence of component to system performance in topological point of view.

$$\mathrm{SI}_{i\downarrow}^{\downarrow} = \mathrm{TD}\left(\frac{\partial\phi(1 \to 0)}{\partial x_i(1 \to 0)}\right),\tag{4}$$

where TD(.) stands for Truth Density, i.e. function described as relatively number of cases function (.) gets value 1 to all possible cases [15]. Function $\frac{\partial\phi(1\to0)}{\partial x_i(1\to0)}$ is partial Boolean derivation and can be defined as following [29]:

$$\frac{\partial\phi(1 \to 0)}{\partial x_i(1 \to 0)} = \phi(x_1, ..., 1, ...x_n) \wedge \overline{\phi(x_1, ..., 0, ...x_n)}.\tag{5}$$

Equation 4 suppose analysed system is coherent. Therefore it is necessary to investigate only cases, when system component failure leads to system failures. There are multiple structure importance for non-coherent systems. The next one takes into account cases, when system component failure leads to system repair. This can be defined using following equation:

$$\mathrm{SI}_{i\uparrow}^{\downarrow} = \mathrm{TD}\left(\frac{\partial\phi(1 \to 0)}{\partial x_i(0 \to 1)}\right)\tag{6}$$

The total influence of system component can be calculated as a sum of Eqs. 4 and 6 [12]:

$$\mathrm{SI}_i^{\downarrow} = \mathrm{SI}_{i\downarrow}^{\downarrow} + \mathrm{SI}_{i\uparrow}^{\downarrow} = \mathrm{TD}\left(\partial\phi(\boldsymbol{x}/\partial x_i)\right)\tag{7}$$

All of previous equations apply for binary-state systems. Structure importance for multi-state systems can be generalized as following:

$$\mathrm{SI}_i^{\downarrow} = \mathrm{TD}\left(\frac{\partial\phi(j \to k)}{\partial x_i(r \to s)}\right),\tag{8}$$

where $\phi(j \to k)$ means system change state from state j to state k; $j, k < m$. Expression $x(r \to s)$ means system component change state from r to state s; $r, s < m_i$. m_i is number of i-th system component states.

Formula 8 can be used for both - coherent and non-coherent systems. In case of coherent systems, condition $j > k \wedge r > s$ has to be met.

For non-coherent systems, there are also multiple structure importance. $\mathrm{SI}_{i\downarrow}^{\downarrow}$ is common with previous case. For the next one, $\mathrm{SI}_{i\uparrow}^{\downarrow}$ investigating decrease of system performance caused by increase of system component performance, one of condition $j > k \wedge r < s$ or $j < k \wedge r > s$ has to be met. Total topological influence of component can be calculated as sum of these two values.

4   Case Study

In this section we will demonstrate application of described methods in dataset obtained from [7]. This dataset contains information about bicycle crashes such as driver age, whether ambulance was called or not, what was the weather like etc., together with information if bicycle driver was killed, injured or without injure. Whole dataset consists of 11 attributes and 162 records. In order to simplify manipulation with data, each attribute value was mapped into numeric value. Complete list of attributes together with possible values and their mapping can be seen in Table 1.

Table 1. Details of Bike Crashes Dataset

Attribute name	Number of values	List of values (mapped into state)
Ambulance	2	Yes (1), No (0)
Age	7	$0-10$ (0), $11-19$ (1), $20-29$ (2),... 70+ (7)
Bike direction	4	With Traffic (0), Facing Traffic (1), Not applicable (2), Unknown (3)
Bike position	7	Travel Line (0), Sidewalk/Crosswalk/Driveway Crossing (1), Non-Roadway (5), Bike Lane/Paved Shoulder (6), Driveway/Alley (3), Multi-use Path (4), Unknown (2)
Sex	2	Male (0), Female (1)
Biker alcohol	2	Yes (1), No (0)
Driver alcohol	3	Yes (2), No (0), Missing (1)
Driver speed	8	$0-10$ (0), $11-20$ (1), $21-30$ (2),..., $61-65$ (6), Unknown (7)
Light condition	5	DayLight (3), Dark - No Light (1), Dark - Lighted (2), Dusk (0), Unknown (4)
Road surface	5	Croashed Asphalt (4), Smooth Asphalt (3), Concrete (0), Gravel (1), Other (2)
Weather	3	Clear (2), Cloudy (1), Rain (0)

This dataset was analysed using methods of datamining presented in [17, 32]. Using these methods, decision tree was created. This tree was in the next step reduced into MDD using methods described in paper [21,24,28]. Resulting MDD can be seen in Fig. 1. Created mathematical model can be used to perform quantitative analysis as described in previous section.

In the first step, structure importance for each component was calculated according to Eq. 4. This contains only cases, when decrease of system component state leads to decrease of system performance. Results of this calculation can be seen in Fig. 2. The x axis contains individual component and system changes. On the y axis there are values of $\text{SI}_{i\downarrow}^{\downarrow}$ for every component. So for example values

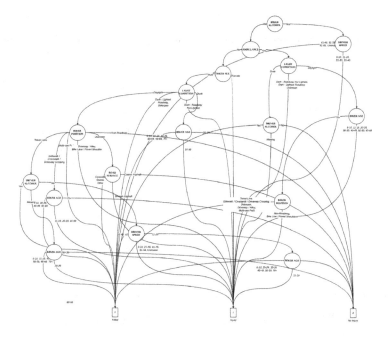

Fig. 1. MDD of Bike Crashes Dataset

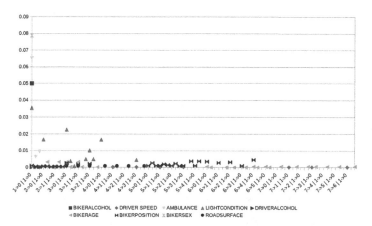

Fig. 2. Results of $SI^{\downarrow}_{i\downarrow}$ for Bike Crashes Dataset

in column "$2 \rightarrow 0|1 \rightarrow 0$" is equal to value of Structure Importance index, when system component state changes from 2 to 0 and system changes from 1 to 0.

From these results we can identify most crucial components according to system structure. These can be seen in Table 2.

Similarly, second structure importance was calculated according to Eq. 6. This contains only cases, when system component performance decrease leads to case system increase its state. Results of this calculation can be seen in Fig. 3. The most crucial components together with value of its structure importance can be seen in Table 3.

Table 2. Attributes with highest values of $\mathrm{SI}_{i\downarrow}^{\downarrow}$ for Bike Crashes Dataset

Component	Component change|System change	Value of $\mathrm{SI}_{i\downarrow}^{\downarrow}$
Biker sex	$1 \to 0\|1 \to 0$	0.0787426
Ambulance	$1 \to 0\|1 \to 0$	0.0651749
Biker alcohol	$1 \to 0\|1 \to 0$	0.0499926
Light condition	$1 \to 0\|1 \to 0$	0.0354167

Table 3. Attributes with highest values of $\mathrm{SI}_{i\uparrow}^{\downarrow}$ for Bike Crashes Dataset

Component	Component change|System change	Value of $\mathrm{SI}_{i\downarrow}^{\downarrow}$
Biker alcohol	$1 \to 0\|0 \to 1$	0.187783
Driver speed	$6 \to 0\|0 \to 1, 6 \to 1\|0 \to 1, 6 \to 2\|0 \to 1$	0.0626488
Light condition	$2 \to 1\|0 \to 1, 4 \to 1\|0 \to 1$	0.025

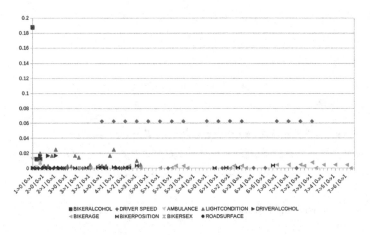

Fig. 3. Results of $\mathrm{SI}_{i\uparrow}^{\downarrow}$ for Bike Crashes Dataset

Finally, structure importance according to Eq. 7 was calculated. This includes both cases - when decrease of system component leads to decrease of system state and decrease of system component leads to increase of system state. Results of this case can be seen in Fig. 4. The components with highest structure importance can be seen in Table 4.

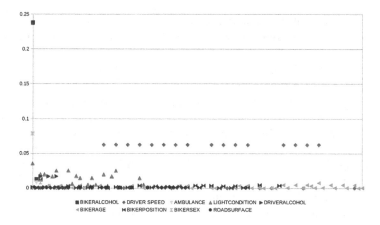

Fig. 4. Results of $SI_i^{\downarrow}$ for Bike Crashes Dataset

Table 4. Attributes with highest values of $SI_i^{\downarrow}$ for Bike Crashes Dataset

Component	Component change|System change	Value of $SI_{i\downarrow}^{\downarrow}$
Biker alcohol	$1 \to 0\|0 \leftrightarrow 1$	0.2377756
Biker sex	$1 \to 0\|0 \leftrightarrow 1$	0.0787426
Ambulance	$1 \to 0\|0 \leftrightarrow 1$	0.0774108
Driver speed	$4 \to 3\|0 \leftrightarrow 1,\ 5 \to 3\|0 \leftrightarrow 1,\ 7 \to 3\|0 \leftrightarrow 1$	0.06264881
Light condition	$1 \to 0\|0 \leftrightarrow 1$	0.0354167

According to Fig. 4, the most crucial attribute of this system is biker alcohol. This can be interpreted as the fact, biker drank alcohol or not is the most significant factor that makes difference between his death or injury. The next crucial attribute is ambulance. The fact ambulance was called to accident has significant impact to result of the accident. The next one is biker sex. The dataset implies, that women has less deaths than men. Significant role in biker survival is caused also by driver speed, where change from 51–55 mps to 31–40 or from 41–50 to 31–40 leads to the fact biker will be alive.

On the other hand, factors as weather or bike direction (whether it is with traffic it) has no impact on result of the accident. However it should be noted, that accuracy of these results depends on amount of available data.

5 Conclusion

This paper contains reliability analysis calculus of multi-state systems based on incompletely specified data. This analysis consists of two steps. The first one is creation of mathematical model. For this purpose we used structure function as it can be used for analysing system behavior based on behavior of its components. Structure function can be represented in multiple ways. In this paper it was represented in form of MDD and it is constructed through the induction of decision tree based on incompletely specified data. MDD can be used for both - topological an probabilistic analysis and can be easily created from decision tree.

The next step in reliability analysis is quantitative analysis using this model. In this paper, we investigate topological analysis of multi-state non-coherent systems, specifically calculus of structure importance of these systems. In difference of other investigations in this paper the non-coherent MSS is considered and mathematical background for calculation of Importance measures is presented.

Mentioned methods was demonstrated on dataset that contains information about bike crashes. Using methods of datamining this dataset was analysed and decision tree was created. This tree was in the next step reduced into MDD from which topological analysis was calculated.

In our future work, we will investigate also probabilistic analysis of multi-state non-coherent systems. This analysis will be based on structure function represented using multi-valued decision diagrams.

References

1. Abdallah, I., et al.: Fault diagnosis of wind turbine structures using decision tree learning algorithms with big data. In: Safety and Reliability – Safe Societies in a Changing World, pp. 3053–3061. CRC Press, June 2018. https://doi.org/10.1201/9781351174664-382
2. Amari, S.V., Xing, L., Shrestha, A., Akers, J., Trivedi, K.S.: Performability analysis of multistate computing systems using multivalued decision diagrams. IEEE Trans. Comput. **59**(10), 1419–1433 (2010). https://doi.org/10.1109/tc.2009.184
3. Aven, T., Baraldi, P., Flage, R., Zio, E.: Uncertainty in Risk Assessment: The Representation and Treatment of Uncertainties by Probabilistic and Non-Probabilistic Methods. Wiley (2013). https://www.amazon.com/Uncertainty-Risk-Assessment-Representation-Non-Probabilistic-ebook/dp/B00HFRG7A8?SubscriptionId=AKIAIOBINVZYXZQZ2U3A&tag=chimbori05-20&linkCode=xm2&camp=2025&creative=165953&creativeASIN=B00HFRG7A8
4. Beeson, S., Andrews, J.: Importance measures for non-coherent-system analysis. IEEE Trans. Reliab. **52**(3), 301–310 (2003). https://doi.org/10.1109/tr.2003.816397
5. Cheushev, V., Simovici, D., Shmerko, V., Yanushkevich, S.: Functional entropy and decision trees. In: Proceedings. 1998 28th IEEE International Symposium on Multiple- Valued Logic (Cat. No.98CB36138), IEEE Computer Society. https://doi.org/10.1109/ismvl.1998.679467
6. Choudhury, M., Mohanram, K.: Reliability analysis of logic circuits. IEEE Trans. Comput. Aided Design Integr. Circuits Syst **28**(3), 392–405 (2009). https://doi.org/10.1109/tcad.2009.2012530
7. Bicycle crashes. https://catalog.data.gov/dataset/bicycle-crashes. Accessed 05 Sept 2019
8. Figueres-Esteban, M., Hughes, P., Rashidy, R.E., van Gulijk, C.: Manifestation of ontologies in graph databases for big data risk analysis. In: Safety and Reliability – Safe Societies in a Changing World, pp. 3189–3193. CRC Press, June 2018. https://doi.org/10.1201/9781351174664-399

9. Gupta, P., Agarwal, S.: A boolean algebra method for reliability calculations. Microelectron. Reliab. **23**(5), 863–865 (1983). https://doi.org/10.1016/0026-2714(83)91014-4
10. Imakhlaf, A.J., Hou, Y., Sallak, M.: Evaluation of the reliability of non-coherent systems using binary decision diagrams. IFAC-PapersOnLine **50**(1), 12243–12248 (2017). https://doi.org/10.1016/j.ifacol.2017.08.2132
11. Kuo, W., Zhu, X.: Importance Measures in Reliability, Risk, and Optimization. Wiley, Hoboken (2012). https://doi.org/10.1002/9781118314593
12. Kvassay, M., Zaitseva, E., Kostolny, J., Levashenko, V.: Reliability analysis of noncoherent systems based on logical differential calculus. In: Risk, Reliability and Safety: Innovating Theory and Practice, pp. 1367–1374. CRC Press, September 2016. https://doi.org/10.1201/9781315374987-205
13. Kvassay, M., Rabcan, J., Rusnak, P.: Multiple-valued logic in analysis of critical states of multi-state system. In: 2017 International Conference on Information and Digital Technologies (IDT), IEEE, July 2017. https://doi.org/10.1109/dt.2017.8024299
14. Kvassay, M., Zaitseva, E., Kostolny, J., Levashenko, V.: Importance analysis of multi-state systems based on integrated direct partial logic derivatives. In: 2015 International Conference on Information and Digital Technologies, IEEE, July 2015. https://doi.org/10.1109/dt.2015.7222970
15. Kvassay, M., Zaitseva, E., Levashenko, V., Kostolny, J.: Minimal cut vectors and logical differential calculus. In: 2014 IEEE 44th International Symposium on Multiple-Valued Logic. IEEE, May 2014. https://doi.org/10.1109/ismvl.2014.37
16. Kvassay, M., Zaitseva, E., Levashenko, V., Kostolny, J.: Reliability analysis of multiple-outputs logic circuits based on structure function approach. IEEE Trans. Comput. Aided Design Integr. Circuits Syst. 1 (2016). https://doi.org/10.1109/tcad.2016.2586444
17. Levashenko, V.G., Zaitseva, E.N.: Usage of new information estimations for induction of fuzzy decision trees. In: Yin, H., Allinson, N., Freeman, R., Keane, J., Hubbard, S. (eds.) IDEAL 2002. LNCS, vol. 2412, pp. 493–499. Springer, Heidelberg (2002). https://doi.org/10.1007/3-540-45675-9_74
18. Lisnianski, A., Frenkel, I., Ding, Y.: Multi-state System Reliability Analysis and Optimization for Engineers and Industrial Managers. Springer, London (2010). https://doi.org/10.1007/978-1-84996-320-6
19. Lisnianski, A., Levitin, G.: Multi-State System Reliability: Assessment, Optimization and Application. Proc. Eng., vol. 6. World Scientific (2003). https://doi.org/10.1142/5221
20. Lloris, A., Gomez, J.F., Roman, R.: Using decision trees for the minimization of multiple-valued functions. Int. J. Electron. **75**(6), 1035–1041 (1993). https://doi.org/10.1080/00207219308907180
21. Miller, D., Drechsler, R.: Implementing a multiple-valued decision diagram package. In: Proceedings. 1998 28th IEEE International Symposium on Multiple-Valued Logic (Cat. No.98CB36138). IEEE Computer Society. https://doi.org/10.1109/ismvl.1998.679287
22. Miller, D., Drechsler, R.: On the construction of multiple-valued decision diagrams. In: Proceedings 32nd IEEE International Symposium on Multiple- Valued Logic, IEEE Computer Society. https://doi.org/10.1109/ismvl.2002.1011095
23. Mo, Y., Xing, L., Amari, S.V.: A multiple-valued decision diagram based method for efficient reliability analysis of non-repairable phased-mission systems. IEEE Trans. Reliab. **63**(1), 320–330 (2014). https://doi.org/10.1109/tr.2014.2299497

24. Mo, Y., Xing, L., Cui, L., Si, S.: MDD-based performability analysis of multi-state linear consecutive- k-out-of-n: F systems. Reliab. Eng. Syst. Saf. **166**, 124–131 (2017). https://doi.org/10.1016/j.ress.2016.08.027

25. Natvig, B.: Multistate Systems Reliability Theory with Applications. Wiley (2011). https://doi.org/10.1002/9780470977088

26. Rabcan, J., Levashenko, V., Zaitseva, E., Chovancova, O.: Generation of structure function based on ambiguous and incompletely specified data using fuzzy random forest. In: 2018 IEEE 9th International Conference on Dependable Systems, Services and Technologies (DESSERT), IEEE, May 2018. https://doi.org/10.1109/dessert.2018.8409170

27. Rashidy, R.A.H.E., Hughes, P., Figueres-Esteban, M., Harrison, C., Gulijk, C.V.: A big data modeling approach with graph databases for SPAD risk. Saf. Sci. **110**, 75–79 (2018). https://doi.org/10.1016/j.ssci.2017.11.019

28. Sedlacek, P., Rabcan, J., Kostolny, J.: Importance analysis of multi-state system based on incompletely specified data by multi-valued decision diagrams. In: 2019 International Conference on Information and Digital Technologies (IDT), IEEE (2019). https://doi.org/10.1109/dt.2019.8813385

29. Tapia, M., Guima, T., Katbab, A.: Calculus for a multivalued-logic algebraic system. Appl. Math. Comput. **42**(3), 255–285 (1991). https://doi.org/10.1016/0096-3003(91)90004-7

30. Zaitseva, E.N., Levashenko, V.G.: Importance analysis by logical differential calculus. Autom. Remote Control **74**(2), 171–182 (2013). https://doi.org/10.1134/S000511791302001X

31. Zaitseva, E., Levashenko, V.: Investigation multi-state system reliability by structure function. In: 2nd International Conference on Dependability of Computer Systems (DepCoS-RELCOMEX), IEEE, June 2007. https://doi.org/10.1109/depcos-relcomex.2007.28

32. Zaitseva, E., Levashenko, V.: Construction of a reliability structure function based on uncertain data. IEEE Trans. Reliab. **65**(4), 1710–1723 (2016). https://doi.org/10.1109/tr.2016.2578948

33. Zaitseva, E., Levashenko, V.: Reliability analysis of multi-state system with application of multiple-valued logic. Int. J. Quality Reliab. Manage. **34**(6), 862–878 (2017). https://doi.org/10.1108/ijqrm-06-2016-0081

34. Zhang, Q., Mei, Q.: Reliability analysis for a real non-coherent system. IEEE Trans. Reliab. **R–36**(4), 436–439 (1987). https://doi.org/10.1109/tr.1987.5222433

35. Zio, E.: An Introduction to the Basics of Reliability and Risk Analysis. World Scientific Publishing Company (2007). https://doi.org/10.1142/6442

Pattern Recognition and Image Analysis

Brands and Caps Labeling Recognition in Images Using Deep Learning

Vladimir Golovko$^{(\boxtimes)}$ (ID), Aliaksandr Kroshchanka (ID), and Egor Mikhno (ID)

Brest State Technical University, Moskovskaya 267, 224017 Brest, Belarus
vladimir.golovko@gmail.com

Abstract. In this paper, we investigate and analyze applying several well-known models to the task of brands detection in images. Besides this we explore applying these models for solution of industrial task of detection objects on running production line.

In first parts of paper we compare and analyze most effective and widely used architectures as Faster R-CNN (based on Inception v2 and ResNet-50/101), SSD (based on Inception v2 and MobileNet). We implement such comparison using dataset of beer brands. The obtained results confirm the effectiveness of applying Faster R-CNN. But such models are resource intensive. In contrast SSD models perform processing faster than Faster R-CNN and can be considered as basic models for detection and segmentation of objects in images and video in real time.

Based on getting results of comparing models in the last parts of paper intelligent system for detection and recognition labeling of bottles in real time is given.

Keywords: Deep neural network · Object detection · Image classification · Beer brands · Real-time detection · Intelligent systems

1 Introduction

The task of object detection on the images is one of the most actively studied tasks of artificial intelligence. Objects search and counting their number on images or video is of a great importance for a business. Routine tasks for the manual assessment of the number of various types of goods take a considerable part of the work-time of specialists. Therefore, the application of recent research in the field of deep convolutional neural networks for the tasks of detection and classification can help to automate such routine work. In this work, we investigated various models for the detection of goods of certain trademarks on images. The obtained results allow us to talk about the degree of applicability of various models to the proposed detection problem.

2 Existing Solutions

Object detection is one of the most popular research areas in machine learning for recent years. To solve this problem, traditional methods based on the usage of

© Springer Nature Switzerland AG 2019
S. V. Ablameyko et al. (Eds.): PRIP 2019, CCIS 1055, pp. 35–51, 2019.
https://doi.org/10.1007/978-3-030-35430-5_4

SIFT (Scale-Invariant Feature Transform) [1] and SURF (Speeded Up Robust Features) feature tags [2] were actively used. The SIFT method is based on extracting key points from a set of objects of interest and comparing them with new analyzed images. SIFT allows you to detect an object in the presence of noise and partial overlap. The SURF method is based on SIFT, but at the same time, it has greater work speed [3]. Both methods have high mathematical complexity and, in general, have low generalizing ability in comparison with modern methods based on using convolutional neural networks [4].

The advances made in learning deep neural networks have influenced on the methods used in the detection of objects. So, ideas and approaches based on the use of various neural network architectures began to develop actively. In 2014, R-CNN [5] was proposed, in 2015 – Fast R-CNN [6], a feature of which was the use of a special ROI-layer, which made it possible to speed up the network. Following it, the Faster R-CNN architecture was developed [7], which differs from Fast R-CNN in the presence of a special RPN network (Region Proposal Network), whose main task is to highlight areas of the applicants. Such changes made it possible not only to speed up the work of the network but also to get better indicators of the generalizing ability compared to Fast R-CNN. In 2016, YOLO [8] and SSD [9] architectures were proposed.

All of meta-architectures are divided into two main categories:

1. Methods with a preliminary selection of candidates (R-CNN, Fast R-CNN, Faster R-CNN);
2. One-way methods (one-look), which include SSD, YOLO, YOLO9000.

The peculiarity of the second group of methods is the detection of objects in the image in one pass (one-look), without the need to solve two independent tasks, namely the localization of the object and its classification. For the methods of the first group, these two problems are solved by separate parts of the neural network architecture or even by separate methods (R-CNN).

All models for detecting objects in images are based on the use of a previously trained deep convolutional neural network. Most often these are neural networks for classification without the last fully connected layer. Then the network is trained on new data. Thus, the pre-trained network plays the role of a "supplier" of features for the layers performing detection.

3 Detection of Brands

3.1 Dataset

We used photographs from supermarkets, provided by LeverX [10], as initial data. Examples of images (RGB) used for training are shown in Fig. 1.

We used a general sample of 650 photographs, with 562 images of this sample used for training and the remaining 88 images for testing. In the marking process, ten of the most frequently encountered beer brands were identified. Sample preparation consisted of manually sorting the images with the definition

Fig. 1. Image from LeverX dataset

for each of the characteristics of rectangular areas that include goods (height, width, coordinates of the upper left corner). These rectangular areas are called bounding boxes. On one image there can be several bounding boxes.

The use of bounding boxes to select some objects does not seem appropriate since objects can have a complex shape far from a rectangular one (Fig. 2). This is explained by the fact that initially, three-dimensional objects (such as boxes) are difficult to place in a rectangular area without including unnecessary elements (such as fragments of other boxes, a background image, etc.). For such objects, it is possible to obtain acceptable detection results if, when marking them out, to focus on the image of the trademark, and not on the container on which it is located.

3.2 Proposed Solution

To solve the problem of detection, we used several different architectures of deep neural networks [11]. All of them showed acceptable results in solving the detection problem. The analysis was carried out for the following architectures: Faster R-CNN, based on the ResNet-50/101 classifier [12] and SSD.

The Faster R-CNN model consists of three parts (Fig. 3). The first part is the feature extractor (we used ResNet-50, ResNet-101 and Inception v2 classifiers), pre-trained on a COCO dataset [13]. The second part is the RPN network that generates the candidate regions. Finally, the third part is the detector, which is represented by additional fully connected layers that generate the coordinates

Fig. 2. Objects with complex bounds

of bounding boxes containing the desired objects, and class labels for each such area. A key feature of the model is the RPN-network, to the input of which the feature maps obtained by the preceding convolutional layer are fed. Due to this, the generation of applicants is faster than using the original full-size image.

The ResNet50/101 classifiers have the classic structure of deep convolutional neural networks with connections for quick access (residual connections). These connections map identifiers by skipping one or more layers and adding their outputs to the outputs of the layer stack. When using such blocks among layers of the same dimension, accuracy increases without increasing the dimension of the model itself.

The SSD model as well, as Faster R-CNN model consists of three parts (Fig. 4). The first part is the feature extractor (we used Inception v2 and MobileNet v2 classifiers) pre-trained on a COCO sample [13]. The second part is the additional convolutional layers after feature extractor. They are used for reducing the dimension of feature maps for different detection and classification blocks. This blocks are the last part of this model, that consists from default box generator, localization and confidence parts. After the end of the last block, the Fast NMS algorithm is used for final detection and classification.

The Inception v2 classifier is interesting using mixed layers consisting of convolutional and pooling layers. Each mixed layer consists of several parallel branches, each of which processes input information in its own way. The processing results of each of the branches are combined into a single output pattern,

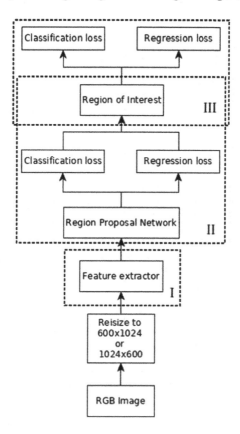

Fig. 3. Faster R-CNN meta-architecture

which can be further processed. An equally important model Inception v2 is the replacement of the classical convolution of the 5×5 format with two equivalent 3×3 formats, which gives a gain in computational speed.

Features of the MobileNetV2 classifier are the presence of residual connections and expansion convolution block. This block consists of 3 consecutive layers. The first is a pointwise convolution with many channels. The second is depthwise convolution with ReLU6 activation function. The first and second layers were used in the MobileNetV2 model as the main unit. And finally, the third layer that distinguishes MobileNetV2 from MobileNet V1 is the convolutional layer with 1×1 linear activation function, which reduces the number of channels. Such organization of the model allowed to increase the accuracy and computational speed of the model compared to the previous version.

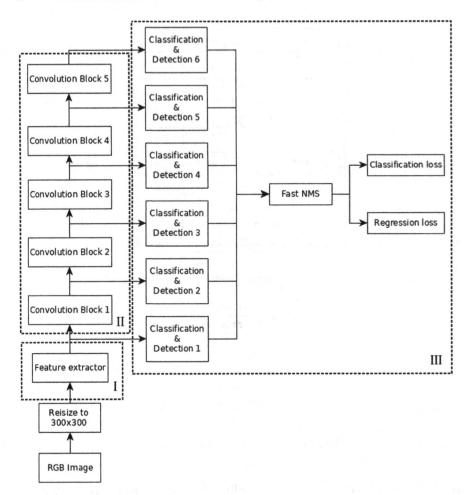

Fig. 4. SSD meta-architecture

3.3   Models Evaluation and Results

To evaluate the effectiveness of the trained models, we used the mAP (mean average precision metric). This metric is the most frequently used for evaluating the quality of detection models. It is used in conjunction with its modifications calculated for various threshold values of IoU (Intersection over Union, a quantity called the Jaccard measure).

The value of IoU is calculated by the following way:

$$IoU = \frac{S_{ground_{true}} \cap S_{box}}{S_{ground_{true}} \cup S_{box}} \tag{1}$$

where $S_{ground_{true}}$ – area of reference box that is used to mark the training set, S_{box} – area of the box generated by the model.

As you know, the proportion of correct detections in the total number of detections obtained by the neural network is P and calculated as follows:

$$P = \frac{TP}{TP + FP} \tag{2}$$

where TP – the number of true-positive, FP – the number of false-positive detection results.

Regarding the task of detecting objects, the number of TP determines the total number of bounding boxes for which the IoU value, calculated relative to the true areas (Ground-true box), is greater than a certain threshold (most often the threshold value is chosen 0.5). Thus, if the IoU value for such predicted area greater than 0.5, then detection is considered as true positive. If there are several detections for this true region, then one detection is selected with the largest IoU value, and the rest are considered as FP (hard non-maximum suppression).

The averaged value for all sensitivity values gives AP:

$$AP = \frac{1}{N} \sum_{i=1}^{N} \frac{TP_i}{TP_i + FP_i} \tag{3}$$

where N – the number of sensitivity values calculated at regular intervals.

Table 1. AP and mAP for each class (*we used next abbreviations: FRIv2 – Faster RCNN Inception v2, FRR101 – Faster RCNN ResNet-101, FRR50 – Faster R-CNN ResNet-50, SIv2 – SSD Inception v2, SMv2 – SSD MobileNet v2*)

Classes	FRIv2	FRR101	FRR50	SIv2	SMv2
blue_moon_belgian_white	0.922	0.896	0.916	0.764	0.780
bud_light	0.770	0.806	0.783	0.624	0.635
budweiser	0.834	0.808	0.843	0.729	0.685
coors_light	0.861	0.826	0.862	0.729	0.745
corona_extra	0.772	0.814	0.846	0.721	0.720
corona_extra	0.860	0.821	0.868	0.671	0.707
heineken	0.802	0.805	0.853	0.651	0.629
michelob_ultra	0.679	0.707	0.799	0.635	0.586
miller_lite	0.883	0.855	0.910	0.783	0.783
modelo_especial	0.746	0.724	0.798	0.568	0.533
Total mAP	0.813	0.806	0.848	0.687	0.680
Steps	32084	11240	8450	16228	22480
Speed of NN (ms) – CPU	863	3483	3055	67	36
Speed of NN (ms) – GPU	211	700	624	32	19

Fig. 5. Detection capability of models

The mAP value is obtained by averaging the AP over all the object classes considered.

All tested models were trained at a different number of iterations. In average, an acceptable result was achieved after 5,000 iterations of training. We used a general approach: the model was trained for 1000 iterations, after which it was tested, then the process was repeated for the next 1000 iterations. If after next stage of learning the results were not improved or became worse, the process was completed.

Table 1 shows results of the detection for each class and architecture. The best results were obtained by Faster R-CNN architecture. SSD architectures showed the worst detection results, regardless of the number of learning iterations. This is explained by the fact that such networks as SSD and YOLO have a poor ability to detect small objects in an image [14] – feature maps for such architectures have low resolution (usually 38×38 or 19×19). For the considered detection problem, this is of a critical importance, since all the images from the sample have a sufficiently high resolution, but the relative size of the objects is small. However, Faster R-CNN architecture is more resource intensive than SSD and YOLO. Time evaluation is given for the case of processing one image.

Table 2. Characteristics of models

Model	Optimizer	Training rate	Batch size
faster rcnn inception v2	momentum	$[2e{-}4; 5e{-}5]$	1
faster rcnn resnet 50	exponential	$1e{-}3$	1
faster rcnn resnet 101	momentum	$[3e{-}4; 5e{-}5]$	1
ssd inception v2	rms prop	$4e{-}3$	5
ssd mobilenet v2	rms prop	$2e{-}3$	10

Table 3. Hardware characteristics

Processor	
Model	Intel Core i7-4790K
Number of cores	4
Number of threads	8
Max frequency	4 GHz
Graphic card	
Model	GeForce GTX 750Ti
Number of CUDA cores	640
Max frequency	1150 MHz
Memory	2 Gb
Memory type	GDDR5

A brief description of main characteristic of used models and parameters of training is presented in Table 2. For all models we have used softmax as activation function on the last layer. We used pretrained versions of models.

Figure 5 visualizes results of detection on test images.

Time estimates have been received on a computer with configuration presented in Table 3.

4   Task of Labeling Recognition

Applications of neural network for industrial purposes have very fascinating perspectives. It is especially refers to object detection tasks in regular production processes. For example, detection of specially classes of objects, which transfer by production line. It is critical important these operations will be executed very quickly.

We are solving the task of detection numbers in labeling of bottles with the milk production (jogurt, kefir, etc.) [15]. This detection is only a part of problem. Additionally system should check labeling and reveal some failure, which can be raised in process of printing. We have videostream as a input data, which arrives from production line's RGB-camera. Such stream has rate 76 frames per second. Example of frame is presented on Fig. 6.

Objects detection is possible in real-time mode, but in this case problem of quick processing by neural network reveals. At processing each frame neural networks can not finish work just in time if videostream with high framerate

Fig. 6. Example of frame

is used. In our case time window, which can be involved for processing one frame from this stream, is about 0.013 s or 13 ms. Neural networks, which are capable for object detection in this time interval with restricted machine resources (e.g., mobile devices), don't exist. Therefore it is necessary to quick evaluate importance of separate frame for detection and drop others irrelevant frames.

Since the bottles appear on production line with defined rate, it can be selected key frames, which will be processed by network, and others, intermediate frames, can be dropped.

As mentioned above during the process of bottle's labeling recognition some accessory tasks should be solved, which is connected with correctness of printing this labeling. First task is to define of existence labeling on the bottle. Second task, which is more general case of first one, is to determine of distortion of labeling (e.g. missing of parts, blur, etc.) Third task is a detection of numbers, forming date and time of producing of good and check of correctness these data in compare to pattern. Failures of labeling are represented schematically in Fig. 7.

4.1   Architecture of Recognition System

Labeling recognition system consists of 4 neural networks, which work in parallel and sequence modes (Fig. 8).

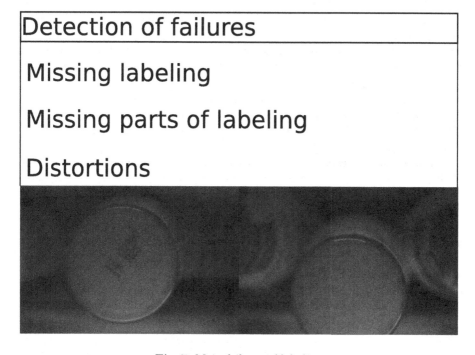

Fig. 7. Main failures of labeling

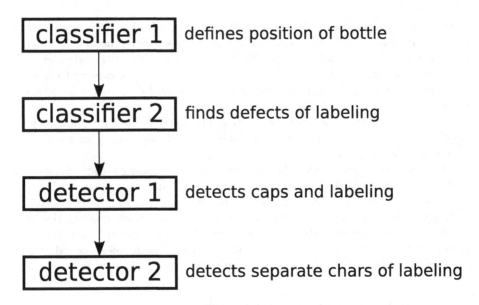

classifier 1 — defines position of bottle

classifier 2 — finds defects of labeling

detector 1 — detects caps and labeling

detector 2 — detects separate chars of labeling

Fig. 8. Scheme of recognition system

First network is a simple classifier based on convolutional neural network, which defines position of bottle with labeling in the frame. We have four main positions according to distance from the center of the frame. First class describes minimum distance from the center of the frame. Only frames from this class are used in subsequent analysis by others networks. Second and third classes describe mean and maximum distance. Finally, fourth class is used in cases, when good with labels is missing in frame (for example, in case of empty production line).

If the frame was assigned to first class, it fed into second neural network. This network is a classifier also and serves for detection of failure of labeling. These failures of labeling include full lack of marking, partially lack of marking, distortion of labeling (blur).

We have trained second classifier for detection only one failure – full lack of labeling.

If failure was detected, system notified operator about this. Else frame is transferred to next network.

Third neural network detects caps of bottle and labeling in frame. We have used SSD with MobileNet as a base classifier for this stage. This model has presented maximum speed in task of brands detection and has become the most acceptable candidate for real-time work.

Finally, fourth neural network is SSD-detector as well. It implements the search for separate numbers in labeling and forms final result of recognition.

Now let us consider these architectures more details.

4.2 Architectures of Used Neural Networks

As already has been said, classifiers on first two stages are simple convolutional neural networks.

First classifier has architecture presented in Fig. 9. It contains 5 layers and has 4 output neurons (one per class for position of bottles in frame). All layers have ReLU as activation function except 3-th and last. They have linear and softmax activation functions respectively. Also network has max pooling after first and second convolutional layers with stride 2.

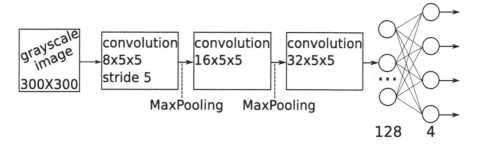

Fig. 9. Architecture of "position-define" classifier

Second classifier has architecture presented in Fig. 10. It contains 6 layers and has 2 output neurons (one per class for two possible states – one for labeling without failures and one for missing labeling). Network has max pooling after first layer and batch normalization after first and second layers.

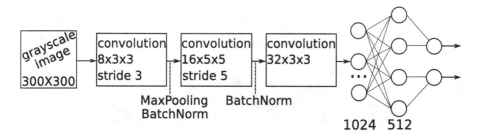

Fig. 10. Architecture of "failures-define" classifier

4.3 Training Sets: Main Properties

We used the auxiliary detector Faster R-CNN based on classifier ResNet-50 for forming training set for first classifier. Task of this network is an accurate mark-up of the general set of images. Measure of such mark-up is a euclidian distance between center of bottle's cap and center of frame. This detector has been trained

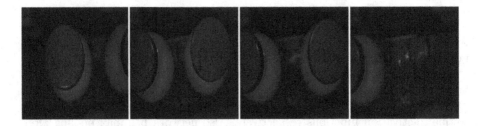

Fig. 11. Samples from all four classes of a bottle's position

in a traditional manner. Then it has been used for an automatically mark-up of the general set. Such way we formed sets for each class of first classifier (Fig. 11).

Training set formation for second classifier was more complex due to missing of sufficient amount of data. Such failure of labeling as full missing is very rare thing. Therefore we prepared hand-made dataset, which contains bottle caps without labels (Fig. 12). For this all frames from first class were been processed to remove labeling. Thus, two groups of caps were obtained, the samples from the first group contain the labeling, and from the second – don't.

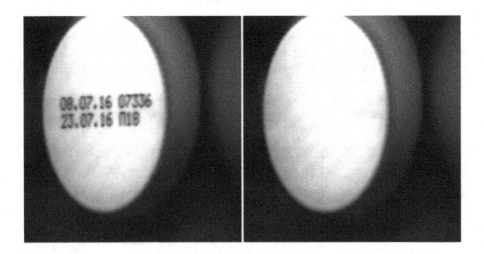

Fig. 12. Example from hand-made dataset

For first and second detectors we use datasets with different count of samples. So, first dataset contains 830 samples and for second – only 95. This is connected with fact that images from second dataset include more objects for detection and it compensates little size of dataset.

Images from these datasets labeled manually.

4.4 Results of Detection

Applying SSD-models allow to reach effectiveness of detection in **99%** **(mAP = 0,99)** for production labeling and **97%** for parts of labeling (numbers). Besides speed of system allows to detect labeling in videostream with rate 76 frames per second. It's was possible with help of parallel functioning neural networks, which are included in system (Fig. 13).

Results of detection for first and second SSD-network are presented in Figs. 14 and 15.

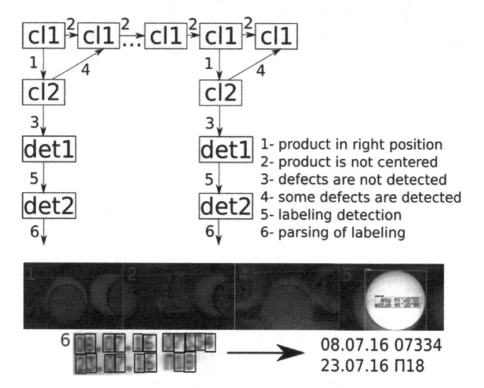

Fig. 13. System functioning

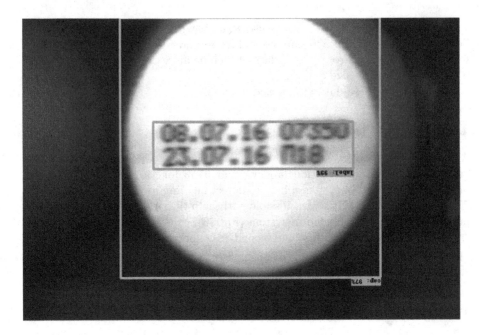

Fig. 14. Labeling detection: images are inputted in inverted form

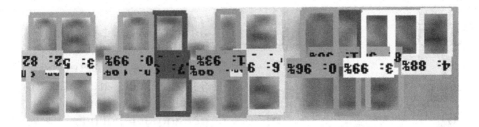

Fig. 15. Parts of labeling (numbers) detection: images are inputted in inverted form

5   Conclusion

This paper discusses the use of various models to solve the problem of detecting goods of different brands in the image.

A comparative analysis of the most efficient and widely used neural network architectures Faster R-CNN (ResNet-50/101), and SSD have been carried out. The results confirm the effectiveness of applying the Faster R-CNN architecture to any image samples. However, it is necessary to note the resource intensity of such architectures and their unsuitability for solving problems, in which the analysis time is an important criterion of efficiency. At the same time, SSD models can be successfully used as part of mobile detection systems, limited in their hardware capabilities. In addition, these neural network architectures perform faster than Faster R-CNN processing and can be considered as basic models for detecting and segmentation of photo and video images in real time.

References

1. Lowe, D.: Object recognition from local scale-invariant features. In: Proceedings of the IEEE International Conference on Computer Vision, Kerkyra, Greece, vol. 2, pp. 1150–1157. IEEE (1999)
2. Bay, H., Tuytelaars, T., Van Gool, L.: SURF: speeded up robust features. In: Leonardis, A., Bischof, H., Pinz, A. (eds.) ECCV 2006. LNCS, vol. 3951, pp. 404–417. Springer, Heidelberg (2006). https://doi.org/10.1007/11744023_32
3. Panchal, P.M., Panchal, S.R., Shah, S.K.: A comparison of SIFT and SURF. Int. J. Innov. Res. Comput. Commun. Eng. 1(2), 323–327 (2013)
4. LobnaRagab, S.: Object detection using histogram and SIFT algorithm vs convolutional neural networks (2014). http://www.academia.edu/24497785/Object_Detection_using_Histogram_and_SIFT_Algorithm_Vs_Convolutional_Neural_Networks. Accessed 30 Aug 2019
5. Girshick, R., Donahue, J., Darrell, T., Malik, J.: Rich feature hierarchies for accurate object detection and semantic segmentation (2014). https://arxiv.org/pdf/1311.2524v5.pdf. Accessed 30 Aug 2019
6. Girshick, R.: Fast R-CNN (2015). https://arxiv.org/pdf/1504.08083.pdf. Accessed 30 Aug 2019
7. Ren, S., He, K., Girshick, R., Sun, J.: Faster R-CNN: towards real-time object detection with region proposal networks (2016). https://arxiv.org/pdf/1506.01497.pdf. Accessed 30 Aug 2019
8. Redmon, J., Divvala, S., Girshick, R., Farhadi, A.: You only look once: unified, real-time object detection (2016). https://arxiv.org/pdf/1506.02640.pdf. Accessed 30 Aug 2019
9. Liu, W., et al.: SSD: Single Shot MultiBox Detector (2016). https://arxiv.org/pdf/1512.02325.pdf. Accessed 30 Aug 2019
10. Hire SAP integrator, long-term SAP service provider—LeverX. https://leverx.com. Accessed 30 Aug 2019
11. Golovko, V., Mikhno, E., Kroschenko, A., Bezobrazov, S.: Deep learning for brands object detection and recognition in images. In: Pattern Recognition and Information Processing (PRIP'2019), Minsk, Belarus, pp. 155–158. BSUIR (2019)
12. Kaiming, H., Xiangyu, Z., Shaoqing, R., Jian, S.: Deep residual learning for image recognition (2015). https://arxiv.org/pdf/1512.03385.pdf. Accessed 30 Aug 2019
13. Lin, T., et al.: Microsoft COCO: common objects in context (2015). https://arxiv.org/pdf/1405.0312.pdf. Accessed 30 Aug 2019
14. Huang, J., et al.: Speed/accuracy trade-offs for modern convolutional object detectors. In: IEEE Conference on Computer Vision and Pattern Recognition (CVPR), Honolulu, HI, USA, pp. 7310–7319. IEEE (2017)
15. Golovko, V., Kroshchanka, A., Ivashenko, V., Kovalev, M., Taberko, V., Ivaniuk, D.: Principles of decision-making systems building based on the integration of neural networks and semantic models. In: Open Semantic Technologies for Intelligent Systems (OSTIS'2019), Minsk, Belarus, pp. 91–102. BSUIR (2019)

Image Semantic Segmentation Based on Convolutional Neural Networks for Monitoring Agricultural Vegetation

Valentin Ganchenko[(⊠)] and Alexander Doudkin

United Institute of Informatics Problems, Surganov st., 6, 220012 Minsk, Belarus
ganchenko@lsi.bas-net.by, doudkin@newman.bas-net.by

Abstract. This paper considers problem of recognition agricultural vegetation state from aerial photographs of various spatial resolutions. Semantic segmentation based on convolutional neural networks is used as a basis for recognition. Two neural networks with SegNet and U-Net architectures are presented and investigated for this aim.

Keywords: Convolutional neural network · Semantic segmentation · Aerial photograph · Agricultural vegetation

1 Introduction

Precision farming implies availability of accurate and promptly updated information about vegetation and soil state. It is possible to obtain such information when remote sensing is used. Remote sensing methods for monitoring agricultural fields make a possibility to quickly identify vegetation areas affected by some diseases. Detection of the diseased areas in early stages of development allows locating and curing the disease promptly and at minimal cost. There are two main approaches to solve the problem of identifying diseased areas - spectrometric and optical [1–7]. The spectrometric approach allows determining many diseases in early stages of development. However, this approach requires multispectral imaging equipment, which is not always possible. In this point of view optical methods are more preferable.

Unmanned aerial vehicles (UAVs) are effective tools of data collection in agriculture because they are cheaper and more efficient in comparison with satellites [8, 9]. UAVs provide visual information about large areas of crops as quickly as possible. Obtained images can import into a GIS database for further processing and analysis, which allows farm managers to make operational decisions.

Convolution neural networks (CNNs) are successfully used for processing of aerial photographs of vegetation in solving various problems of precision farming [10]. In works [11–13], weed extraction in fields with accuracy of more than 90% is shown on

The work was partially supported by Belarusian Republican Foundation for Fundamental Research (project No. Ф18В-005) and the State Committee on Science and Technology of the Republic of Belarus (project no Ф18ПЛШГ-008П).

S. V. Ablameyko et al. (Eds.): PRIP 2019, CCIS 1055, pp. 52–63, 2019.
https://doi.org/10.1007/978-3-030-35430-5_5

data obtained from a robot, where CNN is used for classification of objects and semantic segmentation. Residual CNN is used for semantic segmentation to detect flowers in task of estimating flowering intensity to predict yield [14]. At the same time, detection accuracy is achieved 67–94%, depending on photographed plants. The yield is also estimated for the already growing fruits [15], for which multi-layer perceptron and CNN are used. In [16], CNN model is presented for extracting vegetation from Gaofen-2 remote sensing images. The authors have created two-layer encoder based on CNN, that allows to obtain of 89–90% accuracy of identification. The first layer has two sets of convolutional kernels for selection of features of farmland and woodlands, respectively. The second level consists of two coders that use nonlinear functions to encode the features and to compare codes with corresponding category number. CNNs also can be applied for damage degree evaluation of individual plants. So in [17] U-Net scheme is used, a damage degree of cucumber foliage by powdery mildew is estimated to within 96%. Based on CNN semantic segmentation is also used for thematic mapping. For example, it was shown in [18], where vegetative cover for agricultural land is assessed.

The presented work focuses on recognition of areas of vegetation, state of which has changed due to influence of disease. Two CNNs for implementing of semantic segmentation of color images of agricultural fields is proposed. In this case, disease classification is not performed at this stage. The aim of the work is to develop algorithms for processing of digital color images of various spatial resolutions.

2   Formulation of Problem

Task of the research is to develop transformation algorithm $A : I_{orig} \rightarrow I_{result}$, which allows to obtain image I_{result} from original image of agricultural field I_{orig}. Each pixel $I_{orig}(x, y)$ is a point in RGB space and each pixel $I_{result}(x, y)$ corresponds to one of four classes ("soil", "healthy vegetation", "diseased vegetation" and "other objects").

Materials for research are photographs both of individual plants and an experimental potato field. The pictures were made from a height of 5, 15, 50, and 100 m [19, 20]. To obtain data, small parts of the field were selected using four square marks. The length of the side of the square is one meter; the width of the two black lines is 20 cm (Fig. 1). The marks allow not only to determine area for research, but also to calculate image spatial resolution.

Three groups of plants are observed:

- plants infected with the disease alternaria;
- plants infected with bacterial disease erwinia;
- healthy plants (control group).

The plants were photographed daily at 8, 10, 12, 14 and 16 h during the 8 days in July.

As a result of the diseases mentioned above, chlorophyll is destroyed in potato leaves, what leads to a change in color of plants. Also it should be noted that in clear weather, the sun's glare on leaves also creates yellow effect, what introduces an additional error during automatic processing.

Histogram analysis of color characteristics of various types of photographs shows a noticeable difference between images of soil and vegetation, as well as the difference in blue channel for healthy and disease plants. For example, for the images of healthy, diseased vegetation and soil in respective histograms, it is visible that the histograms for soil are different from histograms for vegetation on each color channel, and histograms for healthy and diseased vegetation channels differ in shape (Fig. 2).

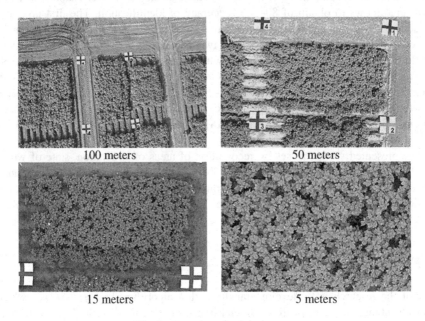

Fig. 1. Samples of origin images

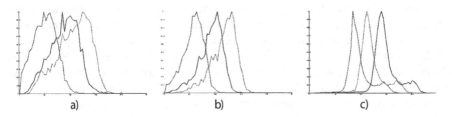

Fig. 2. Histograms: (a) diseased plants; (b) healthy plants; (c) soil

However, presence of several type objects in the selected areas of the images leads to distortion of histogram of the objects – bins will be shifted and there won't be clear peaks. Such distortions, as well as a significant similarity of color characteristics of healthy and diseased vegetation, require information about structure of images of various classes for their recognition. Structural information can be taken into account when CNNs are used as the basis for the proposed algorithms.

3 Preparing of Data for Training and Validation

The training set was obtained by "slicing" existing aerial photographs with labeled areas. At the same time, sections of 256×256 pixels were cut with overlapping, vertical and horizontal reflection, as well as with the addition of turns at angles multiple of $90°$. A class mask is a halftone image that has the same size as the image. A mask image contains the number of brightness levels which equals to the number of the classes in the image. The following brightness values correspond to the classes: 0 – "soil", 1 – "healthy vegetation", 2 – "diseased vegetation", 3 – "other objects".

4 Based on SegNet Segmentation

It is proposed the CNN based on SegNet architecture [21, 22] (denote it by A_s; view of this architecture is presented on Fig. 3) that segments images into four segments: "soil", "healthy vegetation", "diseased vegetation" and "other objects".

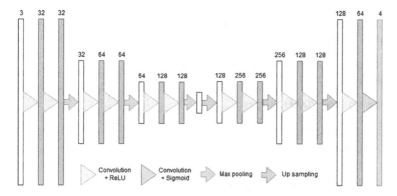

Fig. 3. Implemented SegNet architecture

Empirically selected following parameters of the CNN:

- Input layer size: $256 \times 256 \times 3$ (color image).
- Convolutional layer Conv2D_1.1: filter size $F_s = 3$, filters count $F_c = 32$, activation function – ReLU.
- Convolutional layer Conv2D_1.2: filter size $F_s = 3$, filters count $F_c = 32$, activation function – ReLU.
- Max pooling layer MaxPooling2D_1: filter size $F_s = 2$.
- Convolutional layer Conv2D_2.1: filter size $F_s = 3$, filters count $F_c = 64$, activation function – ReLU.
- Convolutional layer Conv2D_2.2: filter size $F_s = 3$, filters count $F_c = 64$, activation function – ReLU.
- Max pooling layer MaxPooling2D_2: filter size $F_s = 2$.

- Convolutional layer Conv2D_3.1: filter size $F_s = 3$, filters count $F_c = 128$, activation function – ReLU.
- Convolutional layer Conv2D_3.2: filter size $F_s = 3$, filters count $F_c = 128$, activation function – ReLU.
- Max pooling layer MaxPooling2D_3: filter size $F_s = 2$.
- Upsampling layer UpSampling2D_1: scale factor = 2 interpolation – bilinear.
- Convolutional layer Conv2D_4.1: filter size $F_s = 3$, filters count $F_c = 256$, activation function – ReLU.
- Convolutional layer Conv2D_4.2: filter size $F_s = 3$, filters count $F_c = 256$, activation function – ReLU.
- Upsampling layer UpSampling2D_2: scale factor = 2 interpolation – bilinear.
- Convolutional layer Conv2D_5.1: filter size $F_s = 3$, filters count $F_c = 128$, activation function – ReLU.
- Convolutional layer Conv2D_5.2: filter size $F_s = 3$, filters count $F_c = 128$, activation function – ReLU.
- Upsampling layer UpSampling2D_3: scale factor = 2 interpolation – bilinear.
- Convolutional layer Conv2D_6.1: filter size $F_s = 3$, filters count $F_c = 64$, activation function – ReLU.
- Output convolutional layer Conv2D_6.2: filter size $F_s = 3$, filters count $F_c = 4$, activation function – sigmoid, output layer size – $256 \times 256 \times 4$.

Loss function – softmax cross entropy [23].
Training:

- Training set size: 20000 images.
- Validation set size: 4000 images.
- Accuracy for validation set: 92.36%.

5 Based on U-Net Segmentation

The U-Net A_u segmenter is a CNN (Fig. 4), which segments image into four segments: "soil", "healthy vegetation", "diseased vegetation" and "other objects". This architecture differs from SegNet by presence of additional connections between convolution layers, which is technically expressed by the addition of concatenation layers. Empirically selected the following parameters of the CNN:

- Input layer size: $256 \times 256 \times 3$ (color image).
- Convolutional layer Conv2D_1.1: filter size $F_s = 3$, filters count $F_c = 32$, activation function – ReLU.
- Convolutional layer Conv2D_1.2: filter size $F_s = 3$, filters count $F_c = 32$, activation function – ReLU.
- Max pooling layer MaxPooling2D_1: filter size $F_s = 2$.
- Convolutional layer Conv2D_2.1: filter size $F_s = 3$, filters count $F_c = 64$, activation function – ReLU.
- Convolutional layer Conv2D_2.2: filter size $F_s = 3$, filters count $F_c = 64$, activation function – ReLU.

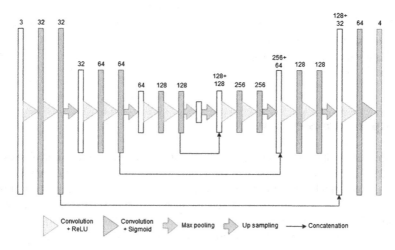

Fig. 4. Implemented U-Net architecture

- Max pooling layer MaxPooling2D_2: filter size $F_s = 2$.
- Convolutional layer Conv2D_3.1: filter size $F_s = 3$, filters count $F_c = 128$, activation function – ReLU.
- Convolutional layer Conv2D_3.2: filter size $F_s = 3$, filters count $F_c = 128$, activation function – ReLU.
- Max pooling layer MaxPooling2D_3: filter size $F_s = 2$.
- Upsampling layer UpSampling2D_1: scale factor = 2 interpolation – bilinear.
- Layer for concatenation of UpSampling2D_1 and Conv2D_3.2.
- Convolutional layer Conv2D_4.1: filter size $F_s = 3$, filters count $F_c = 256$, activation function – ReLU.
- Convolutional layer Conv2D_4.2: filter size $F_s = 3$, filters count $F_c = 256$, activation function – ReLU.
- Upsampling layer UpSampling2D_2: scale factor = 2 interpolation – bilinear.
- Layer for concatenation of UpSampling2D_2 and Conv2D_2.2.
- Convolutional layer Conv2D_5.1: filter size $F_s = 3$, filters count $F_c = 128$, activation function – ReLU.
- Convolutional layer Conv2D_5.2: filter size $F_s = 3$, filters count $F_c = 128$, activation function – ReLU.
- Upsampling layer UpSampling2D_3: scale factor = 2 interpolation – bilinear.
- Layer for concatenation of UpSampling2D_3 and Conv2D_1.2.
- Convolutional layer Conv2D_6.1: filter size $F_s = 3$, filters count $F_c = 64$, activation function – ReLU.
- Output convolutional layer Conv2D_6.2: filter size $F_s = 3$, filters count $F_c = 4$, activation function – sigmoid, output layer size – $256 \times 256 \times 4$.

  Loss function – softmax cross entropy.

Training:

− Training set size: 20000 images.
− Validation set size: 4000 images.
− Accuracy for validation set: 93.65%.

6 Output Data Structure

The output of implemented CNNs is $256 \times 256 \times 4$ matrix, where the dimensions "256×256" correspond to the size of the input image, and "4" – to the number of the required classes: "soil", "healthy vegetation", "diseased vegetation" and "other objects. Thus, the output is four matrices which elements are the values of probability of belonging of pixels of the original image to the particular class. After normalization of the values for each pixel, we obtain a fuzzy value that characterizes belonging of pixel to the desired classes.

7 Recognition Algorithm

In general, the recognition algorithm (transformation $A : I_{orig} \rightarrow I_{result}$) can be represented as follows:

1. Load origin color image I_{orig}.
2. Divide I_{orig} to parts $O_i(I_{orig})$ with size 256×256. For each part:
   2.1 Copy selected part $O_i(I_{orig})$ with size 256×256 as color image.
   2.2 Transform obtained image $O_i(I_{orig})$ by segmenter $A \in \{A_S, A_u\}$ to matrix $Segm_A$ with size $256 \times 256 \times 4$.
   2.3 Obtain class index for each pixel of the image $O_i(I_{orig})(x,y)$: $x \in [0, 255]$, $y \in [0, 255]$:

   $$index = argmax([A(x,y)]),$$

   where $Segm_A(x,y)$ – vector with 4 values which correspond to degree of belonging to the required classes of the origin image $O_i(I_{orig})$.
   2.4 Set values of the pixels of output image $I_{result}(O_i)$. Each value corresponds to pseudocolor of the class index: black – to soil, dark-gray – to healthy vegetation, light-gray – to diseased vegetation, white – to the other objects.
3. Save the obtained image I_{result}.

8 Testing

Segmenters were tested on validation set. At the same time, accuracy was assessed both for each class separately and for all classes as a whole. The obtained test results are shown in Table 1.

Table 1. Segmenter test results

Classes	Accuracy %	
	SegNet	U-Net
Soil	84.88	87.99
Healthy vegetation	95.41	96.89
Diseased vegetation	77.48	74.56
Other objects	88.80	88.90
Average	**92.36**	**93.65**

Due to the imbalance of classes in the origin data, an additional evaluation is required. The result data are summarized in confusion matrix presented in Table 2. The value in the matrix is given as the ratio of the number of pixels belonging to the class to the total number of pixels of all classes in the sample.

Table 2. Confusion matrix

Predicted classes	Real classes			
	SegNet			
	Soil	Healthy	Diseased	Others
Soil	11.51	0.75	0.20	0.02
Healthy	1.41	73.49	1.79	0.03
Diseased	0.62	2.71	6.88	0.00
Other objects	0.03	0.07	0.00	0.48
	U-Net			
Soil	11.93	0.86	0.31	0.02
Healthy	1.34	74.63	1.95	0.04
Diseased	0.27	1.50	6.62	0.00
Other objects	0.02	0.03	0.00	0.48

To assess quality of the segmentation, corresponding values of precision, recall and F_1-score [24] were calculated (TP – True Positives count, FP – False Positives count, FN – False Negatives count):

$$Precision = \frac{TP}{TP+FP}, \ Recall = \frac{TP}{TP+FN}, \ F_1 = 2 \times \frac{Precision \times Recall}{Precision + Recall},$$

Values of these measures are presented in Table 3.

Table 3. Precision, recall and F1-score

Classes	SegNet		
	Precision	Recall	F_1
Soil	0.92	0.85	0.88
Healthy	0.96	0.95	0.96
Diseased	0.67	0.77	0.72
Others	0.83	0.89	0.86
	U-Net		
Soil	0.91	0.88	0.89
Healthy	0.96	0.97	0.96
Diseased	0.79	0.75	0.77
Others	0.90	0.89	0.89

The greatest number of errors occurred in areas that correspond to boundary of healthy vegetation and soil (especially in places where small areas of soil are surrounded by vegetation, what which creates a shadow on this area of soil).

Additionally, Table 4 provides estimations of the number of errors for each class separately. It can be seen that the significant number of errors occurs when the soil is not correctly identified as healthy vegetation (boundaries of vegetation and soil, small patches of soil among vegetation). The greatest number of errors occurs when diseased areas of vegetation are classified as healthy on any image parts where signs of damage are not sufficiently pronounced.

Figure 5 shows an example of the original image part and the corresponding class labels.

Table 4. Error estimation

Predicted classes	Error %			
	SegNet			
	Soil	Healthy	Diseased	Others
Soil	–	0.98	2.31	4.67
Healthy	10.38	–	20.21	6.53
Diseased	4.54	3.52	–	0.01
Other objects	0.2	0.09	0	–
	U-Net			
Soil	–	1.12	3.49	4.28
Healthy	9.85	–	21.96	6.82
Diseased	2.01	1.95	–	0
Other objects	0.15	0.04	0	–

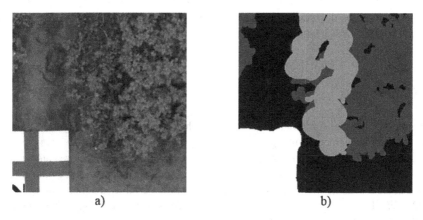

Fig. 5. Example of original aerial image (a) and corresponding labeled classes (b)

Figure 6 shows the classes obtained for this image part. For comparison, the classes are also given labeled by an expert.

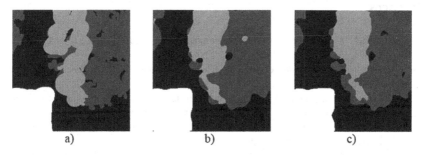

Fig. 6. Labels of classes (a); classes obtained using SegNet (b) and U-Net (c)

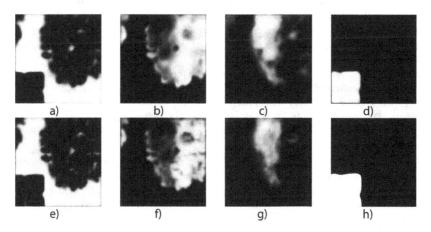

Fig. 7. Degrees of belonging of points of part of a segmented image to classes, obtained using SegNet (a–d) and U-Net (e–h)

Figure 7 shows degrees of belonging of pixels of segmented image to the classes: 7a, 7e – soil, 7b, 7f – healthy vegetation, 7c, 7 g – diseased vegetation, 7d, 7 h – other objects.

9   Conclusions

Semantic segmenters for processing of aerial photographs of agricultural fields were proposed and implemented using the Keras library (the Tensorflow library was used as the backend). The segmenters are built on SegNet and U-Net architectures and trained for obtaining the four classes: "soil", "healthy vegetation", "diseased vegetation" and "other objects". Using the proposed segmenters, it was possible to achieve an accuracy of 92–93%. In this case, the greatest number of errors occurs for diseased vegetation, which can be mistakenly attributed to healthy in the case of small damaged areas, as well as in cases when significantly diseased plants are interspersed with healthy, as well as soil plots.

Further research suggests to reduce errors in problem areas.

References

1. Belyayev, B.I., Katkovskiy, L.V.: Optical remote sensing, 455 p. BSU, Minsk (2006). [in Russian]
2. Schowengerdt, R.A.: Remote Sensing. Models and Methods for Image Processing, 3rd edn, 558 p. Academic Press (2007)
3. Chao, K., Chen, Y.R., Kim, M.S.: Machine vision technology for agricultural applications. Trans. Comput. Electron. Agric. **36**, 173–191 (2002). Elsevier science
4. Kumar, N., et al.: Do leaf surface' characteristics affect agrobacterium infection in tea [camellia sinensis (1.)]. J. Biosci. **29**(3), 309–317 (2004)
5. Wu, L., et al.: Identification of weed, corn using BP network based on wavelet features and fractal dimension. Sci. Res. Essay **4**(11), 1194–1400 (2009)
6. Qin, Z., Zhang, M.: Detection of rice sheath blight for in-season disease management using multispectral remote sensing. Int. J. Appl. Earth Obs. Geoinf. **7**, 115–148 (2005)
7. Aksoy, S., Akcay, H.G., Wassenaar, T.: Automatic mapping of linear woody vegetation features in agricultural landscapes using very high-resolution imagery. IEEE Trans. Geosci. Remote Sens. **48**(1, 2), 511–522 (2010)
8. Abdullahi, H.S., Zubair, O.M.: Advances of image processing in precision agriculture: using deep learning convolution neural network for soil nutrient classification. J. Multidisciplinary Eng. Sci. Technol. (JMEST) **4**(8), 7981–7987 (2017)
9. Wright, D., Rasmussen, V., Ramsey, R., Baker, D., Ellsworth, J.: Canopy reflectance estimation of wheat nitrogen content for grain protein management. GISci. Remote Sens. **41**(4), 287–300 (2004)
10. Khobragade, A., Pooja, M.G., Singh, R.K.: Feature extraction algorithm for estimation of agriculture acreage from remote sensing images, pp. 5–9 (2016)
11. Huang, H., Deng, J., Lan, Y., Yang, A., Deng, X., Zhang, L.: A fully convolutional network for weed mapping of unmanned aerial vehicle (UAV) imagery. PLoS ONE **13**(4), e0196302 (2018)

12. Sa, I., et al.: weedNet: dense semantic weed classification using multispectral images and MAV for smart farming. IEEE Robot. Autom. Lett. **3**(1), 588–595 (2018)
13. Potena, C., Nardi, D., Pretto, A.: Fast and accurate crop and weed identification with summarized train sets for precision agriculture. In: Chen, W., Hosoda, K., Menegatti, E., Shimizu, M., Wang, H. (eds.) IAS 2016. AISC, vol. 531, pp. 105–121. Springer, Cham (2017). https://doi.org/10.1007/978-3-319-48036-7_9
14. Dias, P.A., Tabb, A., Medeiros, H.: Multispecies fruit flower detection using a refined semantic segmentation network. IEEE Robot. Autom. Lett. **3**(4), 3003–3010 (2018)
15. Bargoti, S., Underwood, J.P.: Image segmentation for fruit detection and yield estimation in apple orchards. J. Field Robot. **34**(6), 1039–1060 (2017)
16. Zhang, C., et al.: Segmentation model based on convolutional neural networks for extracting vegetation from Gaofen-2 images. J. Appl. Remote Sens. **12**(4), 042804 (2018)
17. Lin, K., Gong, L., Huang, Y., Liu, C., Pan, J.: Deep learning-based segmentation and quantification of cucumber powdery mildew using convolutional neural network. J. Front. Plant Sci. **10**, 10 p (2019). Article 155
18. Xu, L., Ming, D., Zhou, W., Bao, H., Chen, Y., Ling, X.: Farmland extraction from high spatial resolution remote sensing images based on stratified scale pre-estimation. J. Remote Sens. **11**(2), 10–19 (2019)
19. Sobkowiak, B., et al.: Zastosowanie technik analizy obrazu do wczesnego wykrywania patogenow ziemniaka. Praca nie publicowana. PIMR, Poznan (2006)
20. Sobkowiak, B., et al.: Zastosowanie technik analizy obrazu do wczesnego wykrywania zarazy ziemnechanej w warynkach polowych. Praca nie publicowana. PIMR, Poznan (2007)
21. Goodfellow, I., Bengio, Y., Courville, A.: Deep Learning, 800 p. The MIT Press (2016)
22. Nikolenko, S, Kadurin, A., Archangelskaya, E.: Deep Learning, 480 p. Piter, Saint Petersburg (2018). (in Russian)
23. Tensorflow API documentation. https://www.tensorflow.org/api_docs/python/tf/nn/softmax_cross_entropy_with_logits_v2. Accessed 04 Aug 2019
24. Sokolova, M., Japkowicz, N., Szpakowicz, S.: Beyond accuracy, F-score and ROC: a family of discriminant measures for performance evaluation. In: Sattar, A., Kang, B.-H. (eds.) AI 2006. LNCS (LNAI), vol. 4304, pp. 1015–1021. Springer, Heidelberg (2006). https://doi.org/10.1007/11941439_114

Possible Methodological Options
for Development of Pattern Recognition
Theory

Vladimir Obraztsov[(⊠)] and Moqi Sun

Belarusian State University, 4 Independence Avenue, 220030 Minsk, Belarus
obraztsov@bsu.by

Abstract. The article provides a fresh approach to some problems of the theory of pattern recognition. In particular, an extension variant of the distance-based models is proposed. The estimation questions of decision quality of recognition problem without training are also considered. The experiments have been conducted that show that neural networks can be considered a new standard in the solution of recognition problems.

Keywords: Pattern recognition · Metric algorithm · Recognition problem without training · Neural networks

1 Introduction

Nowadays different areas of artificial intelligence are developing such as machine learning [1], neural networks [2] and others. There are many practical problems in the field of pattern recognition that have been solved with the help of neural networks [3, 9]. Moreover, it is arguable that the research in the last 5–10 years and its results in the machine learning field have forced pattern recognition as a science onto the back burner. Perhaps it can be considered natural if it is remembered about the cyclical development of any scientific knowledge. It should be remembered that all key ideas that are actively used to solve problems based on machine learning methods and using neural networks have arisen and have been the subject of research initially precisely in the framework of the theory of pattern recognition. Moreover, recognition theory as a science includes many potentially interesting questions, the study of which will significantly expand our understanding of the nature of practical recognition problems and improve the quality of their solution. Some simple questions are considered in this article that relate to the concept of similarity of objects, the possibility of assessing the quality of solving a recognition problem without training and using neural networks as a standard in solving practical problems.

This article is sequel to an earlier article [17]. In this paper the terminology is clarified. Besides the examples of likeness and derivability measures are provided.

S. V. Ablameyko et al. (Eds.): PRIP 2019, CCIS 1055, pp. 64–73, 2019.
https://doi.org/10.1007/978-3-030-35430-5_6

2 Relationships in Pattern Recognition Theory

As it is known, object classes are used during formulating any problem of pattern recognition (with or without training). The classes disjoint and its colligation creates a set of objects that will be recognized in the object domain. The class information is given by indicating a finite number of objects with known priori class membership (pattern recognition with training) or with algorithmically obtained class partition of the finite set (pattern recognition without training).

Let X denote the set of objects of arbitrary nature $X_1, \ldots, X_l (l \in \mathbb{N})$ - the classes on which the set X is divided. Let the subset $X^0 \subset X$ is given and $|X^0| < +\infty$. The following predicate is regarded as given $P(x) = (P_1(x), \ldots, P_l(x))$ for the problem of pattern recognition with training for objects from the set X^0. The components $P_i(x)$ $\forall i \in \{1, 2, \ldots, l\}$ are defined as follows:

$$P_i(x) = \begin{cases} 1, & if \ \ x \in X_i, \\ 0, & otherwise \end{cases} \tag{1}$$

The binary relation σ that is an equivalence can be associated [4] with the partition of the set X into the classes $X_1, \ldots, X_l$. By definition, $x_1, x_2 \in X$ belong to the same class from $X_1, \ldots, X_l$. if and only if the relation $x_1 \sigma x_2$ holds for x_1, x_2. In terms of relations, classes from $X_1, \ldots, X_l$ are called adjacent, and its collection for X with respect to σ is denoted by X/σ and called a factor-set on X by σ. Lets introduce the set $= \{B_1, \ldots, B_l\}$, whose elements will be determined by the condition.

$$B_i = \left(b_1^i, \ldots, b_l^i\right) \in \mathbb{B}_2^l \wedge (b_j^i = 1 \Leftrightarrow i = j), \mathbb{B}_2 = \{0, 1\}.$$

Now the recognition problem can be reduced to the problem of constructing of a suitable canonical mapping α_1 or α_2 of the following form

$$X \xrightarrow{\alpha_1} X/\sigma \xrightarrow{\alpha_2} B. \tag{2}$$

It is interesting to note that with respect to pattern recognition theory, the algorithmic implementation of the mapping α_1 can be interpreted as a recognizing operator, and α_2, as a decision rule, respectively [5].

The mappings study of α_1 and α_2 in the form (2) is of interest exclusively from a theoretical perspective. As for the practical implementation, it is logical to use the sample X^0 in the recognition problem with training. It is sufficient to build algorithms that implement mappings (2) on the sample X^0 (or on its part, that is usually called the training one), and then use the obtained algorithms to solve the problem on all of the set X.

It is necessary to proceed from the equivalence relation σ that can be considered as relational similarity on the set X in all cases, when building the algorithms. Nowadays two fundamentally different approaches to the building of the specified algorithms have been formed.

The idea of functional homogeneity of the set X is used in the first approach. Within the framework of this idea, it is assumed that equivalence classes are described by functions of the same type, that differ only in parameters. Moreover an additional constraint is imposed upon the class of functions. They should have combinative properties with respect to objects of one class, and separation ones with respect to objects of different classes. These properties should accept interpretation in terms of the similarity of objects. Such functions are called decision functions in pattern recognition [1, 5].

The second approach directly uses the fact that the equivalence σ is a reflexive, symmetric, and transitive relation on the set $X \times X$. Thus natural idea is to make the set X as metric space inputting a numerical function $\rho : X \times X \to \mathbb{R}$ on it that satisfies the conditions:

$$\rho(x,x) = 0 \qquad \forall x \in X$$

$$\rho(x,y) = \rho(y,x) \qquad \forall x, y \in X$$

$$\rho(x,y) \leq \rho(x,z) + \rho(z,y) \qquad \forall x, y, z \in X$$

It's plain to see the connection between the equivalence of σ and the function ρ. The last function can be considered as a numerical implementation of the relation σ. Such functions are called metrics or distances [6], and in the sense of similarity they define a measure of proximity of objects in the set X. In pattern recognition, models that are based on the use of ρ functions are called metric ones.

The Example. The choice of the metric ρ depends on many factors. The most popular types of ρ are:

- Euclidean metric ($X \subseteq \mathbb{R}^n$)

$$\rho(x_1, x_2) = \left(\sum_{i=1}^{n} (x_{1i} - x_{2i})^2 \right)^{\frac{1}{2}}$$

- Hamming distance ($X \subseteq \mathbb{B}^n$)

$$\rho(x_1, x_2) = \sum_{i=1}^{n} |x_{1i} - x_{2i}|$$

- Minkowski space ($X \subseteq \mathbb{R}^n, p \in \mathbb{N}$)

$$\rho(x_1, x_2) = \left(\sum_{i=1}^{n} (x_{1i} - x_{2i})^p \right)^{\frac{1}{p}}$$

Unquestionably, the diversity of metric recognition models is not limited to the types of metric ρ that is listed above. Moreover, some options for the obvious extension of the metric models set based on similarity and derivability measures will be proposed below.

At the beginning we will turn to the relation of likeness. Intuitively obvious, it also defines a certain equivalence of σ. It is possible to become familiar with the likeness theory in details on [7]. Probably, it is impossible to build likeness measure that could lead to the building of the metric space. However, the likeness relation allows a numerical implementation. To demonstrate this, we introduce a function $\mu: X \times X \to \mathbb{R}^+$ that satisfies the conditions:

$$\mu(x, x) = 1 \qquad \forall x \in X$$

$$\mu(x, y) = (\mu(y, x))^{-1} \quad \forall x, y \in X$$

$$\mu(x, y) = \mu(x, z) \times \mu(z, y) \qquad \forall x, y, z \in X$$

It is clear that the function μ defines a likeness measure of objects in the set X. It may be difficult to introduce such a function for some X, but it will definitely work in some obvious cases.

The Example. Let $X \subseteq \mathbb{R}^n$. The likeness metric can be defined as follows because of the definition $n + 1 \overset{\text{def}}{=} 1$:

$$\mu(x_1, x_2) = \left(\prod_{k=1}^{n} \frac{\max\{x_{1k}, x_{1k+1}\} \cdot (\min\{x_{1k}, x_{1k+1}\})^{-1}}{\max\{x_{2k}, x_{2k+1}\} \cdot (\min\{x_{2k}, x_{2k+1}\})^{-1}} \right)^{\frac{1}{n}}$$

Now some words about a derivability relation. This is a very interesting relation in the formal sense. In particular, if the subsets B_2^n ($n \in \mathbb{N}$) are considered as X. In general, derivability measures of objects can be defined as a function $\delta: X \times X \to [0, 1]$ that satisfies the conditions:

$$\delta(x, x) = 1 \quad \forall x \in X$$

$$\delta(x, y) = \delta(y, x) \quad \forall x, y \in X$$

$$x_1 \sqsubseteq x_2 \Rightarrow \delta(x_1, y) \leq \delta(x_2, y) \quad \forall x_1, x_2, y \in X$$

The Example. For the case $x_1, x_2 \in \mathbb{B}_2^n$, $\mathbb{B}_2 = \{0, 1\}$, the function δ is defined as follows

$$\delta(x_1, x_2) = \max\{0, \left(\sum_{j=1}^{n} a_j \right)^{-1} \times \left(\sum_{j=1}^{n} (-1)^u \cdot a_j \right) \}$$

Where

$$u = \begin{cases} 1, \text{если } x_{1j} \neq x_{2j} \\ 2, \text{иначе} \end{cases}$$

Here $(a_1, \ldots, a_n) \in \mathbb{R}_+^n$ are numerical parameters that can reflect, for example, a relative assessment of the degree of importance of the attribute $i \in \{1, 2, \ldots, n\}$. It is possible to become familiar with the introduction to functions δ options and appropriate recognition algorithm in details on [8]. We will confine ourselves to saying that derivability relation allows to formalizable inductive inference in logical propositional calculus systems. Thus, it is reasonable to expect that appropriate recognition models will significantly expand the understanding of the recognition problems nature.

Nowadays the proximity metric is the most investigated. Nevertheless, other metrics that is introduced in this article have already been received approval. The likeness metric was used to solve data problems that was provided in various repositories. In general, the results are no worse than if using the proximity metric. As for the derivability metric, this is a representative example of inductive inference. This metric was used to solve a number of problems in medical diagnostics.

Thus, one may ask, has everything in recognition theory already been determined and investigated? The answer is No. The above considerations show possible modifications of the existing recognition models that are based on the relational similarity.

3   The Problem of Recognition Without Training – The Quality of Solving

The values of the predicate $P(x)$ on the set X^0 is required to compare with each object $x \in X^0$ in the problem of recognition without training. Moreover, the number of classes $l \in \mathbb{N}$ can be a parameter that needs to be established as a result of problem solving.

It is possible to get completely different statements in this problem, depending on a priori given information. In the first case, the existence of some groups or structures is only implied in the space X [1]. Therefore, the task does not imply entering the input objects (images) $x \in X^0$ into a priori specified classes, but the process of algorithmizing is required that allows to distinguish them in any way according to the attributes specified in the description of the set X (to group or simply structure). The task in this formulation is called the classification (clustering) problem. Schematically, the process of solving this problem class (for the case of splitting X^0 into two disjoint subsets) is presented in Fig. 1.

Pay attention to the fact that the objects $x \in X^0$ are selected from the set X and, thus, have all its properties. The list of these properties does not contain classes.

The second statement implies the classes existence. Therefore, it is assumed that the input objects (images) $x \in X^0$ are entered into a priori specified classes in the problem. It is required that the classes obtained as a result of the partition of X^0 should correspond to the given ones. Note that in this statement, it is assumed to construct a partition of the set X^0, that must be taken into account when algorithmizing the process of solving the problem. Unlike the recognition problem with training, the presence of a priori knowledge about the value of the predicate $P(x)$ for objects $x \in X^0$ is not meant. In general, it is logical to call the task as the recognition of images without training in such formulation.

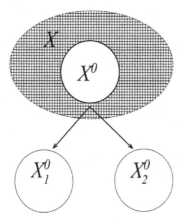

Fig. 1. The process of solving the problem of classification (clustering).

There are two reasons for this. First, it becomes dual in the staged sense to the recognition problem with training in this case. Secondly, the process algorithmization can be considered in the form (2) for such a statement. Schematically, the process of solving this problem class (for the case of splitting X^0 into two classes) is presented in Fig. 2.

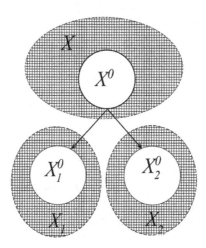

Fig. 2. The process of solving the pattern recognition problem without training.

Let's talk about the quality of solving problems in the above statements. In the first statement, it is obviously wrong to talk about the quality of the problem solution in the sense that is done in the training problem. It is completely determined by the parameters of the algorithmic process. Various methods can be used to evaluate the last. For example, based on the calculation of entropy, as it happens when solving classification problems using decision trees. However, methods for evaluating methods are quite diverse here [1, 9].

Everything is much more complicated in the second statement. It is necessary to evaluate the result and the process of its obtaining. Let's look at the result of solving the problem, which is schematically presented in Fig. 3. and try to answer the question, which result of solving the original problem is better. In the first case, two classes X_1^0, X_2^0 are obtained, and in the second three classes - $X_1^0, X_{21}^0, X_{22}^0$. It is necessary to set the parameter for the number of classes in the model that will be used to solve the problem equal to 3. for getting the last partition. Let's try to find the answer to the following question: which of these two partitions is better and why? Obviously, the answer to this question is very difficult.

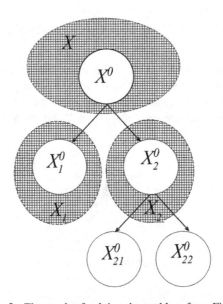

Fig. 3. The result of solving the problem from Fig. 2

But on a brighter note. In fact, after the result of solving the recognition problem without training is obtained, a new problem can be formed - with training. In this sense, there is dualism (or duality) between tasks - both in the sense of results and in the sense of algorithms for solving them. It is also important that it is easy to use standard methods to evaluate the quality of the solution for the recognition problem with training.

Here we can formulate the main question - is it possible to compare the best estimate obtained when solving the recognition problem thus constructed with training as a quality assessment for the results of solving the recognition problem without training? It seems that much more arguments can be expressed for a positive answer.

4 Neural Network as a Standard for Solving Recognition Problems

Each specialist in this field has a certain standard set of methods when solving practical recognition problems. It was always possible to take the first steps in obtaining a solution with the help of that methods. For a long time, a linear model (perceptron) was used in this capacity of standard. Someone could have a probabilistic model. In most cases, the simple logic worked - I knew this model best and I had an experience using it. So, as a first approximation, I will receive the results of solving a specific problem with its help. This, incidentally, is quite normal logic, counting the inductive and empirical nature of the recognition problem.

Currently, a set of methods, which is collectively called a neural network, is rightfully claiming the role of such a standard. With the help of neural networks, many practical problems have been solved and the quality of their solution is more than decent. In addition, the methodology and technology of using neural networks is developing quite rapidly and an increasing number of specialists are involved in the process of their research and use. All this suggests that it may be worth changing priorities and considering neural networks as the new standard. What would be the point in terms of practice? The first steps could be taken quite quickly and unifiedly. In addition, it would allow subject specialists to be involved in the process of solving recognition problems. In other words, a neural network without any stretch looks like a new standard for solving recognition problems.

See that this is so, the second of the authors of this publication was tasked with conducting simple experiments with data obtained from various repositories. The task was set to get a solution using a suitable neural network. Moreover, these were his first steps in the study of neural networks. For comparison, we selected those tasks that were previously solved by more serious methods. The Hopfield neural network [10], which is well adapted for working with vector data, was used as a model.

In the first experiment, ECL [11], C4.5 [12], HIDER [13], and hybrid algorithms described in [14] were chosen to compare the quality of the algorithms. Data taken from Machine Learning Repository for the Congressional Voting Records Data Set task. The results are shown in Table 1.

Table 1. Comparison of the accuracy of the algorithms for congressional voting records data set

Algorithm	Recognition accuracy
Hopfield network	85,7%
Hybrid	93,5%
ECL	95%
C4.5	94%
HIDER	97,0%

In the second experiment, the data set was selected from the repository of UCI recognition tasks [15] for the Automobile task. The Ant Miner, HIDER, and SGERD algorithms [13] were chosen to compare the quality of the work of the algorithms, as well as the hybrid algorithm mentioned above. The results are shown in Table 2.

Table 2. Comparison of the accuracy of the algorithms for Automobile data set

Algorithm	Recognition accuracy
Hopfield network	66%
Hybrid	74,2%
Ant Miner	53,7%
HIDER	62,6%
SGERD	50,7%

Finally, a data set was selected for the Hepatitis task from the repository of UCI recognition tasks [15] for the third experiment. The Bagging and Boosting algorithms [16] were chosen to compare the quality of the algorithms, as well as the hybrid algorithm. The results are shown in Table 3.

Table 3. Comparison of the accuracy of the algorithms for Hepatitis data set

Algorithm	Recognition accuracy
Hopfield network	75,2%
Hybrid	78,6%
Bagging	80,6%
Boosting	83,8%

All missing details in the information description can be found in the UCL repository. As the obtained data indicate, the neural network allows practically without skills to get a result that, in the first approximation, is comparable to the results obtained earlier with more serious studies. What does it give? In general, a lot. It is safe to say that all considered problems can be solved by recognition methods. It is necessary to move on to data analysis. More serious results are possible only in this way.

5 Conclusion

The main conclusion that can be drawn from the discussion is the following. In the theory of pattern recognition, there are still many possibilities that can significantly improve the quality of solving practical problems. As a methodology for empirical generalization, recognition theory contains all the necessary tools - from formalizing the task to assessing the quality of the results. New studies in machine learning and neural networks provide an opportunity to take a fresh look at the results that were previously get in the recognition theory.

References

1. Flach, P.: Machine Learning: The Art and Science of Algorithms That Make Sense of Data, p. 400. Cambridge University Press, New York (2012)
2. Kriesel, D.: A brief introduction to neural networks (2007). http://www.dkriesel.com
3. Goodfellow, Y., Bengio, A.: Courville deep learning. MIT Press (2016). http://www.deeplearningbook.org
4. Maltzev, A.I.: Algebraic systems. Science, 392 p. (1970). (in russian)
5. Zhuravlev, Ju.I.: Selected scientific papers. Magistr, 420 p. (1998). (in russian)
6. Leont'ev, V.K.: On measures of similarity and distances between objects. Comput. Math. Math. Phys. **49**(11), 2041–2058 (2009)
7. Hilpert, R.: Similarity theory. In: Durst, F. (ed.) Fluid Mechanics, pp. 193–219. Springer, Heidelberg (2008). https://doi.org/10.1007/978-3-540-71343-2_7
8. Krasnoproshin, V.V., Obraztsov, V.A.: Problems of solvability and choice of algorithms for decision making by precedence. Pattern Recogn. Image Anal. **16**(2), 155–169 (2006)
9. Raschka, S.: Python Machine Learning, 2nd Edition, 622 p. Packt Publishing, Birmingham (2017)
10. Hopfield, J.J.: Neural networks and physical systems with emergent collective computational abilities. Proc. Nat. Acad. Sci. **79**(8), 2554–2558 (1982)
11. Divina, F., Marchiori, E.: Evolutionary concept learning. In: Proceedings of Genetic and Evolutionary Computation Conference, pp. 343–350 (2002)
12. Anglano, C., et al.: An experimental evaluation of coevolutive concept learning. In: Proceedings of 15th International Conference on Machine Learning, pp. 19–27. Morgan Kaufmann, San Francisco, CA (1998)
13. Alcalá-Fdez, J., et al.: KEEL data-mining software tool: data set repository, integration of algorithms and experimental analysis framework. J. Multiple-Valued Logic Soft Comput. **17** (2–3), 255–287 (2011)
14. Shut, V.O.: A model of solving of pattern recognition problems based on resolution method. Lect. Model. Simul. **14**(1), 7–19 (2012)
15. Lichman, M.: UCI machine learning repository. University of California, School of Information and Computer Science, Irvine, CA (2013). http://archive.ics.uci.edu/ml. Accessed 31 July 2015
16. Li, J., Wong, L.: Using rules to analyse bio-medical data: a comparison between C4.5 and PCL. In: Proceedings of Advances in Web-Age Information Management, pp. 254–265 (2003)
17. Obraztsov, V., Sun, M.: Some methodological remarks on pattern recognition. In: Proceedings of the 14th International Conference – PRIP 2019, Minsk, pp. 350–354 (2019)

Irrelation of Mathematical and Functional Aspects of Descriptive Image Algebras with One Ring Operations Interpretability

Igor Gurevich and Vera Yashina[✉]

Federal Research Center "Computer Science and Control" of the Russian
Academy of Sciences, 44/2, Vavilov Str., Moscow 119333, Russian Federation
igourevi@ccas.ru, werayashina@gmail.com

Abstract. The study is continued investigation of mathematical and
functional/physical interpretation of image analysis and processing operations
used as sets of operations (ring elements) in descriptive image algebras
(DIA) with one ring. The main result is the determination and characterization of
interpretation domains of DIA operations: image algebras that make it possible
to operate with both the main image models and main models of transformation
procedures that ensure effective synthesis and realization of the basic procedures
involved in the formal description, processing, analysis, and recognition of
images. The applicability of DIAs in practice is determined by the realizability
—the possibility of interpretation—of its operations. The interpretation is considered as a transition from a meaningful description of the operation to its
mathematical or algorithmic implementation. The main types of interpretability
are defined, and examples of interpretability of operations of the descriptive
image algebras with one ring, are given.

Keywords: Computer Vision · Descriptive Image Algebras · Algebraic
Interpretation · Physical, semantic, and Functional Interpretability of Image
Processing Operations · Interpretation Domains of Operations · Interpretability
of Operations · Image Analysis, Recognition, and Processing · Automated
Image-mining

1 Introduction

The article is devoted to mathematical and functional/physical interpretation of image
analysis and processing operations used as sets of operations (ring elements) of
descriptive image algebras (DIAs) [3, 4, 6–8].

This article continues the study of interpretability of DIA operations begun in [8].

DIAs are studied in the framework of developing a mathematical apparatus for
analyzing and evaluating information in the form of images. For a structured
description of possible algorithms for solving these problems, a formal tool is needed to
describe and validate the chosen solution path. For the formalization, an algebraic
apparatus was chosen [3] that should ensure the uniformity of procedures for describing
image objects and transformations over these image objects.

© Springer Nature Switzerland AG 2019
S. V. Ablameyko et al. (Eds.): PRIP 2019, CCIS 1055, pp. 74–85, 2019.
https://doi.org/10.1007/978-3-030-35430-5_7

Despite a number of significant works in the field of "algebraization" of image processing, analysis and recognition, it can be argued that there is currently no generally accepted unified approach to solving problems in this subject area.

In the late 1980s and 1990s, Gurevich [3–9] specialized a general algebraic approach to solving recognition, classification and prediction problems [10] (Zhuravlev) in the case of initial data in the form of images (Descriptive approach to the analysis and understanding of images (DA)).

Gurevich introduced DIAs in the framework of the DA and continues to develop them in collaboration with his pupils [3–9]. In order to construct a DIA, it is necessary to select the operations and operands of the algebra. Some transformations in image processing, analysis and recognition can formally be used for mathematical description of the algorithm using DIAs, however, they have no physical meaning specific to image processing and analysis. At the same time, the practical applicability of DIAs is determined by the practical applicability and realizability of operations by which DIAs are constructed.

In our case, we are talking mainly about algebraic interpretation, since DIAs represent an algebraic language for the mathematical description of procedures of processing, analyzing, recognizing, and understanding images using digital image transformation operations and their representations and models.

These procedures are formed and implemented as descriptive algorithmic schemes (DASs) [4], which are correct (valid) expressions of the DIA language. The latter are constructed from image processing and transformation operations and other mathematical operations included in the corresponding DIA ring.

The mathematical and functional (content/semantic) properties of DIA operations are of considerable interest for optimizing the selection and implementation of image processing and analysis procedures and for constructing specialized DAS libraries.

The choice and optimization of operations included in the DAS are essentially related to the specifics of images as a means of representation, carriers, and sources of information. The functional interpretation of image transformation operations should ensure the establishment of a relationship between the image analysis task and the DAS specialized for its solution. In essence, this kind of interpretation is reduced to establishing a correspondence between the content division of the decision process into stages and the mathematical operations of the DAS ensuring the realization of these stages.

This means that the efficiency of model synthesis and recognition processes can be achieved by the choice of "content" (function) of image transformation operations, based on what image representation needs to be obtained with the next transformation. Such a choice, in turn, should be based both on the analysis of the mathematical characteristics of the operation and on the analysis of its functional purpose, in other words, the semantic aspects of the operation, i.e., its content, identification of a "physical equivalent," and its underlying functional heuristics.

Since not all mathematical operations have a direct physical equivalent with respect to the construction of effective DASs for image analysis, there is the problem of interpreting operations for filling the DAS. Research into this problem leads to the selection and study of interpretation domains of DIA operations.

Thus, interpretation is considered as a transition from a meaningful description of the operation to its mathematical or algorithmic realization. As a result, the practical applicability of operations is revealed in the context of the more general concept of interpretability.

The following sections of the article present results related to the interpretability of DIA operations and examples of domains of interpretability for certain types of operations.

The article consists of the Introduction, three sections, the Conclusion, and References.

In Sect. 2 "Descriptive Image Algebras with One Ring", the main specifics of DIAs with one ring are determined, from which the interpretability of operations is formalized and specified.

Section 3, "Types of Interpretability of Operations of Descriptive Image Algebras with One Ring", describes the method and tools for formalizing the types of interpretability of image analysis and processing operations.

To characterize the interpretability of DIA operations, the following concepts are introduced: (1) physical meaning of the operation, (2) physical interpretability in the context of image analysis and processing, (3) visual interpretability in the context of image analysis and processing, (4) weak physical interpretability, (5) strong physical interpretability.

Section 4, "Examples of Interpretability of Descriptive Image Algebra Operations", provides 4 examples of operands with operations, for which the interpretability is studied.

2   Descriptive Image Algebra with One Ring

In this section, let us briefly recall the basic properties of DIAs.

The algebraization of pattern recognition and image analysis was devoted to creating a universal language for the uniform description of images and transformations over them. In [3, 5], the algebraization stages of pattern recognition and image analysis are described in detail and the basic concepts for defining DIAs and DIA with one ring (DIA1R) are introduced. The most significant results of the initial stage of pattern recognition algebraization were Zhuravlev's algebras of algorithms [12] and Grenander's image theory [1]; in image analysis, Sternberg's image algebra [10] and Ritter's standard image algebra [11]. In common sense, by image algebra, we mean a mathematical theory describing image transformations and analysis in continuous and discrete domains [11].

The classical algebra was developed to generalize operations on numbers; however, direct application of an algebra to information in the form of images is not possible for all problems, and a simple interpretation of the results is not always admissible. There are many natural image transformations that are easily interpreted from the user's viewpoint (e.g., rotation, compression, stretching, color inversion), which are difficult to imagine using standard algebraic operations. It becomes necessary to combine the algebraic apparatus and the set of image analysis and processing transformations.

One of the fundamental features of the algebraic approach is the representation of recognition algorithms in the form of algebraic combinations over a certain basis of algorithms. Another necessary prerequisite is algebraization of the representations of the input information of the algorithms, which in its capabilities is comparable to algebraization of the representations of the algorithms proper in the algebraic approach.

Correspondence of the algebraization of representations of algorithms and information is ensured by DA methods. These methods are designed to solve problems associated with obtaining formal descriptions of images as analysis and recognition objects and with the synthesis of procedures for their recognition by studying the internal structure, structure, and content of an image as a result of the generating operations by which the image can be constructed from primitive elements and objects detected in the image at various stages of its analysis [5, 9].

DIAs [3, 6] allow the use of image transformation procedures not only as DIA operations, but also as operands for constructing combinations of basic models of transformation procedures.

Definition 1 [3, 6]. An algebra is called a **descriptive image algebra** if its operands are either representations and models of images (as well, both the image itself and the set of values and characteristics associated with the image can be selected as a model), or operations on images, or simultaneously both.

In order to ensure compliance of the DIA with the requirements that must be met by the mathematical object "algebra," it is necessary to introduce restrictions on the basic DIA operations.

The main research into DIAs was aimed at studying DIA1R (see Definition 2), which is by definition a classical algebra with nonclassical operands.

The subsequent specifics of DIAs are determined by the properties of the algebras.

Definition 2 [3, 6]. The ring, which is a finite-dimensional vector space over some field, is a **DIA1R** if its operands are either representations and models of images, or operations on images and their representations and models.

The ultimate goal in studying DIA1R is to obtain sets of complete systems of operands and DIA operations to describe image analysis tasks. The use of the algebra concept in defining a DIA1R in a strictly classical sense is governed by the fact that in this case, it becomes possible to distinguish the basic DIA operations for various types of operands. The interpretability of DIA1R operations for different types of operands was studied in [8]. In this paper, we present additional examples of strongly and weakly interpretable DIA1R operations.

3   Types of Interpretability of Operations of Descriptive Image Algebras

A problem arises in constructing a DAS for solving applied image analysis and recognition problems: the applicability of some classes of DIA to describe the corresponding problem [4]. Evaluating the applicability of the DIA leads to the problem of interpretability of DIA operations. The formulation of the problem and initial results are presented in [7, 8].

Recall [5] that, according to the DA, the source image in recognition tasks is called an ordered set of recorded initial spatial and contextual data, reflecting the form (form and state) of objects, events, and processes of the depicted scene and allowing application of transformations that produce an image convenient for recognition.

Definition 3 [3]. **Physical meaning of the operation** means a content description of the process of transforming the source image(s) into the final image(s), or the description of putting a certain set of characteristics into correspondence with the source image.

In order to preserve the logic of consideration below, let us recall some notions of the DA associated with description of the image processing and analysis process and leading to the definitions of model/image representation [5, 9].

In image processing and analysis, a certain system of transformations is applied to the source image, ensuring a successive change of "phase states" of the transformed image corresponding to the degree of its current "formalization." The set of valid image representations is defined as the set of phase states of the image.

The system of transformations is given by the DAS image representation (DASIR), written according to DA concepts using DIAs. DASIRs reflect methods of sequential and/or parallel application of transformations from a set of transformations to the initial information from the initial data space. The set of admissible DASIRs is defined as the set of phase states of the DASIR.

To ensure the possibility of applying recognition algorithms to the constructed formal image descriptions, it is necessary to use the constructed DASIRs (to establish specific transformations from fixed DIAs and the parameters included in the transformation schemes) and to apply the implemented schemes to the initial data, i.e., construct image representations and models. In the DA, an image model is a formal (symbolic) description of an image that allows recognition algorithms to be applied to it. An image representation is any element of the set of states of the image in the image formalization space, with the exception of the objects "image model" and "image realization."

A more detailed description of the image formalization space, including both the image phase states and the DASIR phase states, is given in [6].

Definition 4 [3]. An operation on an image(s) or fragments thereof, or on a model(s) of an image(s), or the representation(s) of an image(s) is called a **physically interpretable operation in the context of image analysis and recognition** if

(1) the result of its use is an image or fragments thereof;
(2) the result of its application is an image representation or image model that can be used to reconstruct semantically significant geometric objects, brightness characteristics, and configurations formed due to regular repetitions of geometric objects and brightness characteristics of the source image;
(3) the result of its application is a characteristic(s) of the image(s), which can be unambiguously compared to the properties of geometric objects, brightness characteristics, or configurations formed due to regular repetitions of geometric objects and brightness characteristics of the source image.

Definition 5 [3]. The operation on some objects is called **visually interpretable in the context of image analysis and recognition** if as a result of the operation, an image (s) is obtained with which it is possible to reconstruct a one-to-one correspondence between semantically significant geometric objects, brightness characteristics, and configurations formed due to regular repetitions of geometric objects and brightness characteristics in the resultant image(s) and in source objects.

Statement 1 [3]. A visually interpretable operation is always a physically interpretable operation.

Corollary [3]. If the operation is not a physically interpretable operation, then this operation is also not visually interpretable.

Physical interpretability can be distinguished in a strong and weak sense.

Definition 6 [3]. An operation is called **strongly physically interpretable** if it is also visually interpretable.

Definition 7 [3]. An operation is called **weakly physically interpretable** if it is physically interpretable, but not visually interpretable.

Visually interpretable operations include, e.g., image rotation, image shift, image contrast enhancement, image brightness enhancement, image noise reduction, image smoothing, image contour selection, and other image processing operations. An example of visually interpretable operations can also be image-constructing operations according to a certain specified rule from a set of original objects, e.g., image reconstruction from equations that define the image type.

Physically interpretable operations include certain operations of constructing image representations and models and such operations with images as calculation of the image histogram or the values of the image's statistical characteristics.

Statement 2 [3]. An operation is physically uninterpretable in the context of image analysis and recognition if

(1) its operands are not images, image models, image representations, or image fragments;

(2) as a result of application of an operation to the image(s), an image model(s) is constructed, with which it is not possible to reconstruct semantically significant geometric objects, brightness characteristics, or configurations arising due to regular repetition of geometric objects and brightness characteristics of the source image;

(3) as a result of application of an image operation, characteristics are calculated that cannot be unambiguously compared with the properties of geometric objects, brightness characteristics, or configurations arising due to regular repetition of geometric objects and brightness characteristics of the source image;

(4) an operation is not applicable to images, image models, image representations, or image fragments.

4 Examples of Interpretability of Descriptive Image Algebra Operations

This section provides examples of the DIA listed in Table 1.

Table 1. Examples of DIA1R.

No.	Ring operands	Ring operations
1	Image algebra operations	Standard algebraic operations
2	Operations for constructing numerical estimates	Special operations
3	Rotate and zoom operations	Special operations
4	Standard algebraic operations	Image algebra operations

Example 1. A DIA1R Over Image Algebra Operations

Let us demonstrate an example of a descriptive algebra that is an analog of the recognition algorithm algebra. Let be I an image, F be the field of real numbers, and elements of ring R be the operations of the image algebra [11]. Let $r_1, r_2 \in R, \alpha \in F$.

The following operations are introduced in ring R:

$$(r_1 + r_2)(I) = r_1(I) + r_2(I) \tag{1}$$

Physical meaning of the operation: addition of the elements of the algebra is understood as addition of the results of applying the image algebra operations to the image.

$$(r_1 \cdot r_2)(I) = r_1(I) \cdot r_2(I) \tag{2}$$

Physical meaning of the operation: multiplication of elements of the algebra is understood as multiplication of the results of applying the image algebra operations to the image.

$$(\alpha r_1)(I) = \alpha r_1(I) \tag{3}$$

Physical meaning of the operation: multiplication of an element of the algebra by an element of the field of real numbers is understood as multiplication of an element of the field of real numbers and the result of application of the operation of the image algebra to an image.

As ring elements, it is possible to choose both operations that transfer images to other images and operations that construct certain image models for images, e.g., numerical estimates of their characteristics.

In the first case, the algebra can be considered an apparatus for constructing a chain of image transformations necessary for constructing the final procedural representation/ model of an image [5, 9]. In the second case, the algebra is a convenient tool for representing algorithms as a composite of algorithms from a given basis with given operations over them.

Statement 3. The operations of addition (1) and multiplication (2) of two image algebra operations applied to the image are **weakly physically interpretable operations**.

Proof

1. Physical interpretability of operations: By Definition 5, an operation is physically interpretable if its application results in an image, or an image representation or image model, or characteristics of the source image.
2. Visual interpretability of operations: these operations are not visually interpretable, since their application to arbitrary images obtained before this during application to the image of image algebra operations leads to an unpredictable visual result (Definition 5).
3. By Definition 6, a physically interpretable, but not visually interpretable operation is a weakly physically interpretable operation.

   Q.E.D.

Statement 4. The operation of multiplication of the image algebra applied to the image by field element (3) is **a strongly physically interpretable operation**.

Proof

1. Physical interpretability of operation: By Definition 4, an operation is physically interpretable if its application results in an image, or an image representation or image model, or characteristics of the source image.
2. Visual interpretability of operation: the operation is visually interpretable (Definition 5).
3. By Definition 7, a physically interpretable and visually interpretable operation is a strongly physically interpretable operation.

   Q.E.D.

Example 2. A DIA1R Over Numerical Estimate Construction Operations
Let I be an image, F be the field of real numbers, and the elements of ring R be numerical estimate construction operations. Each operation is represented by a function f, which relates an image to a number or a set of numbers—a feature vector. Let be $r_1, r_2 \in R, \alpha \in F$, where $r_i(I) = f_i(I)$ (i = 1, 2) (in this case $f_1(I)$ and $f_2(I)$ are vectors of the same dimensionality or real numbers). Let the values of all features be considered on the segment [0, 1] of the real number axis. The dimensionality of the feature vector is fixed; unknown feature values are replaced by a value of 0.5.

We introduce the following operations in the ring:

$$(r_1 + r_2)(I) = f_1(I) + f_2(I) - f_1(I) \cdot f_2(I) \tag{4}$$

Physical meaning of the operation: addition of the elements of the algebra is understood as addition of the results of applying the corresponding functions for computing estimates to the image minus multiplication of the results of applying the corresponding functions to the image.

$$(r_1 \cdot r_2)(I) = f_1(I) \cdot f_2(I) \tag{5}$$

Physical meaning of the operation: multiplication of the elements of the algebra is understood as multiplication of the results of applying to the image the corresponding functions for computing estimates.

$$(\alpha \cdot r_1)(I) = \alpha \cdot f_1(I) \tag{6}$$

Physical meaning of the operation: multiplication of an element of the algebra by a field element is understood as multiplication of the field element by the result of applying to the image the corresponding function of computing estimates.

Statement 5. The operations of addition (4) and multiplication (5) of two for numerical estimate construction operations applied to the image are **weakly physically interpretable**.

Proof

1. Physical interpretability of operations: By Definition 4, an operation is physically interpretable if its application results in an image, or an image representation or image model, or characteristics of the source image.
2. Visual interpretability of operations: these operations are not visually interpretable, since their application to the functions of calculating the estimates applied to the image leads to a new estimate that does not have a visual relationship with the image (Definition 5).
3. By Definition 6, a physically interpretable, but not visually interpretable operation is a weakly physically interpretable operation.

   Q.E.D.

Statement 6. The operation of multiplication of the numerical estimate construction operation by field element (6) is **strongly physically interpretable**.

Proof

1. Physical interpretability of operations: By Definition 4, an operation is physically interpretable if its application results in an image, or an image representation or image model, or characteristics of the source image.
2. Visual interpretability of operation: the operation is visually interpretable (Definition 5).
3. By Definition 7, a physically interpretable and visually interpretable operation is a strongly physically interpretable operation.

   Q.E.D.

Example 3. A DIA1R Over Rotation and Scaling Operations

Let I be an image, F be the field of real numbers, and elements of ring R be rotation and scaling operations represented as the pair $r_i = (s_i, t_i), i = 1, 2, \ldots$ Let $r_1, r_2 \in R, \alpha \in F$.

We introduce the following operations in the ring:

$$(r_1 + r_2)(I) = (s_i + s_j, t_i + t_j)(I) \tag{7}$$

Physical meaning of the operation: the addition of the elements of the algebra is understood as the pair of the total angle of rotation and total scale of the image.

$$(r_1 \cdot r_2)(I) = (0, t_1 \cdot t_2)(I) \tag{8}$$

Physical meaning of the operation: multiplication of the elements of the algebra is understood as the pair with an angle of rotation equal to 0 and with multiplication of the image scales.

$$(\alpha \cdot r_1)(I) = (s_i, \alpha \cdot t_i)(I) \tag{9}$$

Physical meaning of the operation: multiplication of an element of the algebra by a field element is understood as the pair of the initial angle of rotation and image scale multiplied by α.

Statement 5. The operations of addition (7) and multiplication (8) of the two rotation and scaling operations applied to the image, as well as the operation of multiplication of the rotation and scaling by field element (9) are **strongly physically interpretable**.

Proof

1. Physical interpretability of operations: By Definition 4, an operation is physically interpretable if its application results in an image, or an image representation or image model, or characteristics of the source image.
2. Visual interpretability of operations: these operations are visually interpretable (Definition 5).
3. By Definition 7, a physically interpretable and visually interpretable operation is a strongly physically interpretable operation.

Q.E.D.

Example 4. A DIA1R Over Standard Algebraic Operations

Let I be an image, F be the field of real numbers, and elements of the ring R be standard algebraic operations. Let $r_1, r_2 \in R, \alpha \in F$. $r_i(I)$ corresponds to a standard algebraic operation over a pair (I, T_i), where T_i is some fixed object (standard, model), $i = 1, 2, \ldots$.

Some of G. Ritter's image algebra operations are introduced in ring R so that the properties of the algebra are fulfilled (e.g., the operations of pointwise addition and multiplication of two images, or the operations of pointwise taking of the maximum and minimum of two images):

$$(r_1 + r_2)(I) = r_1(I) \oplus r_2(I) \tag{10}$$

Physical meaning of the operation: addition of the elements of the algebra is understood as application of the operation of addition of two images obtained after application of standard algebraic operations to the original image and the given template.

$$(r_1 \cdot r_2)(I) = r_1(I) \odot r_2(I) \tag{11}$$

Physical meaning of the operation: multiplication of elements of the algebra is understood as application of the operation of multiplication of two images obtained after application of standard algebraic operations to the original image and a given template.

$$(\alpha r_1)(I) = \alpha r_1(I) \tag{12}$$

Physical meaning of the operation: multiplication of an element of the algebra by an element of the real number field is understood as pointwise multiplication of an element of the real number field and the result of application of a standard algebraic operation to the original image.

Statement 5. The operations of addition (10) and multiplication (11) of two standard algebraic operations applied to the image and the given templates, as well as the operation of multiplication of a standard algebraic operation applied to the image and the given template by field element (12), are **weakly physically interpretable**.

Proof

1. Physical interpretability of operations: By Definition 4, an operation is physically interpretable if its application results in an image, or an image representation or image model, or characteristics of the source image.
2. Visual interpretability of operations: these operations are not visually interpretable, since their application to standard algebraic operations previously applied to the image and given templates generally leads to unpredictable images (Definition 5).
3. By Definition 6, a physically interpretable, but not visually interpretable operation is a weakly physically interpretable operation.

   Q.E.D.

5   Conclusion

This paper continues to study the formal aspects of interpretability for all major DIA operations. The main types of interpretability are defined, and examples of interpretability of operations of the DIA1R are given.

Also of interest is the formulation of the problem of the formalization of interpretability of sets and bases of the standard image-processing operations of DIA1R. This problem is apparently related to the concept of image equivalence [2].

Note that sometimes the interpretation of algorithmic procedures for image processing and analysis is understood as the construction of descriptive algorithmic schemes in the language of DIA1R for solving applied problems [4, 8].

The results of this work can be used to study the interpretability of specialized DIA1R operations designed to solve problems of image analysis.

Acknowledgment. This work was supported in part by the Russian Foundation for Basic Research (Project No. 18-57-00013).

References

1. Grenander, U., Miller, M.: Pattern Theory: From Representation to Inference. Oxford Studies in Modern European Culture. Oxford University Press, Oxford (2007)
2. Gurevich, I.B., Yashina, V.V.: Computer-aided image analysis based on the concepts of invariance and equivalence. Pattern Recogn. Image Anal.: Adv. Math. Theory Appl. **16**(4), 564–589 (2006)
3. Gurevich, I.B., Yashina, V.V.: Operations of descriptive image algebras with one ring. Pattern Recogn. Image Anal.: Adv. Math. Theory Appl. **16**(3), 298–328 (2006)
4. Gurevich, I.B., Yashina, V.V., Koryabkina, I.V., Niemann, H., Salvetti, O.: Descriptive approach to medical image mining. An algorithmic scheme for analysis of cytological specimens. Pattern Recogn. Image Anal.: Adv. Math. Theory Appl. **18**(4), 542–562 (2008)
5. Gurevich, I.B., Yashina, V.V.: Descriptive approach to image analysis: image formalization space. Pattern Recogn. Image Anal.: Adv. Math. Theory Appl. **22**(4), 495–518 (2012)
6. Gurevich, I.B., Yashina, V.V.: Descriptive image analysis. foundations and descriptive image algebras. Int. J. Pattern Recogn. Artif. Intell. **33**(12), 25 p. (2019)
7. Gurevich, I.B., Yashina, V.V.: On the interpretability of operations of descriptive image algebras. In: Proceedings of 14th International Conference on Pattern Recognition and Information Processing, Minsk, "Bestprint", pp. 159–163 (2019)
8. Gurevich, I.B., Yashina, V.V.: Algebraic interpretation of image analysis operations. Pattern Recogn. Image Anal.: Adv. Math. Theory Appl. **29**(3), 389–403 (2019)
9. Gurevich, I.B., Yashina, V.V.. Descriptive image analysis. II. descriptive image models. Pattern Recognition and Image Analysis: Advances in Mathematical Theory and Applications **29**(4) (2019)
10. Haralick, R.M., Sternberg, S.R., Zhuang, X.: Image analysis using mathematical morphology. IEEE Trans. Pattern Anal. Mach. Intell. **9**(4), 532–550 (1987)
11. Ritter, G.X., Wilson, J.N.: Handbook of Computer Vision Algorithms in Image Algebra, 2nd edn. CRC Press Inc., Boca Raton (2001)
12. Zhuravlev Yu.I.: an algebraic approach to recognition and classification problems. Pattern Recogn. Image Anal.: Adv. Math. Theory Appl. **8**, 59–100 (1998)

Cell Nuclei Counting and Segmentation for Histological Image Analysis

Maryna Lukashevich[1]([✉]) and Valery Starovoitov[2]

[1] Belarusian State University of Informatics and Radioelectronics,
Minsk, Republic of Belarus
lukashevich@bsuir.by
[2] The United Institute of Informatics Problem, Minsk, Republic of Belarus
valerystar@mail.ru

Abstract. The paper describes our experiments of automated digital histological image analysis. In our study we investigated two tasks. The primary goal was to develop a simple and effective automated scheme of cell nuclei counting. The second goal was to demonstrate that for histological images with homogeneous background we can apply a binarization technique and approximately calculate the number of nuclei in the image. The experiments were done on two public datasets of histological images. The experiments have demonstrated acceptable level of calculation results.

Keywords: Histological analysis · Image analysis · Cell nuclei counting · Nuclei segmentation

1 Introduction

Visualization and control are key functions of automatic computer vision systems in the field of bioinformatics and biomedical research. In histological image analysis, accurate detection and segmentation of microscopic objects play an important role for cell analysis, identification of morphological changes, diagnosis clarification, appointment and adjustment of treatment. Digital image processing and analysis methods are widely used in morphological studies of cells and are the basis for the development of computer-aided diagnosis (CAD) and content-based image-retrieval (CBIR) systems. It is especially important to automate the analysis of histological images in the context of ever-increasing amount of patient data [1, 2]. Nuclei are distinctive in image and can help researchers locate cell. In computer vision, segmentation is the process of partitioning a digital image into segments. The result of segmentation is a set of segments extracted from the image. Each of the pixels in a region are similar with the respect to some characteristic (color, texture, intensity). An effective solution to the segmentation problem will make it possible to start treating both a simple cold and a serious disease more quickly. Detection is the starting point for analyses process because it allows identifying each individual cell and measuring how cells read to treatments, to analyzing the biological processes. Nuclei detection helps to reduce time-to-market for new drugs (currently 10 years) and improve health and increase quality of life.

© Springer Nature Switzerland AG 2019
S. V. Ablameyko et al. (Eds.): PRIP 2019, CCIS 1055, pp. 86–97, 2019.
https://doi.org/10.1007/978-3-030-35430-5_8

Automatic systems for microscopic analysis consist mainly of pre-processing, segmentation, separation and classification methods. We review relevant work according to solvable task, Table 1. A lot of automated methods for histological image analysis have been developed. The most common and simple approach for cell nuclei segmentation is thresholding. The another way is to use edge detectors (Laplacian of Gaussian filter, Laplacian filtering, etc.). Good reviews about nuclei image processing are presented in [1, 2].

Traditional algorithms of digital image processing (adaptive contour model, watershed, morphological operations, k-means, Support vector machine, etc. [3–12]) have some limitations. Because the task of automated detection and segmentation of cell nuclei is quite challenging for several reasons. The cell nuclei have a complex, no-uniform structures with great number of object variations [13]. Samples of microscopy images and their intensity histograms are presented in Fig. 1. One way to eliminate the limitations of traditional methods is to combine several algorithm and to developed specific methodology. This was the task of our research.

2 Method and Materials for Cell Nuclei Counting

We evaluate our method on the publicly available dataset which contains digital microscopy images stained with H&E [13, 14]. Images were obtained using the Zeiss Mirax Scan slide scanner. The resulting images saved as JPEG image files. The size of the analyzed field of each image is 600 × 600 pixels. Dataset includes 36 color tissue images with 7931 cells. The images of different organs (breast, kidney, gastric mucosa, connective tissue, small intestine, etc.) are presented in dataset. Three expert pathologists manually annotated all visible cell nuclei, Fig. 1. The ground truth information about the nuclei center coordinates are available.

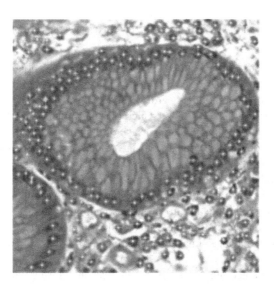

Fig. 1. An example of H&E image with nuclei centers indicated by crosses

2.1 The Main Idea

In proposed approach for cell nuclei counting in histological image analysis there are five mane stages: (1) RGB color space regularization; (2) image intensity adjusting; (3) guided filtering; (4) thresholding; (5) morphological processing. The preprocessing stage includes several steps. The number of colors (pink, purple and shades of blue) presented in the images is limited. It is proposed to reduce the number of colors in the original image palette using minimum variance quantization. Minimum variance quantization cuts the RGB color cube into smaller boxes (not necessarily cubic shape) of different sizes, depending on how the colors are distributed in the image. If the input image actually uses fewer colors than the number specified, the output colormap is also smaller, Fig. 2.

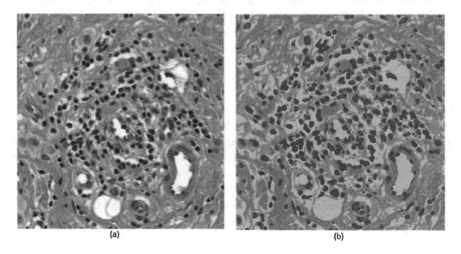

(a)   (b)

Fig. 2. (a) An input image, (b) the image after requantization (Color figure online)

For the tested dataset the result of this stage is almost visible to the human eye because of the limited number of colors in the difference between original images and same images after regularization is hardly visible, but it is crucial for further image analysis stages. After that we try to increase the image quality by a contrast enhancement procedure. The next step is usage of the guided filter. The filter performs edge-preserving smoothing of images, using content of a second image, called a guidance image, to influence the filtering. The guidance image can be the original image itself, a another version of the original image, or a completely different image. Guided image filtering is a neighborhood operation, like other filtering operations, but takes into account pixel statistics in the corresponding spatial neighborhood of the guidance image when calculating the value of the output pixel [15]. Then we apply binarization by Sauvola local image thresholding [16–18] for separation nuclei and background, see Fig. 3.

We clean the obtained binary images by opening and closing with a small structure element. Opening and closing are the basic operations of mathematical morphology.

Mathematical morphology is a tool for extracting some image components, useful for its representation and description (boundaries, skeletons, etc.). The opening smooths out the contours of the object, breaks the narrow isthmus and eliminates projections of a small width. Closing also results in smoothing out sections of the object outlines, but "floods" narrow gaps and long depressions of small width, and also eliminates small "holes" and fills the contours of the contour. After that we count automatically the number of black blobs corresponding to the cell nuclei.

2.2   Counting Method Validation

The have tested software implementations (in Matlab) of the proposed approach in 36 images from the data set described above. The typical parameter values used in our experiments are shown in Table 1. An example of original image and the binary variant with labeled centers of cell nuclei by experts are presented in Fig. 4.

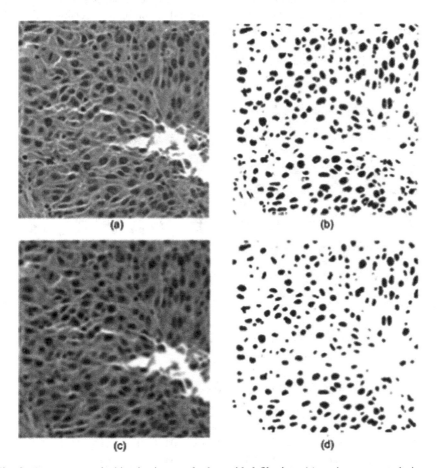

(a)

(b)

(c)

(d)

Fig. 3. Improvement in binarization results by guided filtering: (a) an input grayscale image, (b) thresholding without guided filtering; (c) the input grayscale image after guided filtering; (d) thresholding after guided filtering.

Table 1. Typical parameters values

Processing stage	Parameters	Different values
Minimum variance	Amount of color space	4
Guided filtering	Mask size	33
	Balance between data matching and smoothing	0.5
Sauvola local image thresholding	Local thresholding with M-by-N	45 × 45
	Neighbourhood threshold	0.35
Morphology	Radius of structuring elements	1
	Shape of structuring element	Disk

The performance of calculation was calculated using TP (true positive), FN (false negative) and FP (false positive) events. A measure that combines precision and recall is the harmonic mean of precision and recall, the traditional F-measure or balanced F-score. The detection accuracies of the proposed approach, Wienert's, Al-Kofahi's methods [13, 14] in precision and recall values are presented in Table 2.

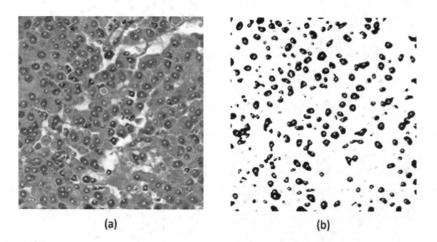

(a)   (b)

Fig. 4. (a) Original image and (b) its labeled cell nuclei

Table 2. Detection results of the Proposed Approach, Wienert's, Al-Kofahi's Methods in Precision and Recall Values

	Proposed	Wienert	Al-Kofahi
Precision	0.833 ± 0.01	0.908 ± 0.04	0.707 ± 0.13
Recall	0.920 ± 0.01	0.859 ± 0.04	0.916 ± 0.04
F-measure	0.8743	0.8828	0.7980

3   Nuclei Segmentation and Counting: Methods and Materials

Segmentation is one of the most important tasks but it is one of the most difficult stage for automated image analysis. In the previous section, we concentrated on cell nuclei counting. Segmentation is implemented by binarization (Sauvola local image thresholding) in proposed method. However, the segmentation accuracy was not taken into account. Cell nuclei counting is a key aspect. In this section, we will focus on the segmentation process and the assessment of its quality.

The investigated images are presented within the framework of the Data Science Bowl Social Media contest 2018 from https://www.kaggle.com [19]. Kaggle is a platform for the world largest community of data scientists and machine learning engineers. On Kaggle you can find high quality data sets, explore build models with that data science environment, connecting learn data scientist and machine learning engineers about problems and new approaches and enterprising competition on challenging skills. Sometimes histological images have a fairly uniform background. This allows us to apply a simpler image analysis scheme. Examples of such images are images from the database Kaggle, Fig. 5.

Each image is represented by an associated ImageId. Files belonging to an image are contained in a folder with this ImageId. Within this folder are two subfolders: images contains the image file; masks contains the segmented masks of each nucleus.

For experiments we have selected 108 color images from dataset and combine individual segmented masks of each nucleus into single mask, Fig. 6. The size of each image is 320×256 pixels.

Jaccard coefficient have been used for measure effectiveness of segmentation process. Objective object segmentation metrics are generally classified into two categories: region-based metrics and boundary-based metrics. Jaccard Index, also known as Intersection over Union and the Jaccard similarity coefficient is a typical region-based metric. Jaccard Index is a ratio of the number of matching pixels to the total number of both matching pixels and mismatching pixels. The Jaccard coefficient measures similarity between finite sample sets, and is defined as the size of the intersection divided by the size of the union of the sample sets.

The result from Sect. 2 algorithm is not satisfying. This means that there is no single approach for all histological images. There is a wide variability within this class of images. Based on this we have performed the analysis of the segmentation accuracy for the following approaches: convert RGB image to indexed image; k-means clustering.

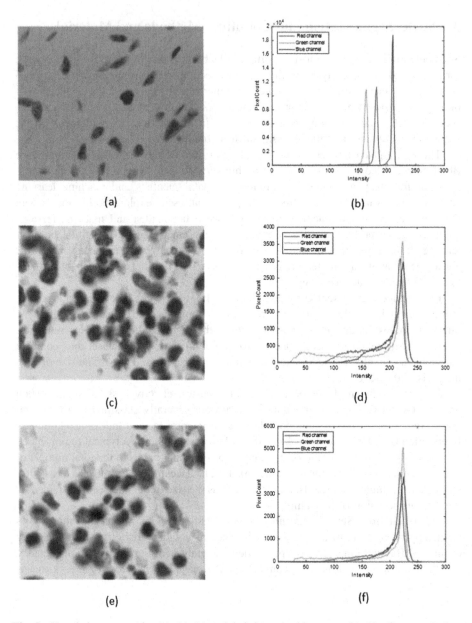

(a)

(b)

(c)

(d)

(e)

(f)

Fig. 5. Kaggle image samples (a), (c), (e) and their intensity histogram (b), (d), (f) respectively.

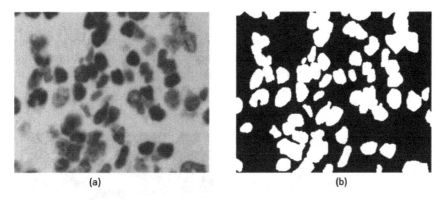

Fig. 6. (a) An original image, (b) its ground truth mask

3.1   Transformation RGB Images into Indexed Images

It is possible to approximately obtain the number of cells through segmentation. For an approximate calculation of the number of cell nuclei, the following empirical algorithm was tested. The simple approach is to convert the RGB image to an indexed image using minimum variance quantization (reducing the number of colors in an image involves quantization). We have performed image indexing on 2 or 3 classes and excluded from consideration a class having a median index. In the case of three classes, if one of the remaining two indices forms a spot of a very large area, it is also excluded. Then we have extracted all connected components (objects) from the binary image, where the area of the objects is in range from 20 pixels up to 10% of the image area. The region area is calculated for each connected components. The median value of region area was calculated. But this approach did not allow obtaining an objective value of the average area of nuclei. We have assumed that the values of nuclei indices is in the interval from 0 to 1. Then a nucleus with an average area on the image has an index about 0.6. This was established empirically. The total area of nuclei on the image is divided by the average nucleus area which was obtained in the previous step. This approach made it possible to determine the number of nuclei in the image.

The ratio of the real nuclei number to the calculated nuclei number was obtained for each image from dataset. This made it possible to obtain an average coefficient, which shows the efficiency of nuclei counting through segmentation. Let us to denote this coefficient as N. N = 0.6831 for Kaggle dataset. The segmentation accuracy is presented in Table 3. An example of histological image segmentation by color indexing is shown in Fig. 7.

Table 3. The segmentation accuracy

The number of colors	Mean Jaccard coefficient
2 colors	0.7310
3 colors	0.6942

3.2   Segmentation by k-means Clustering

One of the traditional approaches for segmentation is k-means clustering. We have performed experiments for segmentation accuracy calculation using k-means algorithm. Our experiments have demonstrated that this type of histological image segmentation is worse that color indexation described above.

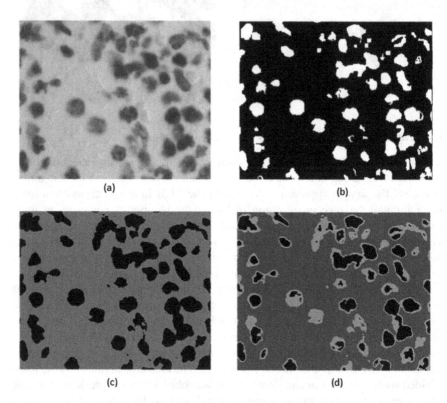

Fig. 7. (a) An original image, (b) ground truth for original image, (c) the result of indexing image into 2 colors and (d) the result of indexing image into 3 colors.

4   Conclusion

Table 2 shows the best parameters for the first image database. The developed approach can be adapted to different nuclei counting task. Its main advantage is automatic approach for cell nuclei counting. In the future, it is necessary to develop automated procedure for selecting the initial parameters settings depending on images.

Unlike the first dataset in the second Kaggle dataset the background of the images were fairly homogeneous. Besides dataset contains ground truth information for calculating the segmentation accuracy. This allowed us to apply a simple empirical scheme of image segmentation. The number of nuclei can be counted through segmentation process. Table 3 shows the segmentation accuracy (mean Jaccard coefficient).

However, this approach does not work if the image has no dominant background and there are large blue or red areas. Examples of such images are shown in Fig. 8. There are several reasons for this: not enough homogeneous background, not very homogeneous nuclei. The experimental results for these images are presented in Table 4. The average coefficient, which shows the efficiency of nuclei counting through segmentation denotes as N. As shown in the table we did not get reasonable segmentation accuracy and cell nuclei counting at the same time.

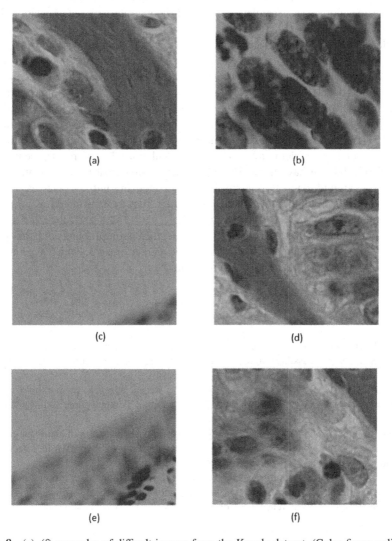

(a)

(b)

(c)

(d)

(e)

(f)

Fig. 8. (a)–(f) examples of difficult images from the Kaggle dataset. (Color figure online)

Table 4. The experimental results for images form Fig. 8

Image	(a)	(b)	(c)	(d)	(e)	(f)
Jaccard coeff.	0.0002	0.0765	0.1428	0.0020	0.2774	0.0039
N	0.0	0.7058	0.5	0.0	0.8333	1.3571

5 Discussion

We have investigated two tasks: counting of cell nuclei and nuclei segmentation on histological images with sufficiently homogeneous background. In the first case, the accuracy of cell nuclei detection has determined. In the second case, the accuracy of nuclei segmentation has calculated and cell counts through segmentation were analyzed.

In this study, a problem of cell nuclei detection and counting was addressed. We have proposed approach that is based on the guided filter and morphological operations. We avoided complex calculations, because realized only the detection and counting of cell nuclei. In this case cell segmentation in the image was not performed. The main goal was to achieve acceptable accuracy.

Another simple empirical algorithm is developed for cell nuclei segmentation and counting. Different to the previous algorithm, this algorithm segments nuclei in images and obtain round cell nuclei number by simple calculations. In general, segmentation is quite difficult, but we have demonstrated that if a histological image has any homogeneous background, one can segment it by color indexing into 2–3 classes.

The software prototype developed in our study may be considered as an experimental automatic tool for a cell nuclei analysis.

A very popular tool for solving of different segmentation problems is U-net neural network [20]. But it requires a large number of marked images, which was not in a case. This is a further direction of our research.

References

1. Irshad, H., Veillard, A., Roux, L., Racoceanu, D.: Methods for nuclei detection, segmentation, and classification in digital histopathology: a review current status and future potential. IEEE Rev. Biomed. Eng. **7**, 97–114 (2014)
2. Chen, S., Zhao, M., Wu, G., Yao, C., Zhang, J.: Recent advances in morphological cell image analysis. Hindawi Publishing (2012). Corporation: Computational and Mathematical Methoda in Medicine
3. Jung, C., Kim, C.: Impact of the accuracy of automatic segmentation of cell nuclei clusters on classification of cell nuclei clusters on classification of thyroid follicular lesions. Cytometry Part A **85A**, 709–719 (2014)
4. Saharma, H., et al.: A multi-resolution approach for combining visual information using nuclei segmentation and classification in histopathological images. In: Proceedings of the 10th International Conference on Computer Vision, Theory and Applications (VISAPP 2015), pp. 37–46 (2015)

5. Alilou, M., Kovalev, V., Taimouri, V.: Segmentation of cell nuclei in heterogeneous microscopy images: a reshapable templates approach. Comput. Med. Imaging Graph. **37**, 488–499 (2013)
6. Kowal, M., Filipczuk, P.: Nuclei segmentation for computer-aided diagnosis of breast cancer. Int. J. Appl. Math. Comput. Sci. **24**(1), 19–31 (2014)
7. Wienert, S., Helm, D., Saeger, K., Stenziger, A., Beil, M., Hufnagl, P., et al.: Detection and segmentation of cell nuclei in virtual microscopy images: a minimum-model approach. Nat. Sci. Rep. **2,** 503 p. (2012)
8. Zang, C., et al.: White blood cell segmentation by color-space-based K-means clustering. Sensors **14**, 16128–16147 (2014). https://doi.org/10.3390/s140916128
9. Song, Y., Cai, W., Huang, H., Wang, Y., Feng, D.D., Chen, M.: Region-based progressive localization of cell nuclei in microscopic images with data adaptive modeling. BMC Bioinf. **14,** 173 p. (2013)
10. Coelho, L.P., Shariff, A., Murphy, R.F.: Nuclear segmentation in microscope cell images: a hand-segmented dataset and comparison of algorithms. In: Proceedings of IEEE International Symposium Biomedical Imaging, pp. 518–521 (2009)
11. Signolle, N., Revenu, M., Plancoulaine, B., Herlin, P.: Wavelet-based multiscale texture segmentation in application to stromal compartment characterization on virtual slides. Signal Process. **90**(8), 2412–2422 (2010)
12. Lezoray, O., et al.: Segmentation of cytological image using color and mathematical morphology. Acta Stereologica **18**, 1–14 (1999)
13. Loukas, C.G., Wilson, G.D., Vojnovic, B., Linney, A.: an image analysis-based approach for automated counting of cancer cell nuclei tissue sections. Cytometry Part A **55A**, 30–42 (2003)
14. Al-Kofahi, Y., Lassoued, W., Grama, K., Nath, S.K., Zhu, J., Oueslati, R., et al.: Cell-basedquantification of molecular biomarkers in histopathology specimens. Histopathology **59**(1), 40–54 (2011)
15. Xu, L., Lu, C., Xu, Y., Jia, J.: Image smoothing via L0 gradient minimization. ACM Trans. Graph. **30**(6). Article 174 (2011)
16. Sauvola, J., Pietikainen, M.: Adaptive document image binarization. Pattern Recogn. **33**, 225–236 (2000)
17. Shafait, F., Keysers, D., Breuel, T.M.: Efficient implementation of local adaptive thresholding techniques using integral images. In: Document Recognition and Retrieval XV (2008)
18. Stathis, P., Kavallieratou, E., Papamarkos, N.: An evaluation technique for binarization algorithms. J. Univ. Comput. Sci. **14**(18), 3011–3030 (2008)
19. Data Science Bowl. https://www.kaggle.com/c/data-science-bowl-2018. Accessed 29 Apr 2018
20. Ronneberger, O., Fischer, P., Brox, T.: U-Net: convolutional networks for biomedical image segmentation. https://arxiv.org/abs/1505.04597. Accessed 29 Apr 2018

Examining the Capability of GANs to Replace Real Biomedical Images in Classification Models Training

Vassili Kovalev and Siarhei Kazlouski[(✉)]

United Institute of Informatics Problems,
Surganova St., 6, 220012 Minsk, Belarus
vassili.kovalev@gmail.com, kozlovski.serge@gmail.com

Abstract. In this paper, we explore the possibility of generating artificial biomedical images that can be used as a substitute for real image datasets in applied machine learning tasks. We are focusing on generation of realistic chest X-ray images as well as on the lymph node histology images using the two recent GAN architectures including DCGAN and PGGAN. The possibility of the use of artificial images instead of real ones for training machine learning models was examined by benchmark classification tasks being solved using conventional and deep learning methods. In particular, a comparison was made by replacing real images with synthetic ones at the model training stage and comparing the prediction results with the ones obtained while training on the real image data. It was found that the drop of classification accuracy caused by such training data substitution ranged between 2.2% and 3.5% for deep learning models and between 5.5% and 13.25% for conventional methods such as LBP + Random Forests.

Keywords: Generative Adversarial Networks · X-ray images · Histology images

1 Introduction

Machine learning (ML) and in particular deep learning (DL) techniques become more and more popular in biomedical image analysis domain during the last several years [1]. Despite of a high efficiency of these approaches (see, for example, [1, 2]) the success of ML methods strongly depends on the availability of large training datasets accompanied by appropriate annotations. At the same time, data specificity clearly implies a number of ethical, legal, and technical challenges in retrieving and sharing datasets of biomedical images. The frequency of natural appearance of patients with particular pathologies limits the possible number of cases with certain pathologies. The image data collecting procedure may be time consuming and often requires advanced equipment. On the top, the data annotation supposes involvement of experienced specialists. This could be costly or even not feasible at all due to a very high cost. Also, ethical and privacy regulations make it difficult or, in some particular cases, entirely impossible to distribute collected biomedical image data publicly as well as between some institutions, or even on-site [3, 4].

© Springer Nature Switzerland AG 2019
S. V. Ablameyko et al. (Eds.): PRIP 2019, CCIS 1055, pp. 98–107, 2019.
https://doi.org/10.1007/978-3-030-35430-5_9

Although a number of projects (e.g., National Biomedical Imaging Archive, OASIS Brains project, OpenNeuro.org and some other) tend to provide public image datasets of some modalities, the problem of data scarcity remains and it constrains possibilities of researchers in the field of biomedical imaging.

In this work, we study the possibility to overcome the problem of biomedical data scarcity by applying modern SOTA image synthesis technique – Generative Adversarial Networks (GANs) [5] for creation of artificial biomedical image datasets that can be used as a publicly available substitute for real images in applied ML tasks.

Recent researches that used GANs in biomedical domain have proven the efficiency of this approach in modality-to-modality translation, image de-noising, reconstruction, enhancement, segmentation and image synthesis itself [6, 7]. Existing works related to the problem of image synthesis can be split into two groups. A majority of works belongs to the first group which puts emphasis on utilizing GANs for augmentation of some existing image dataset as well as transformation and widening them in order to achieve more accurate results in various applied task. The works of the second group aim to replace real image data with artificial ones.

This study belongs to the second group and we are trying to widen the existing research works in the field by involving multiple combinations of data types and methods. In particular, we are working with the two large image datasets of opposite nature, namely, the chest X-rays and histology images. For artificial image synthesis, we are using the following two GAN architectures: the Deep Convolutional generative adversarial networks [8] (DCGAN) and the Progressive Growing generative adversarial networks [9] (PGGAN). Also, we utilizing two different approaches for the quantitative evaluation of the quality of artificial images which include training of convolutional networks for solving image classification tasks and using conventional ML models based on feature extraction followed by traditional classifiers.

Hence, with this work we are trying to provide the results of the assessment of the quality of artificial images as well as to enrich the paper content by way of reporting interesting observations regarding the two GAN architectures mentioned above.

2 Original Image Data

Two kinds of biomedical images were selected in order to cover images of two different modalities of opposite nature. The first image type is represented by chest X-ray images which are grayscale and are holding certain anatomical shape with the relatively high role of spatial, "geometrical" structure. The second image type is represented by histological images which are, on the contrary, color and can be viewed as a "shape-free" random color texture. Both image types are important for medical practice: x-ray images are often used in screening for detecting lung, skeletal and cardiovascular system abnormalities as well as for monitoring various treatment processes; histological images are continuously playing the role of a gold standard in cancer diagnosis.

2.1 Chest X-Ray Images

X-ray image data used in this study were the natively-digital X-ray scans extracted from a PACS system, containing results of a periodic chest screening of adult population of a two-million city. The version of the database we used here contains a total of 1,908,926 X-ray images accompanied by data records which include patients' ID, age, gender and textual radiological reports made by a chief radiologist.

Technically, all the X-ray scans were represented by a one-channel 16-bit non-compressed images. The original image resolution varied from a rarely occurred 520×576 pixels to the size of 2800×2531 pixels. In order to unify dataset and make it usable in our research, images were resized to 512×512 pixels and normalized by the lungs convex hull using 5 and 95 percentiles of brightness. Images were labeled with patient age, gender and abnormality (if any) what was extracted from radiological reports.

Normal Chest X-Ray (X-Norm) included images without visible signs of any type of abnormalities in mediastinum, skeleton and the lungs themselves. A total of 566,712 chest images were included in this image dataset after a technical clearance.

2.2 Histology Images

Histology images used in this study were images of lymph node [10]. The source dataset was composed of 400 whole-slide images of sentinel lymph node, 270 of which were labeled as normal regions and the rest 130 as the regions containing metastases from breast cancer. Technically, all the images were presented by color 3-channel images of tissue samples with resolution up to 200 000 pixels in both width and height. In order to retrieve manageable-sized data, original images were cut into small 256×256 regions, which are referred to as the image "tiles". Each tile inherited a label from its source whole-slide image. The following two data sets were extracted:

Normal Histology (H-Norm) included 50 000 randomly chosen tiles taken from normal regions.

Tumor Histology (H-Tumor) included 50 000 randomly chosen tiles taken from regions containing metastases.

2.3 Study Groups

The image study groups created based on the above mentioned X-ray and histology images which are used in all the experiments are presented in Table 1 along with their major characteristics.

As it can be seen from the Table, the X-Norm-L study group uses not evenly-binned age subgroups. This is caused by a non-equivalent distribution of gender and ages in the original dataset. Due to a well-known social reasons, there is a lack of scans of elderly people. This is especially true for male subjects. In order to maintain the maximum coverage of ages and still get a large, well-balanced dataset, we decided to use non-homogeneous age grouping with smaller group size for younger subjects (what is mostly <50) and larger group size for elderly ages. In order to ensure that this kind of grouping will not cause quality drop in experimental result, a regularly-sampled age groups were also utilized in this study.

Table 1. Study groups and their characteristics

Group name	Subset	Size	Comments
X-Norm	Train	120 570	Images labeled by gender-age group. Age groups are:
	Test	13 410	$18-19, 20-21, \ldots, 67-68$. Balanced by gender and age (30 groups).
X-Norm-L	Train	71 026	Images labeled by gender-age group. Age groups are: 18–
	Test	7 922	19, 20–21, 22–23, 24–25, 26–27, 28–30, 31–33, 34–36, 37– 39, 40–44, 45–49, 50–54, 55–60, 61–66, 67–77. Balanced by gender in 34 age groups.
H-Norm	Train	40 000	None
	Test	10 000	
H-Tumor	Train	40 000	
	Test	10 000	

3 Experimental Setup

3.1 Image Generation

The open-source implementations of two GAN architectures were used as starting points for generation of image datasets including DCGAN [11] and PGGAN [12]. Each model was applied to the training set of each study group we created.

X-Ray. Due to the presence of multiple gender-age groups in the dataset and relatively small amount of samples for each group, we tried both conditional and unconditional model training. In the unconditional setup, a subset of data was extracted from training set of the study group for each label and individual model was trained on this subset without any additional input to discriminator or generator networks. In case of conditional setup, the models were trained on the entire training sets of study group and gender-age label of each image was encoded and passed to generator and discriminator networks during the training. Thus, for unconditional setup a total of 64 DCGAN and 64 PGGAN models were trained. Also, two DCGAN models and two PGGAN models were trained for the conditional setup.

Considering the hardware limitations and based on a visual assessment of generated images during the preliminary experiments, the following setup was used: Latent vector dimensionality: 512; batch size: 32; input and output image size: 256×256 pixels; training epochs: 30 for unconditional setup, 60 for conditional setup; optimizer: Adam. Same batch size and epochs number were used for all layer depths in PGGAN.

Histology. For histology data we used unconditional model training. That means that the one model was trained on the entire training sets of study groups without any additional input to discriminator or generator networks. Thus, two DCGAN models and two PGGAN models were trained. The following setup was used: Latent vector dimensionality: 256; batch size: 32; input and output image size: 256×256 pixels; training epochs: 10; optimizer: Adam. Same batch size and epochs number were used for all layer depths in PGGAN.

After completing training of GANs, the training datasets of artificial images were generated using best checkpoints for each model. The best checkpoints selection criteria were based on visual examination of random samples generated for each epoch during the training procedure.

Finally, the artificial versions of original study groups from Table 1 were generated what is resulted in 12 datasets of artificial images. Generated datasets were of the same size and contain the same labels distribution as corresponding original datasets.

3.2   Artificial Dataset Assessment

Artificial image datasets were first examined visually and then either discarded as obviously unacceptable or passed to further quantitative assessment stage. In case of the use of DCGAN method for generating X-ray images the invalid results were removed with the help of well-known image hash technique (hash size h = 16, hash type = average, distance metric = Hamming) which check images for correct global body shape. Quantitative examination was performed by way of comparing the accuracy achieved on benchmark classification tasks by ML models trained either on real image datasets or on artificial image datasets.

General algorithm of benchmarking can be described as follows:

(a) Formulate the benchmark classification task.
(b) Determine he training sets of real and artificial data and test set of real data.
(c) Determine the model architecture and parameters to use for classification.

For each of selected model:

(d) Train model on the training set of real data.
(e) Train model on the training set of artificial data.
(f) Score models from (d) and (e) on the test set of real data and compare results.

The benchmark tasks and data sets descriptions are presented in Table 2.

Table 2. Benchmark classification tasks

Data type	Classification task	Training set size	Test set size
Histology	By class: norm or tumor	8000	2000
X-ray	By gender: female or male	8000	1000
X-ray	By age group: "young" (18–38) or "mature" (48–68)	8000	1000

All the training and the test image datasets were balanced by target class labels. In case of X-ray datasets, they were also balanced by subjects' gender-age group.

The following ML models were used for classification:
(1) VGG16 deep convolutional network; (2) K-NN; (3) SVM; (4) Random forest.

For conventional methods, the LBP descriptors of images with radius 2, 3, 4 as well as their combination were used as image features. In each classification task, the procedure of selection of the best parameters was performed using 5-Fold cross-validation. In, this experiment, the color histology images were converted to the grayscale versions in order to use LBP method directly.

For VGG16 network, the whole image datasets were used as network input. The training of the model was performed for 20 epochs with the batch size of 32. The best models were selected based on the best validation loss being obtained.

4   Results

X-Ray. Generally, both DCGAN and PGGAN generators were able to produce visually appealing artificial chest X-ray images (see Figs. 1a and 2a respectively). However, it was noticed that in about of 40–60% of cases all the examined DCGAN models produced X-ray images with heavily distorted body shape (Fig. 1b). Contrary to DCGAN, the PGGAN models performed much better in reconstructing global image structure due to their inherent property of "multi-resolution", i.e., the ability of gradual, steady image refinement (Fig. 2a). In context of neural networks, this can be also explained by a much more robust handling of macro structure in progressively growing layers of PGGAN.

Our results suggest that PGGAN achieved the best performance in case of conditional training on X-Norm-L while DCGAN created images of the best quality in case of unconditional training on either X-Norm-L or X-Norm. It should be noted that in all the experiments the training process was not very stable and generator models often passed through phases of dramatic image quality drop. In case of PGGAN this drop appeared only on layers which generated images of resolution 128×128 and higher.

Histology. Here DCGANs have demonstrated faster model collapse than in case of X-ray images. Nevertheless, we were able to generate artificial images of good visual quality on early stage of training, just after 3 epochs for normal histology tiles and after 5 epochs in case of 256×256 tiles of tumor histology images (Fig. 1b, c).

Contrary to the DCGANs, we completely failed to generate good quality histology images using PGGAN model. This is because they were always demonstrating very fast model collapse and produced kind of "averaged" histology image patterns like the ones shown in Fig. 2b. This happened as early as from the first epoch of training. We conclude that in case of texture-like, randomly structured images progressive image size growth leads to a much faster collapse of training since the first layers generate almost solidly filled images and further layers were not able to restore them.

After determining the best models, which were conditional PGGAN for X-ray images trained on X-Norm-L image dataset and DCGAN for histology images trained on Histology, we generated three artificial image datasets as described in Table 2 and used them to train classification models as described in previous section. A summary of these benchmarking results is presented in Table 3. The results demonstrate that in all the cases the classification accuracy of models trained on artificial data is lower than of models trained on real data.

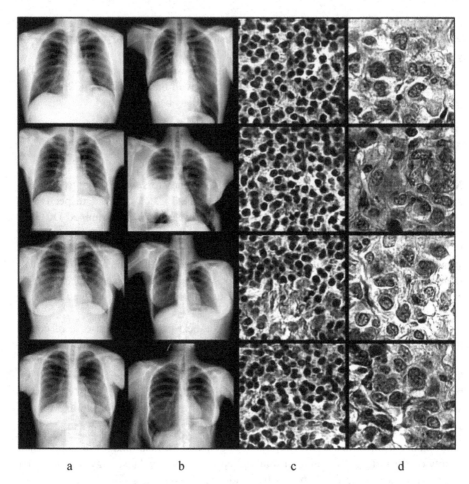

a   b   c   d

Fig. 1. Examples of artificial images created using DCGANS. (a) Visually appealing chest X-ray images. (b) Heavily distorted X-ray images. (c) Histology images of normal tissue. (d) Histology images of malignant tumors.

However, in our view, the performance drop seems to be acceptable for many practical applications and there is still some potential for further improvements.

As it can be seen from the Table 3, both relative and the absolute accuracy drop for DL models is about 2 to 5 times lower than for conventional methods. Since conventional models work with LBP features while DL models treat image "as is", we can assume that generated images may be not very realistic in terms of LBP features. However, still they are much more similar when considered in the feature space of deep convolutional neural networks.

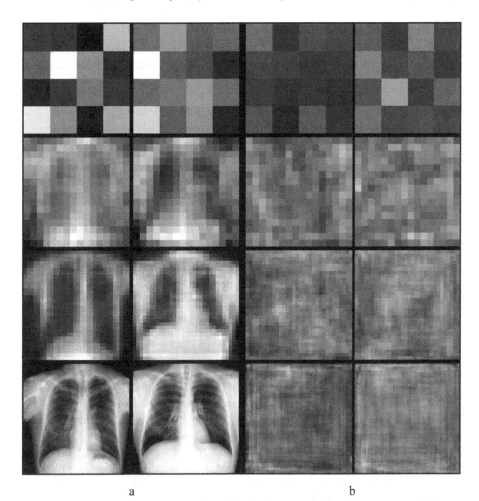

a   b

Fig. 2. Examples of generation of artificial images by progressive refinement (from top to bottom) using PROGAN. (a) Chest X-ray images. (b) Histology images.

Table 3. Benchmarking results (the best scores).

Classification task	ML model	Accuracy, trained on real images	Accuracy, trained on artificial images	Relative accuracy drop
Histology: norm and tumor	VGG16	**0.96**	**0.93**	**3.12%**
	K-NN	0.94	0.87	7.45%
	SVM	0.90	0.85	5.56%
	Random forest	0.93	0.86	7.53%

(continued)

Table 3. (*continued*)

Classification task	ML model	Accuracy, trained on real images	Accuracy, trained on artificial images	Relative accuracy drop
X-ray: by subject's gender	VGG16	**0.90**	**0.88**	**2.22%**
	K-NN	0.84	0.78	7.14%
	SVM	0.82	0.74	9.76%
	Random forest	0.83	0.72	13.25%
X:ray: by subject's age group	VGG16	**0.86**	**0.83**	**3.49%**
	K-NN	0.80	0.73	8.75%
	SVM	0.79	0.71	10.13%
	Random forest	0.80	0.70	12.50%

5 Conclusions

Results on generating artificial images of two different biomedical modalities obtained using two kinds of generative DL models allow drawing the following conclusions.

(1) Artificial X-ray and histology image datasets have a potential to be used as a substitute for real images in the training of classification models of different kinds. The relative accuracy drop was rather acceptable in the majority of benchmarks and ranged between 2.2% and 3.49% in case of DL and between 5.5% and 13.25% in case of conventional methods respectively.

(2) Artificial training data work substantially better when used in recent DL models comparing to the old-fashion models trained on classical LBP features. Probably, this can be generalized to other feature types and explained by conceptual similarity of image presentation in convolutional networks and natural difference between the latter and presentation by any set of conventional features.

(3) We could suggest that progressive GAN architectures may be recommended for generating anatomical images like the chest X-rays while more simple architectures such as DCGANs are better suited for color texture images like the histology ones.

References

1. Litjens, G., et al.: A survey on deep learning in medical image analysis. Med. Image Anal. **42**, 60–88 (2017)
2. Kovalev, V., Liauchuk, V., Kalinovsky, A., Shukelovich, A.A.: Comparison of conventional and deep learning methods of image classification on a database of chest radiographs. Int. J. Comput. Assist. Radiol. Surg. **12**, 139–140 (2017)
3. Ching, T., et al.: Opportunities and obstacles for deep learning in biology and medicine. bioRxiv preprint bioRxiv:142760 (2018)

4. Cunniff, C., et al.: Informed consent for medical photographs. Genet. Med. **2**(6), 353–355 (2000)
5. Goodfellow, I., et al.: Generative adversarial nets. In: Ghahramani, Z., et al. (eds.) Neural Information Processing Systems (NIPS), vol. 2, pp. 2672–2680. MIT Press, Montreal (2014)
6. Kazeminiaa, S., et al.: GANs for medical image analysis. arXiv preprint arXiv:1809.06222 (2018)
7. Yia, X., Waliaa, E., Babyna, P.: Generative adversarial network in medical imaging: a review. arXiv preprint arXiv:1809.07294 (2019)
8. Radford, A., Metz, L., Chintala, S.: Unsupervised representation learning with deep convolutional generative adversarial networks. arXiv preprint arXiv:1511.06434 (2016)
9. Karras, T., Aila, T., Laine, S., Lehtinen, J.: Progressive growing of GANs for improved quality, stability, and variation. arXiv preprint arXiv:1710.10196 (2017)
10. Veta, M., et al.: Predicting breast tumor proliferation from whole-slide images. Med. Image Anal. **54**, 111–121 (2019)
11. DCGAN implementation (2019). https://github.com/carpedm20/DCGAN-tensorflow. Accessed 1 Apr 2019
12. PGGAN implementation (2019). https://github.com/akanimax/pro_gan_pytorch. Accessed 1 Apr 2019

Nearest Convex Hull Classifier with Simplified Proximity Measurement

Anatoly Nemirko[✉] [iD]

Saint Petersburg Electrotechnical University "LETI",
Saint Petersburg, Russian Federation
apn-bs@yandex.ru

Abstract. This text proposes a new classifier of nearest convex hulls characterized by a simplified measurement of convex hull proximity to the test point. It is called a light nearest convex hull classifier (LNCH). The concept of penetration depth is used for measurement of test point proximity to the class convex hull if the test point is within the convex hull. The proximity is defined based on analysis of extremum points projected onto a direction vector from a given point to the class centroid. For the LNCH classifier, a decision rule for multi-class problems is derived, which uses the proposed proximity measurement estimation method. A comparison of LNCH and classifications using nearest neighbour algorithms (kNN) is performed and results of experimental studies based on synthesized numerical data and actual data of breast cancer diagnostic task are presented. Results have shown the high recognition precision of LNCH classifiers in comparison with other types of classifiers.

Keywords: Nearest convex hull · Multi-class classification · Penetration depth · Breast cancer diagnosis

1 Introduction

In recent years the methods of computational geometry for class description as a multi-dimensional convex hull (CH) are used in the area of pattern recognition [1, 2]. There are several methods of CH constructing in 2D and 3D spaces. There are several algorithms for CH computation in high-dimensional attribute spaces, for instance Quickhull [3], however their implementation is currently limited by both attribute space dimension and training set size. Similar problems are inherent for some instance-based classifiers, such as k-Nearest Neighbour (kNN) classifiers, which suffer from "the curse of dimensionality". Despite the fact that multiple methods, reducing computational cost [4], are being proposed for kNN algorithms, when applied they often provide only a small improvement, compared with classic implementation of the method.

In this paper we examine nearest convex hull (NCH) classifiers and nearest neighbours classifiers (kNN). The study [1] describes a new classification model called a soft nearest convex hull classifier (SNCH).

This classifier determines the proximity of the test point to the convex hulls of the classes and assigns this point the mark of the class, the distance to the convex hull of which is minimal. SNCH classifier is based on support vector machine (SVM) [4] for

© Springer Nature Switzerland AG 2019
S. V. Ablameyko et al. (Eds.): PRIP 2019, CCIS 1055, pp. 108–118, 2019.
https://doi.org/10.1007/978-3-030-35430-5_10

performance of proximity measurement. The literature includes application of this type of classifier for remote sensing [6] and face recognition [2]. SNCH classifiers have some features different from other types of classifiers. They are easy to apply in multi-class recognition tasks. They provide a complex, nonlinear surface for the task, providing a good data fit. One of the main disadvantages of SNCH method is the necessity to solve s optimization tasks for test point mark identification, where s is the number of classes. Also one of the disadvantages of the method is uncertainty of optimization parameters and the necessity of their settings.

This article presents the method for measurement of test point proximity to the nearest convex hull, but this measurement is based on the analysis of convex hull vertex projections onto the direction vector from this point to the class centroid. This method is the basis of the proposed lite nearest convex hull classifier (LNCH) algorithm. Here follows the structure of the article. At first we examine kNN method and SNCH method, described in [1], and then we examine the proposed method of measurement of test point proximity to CH, and later we offer the algorithm of such measurement calculation based on analysis of class projection onto direction from test point to class centroid, and in the final we represent LNCH classification algorithm based on simplified measurement of proximity to CH. Experimental study results are presented in the end of the article. Despite the simplified method of measurement of test point proximity to CH, the study's results have shown that compared with kNN, SVM and SNCH methods the LNCH method has a good recognition precision for training set in case of using cross-validation with the leave-one-out (LOO) principle.

2 k-Nearest Neighbours Classifier

The kNN algorithm, examined for comparison, is one of the simplest machine learning algorithms. The algorithm chooses k of the nearest neighbours and returns the class, that is encountered the most among the chosen ones, and assigns the classifiable object to this class. The learning phase of this algorithm consists only in memorizing the feature vectors and class labels of the training samples. At the classification stage, k is a user-defined constant, and the test point is classified by assigning a label that is most often found among the k training samples closest to the test point.

The disadvantage of kNN classification appears for class distributions different from uniform or if there is no class balance. Then the more frequent classes have the tendency to be more prevailing among k of the nearest neighbours. The choice of the best k presents a problem. Usually the greater k values reduce noise impact on classification, but make the boundaries between classes less clear. In binary classification tasks k is chosen as an odd number since it enables prevention of the connected votes. The proper k can be chosen using various heuristic methods. The cross-validation method [15] is often applied for k parameter optimization. In this study we perform control using the leave-one-out (LOO) principle. The disadvantage of LOO is large resource intensity, since the learning is performed s times, where s is the number of training set members.

The most intuitive type of kNN classifier is the one nearest neighbour (1NN) classifier, for which $k = 1$. It assigns the nearest neighbour class in the feature space to the test point. A naive version of the algorithm is easy to implement by means of measuring the distances from the test case to all saved cases, but it requires large computational resources for large training sets. Usage of approximate nearest neighbour search algorithms enables calculation of kNN even for large data sets. A lot of nearest neighbour search algorithms have been proposed over the last years; usually they try to reduce number of actually performed distance measurements. If the training set size is close to infinity, 1NN classifier guarantees an rate no worse than a double minimum achievable rate of Bayesian errors [7]. Measurement of the error rate upper limit for multi-class kNN classification is also performed in this study [7].

1NN method suffers from "the curse of dimensionality" and can have problems with multi-dimensions due to very small size of training data set for sufficient filling of input space. However, the 1NN method is highly adaptive, since it can produce extremely irregular solutions surface, dividing the classes of any data set without errors for disjoined classes. Transition to operation with convex sets smooths "the curse of dimensionality" due to hypothetic points input inside CH, which can be used for filling the input space artificially.

3   Soft Nearest Convex Hull Classifier

A Soft Nearest Convex Hull (SNCH) classifier [1] is a classifier, that defines test point proximity to CH and gives this point a mark of the class, distance to CH of which is smaller. This classifier is based on a support vector machine (SVM) [5] for measurement of point proximity to CH.

Assume the training set of one class is the following: $X = \{\mathbf{x}_i, \ \mathbf{x}_i \in R^d, \ i = 1, 2, \ldots, k\}$. Then convex hull, made by this set, is defined as

$$conv(X) = \left\{ \mathbf{v} : \mathbf{v} = \sum_{i=1}^{k} a_i \mathbf{x}_i, \quad 0 \le a_i, \quad \sum_{i=1}^{k} a_i = 1, \quad \mathbf{x}_i \in X \right\},$$

where a_i are scalar non-negative coefficients. If there are m classes, we have m sets $X_i, \ i = 1, 2, \ldots, m$ and, respectively, m convex hulls $conv(X_i), \ i = 1, 2, \ldots, m$. For a given test point $\mathbf{x}$ its belonging to a class is defined by minimum distance from this point to convex hull, that is set by decision function $class(\mathbf{x}) = \underset{i=1,2,\ldots m}{\arg\min} d_i(\mathbf{x}, conv(X_i))$, where $d_i(\mathbf{x}, conv(X_i))$ designated a distance from $\mathbf{x}$ to convex hull $conv(X_i)$. It is known that in cases with disjoined classes, the support vector machine (SVM) [5] calculates the minimum distance between the convex hulls of classes and defines a corresponding weight vector $\mathbf{w}$, directed along a dividing axis [8]. In [1] the distance from the test point to convex hull is defined, using SVM method, as a norm of weight vector $\mathbf{w}$, that results from using an optimization task solution of the following type:

$$\begin{cases} \|\mathbf{w}\|^2 \to \min \\ \mathbf{w}^T\mathbf{x}_i + w_0 \geq 0, \quad i = 1, 2, \ldots, N, \\ -(\mathbf{w}^T\mathbf{x} + w_0) = 1 \end{cases} \tag{1}$$

where w_0 = hyperplane threshold value, N = number of class members. This is a problem of convex quadratic programming (per $\mathbf{w}$, w_0) in a convex set considering a totality of linear inequalities.

In the case of linearly inseparable classes the direct determination of $d_i(\mathbf{x}, conv(X_i))$ has some difficulties. But also in this case we can use SVM to reach an approximate solution. In study [1] the required distance is determined using slack variables, therefore the method is called the Soft Nearest Convex Hull (SNCH) classifier.

In study [1] with inseparable classes instead of task (1) the optimization task (2) is determined, as presented below

$$\begin{cases} \frac{1}{2}\|\mathbf{w}\|^2 + C\sum_{i=1}^{N}\xi_i \to \min_{\mathbf{w}, w_0, \xi_i} \\ \mathbf{w}^T\mathbf{x}_i + w_0 \geq 0 - \xi_i, \quad i = 1, 2, \ldots, N, \\ \xi_i \geq 0, \quad i = 1, 2, \ldots, N \\ -(\mathbf{w}^T\mathbf{x} + w_0) = 1 \end{cases} \tag{2}$$

where variables $\xi_i \geq 0$ reflect error value on objects $\mathbf{x}_i$, $i = 1, 2, \ldots, N$, and C ratio is a method setting parameter, which allows regulating relation between the maximization of the margin width, and minimization of summary errors. Solution of task (2) (as well as for separable classes) is achieved by task presentation as dual type [9].

Despite some disadvantages of the method: necessity of solving many optimization tasks for multi-class tasks, necessity of setting the optimization parameters and uncertainty of these parameters, SNCH method has good generalization capability and resistance to outliers.

4 New Method of Simplified Measurement of Test Point Proximity to Convex Hull

For any two objects $\{A, B\} \subseteq \mathbb{R}^n$ the Euclidean distance between A and B is determined as $d(A, B) = \min_{\substack{a \in A \\ b \in B}} \|a - b\|$. However, if A and B intersect, this measure is zero and does not show the degree of their intersection. In this case we use an indicator called *penetration depth* (or *mutual intersection depth*), that we adopted from collision detection area [10, 11]. This measure shows intersection level. We will consider that the object A can move, and object B is stationary. For a given direction vector $\mathbf{u}$ *the directional penetration depth* between A and B is determined as a minimum value, for which B shall be moved in the direction of $\mathbf{u}$, so that the inner area A does not intersect with B. The *overall directional penetration depth* between A and B is determined as minimum value, for which *B* shall be moved in any direction, so that the inner area *A* does not intersect with *B*.

Following the same practice, one can conclude that in case of separable classes, the distance between them may be determined as a minimum distance, by which *B* shall be moved in any direction (or in direction **u** for directional penetration depth) for inner area *A* not to intersect with *B* (Fig. 1).

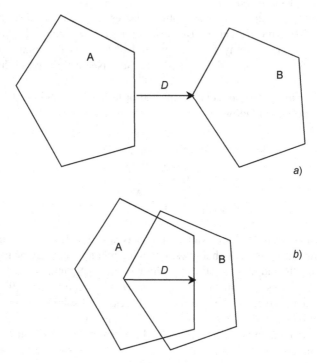

Fig. 1. To the definition of the proximity between two convex hulls: (a) *D* – a minimum distance between A and B and the corresponding weight vector; (b) *D* – a minimum penetration depth between A and B and the corresponding weight vector

In the case of intersection of test point **x** with convex hull $conv(X_i)$ inside intersection area the proximity measure can be determined. In this study, using penetration depth concept, test point **x** proximity to $conv(X_i)$ $d_i(\mathbf{x}, conv(X_i))$ in case of their intersection is determined as a minimum value, to which $conv(X_i)$ shall be moved *in any direction* to stop intersection.

The algorithm of overall penetration depth determination for multidimensional case is a hard and computationally complicated problem. It is significantly simplified when considering projections of convex hulls (or the classes themselves) on some direction *u* in multidimensional space and calculation of directional penetration depth. In this case $d_i^u(\mathbf{x}, conv(X_i))$ is determined as the minimum value, to which $conv(X_i)$ shall be moved in direction *u*, so it does not intersect with **x** on this direction (Fig. 2). In a general case, a minimum penetration depth of **x** in $conv(X_i)$ at their intersection may be found by trying various directions in multidimensional space, and investigating extreme class projection points on these directions. For each direction u, expressed by single vector $\mathbf{u}$, extreme values of projections $conv(X_i)$ onto $\mathbf{u}$ are determined as vertices $conv(X_i)$, which in turn are elements of X_i. Therefore instead of extreme values of projections $conv(X_i)$ it is possible to consider extreme values of projections of a set X_i. Then, in a general case, $d_i^u(\mathbf{x}, conv(X_i))$ is determined according to the following algorithm.

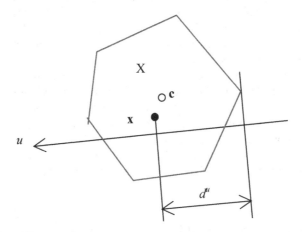

Fig. 2. To the definition of the directional penetration depth d^u of vector $\mathbf{x}$ in convex hull $conv(X)$ of a set X in direction u. In the figure – $\mathbf{x}$ is test vector, $\mathbf{c}$ is the centroid of set X

DISTANCE algorithm

Input: $\mathbf{u}, \mathbf{x}, X_i$ {direction vector, test point, set of elements of i-th class}

Output: F, $d_i^u(\mathbf{x}, conv(X_i))$ {intersection mark, distance to convex hull of i-th class}

1. As per set X_i create a matrix $\mathbf{X}_i$

2. If $\min\left(\mathbf{u}^T\mathbf{X}_i\right) \leq \mathbf{u}^T\mathbf{x} \leq \max\left(\mathbf{u}^T\mathbf{X}_i\right)$

$\quad$ F = 1; $d_i^u\left(\mathbf{x}, conv(X_i)\right) = \left|\mathbf{u}^T\mathbf{x} - \min\left(\mathbf{u}^T\mathbf{X}_i\right)\right|$

$\quad$ else if $\mathbf{u}^T\mathbf{x} \leq \min\left(\mathbf{u}^T\mathbf{X}_i\right)$

$\quad$ F = 0; $d_i^u\left(\mathbf{x}, conv(X_i)\right) = \left|\mathbf{u}^T\mathbf{x} - \min\left(\mathbf{u}^T\mathbf{X}_i\right)\right|$

$\quad$ else F = 0; $d_i^u\left(\mathbf{x}, conv(X_i)\right) = \left|\mathbf{u}^T\mathbf{x} - \max\left(\mathbf{u}^T\mathbf{X}_i\right)\right|$

$\quad$ end

Herein $\mathbf{X}_i$ is a data matrix, formed by a set X_i, F – mark of $\mathbf{u}^T\mathbf{x}$ intersection with the range of function $\mathbf{u}^T\mathbf{X}_i$; F = 1 there is an intersection, F = 0 there is no intersection. It shall be noted that in abovementioned expressions instead of projections of sets X_i onto $\mathbf{u}$ it is possible to use only projections of vertices of convex hulls $conv(X_i)$ onto $\mathbf{u}$, and it gives the same result. It allows you to not use initial sets X_i as classes description, but only vertices of their convex hulls. For that purpose the set of vertices of convex hulls shall be determined as per the initial training set in an explicit form. The determination of vertices list during learning stage is more simple compared with complete forming of convex hull, including its vertices and faces. At the same time in a classification algorithm for chosen directions only found vertices are projected, thus reducing processing time. Usage of only vertices greatly simplifies both learning task and decision making task during test points classification.

For our purposes thereafter the vector $\mathbf{u}$ is always determined as a single vector, directed from test point $\mathbf{x}$ to class centroid $\mathbf{c}$, i.e. $\mathbf{u} = (\mathbf{c} - \mathbf{x})/norm(\mathbf{c} - \mathbf{x})$. This direction is not optimal, since in case of $\mathbf{x}$ intersection with $conv(X_i)$ it determines not general penetration depth, but directional penetration depth. However, considering the greater simplification of calculations, it can be considered as a reasonable alternative to determination of overall penetration depth (actual distance from point to convex hull). Such a simplified measurement of the desired distance gave a basis for the simplified classifier name (lite nearest convex hull classifier – LNCH).

5 Classifier Based on Simplified Measurement of Distance to Nearest Convex Hull

We propose the lite classifier for multi-class tasks based on distance to nearest convex hull (LNCH). It also measures test point proximity to convex hulls, but this measurement is based on abovementioned analysis of projections of convex hull vertices onto direction from this point to class centroid (DISTANCE algorithm).

For this point $\mathbf{x}$ and each class X_i we will define the direction $\mathbf{u}_i$, in which we will measure test point proximity to convex hull: $\mathbf{u}_i = (\mathbf{c}_i - \mathbf{x})/norm(\mathbf{c}_i - \mathbf{x})$, where centroid $\mathbf{c}_i = \frac{1}{k_i}\sum_{j=1}^{k_i}\mathbf{x}_{ij}$, $\mathbf{x}_{ij}$ – elements of set $X_i = \{x_{i1}, x_{i2}, \ldots, x_{ik_i}\}$, and after that we will apply DISTANCE procedure. For m classes X_i, $i = 1, 2, \ldots, m$ we get m pairs (F_i, d_i), $i = 1, 2, \ldots, m$. Then, based on received data, the classification is performed as per the following deciding rule.

1. If neither of pairs contains F = 1, the recognized class number is defined by the formula $class(\mathbf{x}) = \underset{i=1,2,\ldots m}{\arg\min}\, d_i(\mathbf{x}, conv(X_i))$.
2. If only one pair contains F = 1, the number of recognized class is equal to this pair index.
3. If several pairs (may be even all) contain F = 1 and these pairs indices create set G, the number of recognized class is selected from these classes so that $class(\mathbf{x}) = \underset{i \in G}{\arg\max}\, d_i(\mathbf{x}, conv(X_i))$.

This deciding rule is explained using Fig. 3.

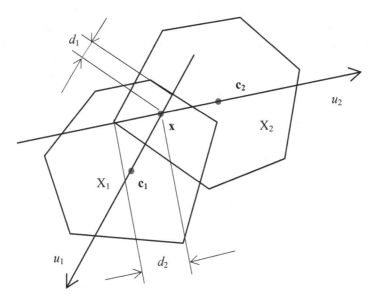

Fig. 3. In the figure – X_1 and X_2 are two classes, c_1 and c_2 are their centroids, x is the test point, u_1 and u_2 are the directions from test point to class centroids, d_1 and d_2 are the directional penetration depth of x in convex hulls of the classes. Since $d_2 > d_1$ (point penetration in X_2 is more than in X_1), according to abovementioned deciding rule the x point refers to class X_2.

The advantage of LNCH classifier is ease of implementation and applying. It does not use optimization procedures and configurable settings. LNCH can be easily applied for multi-class tasks and tasks with configurable training set. Comparing with kNN, LNCH method is more resistant to re-learning, since for learning it uses not single points, but a convex hull. One of the disadvantages of this method is the complexity in classes description for a recognition procedure either as the whole training set or as vertices of calculated convex hulls. To reduce possible retraining of classification algorithm, as with methods of k of nearest neighbours kNN, during determination of distance d it is possible to analyze not convex hulls node projections, but several nearest points of the training set, that came across this projection. The important similarity between 1NN, SNCH and LNCH methods is the fact that in all cases the solution surface between classes is not calculated explicitly.

6 Experimental Studies

The experiments involved synthesized digital data and breast cancer data [12] from a UCI Machine Learning Repository database. The synthesized experiment data included 2 classes in 5-dimensional space with 100 instances per each. Features had values of random numbers, equally distributed in interval (0, 1) for one class and (0.3, 1.3) for another. In the task of breast cancer diagnosis using 9 cytological characteristics [12] the data consist of 683 cases: 444 cases – benign tumour B (1st class), and 239 cases – malignant tumour M (2nd class). Signs are whole numbers in a range from 1 to 10.

For both problems, the estimation of class intersection (intersection of convex hulls) in the original feature space using computational geometry procedures gave the results [13] given in Table 1. Here g is the average intersection of classes, $g = (g_1 + g_2)/2$, $g_i = r_i/k_i$, $i = 1, 2$, r_i is the number of elements of class X_i, that were within convex hull of the other class, k_i is the overall number of class elements X_i. For the problem with digital data it was found that four and seven points of different classes fell into the region of intersection of classes ($g_1 = 4\%$, $g_2 = 7\%$, $g = 5,5\%$).

Table 1. The degree of the class intersection

Data	Degree of the intersection %		
	g_1 (class B)	g_2 (class M)	g
Numeric data	4.00	7.00	5.50
W.B.C. [12]	0.56	0.00	0.28

Visualization of data on breast cancer diagnosis in 2-dimensional reduced space [13] using PCA, FLD and SVM procedures showed almost identical intersection level of classes $g = 13.0\%$.

The study of the intersection of classes B and M using a computational geometry procedure in initial 9-dimensional space showed the following result: neither of the cases from class B entered the class M; 2 cases of class M entered the class B ($g = 0.28\%$, including the exclusion of duplicate points).

Since the training samples used in breast cancer diagnosis are not balanced, the average recognition error p is determined as $p = (p_1 + p_2)/2$, where p_1 and p_2 are recognition errors for classes B and M.

Linear recognition of the synthesized data using SVM (Keerthi modification [14]) for the training set gave the following result. Average classification error was $p = 6.5\%$, and classes errors were: $p_1 = 5.0\%$ and $p_2 = 8.0\%$. LNCH method usage demonstrates 4% errors for each class and 4% average classification error. Results of all studies are shown in Table 2.

Table 2. Recognition errors for various algorithms

Data	kNN ($k = 5$) %			LNCH %		
	p_1	p_2	p	p_1	p_2	p
Numeric data	6.00	8.00	7.00	4.00	4.00	4.00
W.B.C. [12]	2.25	3.15	2.70	2.93	4.18	3.56

Recognition accuracy of classes B and M using SNCH algorithm is presented in [1] and equals to 97.3%. Data on kNN and LNCH usage for solving this task after current

LOO control application are presented in Table 2. The process of cross-validation of algorithm *k*NN using LOO method for determination of optimum value of parameter *k* is shown in Fig. 4.

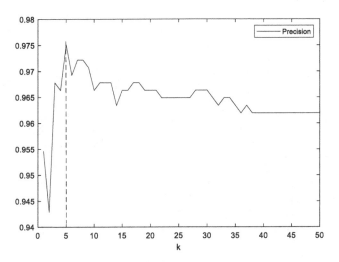

Fig. 4. Dependence of recognition precision on *k* during breast cancer diagnostics using *k*NN algorithm

This figure shows that the best recognition precision value during breast cancer diagnostics is provided if $k = 5$. The study's results show that comparing with *k*NN and SNCH methods the LNCH method has good precision in recognition of the training set in case of using cross-validation with leave-one-out (LOO) principle.

7   Conclusion

The new and simpler method of measurement of test point proximity to convex hulls of classes (DISTANCE algorithm) is proposed in this study. This method is based on analysis of projections of convex hulls vertices onto direction from this point to class centroid. It is the basis of the proposed lite nearest convex hall classifier (LNCH) algorithm. The method differs from earlier proposed soft nearest convex hull classifiers. The main advantage of the method is ease in implementation and application. LNCH can be easily applied for multi-class tasks and tasks with configurable training set. Another advantage of this method is a lack of optimization procedures and absence of necessity of setting these procedures parameters. Recognition precision and its generalization capability are tested using two tasks, one of which is medical diagnostics task based on actual data. The studies' results showed high enough quality of LNCH algorithm.

Acknowledgments. The author wishes to thank the St. Petersburg State Electrotechnical University undergraduate Boris Alekseev for his support in program writing and conducting experimental studies. The study is performed with partial support from the Russian Foundation for Basic Research, grants 18-07-00264 and 19-29-01009.

References

1. Nalbantov, G., Smirnov, E.: Soft nearest convex hull classifier. In: Coelho, H., et al. (eds.) Proceedings of the 19th European Conference on Artificial Intelligence (ECAI-2010), pp. 841–846. IOS Press (2010). https://doi.org/10.3233/978-1-60750-606-5-841
2. Zhou, X., Shi, Y.: Nearest neighbor convex hull classification method for face recognition. In: Allen, G., Nabrzyski, J., Seidel, E., van Albada, G.D., Dongarra, J., Sloot, P.M.A. (eds.) ICCS 2009. LNCS, vol. 5545, pp. 570–577. Springer, Heidelberg (2009). https://doi.org/10.1007/978-3-642-01973-9_64
3. Barber, C.B., Dobkin, D.P., Huhdanpaa, H.: The quickhull algorithm for convex hulls. ACM Trans. Math. Softw. **22**(4), 469–483 (1996). https://doi.org/10.1145/235815.235821
4. Shakhnarovich, G., Darrell, T., Indyk, P.: Nearest-Neighbor Methods in Learning and Vision: Theory and Practice. MIT Press, Cambridge (2005)
5. Vapnik, V.N.: The Nature of Statistical Learning Theory, 2nd edn. Springer, New York (2000). https://doi.org/10.1007/978-1-4757-3264-1
6. Qing, J., Huo, H., Fang, T.: Nearest convex hull classifiers for remote sensing classification. Int. Arch. Photogramm. Remote Sens. Spat. Inf. Sci. **37**, 589–594 (2008)
7. Cover, T.M., Hart, P.E.: Nearest neighbor pattern classification. IEEE Trans. Inf. Theor. **13**(1), 21–27 (1967). https://doi.org/10.1109/TIT.1967.1053964
8. Bennett, K.P., Bredensteiner, E.J.: Duality and geometry in SVM classifiers. In: Proceedings 17th International Conference on Machine Learning (ICML 2000), pp. 57–64. Morgan Kaufmann, San Francisco (2000)
9. Burges, C.J.C.: A tutorial on support vector machines for pattern recognition. Data Min. Knowl. Disc. **2**, 121–167 (1998)
10. Weller, R.: New Geometric Data Structures for Collision Detection and Haptics. Springer, Switzerland (2013). https://doi.org/10.1007/978-3-319-01020-5
11. Lin, M.C., Manocha, D., Kim, Y.J.: Collision and proximity queries. In: Goodman, J.E., O'Rourke, J., Tóth, C.D. (eds.) The Handbook of Discrete and Computational Geometry, 3rd edn, pp. 1029–1056. CRC Press, Boca Raton (2018)
12. Breast Cancer Wisconsin (Original) Data Set. UCI Machine Learning Repository. https://archive.ics.uci.edu/ml/datasets/breast+cancer+wisconsin+(original)
13. Nemirko, A.P.: Multidimensional data visualization based on the minimum distance between convex hulls of classes. Pattern Recogn. Image Anal. **28**(4), 712–719 (2018). https://doi.org/10.1134/S1054661818040247
14. Keerthi, S.S., Shevade, S.K., Bhattacharyya, C., Murthy, K.R.K.: Improvements to Platt's SMO algorithm for SVM classifier design. Technical report CD-99-14, control division, Department of Mechanical and Production Engineering, National University of Singapore (1999)
15. Mitchell, T.M.: Machine Learning. McGraw-Hill, New York (1997)

Shadow Detection in Satellite Images by Computing Its Characteristics

Ye Shiping[1], Henadzi Stantchik[2], Chen Chaoxiang[1],
Olga Nedzved[2,3], Bai Zhicanirst[1], Sergey Ablameyko[2,4],
and Alexander Nedzved[2,4(✉)]

[1] Zhejiang Shuren University, Hangzhou, China
[2] Belarusian State University, Minsk, Belarus
nedzveda@tut.by
[3] Belarusian Medical State University, Minsk, Belarus
[4] United Institute of Informatics Problems, National Academy of Sciences,
Minsk, Belarus

Abstract. The shadows in satellite images have many interesting features. It is possible to define common properties of shadows of buildings. The shadows angle, relation umbra and penumbra, time of image capture for every region include a lot of information for shadow correction and scene reconstruction. In this paper, we propose the algorithm to detect shadows on the base of definition of its structure and features on urban or built-up satellite images by using neural networks.

Keywords: Shadow detection · Satellite image · Segmentation · Image analysis

1 Introduction

The image processing is related to various aspects of working with visual data, such as image segmentation, image analysis, video surveillance, computer vision, motion tracking, commercial software and much more. And one of the most important elements of image processing is the recognition of shadows cast by objects.

A shadow is an area where direct light from a light source does not fall due to obstructions from the object. The shadow properties depend on the size of the objects and the angles of the light source. Shadows played an important role in the problem of image analysis almost as much as the task itself exists. From the very first days of aerial photography, the effects that the shadow creates are used to highlight ground objects in such industries as archeology and aerial reconnaissance.

However, shadows are often seen as a nuisance that hide important details of a space or object texture. Unlike images obtained using aerial surveys, where shadows can be minimized by flying at a specific time during the day, sensors at the Earth's low satellite orbit are limited to acquiring images at a fixed time of day. If at that time the sun is low, then the presence of shadows will be inevitable.

The main problem caused by shadows is the reduction or complete loss of information in the image. Reduction of information can potentially lead to distortion of

S. V. Ablameyko et al. (Eds.): PRIP 2019, CCIS 1055, pp. 119–133, 2019.
https://doi.org/10.1007/978-3-030-35430-5_11

various parameters derived from pixel. Complete loss of information means that image areas cannot be interpreted correctly, and some applications derived from information in the image, such as digital terrain models, cannot be created.

The effects created by the shadows can be slightly reduced by increasing the viewing angle of the camera. This is achieved mainly in areas of the planet where the local solar time is a little later, but this, in turn, increases the likelihood of occlusion of objects in the image.

The effects of shadows are exacerbated in regions where significant changes in altitude occur, namely in urban areas. Tall buildings cast shadows that hide many other features of the surface. Even small buildings cast shadows that hide details in the surrounding streets.

It is ironic that the more accurate the satellite sensors and the higher the resolution of the output image, the more this image is influenced by the shading effects. For comparison, large objects that can be correctly displayed using lower resolution sensors consist of fewer significant height changes and, therefore, less affected by drop shadows.

Removing the shadows from the corresponding image can be used to detect objects such as roads, buildings, trees, military objects, etc. Moreover, after removing shadows, in some cases the objects in the images will be displayed more clearly, so that they can later be correctly recognized.

There are many different methods for detecting and removing shadows in images. The purpose of this work is to obtain a method for detecting shadows on medium-resolution images.

2 Shadow Description in Satellite Images

2.1 A Subsection Sample

As a rule, the structure of shadow depends from features of object. Therefore, the shadow structure is most easily viewed based on images structured objects such as buildings. The shadow phenomenon occurs when an object completely or partially covers a direct light source. Types of shadows are divided into two kinds: attached and cast. The attached shadow falls on the building itself (see Fig. 1). Sometimes this shadow is called as own. Often it is peculiar for buildings with a gable roof.

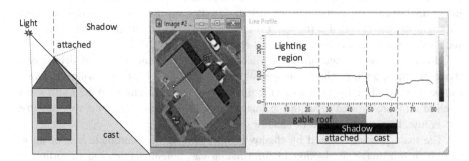

Fig. 1. Representation of shadow structure building with gable roof.

Two types of shadow are characteristic for such buildings. A cast shadow is a projection of a building onto a nearby surface. It could be the result of a high house generating shadow on the street due to the projection of the building outline (see Fig. 2).

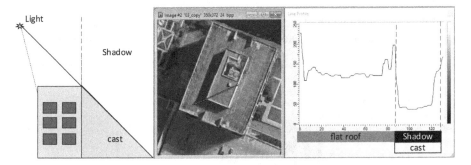

Fig. 2. Representation of shadow structure building with flat roof.

This is the shadow projected by the object away from the light source. Sometimes this shadow is called as dropped. Images of buildings with flat roof usually include it.

The shading belongs to bright and dark contrasts, which are inherent to the form and depend only on the source of light.

In real life, the shadow is a complex structure. In this case, light scattering begins to play a role. For example, for building with hipped roof, there are regions with different lighting (see Fig. 3). There are fragments of roof with direct and slanting rays of light. The first case corresponds to lighting roof. In the second case, the roof is less lit. As result in Fig. 3 the flat roof has a little less brightness.

Fig. 3. Representation of shadow structure building with hipped roof.

The part of the cast shadow in which the light is completely blocked by the object is called umbra, while the part of the object on which the light source is only partially blocked is called penumbra (see Fig. 4). This is strictly dependent on the position and size of the light source:

$$W_{penumbra} = h_{building}\left(\frac{1}{\tan\left(a - \frac{e}{2}\right)} - \frac{1}{\tan\left(a + \frac{e}{2}\right)}\right), \tag{1}$$

where $W_{penumbra}$ is the width of the penumbra, $h_{building}$ is the height of the building, a is the elevation angle of the sun, and e is the angular width of the sun at the top of the building.

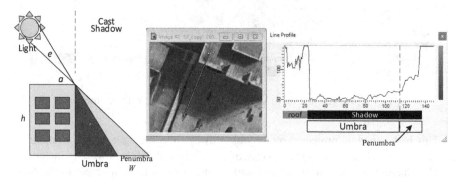

Fig. 4. Structure of cast shadow and umbra/penumbra representation on satellite image with profile of brightness.

However, in the case of real satellite images and aerial photographs, the difference between umbra and penumbra is not so great. It is depending from resolution of image and position of the sun. Sometimes the size of the penumbra is extremely small compared to the size of the umbra. Such way penumbra is attribute of high-rise building on high resolution image (see Fig. 5).

In addition, different parts of the same shadow may have differences in color depth due to the heterogeneity of the background image. In the case of Fig. 6 below, the background of the image is the surface of the earth.

As result different types of building have different pattern for shadow description. For shadow separation on the image it is necessary to select a set of properties (criteria) that differ shadow from object. The main distinguishing feature of the shadow is transparency. And indeed, through the shadow, the features of the background on which it is superimposed clearly appear, although its overall illumination varies significantly. Therefore, to separate the real object and the shadow, you need to check the object for transparency, for which you need to analyze the correlation of the original image and background, taking into account changes in illumination.

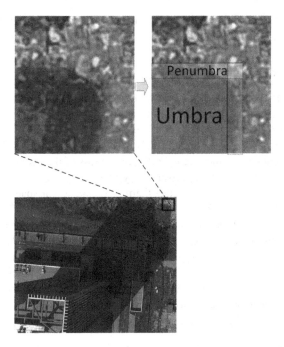

Fig. 5. Umbra and penumbra on high resolution satellite image.

Fig. 6. Sample of shadow with different color characteristics.

3   Modern Methods of Shadow Detection

The task of shadow detection has been investigated in several computer vision applications. The first methods described appear in the field of interpretation of aerial
photographs [1–4]. With the proliferation of digital images in the last decade, there has
been tremendous interest in shadow detection in video streaming applications such as
video surveillance, traffic management, pedestrian monitoring, and so on [5–8].

All the methods proposed by the literature [16] for detecting shadows can be
divided into two classes: methods with training and without training. Methods without

learning, in turn, can be divided into two subclasses: methods based on image properties and methods based on models [29].

3.1   Image-Based Methods

This approach uses such properties of the shadow in the image as color (or intensity),
the structure of the shadow (the assumption that the shadow is always divided into full
shadow and partial shade), borders, etc. This subclass of methods is most common
among shadowless detection methods. The basis of most of these methods is the fact
that the shadow most often simply reduces the brightness of the background to which it
is cast, without changing the pixel chromaticity value.

This shadow property is used to detect them in various color spaces, including hue,
saturation, and value (HSV) [9], red, green, and blue (RGB) [10], C1C2C3 [8], normalized RGB [12, 13], brightness and chromaticity (YUV) [14], the brightness component, red and blue color difference components (YCbCr) [15]. In [9], HSV was
chosen to detect shadows based on how color is perceived by a person (see Fig. 7).
Since the shadow only darkens the background, while the unshadowed part of the
image only changes its color, the HSV values were compared between the background
and each pixel of the input image to detect and remove the shadow. [Convolutional
Neural Network-Based Shadow Detection in Images Using Visible Light Camera
Sensor].

Fig. 7. Extraction of saturation component on image with shadow.

In [10], an algorithm was proposed that calculates brightness and chromaticity in
the RGB color space and uses calculations to detect the shadow. Then the shadow is
recognized by the following principle: a shadow is any area in which chromaticity is
uniform, while the brightness is lower than normal. In [8], normalized color space was
chosen for shadow detection. Along with the photometric color invariant property of
the shadow, the geometric property was also taken into account, which can also be
called the boundary property of the shadow: the shadow appears along the direction of
the light and is located next to the object. Since the usual RGB color space is very
sensitive to light, normalized RGB was used to minimize its impact [11, 12]. The paper

[13] used the YUV color space, which is used in the usual coding of TV, images and video. While other works required conversion to HSV or another color space in order to create a system similar to the way a person perceives the color space, YUV color space was used in [13] to eliminate the processing time required for the conversion.

Thus, in this work, approximate values of color change were obtained, which, however, were not absolute values of hue and saturation. The study [14] chose the YCbCr color space for shadow detection. Y is brightness, and Cb and Cr indicate color information. The brightness value was used to detect the shadow. Channel Y information was used to identify potential shadow areas. Then, a sliding window method was used to detect the shadow. Most of the above studies used only basic information about color or brightness (Y). Therefore, if the object had a color similar to the color of the shadow, then a fairly accurate shadow detection could be expected. Thus, the study did not provide reliable results for more diverse data. To solve this problem, other researchers used additional shadow properties and information [16].

3.2   Model Based Methods

In this approach, simple shadow properties are used in conjunction with some prior knowledge of the scene to obtain the geometry of buildings [2], vehicles [4, 17], pedestrians [6], and so on.

The classification of buildings according to the technology of erection separates buildings into buildings laid out from small-piece materials (bricks, small blocks, etc.), prefabricated, assembled from factory-made industrial structures.

Although buildings can have absolutely any shape depending on the country and region in which they are located, using a classification by specialization can determine that each type of building has certain features according to this classification, for example, height, geometric shape, presence of similar buildings in the neighborhood, etc.

These features can be used to determine the height of the shadow, its direction, or to determine the most shaded part of the image before the analysis [18]. On the other hand, there are studies in which their shadows are used to detect clouds [3, 19]. These methods make assumptions about the observed scenes, and sometimes about some parameters for obtaining images, such as camera orientation, date, daytime and so on. Some examples of how this knowledge is applied in practice:

- One or more edges of the drop shadow are oriented exactly in the direction of the light. In [20] and [21], intensity and geometry restrictions are used to detect and classify shadows in images with limited simple media.
- The size of the shadow depends on the direction of the light source and the height of the object. In [22], the authors present a technique that considers such information as combination with inaccurate terrain maps to determine the likelihood that a given point on aerial images is either in the sunlight or in the shade.

In general, the shadow detection methods proposed in these papers are fairly simplified processes (usually threshold), which are usually part of a more complex system. This system refines the shadow area (along with the model of the object that cast it) using the hypothesis testing framework. The main limitation of these methods is that they are designed for specific applications and for specific types of objects. Therefore, in complex scenes, as is usually the case with high-resolution images, they are not common enough to cope with the wide variety of geometric structures that they can contain.

3.3   Learning-Based Methods

Methods for detecting shadows based on learning have been proposed to eliminate the shortcomings of the methods described earlier. In previous studies [6, 23, 24], the Gaussian shadow model or, as it is called differently, the Gaussian mixture model (further, GMM) was used to build a statistical model of shadow properties. To distinguish the shadow in [23], we used the coefficient of brightness attenuation and chromaticity of shaded surfaces in the YUV color space. Work [24] imitated the shadow and background using physics-based color features. GMM, based on spectral ratio and gradient intensity distortion, was used to study shadow models and then to detect them. Geometric properties of shadows were used in [6]. First, an approximate area where the shadow was located was detected, and its Gaussian modeling was performed using the center of gravity and orientation of the detected area. In [25], it was proposed to detect the shadow by statistical modeling based on the hidden Markov model (Hidden Markovian model (eng), hereinafter-HMM). From histograms of many shaded, background, and foreground images, mean values and deviations for each area were obtained. Each region was then simulated using an independent HMM for shadow detection. In [26], an algorithm for shadow detection using a neuro-fuzzy system was proposed. Based on the color features obtained in the HSV color space, a self-organizing map with Sugeno fuzzy output system was used to detect shadows. In [27], a shadow detection method was proposed using principal component analysis and GMM algorithm. In [28], a shadow detection algorithm was introduced using a support vector machine (SVM) with a Gaussian core. Chromaticity, intensity and margin were used as features for learning.

These learning-based methods, as a rule, show better performance than non-learning-based methods, but they are not capable of recognizing images added manually, and therefore are applicable only to specific environments. Therefore, teaching methods cannot be applied to different types of shadow detection environments [16].

4   Preparation of Fragments of Images with Probable Shadows

The essence of the proposed method of shadow detection is to search for regions in the image that can potentially be shadows and transfer these regions to a convolutional neural network, which will later determine whether a region is a shadow or not.

The satellite image consists of monochrome images (channels). Every satellite includes more than three sensors for image registration by different wavelength. The angles of refraction and reflection are different for these wavelengths. As result shadow has different shape for every wavelength. For color representation image is constructed by mixing channels in three dimensional spaces, such as RGB and other. Color spaces are invariant to changes in the imaging conditions including direction, object surface orientation and direction, lighting conditions, and shadows. Traditional colour spaces such as normalized-RGB, intensity (V) and saturation (S) (see Fig. 8) have revealed some kind of shadow invariant property. Blue component is more interesting for it. The normalization of it is defined as

$$Bc = arctan\left(\frac{B}{max(R,\ G)}\right) \tag{2}$$

However, this equation becomes unstable for low saturation values, which causes the misclassification of non-shadow pixels as shadow.

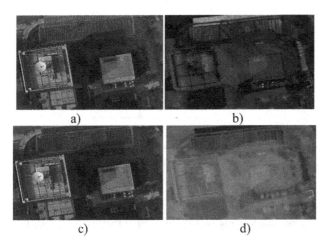

Fig. 8. Color components of image: (a) RGB satellite image, (b) saturation component, (c) intensity component, (d) blue normalized component (Color figure online).

In the original image, regions are selected that are an order of magnitude darker than other pixels in the image. For this, we use the first part of the image-based method proposed by Arevalo et al. [29]. On the first step this part of algorithm is divided into two branches (see Fig. 9): (1) blue component normalization, (2) extraction hue and saturation color component.

The blue component of color normalization (Bc) is convolved with a 3×3 average kernel to minimize the effects of noise, and the magnitude of gradient of the intensity image (V) is computed by a 3×3 Sobel detector.

For segmenting the shadows, we apply a region growing process over the smoothed Bc component. A generic region definition process starts with a group of dark pixels and recursively control neighbor pixels for certain region membership rules. This technique is particularly suitable for our problem because many shadow regions may exist throughout the image, and each may have different radiometric profiles (shadow strength may vary from one zone of the image to another). Obviously, one of the

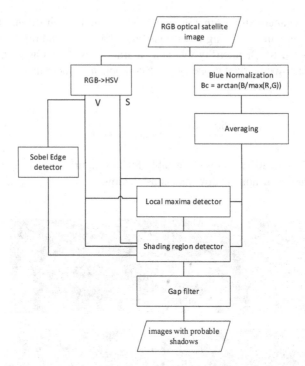

Fig. 9. The part of algorithm for definition of probable shadows regions.

pivotal points when applying this technique is that of reliably placing the seeds in the image: at least one per shadow region (irrespective if they are redundant) and no seed at non-shadow pixels.

Detection of shadow region started from local minimum that is defined by 5×5 pixel's neighborhood with values higher than the mean of the whole Bc image. The size of this window gives the minimum size allowed for the shadows border. The certain region membership rules:

The certain region membership rules include two definitions:

1. The mean of the intensity (V) component of the window's pixels must be lower than a certain threshold (hypothesis of shadow darkness). In the same way, the mean of the saturation (S) component must be higher than a threshold for correction of the instability of Bc for low-saturation color component.
2. None of the window's pixels must belong to another previous seed-window.
   Region growing procedure is recursively executed for all boundary pixels of a region. Starting with the starting region, every pixel is classified as shadow. Then they added to the region if it satisfies the following conditions:
1. It has not previously added to any shadow region already grown.

2. It is below a certain Mahalanobis distance d_0 from the mean of blue normalized component in the region $\left(\widehat{Bc}\right)$, that is:

$$\frac{Bc - \widehat{Bc}}{\sigma} < d_0, \tag{3}$$

Notice that higher values of σ indicate a higher dispersion of Bc within the region, and thus we tolerate larger deviation from the mean $\widehat{Bc}$.

3. The magnitude of the gradient of V is below a given threshold $T_e = 0.30$, that is, it is not a shadow boundary pixel. (We have also tried with the gradient of the Bc smoothed image but because of the noise still present there).

4. It satisfies the conditions imposed to the seed pixels regarding the values of S and V.

If the pixel or neighbor region is incorporated into the region, the Gaussian distribution $N((\widehat{Bc}), \sigma)$ is updated with its Bc value. The process ends when none of the neighbor pixels has been added to the region. Notice that, during the growing process of a particular seed, pixels of different seed-windows not processed yet can be evaluated as any other image pixel. If their inclusion in the region is accepted, that seed is removed from the list of remaining seeds to be grown [29]. Then shape of images with probable shadow's regions are corrected by Gap filtering on base morphological opening operation.

5   Application of Machine Learning Algorithm for Shadow Detection

A shadow is not an independent object. Therefore, for images of urban development, the binding of shadows to objects is one of the key points in the classification. Correction of the shaded region requires an analysis of its environment and consideration of the properties of the object that discards it. Neural network allows to take these features into account. Each region is being cut from the source image and transferred to

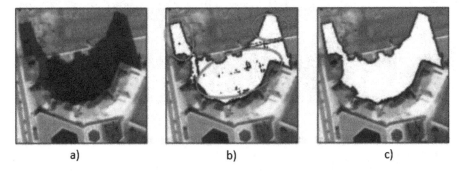

| a) | b) | c) |

Fig. 10. Example of training model: (a) source image, (b) [29] full method, (c) image after human correction.

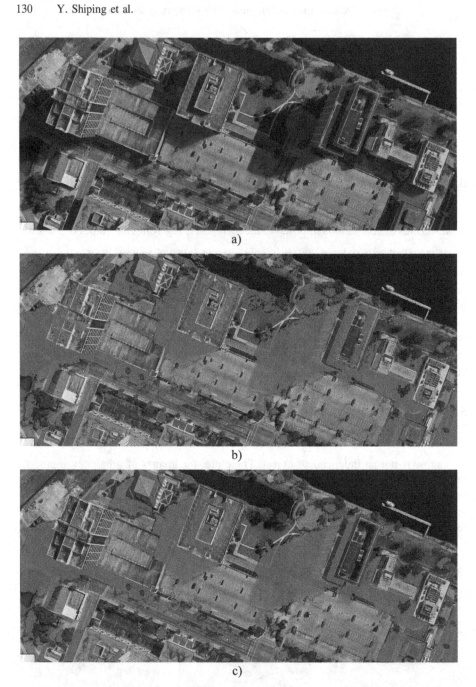

a)

b)

c)

Fig. 11. Results of shadow extraction: (a) source image, (b) *Arevalo* methods, (c) segmentation by VGG Net-16.

pre-trained CNN to determine if the region shadow or not. In this study, VGG Net-16 was used. VGG Net-16 is a convolutional neural network model proposed by K. Simonyan and A. Zisserman from the University of Oxford [30].

For the training and testing shadow recognition by the network on satellite images, a set of 500 images obtained from the Google Maps service was used. This set was divided into two sets: training and testing, with 250 images each.

Network training was performed using human-corrected results of [29] full method work (see Fig. 10).

To determine the accuracy of detection of the shadow region, the result obtained during testing of the pre-trained network was compared with the result obtained with the result of [29] full method work (see Fig. 11).

In the course of the network work on the test set, the determination accuracy varied from 63.43% (minimum match with the standard) to 94.15% (maximum match with the standard). The average accuracy of determination by the test set is 78.68%.

The accuracy of the determination depended on how large an array of buildings was present in the image: the shadow of an isolated building was determined very accurately, while many large and small buildings of various shapes that were close to each other caused difficulties for the network.

In addition, a problem was that, in the case of close building, the shadow sometimes mistakenly considered shadow buildings of a dark color, partially in the shadow, as well as particularly dark patches of vegetation. It possible to correct vegetation problems by NDVI (Normalized Difference Vegetation Index).

6 Conclusion

In this study, a shadow detection method was proposed that uses the VGG Net-16 convolutional artificial neural network and showed relatively high accuracy even with a small pre-training set. The proposed method has the advantage of the definition accuracy over many of the existing methods, but is not universal, as some of the non-learning-based methods.

In addition, with an increase in the pre-training set, an even greater increase in the accuracy of determining shadows can be expected.

It is also worth noting that a more complex network, such as ResNet or DenseNet, can improve the accuracy of shadow classification. However, there are many additional links between the layers with parameters that can significantly increase processing time.

Thus, the method can be improved both by increasing the test suite and by complicating the structure of the neural network used.

Acknowledgement. This work was supported by Public Welfare Technology Applied Research Program of Zhejiang Province (grant number LGJ18F020001, LGJ19F020002 and LGF19F020016) and project of BRFFI F18R-218 "Development and experimental research of descriptive methods for automatization of biomedical images analysis".

References

1. Huertas, A., Nevatia, R.: Detecting buildings in aerial images. Comput. Vis. Graph. Image Process. **41**, 131–152 (1988)
2. Irvin, R.B., McKeown, D.M.: Methods for exploiting the relationship between buildings and their shadows in aerial imagery. IEEE Trans. Syst. Man Cybern. **19**, 1564–1575 (1989)
3. Wang, C., Huang, L., Rosenfeld, A.: Detecting clouds and cloud shadows on aerial photographs. Pattern Recogn. Lett. **12**, 55–64 (1991)
4. Roller, D., Daniilidis, K., Nagel, H.: Model-based object tracking in monocular image sequences of road traffic scenes. Int. J. Comput. 11263on **10**, 257–281 (1993)
5. Rosin, P.L., Ellis, T.J.: Image Difference Threshold Strategies and Shadow Detection. In: BMVC (1995)
6. Hsieh, J., Hu, W., Chang, C., Chen, Y.: Shadow elimination for effective moving object detection by Gaussian shadow modeling. Image Vis. Comput. **21**, 505–516 (2003)
7. Prati, A., Mikic, I., Trivedi, M.M., Cucchiara, R.: Detecting moving shadows: algorithms and evaluation. IEEE Trans. Pattern Anal. Mach. Intell. **25**, 918–923 (2003)
8. Salvador, E., Cavallaro, A., Ebrahimi, T.: Cast shadow segmentation using invariant color features. Comput. Vis. Image Underst. **95**, 238–259 (2004)
9. Cucchiara, R., Grana, C., Piccardi, M., Prati, A., Sirotti, S.: Improving shadow suppression in moving object detection with HSV color information. In: ITSC 2001. 2001 IEEE Intelligent Transportation Systems. Proceedings (Cat. No. 01TH8585), pp. 334–339 (2001)
10. Horprasert, T., Harwood, D., David, L.S.: A statistical approach for real-time robust background subtraction and shadow detection. In: Proceedings of the IEEE Frame Rate Workshop, pp. 334–339, Kerkyra (1999)
11. Cavallaro, A., Salvador, E., Ebrahimi, T.: Shadow-aware object-based video processing. IEE Proc. – Vis. Image Signal Process. **152**, 398–406 (2005)
12. Wang, H., Suter, D.: A consensus-based method for tracking: modelling background scenario and foreground appearance. Pattern Recogn. **40**, 1091–1105 (2007)
13. Schreer, O., Feldmann, I., Golz, U., Kauff, P.: Fast and robust shadow detection in videoconference applications. In: International Symposium on VIPromCom Video/Image Processing and Multimedia Communications, pp. 371–375 (2002)
14. Deb, K., Suny, A.H.: Shadow detection and removal based on YCbCr color space. SmartCR **4**, 23–33 (2014)
15. Sanin, A., Sanderson, C., Lovell, B.C.: Improved shadow removal for robust person tracking in surveillance scenarios. In: 2010 20th International Conference on Pattern Recognition, pp. 141–144, Instanbul (2010)
16. Kim, D.S., Arsalan, M., Park, K.R.: Convolutional neural network-based shadow detection in images using visible light camera sensor. Sensors **18**(4), 960 (2018)
17. Hinz, S., Baumgartner, A.: Vehicle detection in aerial images using generic features, grouping, and context. In: Radig, B., Florczyk, S. (eds.) DAGM 2001. LNCS, vol. 2191, pp. 45–52. Springer, Heidelberg (2001). https://doi.org/10.1007/3-540-45404-7_7
18. Stantchik, H., Nedzved, A., Belotsarkouski, A.: Preparation of the image's fragment with building shadow present for machine learning algorithms. In: Proceeding of 10th International Conference Information Technologies in Industry, Logistics and Social Sphere ITI*2019, pp. 196–202, Minsk (2019)
19. Simpson, J.J., Jin, Z., Stitt, J.R.: Cloud shadow detection under arbitrary viewing and illumination conditions. IEEE Trans. Geosci. Remote Sens. **38**, 972–976 (2000)
20. Jiang, C., Ward, M.O.: Shadow segmentation and classification in a constrained environment. CVGIP: Image Underst. **59**(2), 213–225 (1994)

21. Massalabi, A., Benie, G., Beaudry, E.: Restitution of information under shadow in remote sensing highs pace resolution images: application to IKONOS data of Sherbrooke City, vol. 35 (2004)
22. Stevens, M.R., Pyeatt, L.D., Houlton, D.J., Goss, M.E.: Locating shadows in aerial photographs using imprecise elevation data (1999)
23. Martel-Brisson, N., Zaccarin, A.: Moving cast shadow detection from a Gaussian mixture shadow model. In: 2005 IEEE Computer Society Conference on Computer Vision and Pattern Recognition (CVPR 2005), vol. 2, pp. 643–648 (2005)
24. Huang, J., Chen, C.: Moving cast shadow detection using physics-based features. In: CVPR (2009)
25. Rittscher, J., Kato, J., Joga, S., Blake, A.: A probabilistic background model for tracking. In: Vernon, D. (ed.) ECCV 2000. LNCS, vol. 1843, pp. 336–350. Springer, Heidelberg (2000). https://doi.org/10.1007/3-540-45053-X_22
26. Murguia, M.I., Gonzalez-Duarte, S.: An adaptive neural-fuzzy approach for object detection in dynamic backgrounds for surveillance systems. IEEE Trans. Ind. Electron. **59**, 3286–3298 (2012)
27. Pei, L., Wang, R.: Moving cast shadow detection based on PCA. In: 2009 Fifth International Conference on Natural Computation, vol. 2, pp. 581–584 (2009)
28. Joshi, A.J., Papanikolopoulos, N.: Learning to detect moving shadows in dynamic environments. IEEE Trans. Pattern Anal. Mach. Intell. **30**, 2055–2063 (2008)
29. Arévalo, V., González, J., Ambrosio, G.: Shadow detection in colour high-resolution satellite images. Int. J. Remote Sens. **29**(7), 1945–1963 (2008)
30. Simonyan, K., Zisserman, A.: Very deep convolutional networks for large-scale image recognition. CoRR. arXiv:1409.1556 (2014)
31. Russakovsky, O., et al.: ImageNet large scale visual recognition challenge. Int. J. Comput. Vis. **115**, 211–252 (2014)

Method of Creating the 3D Face Model
of Character Based on Textures Maps Module

Denys Zolotukhin[2], Anatoliy Sachenko[1,2(✉)], Artur Hermanowich[1],
Myroslav Komar[2], and Pavlo Bykovyy[2]

[1] Department of Computer Science, Kazimierz Pulaski University of
Technology and Humanities, ul. Malczewskiego 29, 26-600 Radom, Poland
artur.hermanowicz@uthrad.pl
[2] Research Institute for Intelligent Computer Systems, Ternopil National
Economic University, 11, Lvivska, Ternopil 46020, Ukraine
grakinoua@gmail.com, {as,mko,pb}@tneu.edu.ua

Abstract. The 3D character development process is long, heavy and requires a
high level of professional skills. For today, traditional approaches require from
the developer a lot of time, resources and high-professional skills for making a
3D character model. To facilitate this work, we propose the approach with using
the textures maps module. This module includes a set of prepared and it has
divided into segments textures of different types (diffuse, specular, displacement, bump, SSS). It enables to simplify the texture stage and requires less
professional skills, since the developer no longer needs to create a new texture.
In addition, the module enables to skip the stages of sculpting and retopology,
and get various visual outcomes for same 3D model geometry. The result of
texturing affects directly the quality of both shader and visualization. The
implementation of the proposed approach is described, and case-study results
are presented.

Keywords: 3D character · Texturing · Computer graphic · Foundry Mari

1   Introduction

Today, 3D graphics are an integral part of many spheres of human activity, namely:
construction, TV and film industry, gaming industry, advertising. Every year there is an
increase in the production of media products [1, 2]. The reasons are different: the
development of technologies for designing computer graphics, compressed terms, high
competition, stamping out the development of multimedia products. One of the most
important and time-consuming stages of developing 3D character models is texturing.
It should be noted we have no enough time or resources to texturing the model within
the given requirements by using traditional approaches [3–5].

During the development, the 3D model passes the following stages: data collection,
sculpting, retopology, modeling, texturing, material creation, visualization, post-
production. Each stage requires a lot of time, resources and high professional skills for
its implementation. To simplify some of them, a texture map module was developed.

S. V. Ablameyko et al. (Eds.): PRIP 2019, CCIS 1055, pp. 134–146, 2019.
https://doi.org/10.1007/978-3-030-35430-5_12

This article describes the work of the module of texture maps and its influence on the stages of 3D character model development.

A structure of this paper includes following chapters: related works, structure of textures maps module, textures maps module influence on stages of 3D character model development, conclusion and references.

2 Related Work

In 2014, Jeremy Celeste designed a website [6] developing professionally the XYZ textures and photo references of various types, for different objects (mostly for the face). This site offers a high-quality texture. They make diffuse and SSS map channels by photographing ultra-high quality by photographing photo-references with minimizing glare, saturation and shadow. Texturing XYZ provides displacement resources as well as albedo, specular and specular roughness and even more data. It is one of the only websites that ensures references of pure color accurate specular captured directly from the subject. In work [7] Gael Kerchenbaum described how to combine XYZ files into one projection texture for creature making for VFX.

Substance Source service [8] contains more than 1500 of high-quality classic, PBR metallic, roughness, specular and gloss materials for 3D model texturing in Substance Painter program. Its library enables to export materials at any resolution and up to 8 k to use in any situation or platform. Many materials have been developed with physically based workflows in mind. Substance Source materials can be used for renderers (VRay, Corona, Arnold, Mental Ray, Iray, OctaneRender, Cinema 4D and other) or game engines (Unity, UnrealEngine, Lumberyard engine and other).

In work [9] authors, present a technique for synthesizing the effects of skin microstructure deformation by anisotropically convolving a high resolution displacement map to match normal distribution changes in measured skin samples. They used 10-micron resolution scanning technique to measure several in vivo skin samples as they are stretched and compressed in different directions, quantifying how stretching smooths the skin and compression makes it rougher. They implement the spatially-varying displacement map filtering on the GPU to interactively render the effects of dynamic microgeometry on animated faces obtained from high-resolution facial scans.

In work [10] authors invented a new way to improve the Monte Carlo pixel sampling on the example rendering Glints. Complex specular surfaces under sharp point lighting show a fascinating glint appearance, but rendering it is an unsolved problem. Their results show the complex, temporally varying glints from materials such as bumpy plastics, brushed and scratched metals, metallic paint and ocean waves.

In work [11] the authors describe a joint project using Augmented Reality (AR) to enrich the Konzerthaus printed media. The project contains images, illustrations, audio, video, simple 2D and 3D animations, interactive media as well as 3D objects. The application was implemented using Vuforia and Unity.

IClone Character Creator [12] enables to make the three-dimensional models and animation of the character in real-time. It includes a wide array of tools that enables to create easily and quickly a complete animation of the human face and skeleton, lip sync, importing standard types of 3D files, periods for editing and combining movements. Moreover, the program contains many harvested patterns of textures and models, and it has a wide functionality that enables to make own 3D character models for non-professionals in this industry.

In work [20] the authors present the second part of a two-part study which considers the Intellectual property implications of 3D printing and scanning. This work considers "the current status and impact of 3D printing within the industrial sector" through an analysis of six case studies. The document accompanies the first part of the study (Study I) "A Legal and Empirical Study of 3D Printing Online Platforms and an Analysis of User Behaviour" written by Dr Dinusha Mendis and Dr Davide Secchi from the Centre for Intellectual Property Policy & Management (CIPPM) at Bournemouth University.

In work [21] the authors study a general overview of 3DP in fashion and its integration in fashion education and a pedagogical guidance to educators in the fashion discipline by presenting one case of 3D printing education in fashion design courses. This case study focused on the importance of 3D printing in fashion design curricula and the way to strategically integrate this technology into the curriculum. Rhinoceros (Rhino) and FINEBOT were used for 3D object design and printing, respectively. The coursework consisted of theoretical lectures including definition and application of 3D printing; training of Rhino use; methods of producing objects; 3D modeling of creative objects; and 3D printing practice.

Despite the abovementioned advantages, all the existing services and programs require from the developer to make efforts to split, layout and edit textures.

A goal of this paper is to improve the production of the 3D model by using a proposed method of the simplified texturing. An idea of this method has described shortly in the previous works of authors [13, 27], and it's exploring deeper below.

3 Structure of the Textures Maps Module

Textures maps module – is a set of prepared map fragments: diffuse [16] – contains color information; displacement [15] – map for biasing 3D model geometry; specular [16] – simulates surface reflection of the model; bump [15] – simulates small relief of the surface; SSS (Sub Surface Scattering) [14] – three textures that imitate dermis, epidermis skin and blood. All textures can be combined with each other, to achieve the desired shader result. Technically this module consists of folders that contain a set of fragmented textures of the corresponding categories (see Fig. 1).

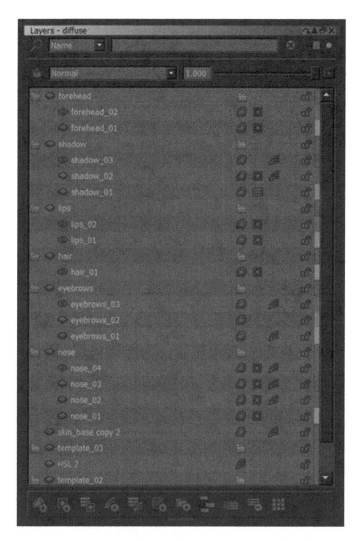

Fig. 1. Visual view of the textures maps complex in the Mari.

As can see in Fig. 1, each folder contains a set of textures that contains color information about certain part of face. For example, the "nose" folder contains 4 patterns of nose texture, the "shadow" folder contains three samples of static shadows, which have been created by using ambient occlusion technology, which approximates the amount of light reaching a point on a diffuse surface based on its directly visible occluders. It gives perceptual clues of curvature and spatial proximity. We used the following form of the ambient occlusion illumination [26]:

$$A = 1 - \frac{1}{2\pi} \int_\Omega V(\vec{\omega})\, W(\vec{\omega}) d\omega \tag{1}$$

where V is the visibility function over the normal-oriented unit hemisphere Ω, which returns 1 if a ray starting from surface point in direction $\vec{\omega}$ intersects an occluder and 0 otherwise, and W is a linear attenuation function.

This technique can be used like shadows or like color fill for other maps or channels. Each texture can be combined by turning on and off the required maps, they can also be edited by using the tool of the selected software (see Fig. 2).

Fig. 2. Samples of nose textures.

These four textures are in the corresponding folder "nose". Similarly, other maps of the same and other channels look like. Every folder contains a number of different textures of the same subject. The developer takes the need one, combines it with other textures and edits. This process is relevant for all channels (diffuse, SSS, specular, bump, displacement).

An algorithm of texturing 3D characters by using the proposed textures maps complex is shown in Fig. 3.

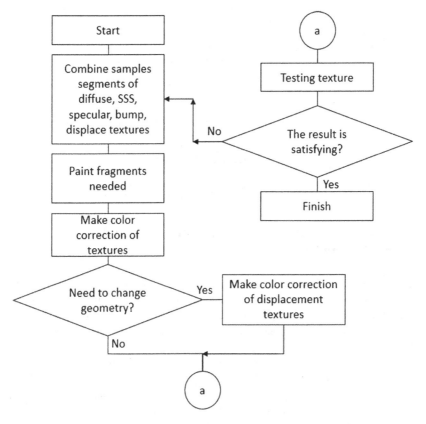

Fig. 3. Texturing algorithm by using the textures maps complex.

Each texture is sorted in the appropriate folders. These textures can be selected in any order. After the desired combination has found the developer can make a color editing and add all the necessary details. This process is carrying out until the desired result is obtained. It should be noted that textures change not only the color information, but also the ability to edit the geometry of the 3D model, by using techniques based on raytracing and render-to-displacement map approach [25]. The Fig. 4 shows principles of this technique: rays, corresponding to each pixel of the mapped displacement map area, are casted towards the direction of the normal vector in the corresponding point of the low-poly model surface to determine an actual displacement amount value. Given the fact that maximum displacement value is correctly set the way that high-poly backface surface is beyond the reach of the distance rays, this allows to accurately obtain desired measurements.

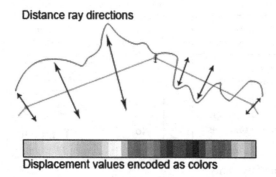

Fig. 4. Casting rays to determine displacement amount [25].

4 Textures Maps Module Influence on Stages of 3D Character Model Development

The development of 3D character model is a module and lengthy process that runs through a series of stages: data collection, sculpting, retopology, modeling, texturing, material creation, visualization, post-production [17]. Using the proposed texture maps module helps to simplify and accelerate some of the steps in this process in a way described below.

Data collection – there are various sources of ideas, information, sketches and templates for project development. The proposed module contains a database of ready textures that can also serve as basic materials for developing own maps, which will shorten the search time for the necessary materials.

Sculpting – traditionally this stage is used to get from hi-poly model bump, normal and displacement maps for their subsequent low-poly model overlay. The proposed module contains ready-made templates for data map types. The all of them may serve as a good addition to editing already created maps. Therefore, the stage of sculpting is skipped completely, and then a developer can proceed to texture the low-poly model without the need to create hi-poly.

Since the proposed module enables to skip the stage of sculpting and proceed directly to texture then retopology stage can be eliminated.

By contrast to the traditional texturing the proposed module enables to pick up already prepared textures fragment of many type (for example: diffuse, SSS, specular, bump, displacement). Each texture is sorted into the appropriate folders, and then they can be selected in any order. To find the desired combination it is necessary to make a color editing and add the all required details. This process is carried out until the desired result is obtained.

On the stage of material creation, we use a combination of the completed fragments for the proposed module. That enables to run experiments more compact and convenient with different textures as well as create good shades, because the color and texture location directly affects its quality.

Visualization – since the texture and shader quality of the previous steps directly affect the quality of the result then the proposed module enables to achieve the desired result quicker and more conveniently.

To get started with the texture's maps module, we need to connect into a graphic editor that supports layers (in this example, it's Mari program [18]). Textures should be imposed on a low-poly model (see Fig. 5).

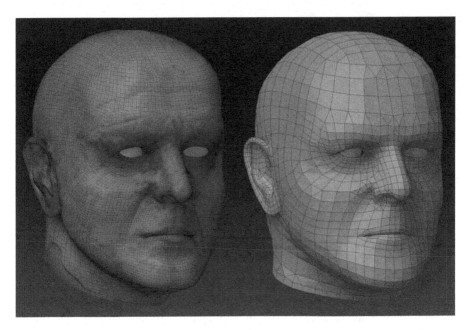

Fig. 5. 3D character geometry, hi-poly (left), low-poly (right).

The low-poly character model is obtained from Hi-poly (if necessary) [19], which is usually prepared in the ZBrush program [5]. Next you need to select the required textures of each type and category in the relevant folders, until the desired result is obtained. Any texture segments the developer can be deformed and edited using the tool of the selected software. The result of the experiment is shown in Fig. 6.

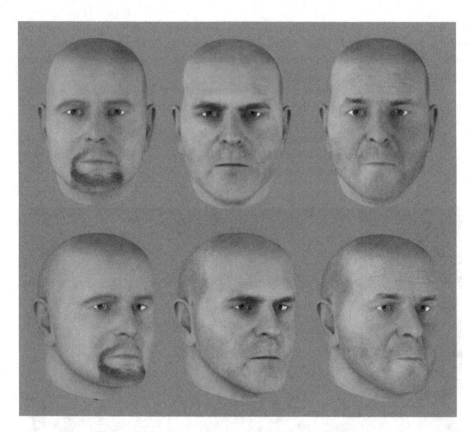

Fig. 6. Three versions of the character's head. Two angles.

As it can be seen on Fig. 6, the result of the experiment is three versions of the 3D character head model. All the three models have the similar geometry and the same topology. In the same time, they have different textures, so they visually look differently. If we created one original geometry of the model and made the necessary textures for it then we can modify it using the proposed module of texture maps. To do this, we need to overcome and combine the finished textures and edit that. We may create visually different models in this way and then to make their 3D geometry "from scratch".

The experiment used a texturing technique using a Multi-Tile UV Mapping [23] (see Fig. 7).

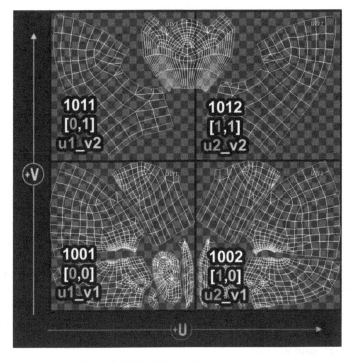

Fig. 7. Multi-Tile UV Mapping of character head

We used Multi-Tile UV Mapping to better optimize your text tours and achieve better texture quality. The result is 4 tiles with numbers (1001, 1002, 1011, 1012), each tile has a map size of 4096 × 4096.

VRaySkinMtl material was used for the skin shader, based on the bidirectional surface scattering distribution function (BSSRDF) technology [22] (see Fig. 8), which is described by the formula:

$$f_r\left(\vec{x}, \overrightarrow{\omega_l}, \overrightarrow{\omega_o}\right) = \frac{dL_r\left(\vec{x}, \overrightarrow{\omega_o}\right)}{dE_i\left(\vec{x}, \overrightarrow{\omega_l}\right)} = \frac{dL_r\left(\vec{x}, \overrightarrow{\omega_o}\right)}{L_i\left(\vec{x}, \overrightarrow{\omega_l}\right)\left(\overrightarrow{\omega_l} * \vec{n}\right)d\overrightarrow{\omega_l}},$$ (2)

where:

$\overrightarrow{\omega_l}$ – the direction from which the ray is coming;
$\vec{x}$ – location of surface striking;
L_i – incoming radiance;
L_r – reflected radiance;
$\vec{n}$ – the surface normal.

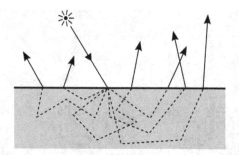

Fig. 8. Light scattering model for BSSRDF [24]

BSSRDF describes the relation between outgoing radiance and the incident flux, including the phenomena like subsurface scattering (SSS). The BSSRDF describes how light is transported between any two rays that hit a surface. This technology is well suited for the skin shader.

Given that, the developer does not need to create textures "from scratch", the speed of texture development for the 3D model has grown significantly. For example, when applying the traditional way (from search to texture editing), the texture developer would spend 6 days. Using textures maps module enabled to shorten this period to need the about two days. It should be mentioned that additional manipulations are required to provide such texture's maps.

The proposed approach by using the textures maps module has the practical value and it can be used in the field of the gaming and film industry, to accelerate development of the 3D character model. Moreover, it can implement as basis for 3D Modelling in other areas like interior, furniture, and landscape designers, automobile makers, web design, clothing, shoe, and jewelry [20, 21].

5   Conclusion

In this paper, the following results were obtained:

- simplifying the process of developing a 3D model due to skipping such stages as sculpting and retopology, and facilitating the stage of information gathering;
- improving the stage of texturing the 3D model. The texture maps module enables to scroll and combine already crafted patterns of textures, thereby eliminating the need to design them "from the scratch";
- reducing the input threshold to develop a 3D model. The process of creating a 3D model by using a texture map module does not require the developer high skill in comparison with the traditional approach. Because the developer does not need to design the necessary textures itself, in some cases, there is no need to make a hi-poly model to create bump, normal, displace maps.

One of promising directions of the further research may be the developing own interface to improve the comfortability of textures design.

References

1. 2019 Video Game Industry Statistic, Trends & Data. https://www.wepc.com/news/video-game-statistics/. Accessed 20 July 2019
2. Film Industry - Statistics & Facts. https://www.statista.com/topics/964/film/. Accessed 20 July 2019
3. Lappa, D.: Photorealistic Texturing for Modern Video Games, p. 45. South-Eastern Finland University of Applied Sciences, Kouvola (2017)
4. Luhtapuro, T.M.: Surface Detail Mapping in 3D Modelling, p. 33. Lahti University of Applied Sciences, Lahti (2014)
5. Bubenová, Z.: Texturing a 3D Character in Hand-painted Style, p. 30. Helsinki Metropolia University of Applied Sciences, Helsinki (2016)
6. High-End contest for artist. The finest art of detail. https://texturing.xyz/. Accessed 22 July 2019
7. Kerchenbaum, G.: How to make high detailed model for VFX, p. 41. ArtStation, Ottawa (2018)
8. Substance Source by Adobe. https://www.allegorithmic.com/products/substance-source/. Accessed 21 July 2019
9. Nagano, K., et al.: Skin microstructure deformation with displacement map convolution. ACM Trans. Graph. (TOG) **34**(4), 109 (2018)
10. Yan, L.-Q., Hašan, M., Jakob, W., Lawrence, J., Marschner, S., Ramamoorthi, R.: Rendering glints on high-resolution normal-mapped specular surfaces. ACM Trans. Graph. (Proc. SIGGRAPH) **33**(4), 116:1–116:9 (2014)
11. Letellier, J., Reinhardt, J., Scholl, P., Sieck, J., Thiele-Maas, M.: Providing aditttional content to print media using augmented reality. Int. J. Comput. **17**(3), 180–189 (2018)
12. Reallusion Character Creator 3. https://www.reallusion.com/character-creator/. Accessed 23 July 2019
13. Zolotukhin, D.V., Sachenko, A.A.: Methods and algorithm for developing 3D models for videoimages. Int. Sci. J. «Internauka» **61**(3), 55–57 (2018)
14. Jimenez, J., et al.: Separable subsurface scattering. Comput. Graph. Forum **34**(6), 188–197 (2015). The Eurographics Association and John Wiley & Sons Ltd.
15. Gustavson, S.: Recomputing normals for displacement and bump mapping, procedural style, p. 4. Department of Science and Technology, Gauteng (2016)
16. Ma, W.-C., Hawkins, T., Peers, P., Chabert, C.-F., Weiss, M., Debevec, P.: Rapid acquisition of specular and diffuse normal maps from polarized spherical gradient illumination. In: Proceedings of the Eurographics Symposium on Rendering Techniques, Grenoble, France, pp. 183–194 (May 2007)
17. Terävä, T.: Workflows for Creating 3D Game Characters, p. 154. Kajaanin ammattiko-rkeakoulu University of Applied Sciences, Kajaani (2017)
18. Foundry Mari. Layers. https://learn.foundry.com/mari/Content/user_guide/layers/layers.html. Accessed 23 July 2019
19. Webster, N.L.: High poly to low poly workflows for real-time rendering. J. Vis. Commun. Med. **40**(1), 40–47 (2017)
20. Reeves, P., Mendis, D.: The Current Status and Impact of 3D Printing Within the Industrial Sector: An Analysis of Six Case Studies. The Intellectual Property Office, London, p. 86 (2015)
21. Kwon, Y.M., Lee, Y.A., Kim, S.J.: Case study on 3D printing education in fashion design coursework. Fash. Text. **4**, 26 (2017). https://doi.org/10.1186/s40691-017-0111-3

22. Bitterli, B.: BSSRDF Explorer: A rendering framework for the BSSRDF. Swiss Federal Institute of Technology Zurich, Zürich, p. 68 (2012)
23. UDIM UV Mapping. https://www.fxguide.com/fxfeatured/udim-uv-mapping/. Accessed 10 July 2019
24. Jimenez, J., Whelan, D., Sundstedt, V., Gutierrez, D.: Real-time realistic skin translucency. IEEE Comput. Graph. Appl. **30**(4), 32–41 (2010)
25. Tisevich, I., Ignatenko, A.: Displacement and normal map creation for pairs of arbitrary polygonal models using GPU and subsequent model restoration. In: Proceedings of GraphiCon 2007, pp. 61–68 (2007)
26. Bavoil, L., Sainz, M., Dimitrov, R.: Image-space horizon-based ambient occlusion. In: ACM SIGGRAPH 2008 Talks, pp. 22:1–22:1 (2008)
27. Zolotukhin, D., Sachenko, A., Hermanowich, A., Komar, M., Bykovyy, P.: Developing the 3D model characters based on textures maps module. In: Lukashevich, M., Doudkin, A., Krasnoproshin, V. (eds.) Proceeding of the 14th International Conference on Pattern Recognition and Information Processing, pp. 338–341. Belarusian State University of Informatics and Radioelectronics, Minsk (2019)

Thresholding Neural Network Image Enhancement Based on 2-D Non-separable Quaternionic Filter Bank

Vladislav V. Avramov⬤, Eugene V. Rybenkov⬤, and Nick A. Petrovsky$^{(\boxtimes)}$⬤

Computer Engineering Department,
Belarusian State University of Informatics and Radioelectronics,
P. Brovky 6, 220013 Minsk, Belarus
avramov.vladislav@gmail.com, {rybenkov,nick.petrovsky}@bsuir.by

Abstract. The thresholding neural network with a 2-D non-separable paraunitary filter bank based on quaternion multipliers (2-D NSQ-PUFB) for image enhancement is proposed. Due to the high characteristics of the multi-bands 2-D NSQ-PUFB (structure "64in-64out", $CG_{2D} = 17.15\,\mathrm{dB}$, prototype filter bank (8×24) Q-PUFB), which forms the basis of the TNN, the results of noise editing in comparison with the approaches based on the two-channel wavelet transform in terms of PSNR are $1\,\mathrm{dB}$–$1.5\,\mathrm{dB}$ higher.

Keywords: Image enhancement · Thresholding neural network · 2-D non-separable quaternionic filter bank

1 Introduction

Different types of noise and artifacts in imaging methods degrade image quality and as a result human interpretation of them, as well as the accuracy of computer methods in the case of medical imaging. Therefore, the editing of noise in the image becomes the main requirement for many practical applications.

In the general case, the noise reduction is aimed to obtain a reconstructed copy of the real signal x from its distorted version $y = x + \xi$, where ξ is, for example, additive Gaussian white noise. Thus, the purpose of processing is to obtain at the output of the noise reduction system $f(\cdot)$ the reconstructed signal $\hat{x} = f(y)$ as close as possible to the original signal x. Analytically it can be expressed as minimization of the loss function $E(x, \hat{x})$ by the following equation

$$\min_{x,\hat{x}\in\Re} E(x,\hat{x}) = \min_{x,\hat{x}\in\Re} ||x - \hat{x}||^2 \tag{1}$$

Any available a priori information about the signal energy and noise distribution should be used when estimating the noise ξ. The redistribution of signal

---

Supported by Belarusian Republican Foundation for Fundamental Research (project no. F18MV-016).

S. V. Ablameyko et al. (Eds.): PRIP 2019, CCIS 1055, pp. 147–161, 2019.
https://doi.org/10.1007/978-3-030-35430-5_13

energy can be accomplished by transferring the original signal to another sub-space based on a linear orthogonal transformation T, as shown in [2]. The use of such transformation for a distorted version of the signal allows to change the original distribution of the signal and provides important information for the implementation of signal and noise separation. Therefore, the useful signal can be extracted from its distorted version by processing in the transform domain with a thresholding function, which preserves the energy of the transformation coefficients $T(x+n)$ that fall into the range of the distribution of the useful signal, and suppressing energy of noisy coefficients that do not fall into this area. Thresholding methods are based on this concept (see Fig. 1) and use nonlinear activation functions to reduce the noise. The most commonly mentioned thresholding functions are the soft-thresholding function and the hard-thresholding function.

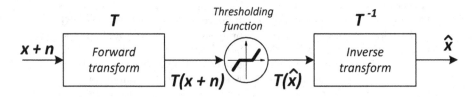

Fig. 1. The structure of thresholding noise reduction approach.

The idea behind the thresholding neural network (TNN) [10] is significantly different from the conventional neural networks concept. TNN training process is aimed at adjusting the threshold activation function in order to achieve the optimal truncation threshold while in classical neural networks the activation functions are fixed, and training consists in adjusting the weights. The term "neural network" is used here because this structure is based on the basic elements of classical neural networks such as interconnection, nonlinear activation function and it is adaptable to the input. The goal of the training process of the TNN is to adapt a thresholding function to the distribution of the transform domain coefficients. Thresholding activation functions are used as nonlinear neural network activation functions. The inverse transform is used to restore the signal from the coefficients with a reduced noise level in the transform space.

2   Transform Selection

The image denoising research is broadly divided into two domains, viz. spatial domain and transform domain. In the last time, in the transform domain, more research has been conducted in the wavelet domain because of its primary properties like sparsity and decomposition of wavelet coefficients [10]. Owing to this property of wavelet coefficients, effective and simplified implementation of the thresholding ideas in the wavelet domain became easy. Later efforts in this area [9] have suggested that perceptual quality obtained in wavelet transform domain could be substantially improved using further spatial operation like the contrast-enhancement technique or additional filtering techniques in the spatial domain.

For a particular class of signals, appropriate orthogonal transformations can be chosen to localize the signal energy with respect to noise. Besides perfect reconstruction and linear phase (LP), regularity is essential desirable property of transformations for image processing as it is associated with the smoothness of the related wavelet basis. Paraunitary filter banks (PUFBs) are of great interest in recent years, especially in image coding. For linear phase responses of analysis paraunitary filter bank with linear phase (LP PUFB), the best known factorization of the polyphase transfer matrix $\mathbf{E}(z)$ assumes number of channel M to be an even number and has the following form [8]:

$$\mathbf{E}(z) = \mathbf{G}_{N-1}(z)\mathbf{G}_{N-2}(z)\ldots\mathbf{G}_1(z)\mathbf{E}_0,$$

$$\mathbf{E}_0 = \frac{1}{\sqrt{2}}\boldsymbol{\Phi}_0 \cdot \mathbf{W} \cdot \operatorname{diag}\left(\mathbf{I}_{M/2}, \mathbf{J}_{M/2}\right),$$

$$\mathbf{G}_i(z) = \frac{1}{2}\boldsymbol{\Phi}_i \cdot \mathbf{W} \cdot \boldsymbol{\Lambda}(z) \cdot \mathbf{W}, \quad i = 1,\ldots,N-1, \tag{2}$$

$$\mathbf{W} = \begin{bmatrix} \mathbf{I}_{M/2} & \mathbf{I}_{M/2} \\ \mathbf{I}_{M/2} & -\mathbf{I}_{M/2} \end{bmatrix}, \quad \boldsymbol{\Lambda}(z) = \operatorname{diag}\left(\mathbf{I}_{M/2}, z^{-1}\mathbf{I}_{M/2}\right)$$

where N is the factorization order; $\mathbf{I}_{M/2}$ and $\mathbf{J}_{M/2}$ denote the $(M/2) \times (M/2)$ identity and reversal matrices, respectively; $\boldsymbol{\Gamma}_{M/2}$ is a diagonal matrix whose elements are defined as $\gamma = (-1)^{m-1}, m = 1,\ldots,M-1$.

The polyphase transfer matrix $\mathbf{D}(z)$ of the synthesis filter bank is constructed on the basis of the reverse inclusion of the factorization components of the polyphase transfer matrix $\mathbf{E}(z)$ of the analysis bank:

$$\mathbf{D}(z) = \hat{\mathbf{E}}_0 \cdot \hat{\mathbf{G}}_1(z) \cdot \ldots \cdot \hat{\mathbf{G}}_{N-2}(z) \cdot \hat{\mathbf{G}}_{N-1}(z),$$

$$\hat{\mathbf{E}}_0 = \operatorname{diag}\left(\mathbf{I}_{M/2}, \mathbf{J}_{M/2}\right) \cdot \mathbf{W} \cdot \hat{\boldsymbol{\Phi}}_0 \cdot \frac{1}{\sqrt{2}},$$

$$\hat{\mathbf{G}}_i(z) = \mathbf{W} \cdot \hat{\boldsymbol{\Lambda}}(z) \cdot \mathbf{W} \cdot \hat{\boldsymbol{\Phi}}_i \cdot \frac{1}{2}, \quad i = 1,\ldots,N-1, \tag{3}$$

$$\hat{\boldsymbol{\Lambda}}(z) = \operatorname{diag}\left(z^{-1}\mathbf{I}_{M/2}, \mathbf{I}_{M/2}\right).$$

However, a fixed-point implementation of the above lattice is vulnerable to coefficients quantization. Namely, the matrices $\boldsymbol{\Phi}_i$ (parameterized with Givens rotations) lose their orthogonality under quantization. Regularly new factorizations and structures appear, offering new useful features, design flexibility and ease, or computational efficiency [4].

Digital image is two dimensional signal and one-dimensional LP PUFB's can be applied to the construction of multidimensional separable systems. 2-D signals (images) are separately transformed along vertical and horizontal directions. However, multidimensional signals are generally non-separable, and this approach does not exploit their characteristics effectively. 2-D non-separable

PUFBs perform more efficiently for image processing than separable PUFBs, because non-separable PUFBs may have better frequency characteristics.

In research [4] presented concept of a quaternionic building block applicable to many existing structures of FBs (Q-PUFB) and transforms, especially to the 4- and 8-channel ones, commonly used in imaging applications. The main results were: structurally guaranteed perfect reconstruction (up to scaling) under a rough coefficient quantization, reduced memory requirements, and good suitability for FPGA and VLSI implementations.

Taking into account the advantages of the Q-PUFB the aim of this contribution is to show using a 2-D non separable quaternionic paraunitary filter banks (2D NSQ-PUFB) in image enhancement based on the TNN and evaluate their performance.

3   Definition of 2D-NSQ-PUFB

3.1   Quaternionic PUFBs

Among LP PUFBs, there are systems with pairwise-mirror-image (PMI) symmetric frequency responses. As the number of the degrees of design freedom is reduced, the optimization of filter bank coefficients is easier. A 4-channel PMI LP Q-PUFB is realized according to the following factorization of the matrices $\mathbf{\Phi}_i$ and $\mathbf{\Phi}_{N-1}$ [4]:

$$\mathbf{\Phi}_i = \mathbf{M}^+ (P_i), \tag{4}$$

$$\mathbf{\Phi}_{N-1} = \mathbf{M}^+ (P_{N-1}) \cdot \text{diag} \left(\mathbf{J}_{M/2} \cdot \mathbf{\Gamma}_{M/2}, \mathbf{I}_{M/2} \right). \tag{5}$$

The matrices $\mathbf{M}^+ (P_i)$ and $\mathbf{M}^- (Q_i)$ are left and right 4 by 4 multiplication matrices, accordingly: $P \cdot Q = \mathbf{M}^+ (P) \cdot \mathbf{Q} = \mathbf{M}^- (Q) \cdot \mathbf{P}$; $Q = q_1 + q_2 i + q_3 j + q_4 k$ and $P = p_1 + p_2 i + p_3 j + p_4 k$ are unit quaternions, where the orthogonal imaginary numbers obey the following multiplicative rules: $ij = -ji = k$, $jk = -kj = i$, $ki = -ik = j$, $i^2 = j^2 = k^2 = ijk = -1$. The corresponding factorization of the matrices $\mathbf{\Phi}_i$ and $\mathbf{\Phi}_{N-1}$ for a 8-channel PMI LP Q-PUFB is shown below [6]:

$$\mathbf{\Phi}_i = \text{diag} \left\{ \mathbf{\Gamma}_{M/2}, \mathbf{I}_{M/2} \right\} \cdot \text{diag} \left\{ \mathbf{M}^- (Q_i), \mathbf{M}^- (Q_i) \right\}$$
$$\times \text{diag} \left\{ \mathbf{M}^+ (P_i), \mathbf{M}^+ (P_i) \right\} \cdot \text{diag} \left\{ \mathbf{\Gamma}_{M/2}, \mathbf{I}_{M/2} \right\}, \tag{6}$$

$$\mathbf{\Phi}_{N-1} = \text{diag} \left\{ \mathbf{J}_{M/2}, \mathbf{I}_{M/2} \right\} \cdot \text{diag} \left\{ \mathbf{M}^- (Q_{N-1}), \mathbf{M}^- (Q_{N-1}) \right\}$$
$$\times \text{diag} \left\{ \mathbf{M}^+ (P_{N-1}), \mathbf{M}^+ (P_{N-1}) \right\} \cdot \text{diag} \left\{ \mathbf{\Gamma}_{M/2}, \mathbf{I}_{M/2} \right\}; \tag{7}$$

Compared these factorizations to general LP PUFBs, there are 50% less coefficients and computations on the initial stage.

3.2   2-D Non-separable Q-PUFB

Two-dimensional separable transform of image signal when the analysis PMI LP PUFB matrix $\mathbf{E}(z)$ is applied to a 2-D input signal $\mathbf{x}_{n,n}$ in horizontal and vertical directions, the output $\mathbf{y}_{n,n}$ is expressed as:

$$\mathbf{y}_{n,n} = \mathbf{E}(z) \cdot \mathbf{x}_{n,n} \cdot \mathbf{E}(z)^T = \mathbf{G}_{N-1}(z) \cdot \ldots \cdot \mathbf{G}_1(z) \cdot \mathbf{E}_0$$
$$\times \mathbf{x}_{n,n} \cdot \mathbf{E}_0^T \cdot \mathbf{G}_1^T(z) \cdot \ldots \cdot \mathbf{G}_{N-1}^T(z)$$

Based on the [5,6] 2-D non-separable transformation result $\mathbf{y}_{n,n}$ can be represented as vector:

$$\mathbf{y}_{n^2,1} = \ddot{\mathbf{E}}(z) \cdot \mathbf{x}_{n\cdot n,1} = \ddot{\mathbf{G}}_{N-1}(z) \cdot \ldots \cdot \ddot{\mathbf{G}}_1(z) \cdot \ddot{\mathbf{E}}_0 \cdot \mathbf{x}_{n^2,1},$$
$$\ddot{\mathbf{E}}_0 = \frac{1}{2} \cdot \ddot{\mathbf{\Phi}}_0 \cdot \ddot{\mathbf{W}} \cdot \mathfrak{D}\left(\mathrm{diag}\left(\mathbf{I}_{M/2}, \mathbf{J}_{M/2}\right)\right) \cdot \mathbf{P} \cdot \mathfrak{D}\left(\mathrm{diag}\left(\mathbf{I}_{M/2}, \mathbf{J}_{M/2}\right)\right) \cdot \mathbf{P}, \quad (8)$$

$$\ddot{\mathbf{G}}_i(z) = \frac{1}{4} \cdot \ddot{\mathbf{\Phi}}_i \cdot \ddot{\mathbf{W}} \cdot \ddot{\mathbf{\Lambda}}(z) \cdot \ddot{\mathbf{W}}; \quad \ddot{\mathbf{W}} = \mathfrak{D}(\mathbf{W}) \cdot \mathbf{P} \cdot \mathfrak{D}(\mathbf{W}) \cdot \mathbf{P},$$
$$\ddot{\mathbf{\Lambda}}(z) = \mathfrak{D}(\mathbf{\Lambda}(z)) \cdot \mathbf{P} \cdot \mathfrak{D}(\mathbf{\Lambda}(z)) \cdot \mathbf{P}.$$

where $\mathfrak{D}(\mathbf{W})$ denotes the matrix with transform matrices $\mathbf{W}_{n,n}$ on the main diagonal (the number of matrices $\mathbf{W}_{n,n}$ is n), $\mathfrak{D}(\mathbf{W}) = \mathrm{diag}\underbrace{(\mathbf{W}, \ldots, \mathbf{W})}_{n \text{ times}} =$ $\mathbf{I}_n \otimes \mathbf{W}_{n,n}$ also can be described using Kronecker tensor product $\otimes$ with identity matrix $\mathbf{I}_n$; double dots $^{\cdot\cdot}$ denotes the 2D transformation matrix size $n^2 \times n^2$; $\mathbf{P}$ is the permutation matrix.

The corresponding 2-D non-separable factorization of the PUFB synthesis matrix $\mathbf{D}(z)$ is shown below:

$$\mathbf{y}_{n^2,1} = \ddot{\mathbf{D}}(z) \cdot \mathbf{x}_{n\cdot n,1} = \ddot{\bar{\mathbf{E}}}_0 \cdot \ddot{\bar{\mathbf{G}}}_1(z) \cdot \ldots \cdot \ddot{\bar{\mathbf{G}}}_{N-1}(z) \cdot \mathbf{x}_{n^2,1},$$
$$\ddot{\bar{\mathbf{E}}}_0 = \mathfrak{D}\left(\mathrm{diag}\left(\mathbf{I}_{M/2}, \mathbf{J}_{M/2}\right)\right) \cdot \mathbf{P} \cdot \mathfrak{D}\left(\mathrm{diag}\left(\mathbf{I}_{M/2}, \mathbf{J}_{M/2}\right)\right) \cdot \mathbf{P} \cdot \ddot{\mathbf{W}} \cdot \ddot{\bar{\mathbf{\Phi}}}_0 \cdot \frac{1}{2},$$
$$\ddot{\bar{\mathbf{G}}}_i(z) = \ddot{\mathbf{W}} \cdot \ddot{\bar{\mathbf{\Lambda}}}(z) \cdot \ddot{\mathbf{W}} \cdot \ddot{\bar{\mathbf{\Phi}}}_i \cdot \frac{1}{4},$$
$$\ddot{\bar{\mathbf{\Lambda}}} = \mathfrak{D}\left(\hat{\mathbf{\Lambda}}(z)\right) \cdot \mathbf{P} \cdot \mathfrak{D}\left(\hat{\mathbf{\Lambda}}(z)\right) \cdot \mathbf{P}$$

where $^{=}$ denotes the synthesis 2-D transformation matrix.

For a **4-channel analysis** PMI LP Q-PUBF the two dimensional analogues of the matrices and $\mathbf{\Phi}_i$ (4) and $\mathbf{\Phi}_{N-1}$ (5) are defined as follows (See Fig. 2):

$$\ddot{\mathbf{\Phi}}_i = \mathfrak{D}\left(\mathbf{M}^+(P_i)\right) \cdot \mathbf{P} \cdot \mathfrak{D}\left(\mathbf{M}^+(P_i)\right) \cdot \mathbf{P},$$
$$\ddot{\mathbf{\Phi}}_{N-1} = \ddot{\mathbf{\Phi}}_i \cdot \ddot{\mathbf{S}}_1; \quad \ddot{\mathbf{S}}_1 = \mathfrak{D}(\mathbf{S}_1) \cdot \mathbf{P} \cdot \mathfrak{D}(\mathbf{S}_1) \cdot \mathbf{P}, \quad (9)$$
$$\mathbf{S}_1 = \mathrm{diag}\left(\mathbf{J}_{M/2} \cdot \mathbf{\Gamma}, \mathbf{I}_{M/2}\right).$$

The corresponding two dimensional analogues of the matrices $\mathbf{\Phi}_i$ (6) and $\mathbf{\Phi}_{N-1}$ (7) for **8-channel analysis** PMI LP Q-PUBF is shown below:

$$\ddot{\mathbf{\Phi}}_i = \ddot{\mathbf{S}}_2 \cdot \ddot{\mathbf{M}}_d^+(Q_i) \cdot \mathbf{P} \cdot \ddot{\mathbf{M}}_d^+(Q_i) \cdot \mathbf{P} \cdot \ddot{\mathbf{M}}_d^+(P_i) \cdot \mathbf{P} \cdot \ddot{\mathbf{M}}_d^+(P_i) \cdot \mathbf{P} \cdot \ddot{\mathbf{S}}_2,$$

$$\ddot{\mathbf{\Phi}}_{N-1} = \ddot{\mathbf{S}}_3 \cdot \ddot{\mathbf{M}}_d^-(Q_{N-1}) \cdot \mathbf{P} \cdot \ddot{\mathbf{M}}_d^+(Q_{N-1}) \cdot \mathbf{P}$$

$$\times \ddot{\mathbf{M}}_d^-(P_{N-1}) \cdot \mathbf{P} \cdot \ddot{\mathbf{M}}_d^+(P_{N-1}) \cdot \mathbf{P} \cdot \ddot{\mathbf{S}}_2,$$

$$\ddot{\mathbf{M}}_d^{\pm}(P) = \mathfrak{D}\left(\mathrm{diag}\left(\mathbf{M}^{\pm}(P), \mathbf{M}^{\pm}(P)\right)\right), \tag{10}$$

$$\ddot{\mathbf{S}}_2 = \mathfrak{D}(\mathbf{S}_2) \cdot \mathbf{P} \cdot \mathfrak{D}(\mathbf{S}_2) \cdot \mathbf{P}; \; \mathbf{S}_2 = \mathrm{diag}\left(\mathbf{\Gamma}_{M/2}, \mathbf{I}_{M/2}\right),$$

$$\ddot{\mathbf{S}}_3 = \mathfrak{D}(\mathbf{S}_3) \cdot \mathbf{P} \cdot \mathfrak{D}(\mathbf{S}_3) \cdot \mathbf{P}; \; \mathbf{S}_3 = \mathrm{diag}\left(\mathbf{J}_{M/2}, \mathbf{I}_{M/2}\right),$$

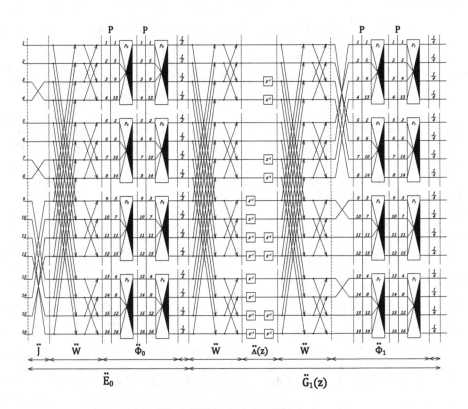

Fig. 2. 2-D NS Q-PUFB 4-channel analysis structure.

The 2-D analogues of the matrices $\hat{\mathbf{\Phi}}_i$ and $\hat{\mathbf{\Phi}}_{N-1}$ of a **4-channel synthesis** PMI LP Q-PUBF are defined as follows (see Fig. 3):

$$\ddot{\hat{\mathbf{\Phi}}}_i = \mathfrak{D}\left(\mathbf{M}^+\left(\overline{P}_i\right)\right) \cdot \mathbf{P} \cdot \mathfrak{D}\left(\mathbf{M}^+\left(\overline{P}_i\right)\right) \cdot \mathbf{P}\cdot,$$

$$\ddot{\hat{\mathbf{\Phi}}}_{N-1} = \ddot{\hat{\mathbf{S}}}_1 \cdot \ddot{\hat{\mathbf{\Phi}}}_i; \; \ddot{\hat{\mathbf{S}}}_1 = \mathfrak{D}\left(\hat{\mathbf{S}}_1\right) \cdot \mathbf{P} \cdot \mathfrak{D}\left(\hat{\mathbf{S}}_1\right), \tag{11}$$

$$\hat{\mathbf{S}}_1 = \mathrm{diag}\left(\mathbf{\Gamma}_{M/2} \cdot \mathbf{J}_{M/2}, \mathbf{I}_{M/2}\right).$$

The corresponding two dimensional analogues of the matrices $\hat{\mathbf{\Phi}}_i$ and $\hat{\mathbf{\Phi}}_{N-1}$ for **8-channel synthesis** PMI LP Q-PUBF are shown below:

$$\begin{aligned}
\bar{\bar{\mathbf{\Phi}}}_i &= \ddot{\mathbf{S}}_2 \cdot \ddot{\mathbf{M}}_d^+ \left(\overline{P}_i\right) \cdot \mathbf{P} \cdot \ddot{\mathbf{M}}_d^+ \left(\overline{P}_i\right) \cdot \mathbf{P} \\
&\times \ddot{\mathbf{M}}_d^- \left(\overline{Q}_i\right) \cdot \mathbf{P} \cdot \ddot{\mathbf{M}}_d^- \left(\overline{Q}_i\right) \cdot \mathbf{P} \cdot \ddot{\mathbf{S}}_2, \\
\bar{\bar{\mathbf{\Phi}}}_{N-1} &= \ddot{\mathbf{S}}_2 \cdot \ddot{\mathbf{M}}_d^+ \left(\overline{P}_{N-1}\right) \cdot \mathbf{P} \cdot \ddot{\mathbf{M}}_d^+ \left(\overline{P}_{N-1}\right) \cdot \mathbf{P} \\
&\times \ddot{\mathbf{M}}_d^- \left(\overline{Q}_{N-1}\right) \cdot \mathbf{P} \cdot \ddot{\mathbf{M}}_d^- \left(\overline{Q}_{N-1}\right) \cdot \mathbf{P} \cdot \ddot{\mathbf{S}}_3.
\end{aligned} \tag{12}$$

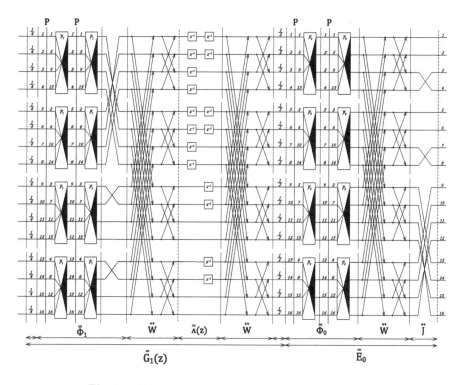

Fig. 3. 2-D NS Q-PUFB 4-channel synthesis structure.

Thus, the factorization components of the 2-D non separable 4-channel PMI LP Q-PUFB for analysis and synthesis parts, whose prototype filters are given by the relations (4, 5), are represented by the following expressions (9, 11). Similarly, the 2-D non-separable factorization for the 8-channel PMI LP Q-PUFB are represented as (10, 12). The given factorization structures called "16in-16out" and "64in-64out" respectively for 4-channel and 8-channel PMI LP Q-PUFBs.

The image enhancement system consists of the thresholding neural network, analysis and synthesis 2-D non separable quaternionic filter bank (2-D NS Q-PUFB). The dataflow of the system is shown in Fig. 4. The forward and inverse

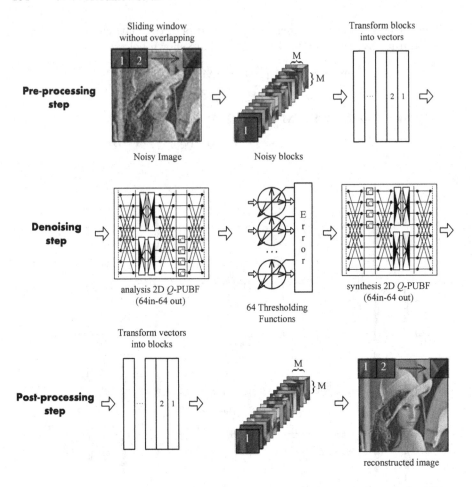

Fig. 4. Dataflow of the image enhancement system by (2-D NS Q-PUFB)-TNN

transformations are implemented on the structure "64in-64out", $N = 2$, the core of which is a multiplier of quaternions (the rectangles with a black triangle). A block of a noisy image of size 8×8 pixels is the input of the system, and a block of a reconstructed image of size 8×8 is formed at the output of the inverse transform. The given structure can be mapped to parallel-pipeline processor architecture with a minimum latency time $2N$ quaternion multiplication operations. The latency of parallel pipeline processing does not depend on the size of the original image in contrast to the conventional 2-D transform.

4   Formulation of the Thresholding Neural Network

It is well known that most learning algorithms of a neural network use the gradients and higher derivatives of the network activation function to adjust the parameters. Since gradient optimization methods require differentiability of activation functions, a necessary condition is the continuity of a function on a given set of arguments. Therefore, the classic hard and soft thresholding functions, shown with bold lines in Fig. 5a and b respectively, cannot be applied and varieties of differentiable versions of thresholding functions were proposed in [1, 10, 11]. For example, the function introduced in [1], besides the threshold value t also has two shape tuning parameters m and k

$$f\left(x, t, m, k\right) = \begin{cases} x + (k-1)t - \frac{kt^m}{2x^{m-1}}, & x > t \\ \frac{k|x|^{m+(2-k)/k}}{2t^{m+2(1-k)/k}}\text{sign}\left(x\right), & |x| \leq t \\ x - (k-1)t + \frac{k(-t)^m}{2x^{m-1}}, & x < -t \end{cases} \tag{13}$$

Figure 5a and b show the function shape for different values of extra tuning parameters.

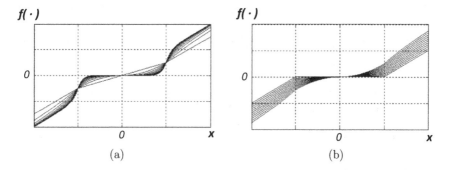

Fig. 5. Shape of thresholding function $f(\cdot)$ with respect to variation of parameter k – (a), m – (b)

From the figures above it can be seen that the shape tuning parameters are responsible for the form of the function and brings it closer to "hard" or "soft" shape depending on the values of m and k.

Training of the TNN with the activation function expressed in (13) consists in finding the optimal values of t, m, k that provide the best solution to the optimization problem established in (1). Then the process of adjusting the function parameters based on the gradient descent can be expressed by the following iterative expressions:

$$t(i+1) = t(i) - \alpha(i)\frac{\partial E(x, \hat{x})}{\partial t(i)},$$

$$m(i+1) = m(i) - \beta(i)\frac{\partial E(x, \hat{x})}{\partial m(i)}, \tag{14}$$

$$k(i+1) = k(i) - \gamma(i)\frac{\partial E(x, \hat{x})}{\partial k(i)},$$

where α, β, γ are the parameters controlling learning rate of t, m, k respectively; $E(x, \hat{x})$ is the loss function (1) defined in the transform domain.

From the expression above, it is clear that parameters α, β, γ affect the speed and stability of the training process in the following way: if one of the parameters is too large then the training process becomes unstable and it is impossible to obtain appropriate local minima of the function, on the other hand when they are small the convergence response is over damped, and thus training takes much more time. Hence, learning rate parameters play a vital role in convergence of the training process and choosing proper values for them becomes the main task during the training.

The aforementioned problem can be solved if each of the learning rate parameters is chosen so that

$$\eta(i) = \arg\min\left(E(x, \hat{x})\right) \tag{15}$$

where η is one of the parameters controlling learning rate. Now the training process can be formulated as follows (Algorithm 1).

Algorithm 1

1: Given an initial values of t, m, k, data x, maximum number of iterations $maxiter$ and expected tolerance tol.
2: **for** $i = 0$ to $maxiter$ **do**
3:     Compute partial derivatives $\frac{\partial E(x, \hat{x})}{\partial t(i)}$, $\frac{\partial E(x, \hat{x})}{\partial m(i)}$, $\frac{\partial E(x, \hat{x})}{\partial k(i)}$ to obtain gradient vector.
4:     Perform linear search expressed in Eq. 15 for parameters $\alpha(i)$, $\beta(i)$, $\gamma(i)$ using pre-computed gradient vector as search direction.
5:     Update t, m and k using Eq. 14
6:     **if** $(E(x, \hat{x})) \leq tol$ **then**
7:         converged
8:     **end if**
9: **end for**

---

5   Experimental Results

The conversion in the image enhancement system was implemented on the two dimensional non-separable critically sampled 8-channels (24 taps) PMI LP Q-PUFB: structure "64in-64out", factorization order $N = 2$, coding gain CG_{2D}=17.15 dB, magnitude response is shown on Fig. 6. To evaluate the performance of the proposed approach test image Lena (Fig. 7a), Barbara (Fig. 7b), Boat (Fig. 7c), synthetic image (Fig. 7d) and ultrasound medical image (Fig. 7e) were used. To investigate denoising method all the images were corrupted by Gaussian noise of various power. Noise signals with standard deviation of 10, 20 and 30 are chosen as basic levels of the noise power.

TNN was trained in supervised manner using clean and noisy images in transform domain as training data. Values of the constants controlling the training process $maxiter$ and tol set to 50 and 10^{-6} were found to be appropriate for achieving the desired results. Parameters m and k have been initialized as 2 and

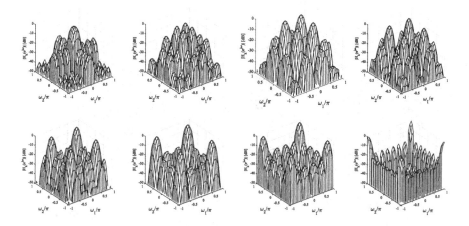

Fig. 6. Magnitude response of 2-D NS Q-PUFB (channels 1–8 are shown from top to bottom from left to right)

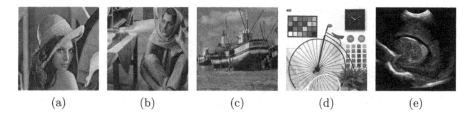

Fig. 7. Original test images: a – Lena, b – Barbara, c – Boat, d – Synthetic, e – Ultrasound

1 respectively. The initial threshold value t was set using the universal threshold value for each transformation subband which is expressed as

$$t = \sigma\sqrt{2\log(n)/n} \tag{16}$$

where σ is the computed standard deviation of the transformation subbands coefficients and is a subspace dimension. The most commonly used performance metrics in image processing like PSNR and SNR are used in this work to evaluate the obtained results.

Table 1 shows the denoising results obtained in this work. The denoised images for different noise levels are shown in Fig. 8. Images on the figure below are arranged in columns by the noise level as follows: Fig. 8a, b and c correspond to noise standard deviation of 10, 20 and 30 respectively.

A detailed view of a noisy test image Barbara and its denoised reference can be seen in Fig. 9.

To analyze the performance of the proposed noise reduction system in speckled image denoising applications we use MSE, S/MSE, β and ρ as it is proposed

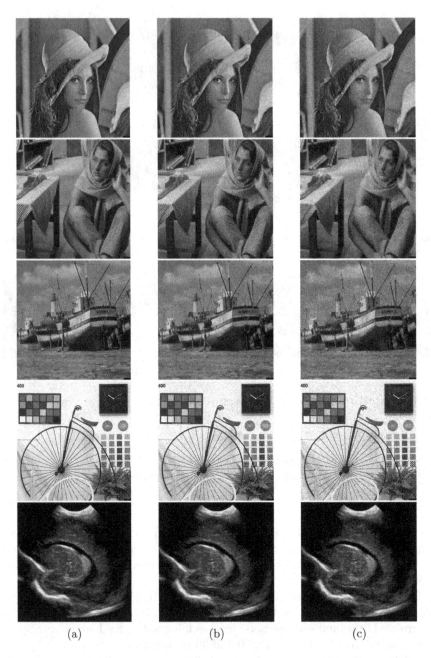

(a)   (b)   (c)

Fig. 8. Denoised test images with different input noise standard deviation: a – 10, b – 20, c – 30

Table 1. PSNR results of proposed approach versus existing.

Image	σ	Noisy	Zhang [11]	Zhang [10]	Narsi [3]	Proposed
Lena	10	28.16	28.74	28.09	31.67	**32.30**
	20	22.14	26.31	25.76	29.01	**29.82**
	30	18.62	25.10	24.63	27.03	**28.25**
Barbara	10	28.16	25.32	24.58	28.42	**29.77**
	20	22.14	23.04	22.55	25.30	**25.40**
	30	18.62	22.12	21.75	**23.84**	23.56
Boat	10	28.16	27.05	26.42	29.97	**30.11**
	20	22.15	24.79	24.19	27.01	**27.82**
	30	18.62	23.57	23.10	25.50	**26.34**
Synthetic	10	28.67				29.20
	20	22.98				28.25
	30	18.62				24.28
Ultrasound	10	29.29				34.08
	20	23.41				31.16
	30	20.05				29.45

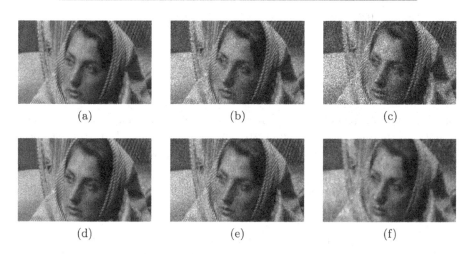

(a)   (b)   (c)

(d)   (e)   (f)

Fig. 9. A detailed view of the noisy (a – 10, b – 20, c – 30) and denoised (d – 10, e – 20, f – 30) image Barbara with different input noise standard deviation.

in [7], where last two parameters are defined as edge preservation criteria and a measure of noise suppression respectively (Table 2).

Table 2. Experimental results of proposed approach of speckle denoising versus existing.

	Noisy	Universal method Nasri [3]	TNN method Nasri [3]	Proposed	σ	Image
MSE	1622.5	184.77	134.33	216.83	0.1	Lena
S/MSE	10.339	18.435	19.92	19.12		
β	0.1176	0.1699	0.240	0.1402		
ρ	0.7542	0.9608	0.9716	0.9520		
MSE	3053.5	299.25	245.99	319.21	0.2	
S/MSE	7.5867	14.761	15.84	17.44		
β	0.0822	0.0797	0.1162	0.0947		
ρ	0.6247	0.9413	0.95	0.9305		
MSE	790.79	265.99	186.68	223.82	0.05	Barbara
S/MSE	13.261	17.621	19.320	18.77		
β	0.4148	0.5806	0.6530	0.6222		
ρ	0.8863	0.9554	0.9680	0.9618		
MSE	166.65	128.58	94.97	83.80	0.01	
S/MSE	20.025	21.068	22.48	23.04		
β	0.7109	0.7975	0.8040	0.8323		
ρ	0.9731	0.9784	0.9845	0.9859		

6   Conclusion

Comparison of the results obtained in this work with known approaches to editing noise in the image shows the perspective of this scheme. In further studies, it is proposed to integrate the processes of editing noise and quantizing the 2-D NSQ-PUFB coefficients in the image encoder scheme.

References

1. Bhutada, G., Anand, R., Saxena, S.: Image enhancement by wavelet-based thresholding neural network with adaptive learning rate. IET Image Process. **5**(7), 573 (2011). https://doi.org/10.1049/iet-ipr.2010.0014
2. Krim, H., Tucker, D., Mallat, S., Donoho, D.: On denoising and best signal representation. IEEE Trans. Inf. Theory **45**(7), 2225–2238 (1999). https://doi.org/10.1109/18.796365
3. Nasri, M., Nezamabadi-pour, H.: Image denoising in the wavelet domain using a new adaptive thresholding function. Neurocomputing **72**(4–6), 1012–1025 (2009). https://doi.org/10.1016/j.neucom.2008.04.016
4. Parfieniuk, M., Petrovsky, A.: Inherently lossless structures for eight- and six-channel linear-phase paraunitary filter banks based on quaternion multipliers. Signal Process. **90**, 1755–1767 (2010). https://doi.org/10.1016/j.sigpro.2010.01.008

5. Petrovsky, N.A., Rybenkov, E.V.: 2-D non-separable integer implementation of paraunitary filter bank based on the quaternionic multiplier block-lifting structure. In: 2019 27th European Signal Processing Conference (EUSIPCO). IEEE, September 2019

6. Petrovsky, N.A., Rybenkov, E.V., Petrovsky, A.A.: Two-dimensional non-separable quaternionic paraunitary filter banks. In: 2018 Signal Processing: Algorithms, Architectures, Arrangements, and Applications (SPA). IEEE, September 2018. https://doi.org/10.23919/spa.2018.8563311

7. Sattar, F., Floreby, L., Salomonsson, G., Lovstrom, B.: Image enhancement based on a nonlinear multiscale method. IEEE Trans. Image Process. **6**(6), 888–895 (1997). https://doi.org/10.1109/83.585239

8. Vaidyanathan, P.P.: Multirate Systems and Filter Banks. Prentice Hall, Englewood Cliffs (1992)

9. Yu, H., Zhao, L., Wang, H.: Image denoising using trivariate shrinkage filter in the wavelet domain and joint bilateral filter in the spatial domain. IEEE Trans. Image Process. **18**(10), 2364–2369 (2009). https://doi.org/10.1109/tip.2009.2026685

10. Zhang, X.P.: Thresholding neural network for adaptive noise reduction. IEEE Trans. Neural Netw. **12**(3), 567–584 (2001). https://doi.org/10.1109/72.925559

11. Zhang, X.P., Desai, M.: Adaptive denoising based on SURE risk. IEEE Signal Process. Lett. **5**(10), 265–267 (1998). https://doi.org/10.1109/97.720560

Information Processing and Applications

Semantic-Based Linguistic Platform for Big Data Processing

A. Bobkov[1], S. Gafurov[2], Viktor Krasnoproshin[1(✉)], and H. Vissia[2]

[1] Belarusian State University,
4 Nezavisimosti Av., 220030 Minsk, Republic of Belarus
anatoly.bobkov@gmail.com, krasnoproshin@bsu.by
[2] ByeleX BV, Argon 1, 4751 XC Oud Gastel, The Netherlands
sergey_gafurov@by.byelex.com, h.vissia@byelex.com

Abstract. The paper deals with the development of a semantic-based linguistic platform. Special attention is paid to semantic patterns.

Keywords: Big data · Natural language processing · Semantic patterns · Ontology-based approach

1 Introduction

Big data has been a widely discussed topic for the past five years [1–5]. The term "Big Data" refers to the large amounts of data in which traditional data processing procedures and tools would not be able to handle. The idea is that mass quantities of gathered data give us unprecedented insights and opportunities across all industries and businesses for solving problems and decision making. Big data is not only an area of potential innovation but is also a crucial factor that companies address to survive in the modern marketplace.

There's no doubt that big data will continue to play an important role in many different industries around the world.

Currently, information extraction from big data becomes predominant. The information can come from various sources, e.g. media, blogs, personal experiences, books, newspaper and magazine articles, expert opinions, encyclopedias, web pages, etc.

Today, big data gives us unprecedented insights and opportunities across all industries from healthcare to financial to manufacturing and more.

Businesses can make a lot out of big data, making it an important resource.

The use and adoption of big data within governmental processes allows efficiencies in terms of cost, productivity, and innovation.

2 Problem Statement and Solution

Information extraction from big data comprises methods, algorithms and techniques for finding the desired, relevant information and for storing it in appropriate form for future use.

© Springer Nature Switzerland AG 2019
S. V. Ablameyko et al. (Eds.): PRIP 2019, CCIS 1055, pp. 165–179, 2019.
https://doi.org/10.1007/978-3-030-35430-5_14

The field of information extraction is well suited to various types of business, government and social applications [6, 7]. Diverse information is of great importance for decision making on products, services, events, persons, organizations.

Creation of systems that can effectively extract meaningful information requires overcoming a number of challenges: identification of documents, knowledge domains, specific opinions, opinion holders, events, activities, mood state, as well as representation of the obtained results.

Numerous models and algorithms are proposed for web information processing and information extraction [8, 9]. But traditional data processing technologies and tools are not able to adequately deal with large amounts of data. Big data is too voluminous and requires the use of new technologies and data-processing applications to effectively capture, store, analyze, and present big data. Thus, the problem of effective information extraction from texts in a natural language still remains unsolved.

The purpose of this paper is to describe the developed and integrated semantic-based linguistic platform for solving the problem of effective extraction of meaningful, user-oriented information from big data.

Semantic relations [10, 11] play the major role in extracting meaningful information.

Semantic relations (lexical-semantic relations) are meaningful associations between two or more concepts or entities. They can be viewed as links between the concepts or entities that participate in the relation. Associations between concepts can be categorized into different types.

In information extraction and text mining, word collocations show a great potential [12] to be useful in many applications (machine translation, natural language processing, lexicography, word sense disambiguation, etc.).

"Collocations" are usually described as "sequences of lexical items which habitually co-occur, but which are nonetheless fully transparent in the sense that each lexical constituent is also a semantic constituent" [13].

The traditional method of performing automatic collocation extraction is to find a formula based on the statistical quantities of words to calculate a score associated to each word pair. The formulas are mainly: "mutual information", "t-test", "z test", "chi-squared test" and "likelihood ratio" [14].

Word collocations from the point of semantic constituents have not yet been widely studied and used for extracting meaningful information, especially when processing texts in a natural language.

The developed approach is based on word collocations on the semantic level and contextual relations forming a "semantic pattern".

A semantic pattern is a kind of a knowledge model. Knowledge modeling describes what data means and where it fits. It allows us to understand how different pieces of information relate to each other. A semantic pattern can be viewed as containing slots that need to be filled. Though most patterns are binary ones having two slots, a pattern may have three or more slots.

Semantic patterns help users to ask questions in a natural way and discover relationships between disparate pieces of information.

In general, the proposed semantic patterns include: (1) *participants* (a person, company, natural/manufactured object, as well as a more abstract entity, such as a plan, policy, etc.) involved in the action or being evaluated; (2) *actions* - a set of verb semantic groups and verbal nouns ("buy", "manufacture", "arrival", etc.); (3) *rules for semantic patterns actualization.*

The patterns cover different types of semantic relations: (1) semantic relations between two concepts/entities, one of which expresses the performance of an operation or process affecting the other ("Much remains to be learned about how nanoparticles affect the environment"); (2) synonymous relationships ("beautiful – attractive - pretty"); (3) antonymy ("wet - dry"); (4) causal relations ("Research identifies new gene that causes osteoporosis"); (5) hyponymous relations ("Jaguar is a powerful vehicle"); (6) locative relations ("Amsterdam is located in the western Netherlands, in the province of North Holland"); (7) part-whole relations ("car transmission - car"); (8) semantic relations in which a concept indicates a time or period of an event designated by another concept ("Second World War, 1939–1945"); (9) associative relations ("baker – bread": "The baker produced bread of excellent quality"); (10) "made-of" relations ("This ring is made of gold"); (11) "made-from" relations ("Cheese made from raw milk imparts different flavors and texture characteristics to the finished cheese"); (12) "used-for" relations ("Database software is used for the management and storage of data and databases"); (13) homonym relations ("bank of the river – bank as a financial institution"), etc. A semantic relation can be expressed in many syntactic forms. Besides words, semantic relations can occur at higher levels of text (between phrases, clauses, sentences and larger text segments), as well as between documents and sets of documents. The variety of semantic relations and their properties play an important role in web information processing for extracting relevant fragments of information from unstructured text documents.

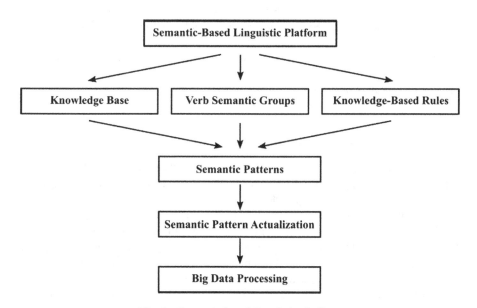

Fig. 1. Semantic-based linguistic platform

An ontology-based approach is used for semantic patterns recognition and extraction [15, 16].

Semantic patterns and the ontology-based approach form the basis for the developed semantic-based linguistic platform (Fig. 1). The platform is a group of technologies that are used as a base upon which applications, processes and technologies are developed.

3 Implementation of the Developed Linguistic Platform

The developed semantic-based linguistic platform has been successfully realized in BuzzTalk portal [17]. BuzzTalk gathers meaningful information from extensive sources of textual information (i.e. news, scientific articles, Web pages, tweets, reports, online encyclopedias, etc.) on the level of single words, phrases and sentences. BuzzTalk is offered to companies as a SaaS (Software as a Service) model.

The difference between a traditional search engine and a discovery engine such as BuzzTalk, is that search engines list all results for a specific search whereas BuzzTalk allows you to monitor topic-specific developments within your search. BuzzTalk discovers the latest information about a particular brand, competitors or industry, thus facilitating to make better decisions.

BuzzTalk collects all text documents from over 58 000 of the most active websites around the globe, two thirds are news sites and one third is blog sites. The authors of these documents are mainly scientists, journalists and opinion leaders.

BuzzTalk finds and links relevant information in natural-language documents while ignoring extraneous, irrelevant information.

BuzzTalk presents a list of articles in chronological order based on publication date. This list grows each day. You can sort and filter this list based on a variety of criteria such as sentiment, mood state, happenings, etc., thus to experience the wealth of real time information without the pain of information overload. For example, you can easily find all publications within your theme that relate to product releases, employment changes, merger & acquisitions and many more.

Below are examples of information extraction in BuzzTalk.

3.1 Economic Activities Detection

Semantic patterns approach helps to extract information dealing with economic activities. The information could be valuable in many subject areas, including medicine, biology, science, technology, etc.

Recognition of economic activities is closely connected with big data.

The recognition of economic phenomena is rather difficult within natural language processing. Certain elements need to be chosen and grouped according to particular characteristics. Thus, all economic phenomena that are to be described and processed require systematic classification especially when processing big data.

BuzzTalk detects economic activities from texts in a natural language. The economic activities cover all major activities represented in NACE classification (Statistical Classification of Economic Activities in the European Community), which is similar to the International Standard Industrial Classification of all economic activities (ISIC) reflecting the current structure of the world economy. NACE classification provides the internationally accepted standard for categorizing units within an economy. Categories of the classification have become an accepted way of subdividing the overall economy into useful coherent industries that are widely recognized and used in economic analysis, and as such they have become accepted groupings for data used as indicators of economic activities.

While extracting and analyzing economic activities, BuzzTalk ensures a continuing flow of information that is indispensable for the monitoring, analysis and evaluation of the performance of an economy over time. Moreover, BuzzTalk facilitates information extraction, presentation and analysis at detailed levels of the economy in an internationally comparable, standardized way.

Examples of economic activities detection:

- *Toyota has maintained its position as the world's biggest car manufacturer.*

  Extracted instances:
  Economic activities = *Manufacture of motor vehicles* (NACE code C291)

- *Goat cheese has been made for thousands of years, and was probably one of the earliest made dairy products.*

  Extracted instances:
  Economic activities = *Manufacture of dairy products* (NACE code C105)

- *This invention relates to a process for the hardening of metals.*

  Extracted instances:
  Economic activities = *Treatment and coating of metals* (NACE code C256)

- *India is the largest grower of rice.*

  Extracted instances:
  Economic activities = *Growing of rice* (NACE code A0112)

- *OCBC Bank operates its commercial banking business in 15 countries.*

  Extracted instances:
  Economic activities = *Monetary intermediation* (NACE code K641)

- *It is even more important to properly plan the preparation of legal documents.*

  Extracted instances:
  Economic activities = *Legal activities* (NACE code M691)

- *Florida's aquafarmers grow products for food (fish and shellfish).*

  Extracted instances:
  Economic activities = *Aquaculture* (NACE code A032)

3.2 Subject Domains Recognition

In BuzzTalk a subject domain is recognized on the basis of a particular set of noun and verb phrases unambiguously describing the domain.
   Examples:

- *The goal of the pollution prevention and reduction program is to prevent or minimize polluting discharges.*

  Extracted instances:
  Subject domain = *Ecology*

- *Mozzarella cheese is a sliceable curd cheese originating in Italy.*

  Extracted instances:
  Subject domain = *Food*

- *Fresh milk is the common type of milk available in the supermarket.*

  Extracted instances:
  Subject domain = *Beverage*

- *Distance education includes a range of programs, from elementary and high school to graduate studies.*

  Extracted instances:
  Subject domain = *Education*

- *The biathlon is a winter sport that combines cross-country skiing and rifle shooting.*

  Extracted instances:
  Subject domain = *Biathlon*

- *The aim of nanoelectronics is to process, transmit and store information by taking advantage of properties of matter that are distinctly different from macroscopic properties.*

  Extracted instances:
  Subject domain = *Sustainable Business*

- *Britain has made a political decision that will have economic effects.*

  Extracted instances:
  Subject domain = *Politics*

- *Economy from then on meant national economy as a topic for the economic activities of the citizens of a state.*

  Extracted instances:
  Subject domain = *Economics*

- *The law-making power of the state is the governing power of the state.*

  Extracted instances:
  Subject domain = *Law*

- *The president called for collective efforts to fight world terrorism.*

  Extracted instances:
  Subject domain = *Terrorism*

- *Japan was hit by a magnitude 6.5 earthquake followed by an M7.3 quake on Saturday.*

  Extracted instances:
  Subject domain = *Disaster*

For solving the problem of disambiguation special filters, based on the contextual environment (on the level of phrases and the whole text), are introduced.

Subject domains and their concepts are organized hierarchically to state "part-of", "is a kind of" relations.

3.3 Named Entities Recognition

Named-entity recognition is a subtask of information extraction that seeks to locate and classify named entities in a text into pre-defined categories such as names of persons, organizations, locations, etc.

BuzzTalk recognizes the following main named entities:

- "Person" (first, middle, last names and nicknames, e.g. Steve Jobs, Cristina Fernandez de Kirchner);
- "Title" (social, academic titles, etc.);
- "Position" (a post of employment/office/job, e.g. president, CEO);
- "Organization" (a company, governmental, military or other organizations, e.g. Microsoft, Wells Fargo, The University of Oxford);
- "Location" (names of continents, countries, states, provinces, regions, cities, towns, e.g. Africa, The Netherlands, Amsterdam);
- "Technology" (technology names or a description of the technology, e.g. 4D printing, advanced driver assistance, affinity chromatography, agricultural robot, airless tire technology);
- "Product" (e.g. Sikorsky CH-148 Cyclone, Lockheed Martin F-35 Lightning II, Kalashnikov AKS, Windhoek Lager, Mercedes S550, Apple iPhone 6S Plus, Ultimate Player Edition, Adenosine);
- "Event" (a planned public/social/business occasion, e.g. Olympic Summer Games, World Swimming Championship, Paris Air Show, International Book Fair);
- "Industry Term" (a term related to a particular industry, e.g. advertising, finance, aviation, automotive, education, film, food, footwear, railway industries);
- "Medical treatment" (terms related to the action or manner of treating a patient medically or surgically, e.g. vitamin therapy, vaccination, treatment of cancer, vascular surgery, open heart surgery), etc.

3.4 Event Extraction

A specific type of knowledge that can be extracted from texts is an event, which can be represented as a complex combination of relations. Event extraction is beneficial for accurate breaking news analysis, risk analysis, monitoring systems, decision making support systems, etc.

BuzzTalk performs real-time extraction of 35 events, based on lexical-semantic patterns, for decision making in different spheres of business, legal and social activities. The events include: "Environmental Issues", "Natural Disaster", "Health Issues", "Energy Issues", "Merger & Acquisition", "Company Reorganization", "Competitive Product/Company", "Money Market", "Product Release", "Bankruptcy", "Bribery & Corruption", "Fraud & Forgery", "Treason", "Hijacking", "Illegal Business", "Sex Abuse", "Conflict", "Conflict Resolution", "Social Life", etc.

For example:

- *Contract medical research provider, Quintiles, agreed to merge with healthcare information company, IMS Health to make a giant known as Quintiles IMS in an all-stock deal.*

  Extracted instances:
  Event = *Merger & Acquisition*

- *Mazda Motor Corporation unveiled the all-new Mazda CX-5 crossover SUV.*

  Extracted instances:
  Event = *Product Release*

- *TCS ranked as top 100 U.S. brand for second consecutive year.*

  Extracted instances:
  Event = *Competitive Product/Company*

- *Two Hong Kong men arrested for drug trafficking.*

  Extracted instances:
  Event = *Illegal Business*

- *A former President of Guatemala, already in jail, has been accused of taking bribes.*

  Extracted instances:
  Event = *Bribery & Corruption*

- *Yet another green-energy giant faces bankruptcy.*

  Extracted instances:
  Event = *Bankruptcy*

- *Two Afghans held for attempted rape of woman on Paris train.*

  Extracted instances:
  Event = *Sex Abuse*

- *A New York woman faced charges for faking cancer to solicit money from unsuspecting donors and a relative.*

  Extracted instances:
  Event = *Fraud & Forgery*

The extracted events play a crucial role in daily decisions taken by people of different professions and occupation.

3.5 Opinion Mining

Creation of systems that can effectively process subjective information requires overcoming a number of new challenges: identification of opinion-oriented documents, knowledge domains, specific opinions, opinion holders, representation of the obtained results.

Opinion mining is gaining much popularity within natural language processing [18]. Web reviews, blogs and public articles provide the most essential information for opinion mining. This information is of great importance for decision making on products, services, persons, events, organizations.

Opinion words are the main constituents of opinion mining and sentiment analysis.

Numerous models and algorithms are proposed to identify and extract opinion words, positive or negative assessment of the object being evaluated [18–20]. But the problem of effective identification and extraction of opinion words and phrases from an arbitrary text, irrespective of the knowledge domain, still remains unsolved.

We propose an ontology-based approach [15] that helps to identify and process opinion words expressing:

(1) appreciation (e.g. flexible, efficient, stable, reduced, ideal, backward, poor, highest)
(2) judgement (e.g. active, decisive, caring, dedicated, intelligent, negligent, evil)

While "judgement" evaluates human behaviors, "appreciation" typically deals with natural objects, manufactured objects, as well as more abstract entities, such as plans and policies. Humans may also be evaluated by means of "appreciation", rather than "judgement", when viewed more as entities than as participants, e.g. *lovely medical staff*.

Opinion words can be expressed by: an adjective (*brilliant, reliable*); a verb (*like, love, hate, blame*); a noun (*garbage, triumph, catastrophe*); a phrase (*easy to use, simple to use*). Adjectives derive almost all disambiguating information from the nouns they modify, and nouns are best disambiguated by directly adjacent adjectives or nouns.

Information about the force of evaluation (low, high, the highest) and orientation (positive/negative) is also taken into consideration. For example, *safe* (low force, positive orientation), *safer* (high force, positive orientation), *the safest* (the highest force, positive orientation), *unsafe* (low force, negative orientation).

Opinion words go together with their accompanying words, thus forming "opinion collocations" (e.g. *deep depression*, *deep devotion*, *warm greetings*, *discuss calmly*, *beautifully furnished*). By an "opinion collocation" we understand a combination of an opinion word and accompanying words, which commonly occur together in an opinion-oriented text. The use of opinion collocations is a way to solve the problem of opinion word sense disambiguation (e.g. *well-balanced political leader* and *well-balanced wheel*) and to exclude words that do not relate to opinions (cf. *attractive idea* and *attractive energy*).

We assume that the number of opinion collocations, which can be listed in a knowledge base, is fixed.

Processing of the extracted opinion collocations is carried out in their contextual environment. The developed algorithm checks for the presence of modifiers that can change the force of evaluation and orientation indicated in the knowledge base.

Based on the proposed ontology approach, an object of the particular class of interest may have its own specific sets of sub-classes, opinion collocations and evaluation. In the automobile domain, for a car model they can be: engine, transmission, suspension, size, color, design, condition under which an evaluation applies (e.g. driving on slippery roads), a supporting factor for the evaluation.

The results of opinion collocations processing are grouped and evaluated to recognize the quality of the opinion-related text. The results are also visualized.

3.6 Mood State Detection

A valuable addition to opinion mining is detection of individual/public mood states. BuzzTalk mood detection uses the classification of the widely-accepted "Profile of Mood States" (POMS), originally developed by McNair, Lorr and Droppleman. The relationship between mood states and different human activities has proven a popular area of research [21].

BuzzTalk mood detection uses the classification of the widely-accepted "Profile of Mood States" (POMS), originally developed by McNair, Lorr and Droppleman [22].

In BuzzTalk, mood state detection is based on: (1) mood indicators (e.g. "I feel", "makes me feel", etc.); (2) mood words (e.g. anger, fury, horrified, tired, taken aback, depressed, optimistic); (3) special contextual rules to avoid ambiguation. BuzzTalk automatically recognizes the following mood states: "Anger", "Tension", "Fatigue", "Confusion", "Depression", "Vigor".

For example:

- *Despite these problems, I feel very happy.*

  Extracted instances:
  Mood state = *Vigor*

- *I'm feeling angry at the world now.*

  Extracted instances:
  Mood state = *Anger*

- *I feel fatigued and exhausted.*

  Extracted instances:
  Mood state = *Fatigue*

- *I have suicidal thoughts every day.*

  Extracted instances:
  Mood state = *Depression*

Mood state detection alongside with opinion mining can give answers to where we are now and where will be in future.

3.7   Predictive Analytics

With the use of information technologies a decision maker has a great possibility to know and investigate what is happening, when and where, closely monitor the existing current situation in the world and make predictions. Predictive analytics [23, 24] is used to make predictions about unknown future events. Predictive analytics is used in marketing, financial services, insurance, telecommunications, retail, travel, mobility, healthcare, child protection, pharmaceuticals, capacity planning and other fields. The goal is to go beyond the knowledge of what has happened to provide the best assessment of what will happen in future.

Organizations are turning to predictive analytics to solve difficult problems and uncover new opportunities. Analytical methods can improve crime detection and prevent criminal behavior. As cybersecurity becomes a growing concern, high-performance behavioral analytics examines all actions on a network in real time to spot abnormalities that may indicate fraud, zero-day vulnerabilities and advanced persistent threats. In addition to detection of claims fraud, the health insurance industry is taking steps to identify patients most at risk of chronic disease and to find what interventions are best. Predictive analytics is used to determine customer responses, as well as to promote cross-sell opportunities. Predictive models help businesses to attract, retain and grow their most profitable customers. Many companies use predictive models to forecast equipment failures and future resource needs. Airlines use predictive analytics to set ticket prices. Hotels try to predict the number of guests for any given time to maximize occupancy and increase revenue. Predictive analytics enables organizations to function more efficiently. It helps to detect earthquakes, floods, hurricanes, as well as to forecast future occurrences of such hazards and their various characteristics (magnitude of an earthquake, track and intensity of a cyclone, etc.). Predictive analytics can fix small problems before they become big ones.

Endless flood of Internet data calls for substantial analytical work. Thus, of great importance is the development of effective computer systems for predictive analytics within natural language processing. Predictive analytics, as an area of big data mining, involves extraction of information and its use to predict events, trends, behavior patterns, etc.

We consider that extraction and processing of "cause-effect" relations from texts form the basis for predictive analytics. Knowledge of "cause" and "effect" ensures rational decision making and problem solving. It is important in all areas of science and technology.

A "cause-effect" [25, 26] is a relation in which one event ("cause") makes another event happen ("effect"). "Effect" is defined as what happened. "Cause" is defined as why something happened.

For example:

- *Insecticide lindane found to cause cancer*
- *Culprit identified as a major cause of vision loss*
- *Stiff and oxygen-deprived tumors promote spread of cancer*
- *The car accident was due to the adverse driver's negligence*

The "cause-effect" relation affects all aspects of our lives. For every "effect" there is a definite "cause", likewise for every "cause", there is a definite "effect". This means that everything that we currently have in our lives is an "effect" that is a result of a specific "cause".

Though many of the cause-effect relations in texts are implicit and have to be inferred by the reader, the English language actually possesses a wide range of linguistic expressions for explicitly indicating "cause" and "effect" [27–29].

The following main means are identified:

1. causative verbs (cause, result in, lead to, make happen, provoke, encourage, etc.)

   For example:
   Lung cancer, brain disease caused death
   The crash resulted in the deaths of 15 passengers
   E-cigarettes may lead to cancer and heart disease

2. causal links (so, hence, therefore, because of, on account of, that's why, due to, as a result of, owing to, thanks to, by reason of, by cause of, etc.)

   For example:
   Schools are closed because of flu
   He knew he could not win the election - hence his decision to withdraw
   US Postal Service suspends services due to Hurricane Irma

3. conditionals (i.e. "if ..., then" constructions)

   For example:

   If the demand for a product is elastic, then a business owner can cut the price
   If you use correct punctuation, then you will include commas where necessary
   If an economy is producing efficiently, then it is possible for that economy to produce more of one good without producing less of the other.

4. causative nouns *(cause of, reason for, result of, consequence of, influence of, impact of, etc.)*

   For example:

   Probably the most serious and most short-sighted consequence of deforestation is the loss of biodiversity
   Warm, wet winters during recent decades in the Northern Hemisphere can be explained by the influence of greenhouse gases on atmospheric winds
   In coming decades, global warming will have a dramatic impact on regional water supplies.
   The most common cause of dehydration in young children is severe diarrhea and vomiting.

Knowledge of "cause-effect" provides the basis for decision making [30] and predictive analytics in particular.

Causal reasoning, as a "process of observing an event and reasoning about future events that might be caused by it" [31], can be extremely helpful in solving complex problems such as identification and prediction of a particular event, crime suspects, fraud cases, detection of trends, question answering, support of decision making by politicians, businessmen, and individual users. An important feature of causality is the continuity of the cause-effect connection.

Many efforts have been made to extract "cause-effect" relationships from texts utilizing constraints and machine learning techniques [25].

In spite of the existing algorithms, dealing with causal reasoning [26, 31–33], there isn't a reliable computer system that can process big data and show good results in giving answers to such questions as:

What may cause cancer?

unhealthy diet
wireless devices
stress
implants

What may help fight cancer?

ultrasound
nanoparticles
broccoli sprouts

As a way for solving the problems we propose extraction and processing of "cause-effect" relations on the basis of semantic patterns described above.

Semantic patterns approach helps to extract information dealing with "cause-effect" in order to make predictions for decision making. The information could be valuable in many subject areas, including medicine, biology, science, technology, etc.

The constructed rules use causality connectors [34–36] such as "cause", "due to", "lead to", "result from", "result in", "owing to", "therefore", "if-then constructions", etc.

BuzzTalk submits information for predictive analytics after processing thousands of texts in the natural language.

"Cause-effect" is often the next step after the extraction of objects or events from texts.

"Cause-effect" relations help to reason about the detected events and is vitally important for problem solving.

4   Conclusion

Processing of texts in a natural language necessitates the solution of the problem of extracting meaningful information from big data. Diverse information is of great importance for decision making on products, services, events, persons, industries, organizations. Semantic relations play a major role in solving different problems ensuring interaction with the information in a natural way. Semantic relations ensure tracing of interrelated knowledge. Semantic knowledge modeling can answer diverse questions about persons, their motives and patterns of behavior.

Semantic patterns approach is proposed as a solution to the problem of processing big data.

The approach can effectively capture, store, analyze, and present big data.

The developed semantic-based linguistic platform has been successfully realized in BuzzTalk portal for opinion mining, mood state detection, event extraction, economic activities detection, subject domain recognition, named entity recognition and predictive analytics, thus helping to solve the problem of automated reasoning for decision making. The approach ensures high accuracy, flexibility for customization and future diverse applications for information extraction.

Implementation results show that the proposed knowledge-based approach (with statistical methods involved to prevent unwanted results) is correct and justified and the technique is highly effective.

References

1. Simon, Ph.: Too Big to Ignore: The Business Case for Big Data, 256 p. Wiley, Hoboken (2015)
2. Davenport, Th.: Big Data at Work: Dispelling the Myths, Uncovering the Opportunities, 228 p. Harvard Business Review Press, Boston (2014)
3. Mayer-Schönberger, V., Cukier, K.: Big Data: A Revolution that will Transform How We Live, Work, and Think, 242 p. Houghton Mifflin Harcourt, Boston (2013)
4. Marr, B.: Big Data - Using SMART Big Data, Analytics and Metrics to Make Better Decisions and Improve Performance, 256 p. Wiley, Hoboken (2015)
5. Marr, B.: Data Strategy: How to Profit from a World of Big Data, Analytics and the Internet of Things, 200 p. Kogan Page, London (2017)
6. Moens, M.: Information Extraction: Algorithms and Prospects in a Retrieval Context, 246 p. Springer, Berlin (2006)
7. Baeza-Yates, R., Ribeiro-Neto, B.: Modern Information Retrieval: the Concepts and Technology Behind Search. Addison-Wesley Professional, Boston, 944 p. (2011)
8. Buettcher, S., Clarke, C., Cormack, G.: Information Retrieval: Implementing and Evaluating Search Engines, 632 p. MIT Press, Cambridge (2010)
9. Machová, K., Bednár, P., Mach, M.: Various approaches to web information processing. Comput. Inf. **26**, 301–327 (2007)
10. Khoo, C., Myaeng, S.H.: Identifying semantic relations in text for information retrieval and information extraction. In: Green, R., Bean, C.A., Myaeng, S.H. (eds.) The Semantics of Relationships. Information Science and Knowledge Management. ISKM, vol. 3, pp. 161–180. Springer, Berlin (2002). https://doi.org/10.1007/978-94-017-0073-3_10
11. Bobkov, A., Gafurov, S., Krasnoproshin, V., Romanchik, V., Vissia, H.: Information extraction based on semantic patterns. In: Proceedings of the 12-th International Conference – PRIP 2014, Minsk, pp. 30–35 (2014)
12. Barnbrook, G., Mason, O., Krishnamurthy, R.: Collocation: Applications and Implications, 254 p. Palgrave Macmillan, London (2013)
13. Cruse, D.A.: Lexical Semantics, 310 p. Cambridge University Press, Cambridge (1986)
14. Manning, C.D., Schütze, H.: Foundations of Statistical Natural Language Processing, 620 p. MIT Press, Cambridge (1999)

15. Bilan, V., Bobkov, A., Gafurov, S., Krasnoproshin, V., van de Laar, J., Vissia, H.: An ontology-based approach to opinion mining. In: Proceedings of 10-th International Conference PRIP 2009, Minsk, pp. 257–259 (2009)
16. Fensel, D.: Foundations for the Web of Information and Services: A Review of 20 Years of Semantic Web Research, 416 p. Springer, Berlin (2011)
17. http://www.buzztalkmonitor.com
18. Pang, B., Lee, L.: Opinion Mining and Sentiment Analysis, 148 p. Now Publishers Inc., Boston (2008)
19. Devitt, A., Ahmad, K.: Sentiment analysis in financial news: a cohesion-based approach. In: Proceedings of the Association for Computational Linguistics (ACL 2007), pp. 984–991 (2007)
20. Eguchi, K., Lavrenko, V.: Sentiment retrieval using generative models. In: Proceedings of the Conference on Empirical Methods in Natural Language Processing (EMNLP 2006), pp. 345–354 (2006)
21. Clark, A.V.: Mood State and Health, 213 p. Nova Publishers, Boston (2005)
22. McNair, D.M, Lorr, M., Droppleman, L.F.: Profile of Mood States - San Diego. Educational and Industrial Testing Service, California (1971)
23. Siegel, E.: Predictive Analytics: The Power to Predict Who Will Click, Buy, Lie, or Die, 320 p. Wiley, Hoboken (2013)
24. Mishra, N.: Predictive analytics: a survey, trends, applications, opportunities & challenges. Int. J. Comput. Sci. Inf. Technol. 3, 4434–4438 (2012)
25. Asghar, N.: Automatic extraction of causal relations from natural language texts: a comprehensive survey. arXiv preprint arXiv:1605.07895, May 2016
26. Sorgente, A.: Automatic extraction of cause-effect relations in natural language text. In: Proceedings of the 13th Conference of the Italian Association for Artificial Intelligence, pp. 37–48 (2013)
27. Darian, S.: Cause and effect in a corpus of science textbooks. ESP. Malaysia 4, 65–83 (1996)
28. Khoo, C.S.G.: Automatic identification of causal relations in text and their use for improving precision in information retrieval. Doctoral dissertation, Syracuse University (1995). Dissertation Abstracts International, 5704A, 1364
29. Xuelan, F., Kennedy, G.: Expressing causation in written English. RELC J. 23(1), 62–80 (1992)
30. Chan, K., Lam, W.: Extracting causation knowledge from natural language texts. Int. J. Intell. Syst. 20(3), 327–358 (2005)
31. Radinsky, K., Davidovich, S.: Learning to predict from textual data. J. Artif. Intell. Res. 45, 641–684 (2012)
32. Radinsky, K.: Learning causality for news events prediction. In: Proceedings of the 21st International Conference on World Wide Web ACM, pp. 909–918 (2012)
33. Kaplan, R., Berry-Rogghe, G.: Knowledge-based acquisition of causal relationships in text. Knowl. Acquisition 3(3), 317–337 (1991)
34. Wolff, P., Song, G., Driscoll, D.: Models of causation and causal verbs. In: Meeting of the Chicago Linguistics Society, main session, vol. 1, p. 607–622 (2002)
35. Levin, B., Hovav, M.A.: Preliminary analysis of causative verbs in English. Lingua 92, 35–77 (1994)
36. Altenberg, B.: Causal linking in spoken and written English. Studia Linguistica 38(1), 20–69 (1984)

Video-Based Content Extraction Algorithm from Bank Cards for iOS Mobile Devices

Rykhard Bohush[1]([✉]) [iD], Alexander Kurilovich[1],
and Sergey Ablameyko[2] [iD]

[1] Polotsk State University,
Blokhina Street 29, Novopolotsk, Republic of Belarus
bogushr@mail.ru, cfif921@yandex.ru
[2] Belarusian State University,
Nezavisimosti Avenue 4, Minsk, Republic of Belarus
ablameyko@bsu.by

Abstract. This paper proposes an algorithm for information fields detection and recognition of bank cards in video sequences, obtained from the iOS mobile device camera. For this, we use two basic steps. The first step is preprocessing for localization of symbols. The second step is symbol block recognition using OCR system. Preprocessing algorithm includes card edge detection, information fields segmentation, segments enhancement, symbols edge emphasizing and the final step is symbol block recognition using OCR system. Based on our approach and iPhone SDK frameworks, OpenCV and Tesseract library the bank card details recognition software is implemented. For experiments our database of the real static images and video sequences was used.

Keywords: Bank card · Flexible forms · Video sequences · Card detail recognition · Mobile device

1 Introduction

The rapid growth of wireless technology has increased the number of mobile device users, which in turn has given pace to the fast development of e-commerce. The new type of e-commerce transactions, conducted through mobile devices is called mobile commerce, increasingly known as m-commerce. Mobile commerce takes a special place among innovative systems and gives an opportunity to manage banking account with the help of a mobile device effectively. Many payment apps or websites with bank card forms require manual entry of card details for payment transactions which always creates a monotonous and boring user experience. It is a time-consuming process, which requires attentiveness and diligence. Therefore, algorithms and software development for the recognition of bank card details for mobile devices is relevant.

Bank cards are usually issued by banks. However, designing them may be done by different partner merchants or organizations who partners up with the bank, which gives freedom to their designers. That is why it is impossible to rely on any graphic bank card characteristics. It can have any color and this color can coincide with color of the background on which it is placed. It leads to insufficient contrast at card borders and

S. V. Ablameyko et al. (Eds.): PRIP 2019, CCIS 1055, pp. 180–191, 2019.
https://doi.org/10.1007/978-3-030-35430-5_15

"false" borders or gaps. Glossy surface plastic is the main material of which bank cards are made. It has strong reflective characteristics and with the bright light, it gives highlights and flashings. In addition, if there is not enough light the image can be underexposed.

Bank card is a typical example of document with flexible form, so any data recognition algorithm can be applied during its processing. In [1] an approach for flexible form fields recognition is described using an example of credit card expiration date, which focused on the template search of data fields on card surface. Canny edge detector was used to obtain the rectangular areas and Radon Transform was used for line detection. This approach has a large computational complexity that could hardly be applicable on mobile devices in real time. In [2] an algorithm to detect business card in an image is presented. It is based on the Sobel edge detection method and Hough transformation, which is used to transform detected edges into parametrical form for further processing. However, it also has a large computational cost. The method [3] uses the classical Hough transform to receive a set of traversing lines and perform boundary detection at later stage. But the authors use a very intensive information suppressed technique at first, with downsizing the image to 180×100 and performing watershed transform. All the steps of this method allow document boundaries detection in every frame of a video acquired by a smartphone or a tablet in real time.

There is a description of business cards processing in [4] and there are two stages at the pre-processing step of this algorithm. At the first stage, it excludes background by crude approximation and extracts the business card; at the second stage, the connected components on the card surface are classified. Then there is a process of threshold binarization which separates text from the image background. However, this algorithm can only be applied to simple images without any background or monotone images. Moreover, background text is not taken into account and projective transformations are not made.

In [5] an approach for optical character recognition on Android platform using an example of business card is presented. Otsu adaptive binarization makes an image black-and-white. Then the connected components analysis is used in order to clear the foreground noise and merge potential characters into blobs. With the help of X- and Y-projections of the binary image, the algorithm approximately detects the text lines and characters. After detection all of the possible text lines in the document, Tesseract [6] is used for word recognition line by line.

A very similar method was used in [7]. It also uses a connected component-based approach to detect text in color image and the segmentation is done horizontally and vertically by using histogram projection approach.

Another Business Card processing method for Android with downsizing the input information coupled with classic transformations is considered in [8]. Canny edge detection for small grayscale image and probabilistic Hough line transform to find line segments in the detected edges are used. All the lines are analyzed for intersections and the largest quadrilateral is selected. After that a sliding window with fixed size was used to locate text boundary. Each bounding box is binarized independently using Otsu's method. The classical transformations are performed with the help of OpenCV library, and the OCR system is presented by Tesseract.

Automatic segmentation of business card region is performed by minimizing local-global variation energy in [9]. Based on this, so-called boundary "chain code" of the business card image region and the binary masks of both the business card and background regions are formed. Then, the algorithm fits a quadrangle on the business card region. This step will identify four corner points of the quadrangle shaped business card region. With the four corner points, they estimate the physical aspect ratio of the business card, thus rectify it to be rectangular by homography.

Using video instead of static images can improve content detection and recognition of bank cards. Because the usage of video sequences allows to process bank card image for a sufficiently large number of times, which is an advantage compared to using static images. Video sequences are less susceptible to incorrect orientation, as well as lack of brightness and glare. Using this approach we can significantly increase probability of positive recognitions.

This paper is organized as follows. In Sect. 2, a bank card content detection and recognition algorithm for video sequences obtained by mobile device video camera is illustrated. A software implementation description, the process of determining algorithm constants, experimental results using database of bank cards for content recognition and comparison of our approach and CardIO SDK are presented in Sect. 3. Finally, in Sect. 4, the conclusion and future work are provided.

2 Algorithm Description

The proposed algorithm for Bank Cards Details Recognition in iOS Mobile Devices is a group of different modules that require the following steps described below.

A frame sequence obtained from the mobile video camera is given on the input of the rectangles detection block. This block detects all the rectangles in the frame and returns only that variant that satisfies the conditions of a bank card. The rectangular area is converted into grayscale and sent to segmentation block, in which the card image is separated into parts by the type of information fields. The next block carries out some transformations that improve contrast qualities of the input images and reduce the noise. Then the adaptive binarization coupled with morphological operations is applied to reduce the amount of information and calculations. After this, the sliding window is applied to images to accurately determine the symbol boundaries. Next, the separated and adjusted regions are sent to the OCR system block for the textual data extracting. Finally, the data evaluation block processes this information to obtain the result of card details recognition.

2.1 Card Detection

The input for the algorithm is a video stream received from a video camera of mobile device. Given the characteristics of iPhone 6, the camera has an 8-megapixel CCD and dual-LED flash. The frame size can vary depending on particular device model, and can reach 3840×2160 pixels. The operating system is capable of automatically holding focus, adjusting brightness and white balance. These indicate that the image received directly from the camera will have effective parameters: depth of field, brightness, sufficient frame size for accurate perception of bank card details.

Separation of bank card image from background is carried out with algorithms based on Viola-Jones high-speed object detection method [10] and deep learning technique using the OverFeat method [11].

The main selection criterion from set of detected rectangles R, where the number of founded rectangular areas - N, is a ratio of its sides. Because, dimensions of a card sides $m_0 \times n_0$, the ratio of its sides is a constant value $\frac{n_0}{m_0}$. At the first, we represent the object of the found rectangle r_i as $R_i(m_i, n_i)$, where $i = 0, 1, ..., N-1$. Then all the rectangles belong to the regions of interest if they satisfy the condition:

$$\frac{n_i}{m_i} = \frac{n_0}{m_0}.$$

(1)

The rectangle with the longest side n_{max} among all selected is the exact match. The size of the rectangular region $r_0(m_{max}, n_{max})$ and its location relative to the whole image $p_0(x_0, y_0)$ are used to extract the card region from the original frame.

2.2   Regions of Interest Segmentation

Regions of interest (ROI), which contain information about the bank card number, the expiration date, the cardholder name, are being separated from the card image I with size $m_{max} \times n_{max}$ (further as $m_I \times n_I$). The size and location of these regions are defined by ISO/IEC7811-5.4:2018 and can be written as:

$C(x_C, y_C, n_C, m_C)$ - the bank card number;
$D(x_D, y_D, n_D, m_D)$ - the expiration date;
$E(x_E, y_E, n_E, m_E)$ - cardholder name.

Because obtained image size $m_I \times n_I$ of a card I can vary, it is necessary to convert C, D and E to forms that will be applicable for their correct extraction from I. This requires defining two scaling factors, by width (2) and by height (3) as:

$$C_{scale.width} = \frac{n_I}{n_0},$$

(2)

$$C_{scale.height} = \frac{m_I}{m_0},$$

(3)

Multiplying each parameter of these regions by the corresponding scaling factor, we can obtain the size of these regions relative to the size of input card I: C_I, D_I, E_I.

Receiving fragments of the regions C_I, D_I, E_I from the bank card image I, we extract images for card number (I_C), expiration date (I_D) and cardholder name (I_E).

A bank card number contains 16 digits distributed into 4 groups, with 4 digits each. Based on this, I_C selected in the previous step with the card number region C_I is being divided into 4 equal regions $C_{I1}, C_{I2}, C_{I3}, C_{I4}$:

$$C_{ij}\left(x_{CI} + \left(\frac{n_{CI}}{4} \times (j-1)\right), y_{CI}, \frac{n_{CI}}{4}, m_{CI}\right),$$

(4)

For $j = 1, 2, 3, 4$ we extract images I_{C1}, I_{C2}, I_{C3}, and I_{C4}, known as card number groups, respectively.

2.3   Image Segment Enhancement

Image enhancement belongs to image preprocessing methods. The first step is to convert an image to grayscale. After that, in order to increase the contrast between the symbol contours and the background, we should make some adjustments of the image.

There are several basic methods for contrast adjustment: linear contrast enhancement, histogram normalization, histogram equalization, etc.

Histogram equalization is a nonlinear process aimed to highlight image brightness in a way more suited for human visual analysis than for this task. It leads to an output image with after histogram, where all levels are equiprobable. In addition, subtle details and noise may appear on the image. All of the above are contrary to the current purpose - to increase the difference in brightness between the characters and card background.

The linear contrast enhancement method takes into account the brightness value for all pixels in the original image. This gives insufficient contrasting effect for cases with low-contrast images that have pronounced intensity areas on the histogram, and smooth attenuation regions. Therefore, it also cannot be applied.

Histogram normalization is the most effective method for our task, because it does not stretch the entire intensity range, but only the most informative part. This approach allows us not to consider all the extremal brightness values but to designate the conditions for their determination with a given accuracy; it enhances contrast effect due to loss of noise regions with rarely encountered intensities [12].

According to the current brightness Y of each image pixel, the output brightness g is defined as:

$$g_{x,y} = \frac{255 \cdot \left(Y_{x,y} - Y_{\min}\right)}{Y_{\max} - Y_{\min}},$$

(5)

where x, y - coordinates, Y_{min} - the minimum input brightness and Y_{max} the maximum input brightness.

To improve the processing results, it is allowed to deviate Y_{min} and Y_{max} from their immediate values, adjusting them by a certain percentage within the specified margin of error. This allows us to neglect an insignificant number of noise pixels along the edges of the histogram. Y_{minadj} and Y_{maxadj} values can be defined as:

$$Y_{\text{minadj}}(i) = \begin{cases} Y_{\text{minadj}}(i+1), & if \sum_{j=0}^{i} f_{total}(Y_j) < T; \\ Y_i, & otherwise, \end{cases}$$

(6)

where $i = 0 \ldots 255$.

$$Y_{\text{maxadj}}(i) = \begin{cases} Y_{\text{maxadj}}(i-1), & if \sum_{j=255}^{i} f_{total}(Y_j) < T; \\ Y_i, & otherwise, \end{cases}$$

(7)

where $i = 255 \ldots 0$. The f_{total} is a function for pixel counting in an image with a specified brightness Y_j. With an error margin of $e(\%)$ and image size of $m \times n$, the threshold T is define as:

$$T = m \cdot n \cdot e. \tag{8}$$

To determine hue of background and symbols, we calculate the average gray value Y_{aver}. The $Y_{aver\psi} > \psi\,127$ means background color is light and symbols color is dark, and vice versa. To emphasize the edges of symbols, mathematical morphology is used [13].

If the color of the symbols is light, morphological transformation is based on the WhiteTopHat. It subtracts the open image from the original:

$$T_w(I) = I - I \circ b, \tag{9}$$

where I - original image, b - structuring element. This filter emphasizes edge details of light symbols.

The BlackTopHat is used to emphasize dark symbols. The filter subtracts the original image from the closed:

$$T_w(I) = I \bullet b - I. \tag{10}$$

The kernel b of both filters has a rectangular shape and the $(n_b \times m_b)$ size, calculated as:

$$n_b = n_l \cdot 0.06; \; m_b = \frac{n_b}{3}, \tag{11}$$

where n_l is an image width.

2.4 Binarization

The next step is binarization of the given segments. Radical reduction in the amount of information is the main purpose of this operation. Given that symbol boundaries should be preserved, we choose the method of image binarization with an adaptive threshold, based on local region analysis.

Since the background of bank cards is very diverse, the brightness level of the background areas containing symbols can vary significantly throughout the image. This means that binarization methods with global thresholding technique are not suitable for solving this problem. Because they do not take into account the characteristics of neighborhood points, this affects the quality of the result. Binarization with an adaptive threshold based on local region analysis is described as [14]:

$$bin_{x,y} = \begin{cases} g_{\max}, & \text{if } Y_{x,y} > T(x,y); \\ 0, & \text{otherwise}, \end{cases} \tag{12}$$

where $Y_{x,y}$ is the brightness of $I(x, y)$, $g_{max} = 255$ and $T(x, y)$ is a threshold. The value of $T(x, y)$ is considered individually for each pixel as a weighted sum (cross-correlation with a Gaussian window) of the $block\_size \times block\_size$ neighborhood of (x, y) minus c. Gaussian window coefficient matrix with size $block_{size} \times 1$ is calculated as:

$$G_i = \alpha \cdot e^{-\frac{\left(i - \frac{(block_{size} - 1)}{2}\right)}{2 \cdot \sigma^2}}, \tag{13}$$

$$\sigma = 0.3 \cdot ((block_{size} - 1) \cdot 0.5 - 1) + 0.8, \tag{14}$$

where $i = 0 \ldots block_{size} - 1$, and α is the scale factor chosen so that $\sum_i Ci = 1$ [15].

To reduce the noise and remove non-informative details from the binary image, and also to isolate the symbols from the background, morphological operations of closing and erosion are applied.

The both filter kernels b have an ellipse shape, which is better applied for OCR-B symbols (ISO/IEC 7811-6.1:2018). The kernel size is $n_b \times n_b$, where n_b - should not exceed $(1/3)$ of the symbol thickness ($w_{symb}/3$). Otherwise, there is a probability of losing symbol outline during processing. Otherwise, there is a probability of losing symbol outline during processing.

The symbol thickness w_{symb} doesn't depend on the card fragment, and it is strictly specified for OCR-B. The font size projection (mm) to the size in pixels, relative to the full bank card region size is constant and calculated based on its full width as:

$$h = \frac{H \cdot m_0}{54}, \tag{15}$$

2.5   Symbol Localization

To localize the symbol edges, the vertical sliding window method is used. The height of the window varies according to the font size, H_{cn} - card number font size (4,0 mm), H_{exd} - expire date font size (2,85 mm), H_{hn} - cardholder's name font size (2,65 mm). Then its projections onto a height (px) relative to the size of the full card region are: h_{cn}, h_{exd}, h_{hn}. The general form of the calculation is represented:

$$w_{symb} = n_0 \cdot 0.004884. \tag{16}$$

where 54 mm is the card height (ISO/IEC 7811-6.3:2018), and m_0 is height of detected region of card (px).

Localized symbol area from the previous step, black and white symbol lists and language identifier for the card are sequentially transmitted to the Tesseract OCR system.

A white list consisting of a set of numbers from 0 to 9 and the language identifier "eng" are transmitted as parameters for a card number image. For an expiration date image: numbers from 0 to 9 and the symbol "/" form white list, "eng" is the language identifier. For a cardholder name image: "rus" and "eng" are language identifiers and a set of characters including punctuation marks, special characters and numbers form a black list. This approach will contribute to increasing the recognition rate and accelerating all the process.

3 Experimental Results

3.1 Software Implementation

The proposed approach is implemented using Objective-C programming language, and based on OpenCV 2.4.13 computer vision library, Tesseract OCR system and iPhone SDK frameworks, such as: CoreMedia and AVFoundation - media data management; UIKit - work with application interfaces; CoreGraphics - low-level, lightweight processing of 2D images based on the Quartz engine.

Video stream capture by the main device camera, using the AVFoundation framework, and the frame processing operations are implemented in separate threads with NSOperationQueue. The video data frequency is 30 fps (frames per second). The first thread obtains video frames and puts them in serial queue for processing if the last one is not busy. Otherwise, received frames are ignored. The second thread sequentially receives frames from the capture queue and starts processing them until the results are obtained. After the algorithm is finished the current frame is removed, the queue is freed and the processing iteration is repeated for new frame.

Tesseract OCR library also performs its calculations asynchronously in the background. After the algorithm is finished, we get the results using callback function in the main thread and display them in the user interface.

The mobile application interface is shown in Fig. 1.

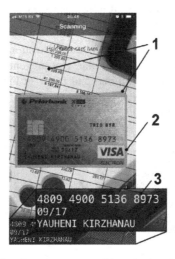

Fig. 1. Our mobile app interface for content recognition: 1 - the viewing area; 2 - highlighting of bank card successful detection; 3 - the data output area (Color figure online)

The interface is equipped with an image viewing area, captured by the mobile device camera in real-time, a data output area, a mark of successful fixation on the recognition object. The capture area has a proportion of 4:3, which is the standard for a vertically oriented iPhone. The data output area contains three text fields, arranged vertically. Information recognized by the algorithm (card number, expiration date, cardholder name) is sequentially displayed therein. The card detection mark is made in the form of a bright green rectangle with a fixed thickness of borders. When a bank card position is successfully determined the mark repeats its boundaries.

3.2   Content Extraction and Recognition

The proposed algorithm has been evaluated using data set utilizing the images and video snippets having real bank card pictorial with ground-truths and degradations. Especially for algorithm result evaluation a database of 180 static test images with characteristics and final results known in advance was formed. Figure 2 presents the results of correct card detection and recognition, (b) – (d) show that the card area is intersected by the external contour of foreign objects (b, d - fingers; c - pen). But this does not affect the detection of the card and the further recognition process.

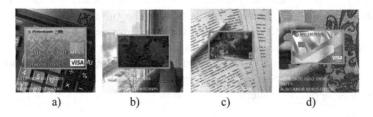

a)   b)   c)   d)

Fig. 2. Examples of correct detection and recognition of bank cards

Figure 3 shows some error examples for card detection and recognition. Colors of card surface and background are very similar, that prevent to recognize its borders in Fig. 3a and b. The input image is blurred and fuzzy in Fig. 3c. There is not enough light and the image is underexposed, furthermore color of symbols is completely the same as the background in Fig. 3d.

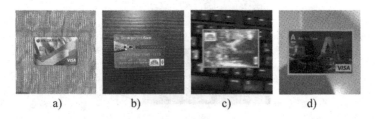

a)   b)   c)   d)

Fig. 3. Examples for bank cards detection and recognition with errors (Color figure online)

From the experimental data it can be seen that a number of drawbacks inherent in static images are partially applicable to video sequences. For example, the completely damaged characters of the card number cannot be identified in the video as well, and the problem of matching the background also remains. Video sequences are less susceptible to problems with incorrect orientation, low light conditions and the presence of flares.

Table 1 shows partial results of the study of card data recognizing process in video sequences. The first column of the table contains examples of test video sequences frames. The second column reflects the number of frames from their total number on which the card region was successfully detected with the algorithm. The third column contains data on the number of frames in which all card details were recognized correctly, compared with the total number of frames. And the last column reflects the time from the start of the frame processing to the first correct result.

Table 1. Algorithm experimental results

Frame image	Card detected (frame count)	Symbols are recognized correctly (frame count)/total frame count	The total time processing (ms)
	22	9 / 90	1217
	-	- / 90	-
	26	10 / 90	1221
	23	10 / 90	1284
	26	11 / 90	1149
	31	13 / 90	1265
	24	- / 90	-
	21	7 / 90	1344
	-	- / 90	-

The results show acceptable adaptation into different defect types such as noise, resolution and illumination changes. Our algorithm showed robust behavior in most situations and performed rather well against the comparison techniques. For example,

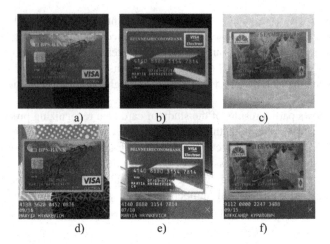

Fig. 4. Content card bank extraction: (a, b, c) using CardIO SDK; (d, e, f) using proposed algorithm

the results presented in this paper were compared with the well-known CardIO SDK [16] and proved our method superiority in recognizing cards with Cyrillic and non-embossing characters, as can be seen from the Fig. 4.

4 Conclusion

In the paper, we have developed a fairly accurate and effective methodology for bank card information recognition. The proposed algorithm, represents the processing of frame sequence received from the mobile device camera and includes: bank card detection using the Viola-Jones high-speed object detection algorithm and the OverFeat method; ROI segmentation; improving the quality of symbols using the method of histogram normalization and morphological transformations TopHat; emphasizing the boundaries of symbols using the binarization with the adaptive threshold, performing morphological transformations on the results and searching for the most suitable region using a vertically sliding window. The Tesseract OCR engine is used to recognize characters within determined and adjusted text regions.

During the experiments, it was observed that the developed algorithm is robust to difficult conditions such as various backgrounds, light reflections and card borders, partially occluded by the user's hand, moreover, there are no false detections along with card movement. It was further noted that the performance of Tesseract OCR engine is highly dependent on the quality of the preprocessed image.

The developed preprocessing algorithm works reasonably well. It is worth noting that when we deal with symbols located on a background with low contrast, the qualitative characteristics of the algorithm are reduced. In further work, the algorithm needs to improve the quality characteristics for a low-contrast card background.

References

1. Sheshkus, A., Nikolaev, D., Ingacheva, A., Skoryukina, N.: Approach to the recognition of flexible forms on the example of the credit card date recognition. In: Proceedings SPIE 9875, Eighth International Conference on Machine Vision (ICMV 2015), Barcelona, pp. 83–88 (2015)
2. Christian, T., Gustavsson, D.: Content recognition of business cards. In: Summer Project, IT University of Copenhagen, Copenhagen (2007)
3. Puybareau, E., Geraud, T.: Real-time document detection in smartphone videos. In: Proceedings of the 24th IEEE International Conference on Image Processing (ICIP), France, pp. 1498–1502 (2018)
4. Mollah, A., Basu, S., Das, N., Sarkar, R., Nasipuri, M., Kundu, M: Text region extraction from business card images for mobile devices. In: Proceedings of International Conference on Information Technology and Business Intelligence (ITBI-09), Nagpur, pp. 227–235 (2009)
5. Bhaskar, S., Lavassar, N., Green, S.: Implementing optical character recognition on the android operating system for business cards. In: IEEE 2010, EE 368 Digital Image Processing, pp. 1–5 (2010)
6. Smith, R.: An overview of the tesseract OCR engine. In: Proceedings of Ninth International Conference on Document Analysis and Recognition (ICDAR), Curitiba, Paraná, pp. 629–633 (2007)
7. Ryan, M., Hanafiah, N.: An examination of character recognition on ID card using template matching approach. In: International Conference on Computer Science and Computational Intelligence (ICCSCI 2015), Jakarta, pp. 520–529 (2015)
8. Sharma, P., Fujii, K.: Automatic Contact Importer from Business Cards for Android. Stanford University, Stanford (2013)
9. Hua, G., Liu, Z., Zhang, Z., Wu, Y.: Automatic business card scanning with a camera. In: Processing of International Conference on Image Processing, Atlanta, pp. 373–376 (2006)
10. Viola, P., Jones, M.: Rapid object detection using a boosted cascade of simple features. In: Proceedings of the 2001 IEEE Computer Society Conference on Computer Vision and Pattern Recognition, Kauai, pp. 511–519 (2001)
11. Sermanet, P., Eigen, D., Zhang, X., Mathieu, M., Fergus, R., LeCun Y.: OverFeat: integrated recognition, localization and detection using convolutional networks. In: Processing of International Conference on Learning Representations (ICLR), Banff, Canada, pp. 1055–1061 (2014)
12. Bovyrin, A., et al.: Development of Multimedia Applications Using OpenCV and IPP Libraries. Course of the Intel Academy, Nizhny Novgorod (2017)
13. Gonzalez, R., Woods, R.: Digital Image Processing, 4th edn. Pearson Education, New Delhi (2017)
14. Singh, R., Roy, S., Singh, I., Sinam, T., Singh, M.: A new local adaptive thresholding technique in binarization. IJCSI Int. J. Comput. Sci. Issues **8**(6), 271–277 (2011)
15. Bradski, G., Kaehler, A.: Learning OpenCV 3 Computer Vision in C++ with the OpenCV Library, 2nd edn. O'Reilly Media, Sebastopol (2016)
16. CardIO official site. https://www.card.io. Accessed 24 Jan 2019

Detection of Bulbar Dysfunction in ALS Patients Based on Running Speech Test

Maxim Vashkevich[1]($\boxtimes$) (iD), Artyom Gvozdovich[1], and Yuliya Rushkevich[2] (iD)

[1] Belarusian State University of Informatics and Radioelectronics,
220013 Minsk, Belarus
vashkevich@bsuir.by

[2] Republican Research and Clinical Center of Neurology and Neurosurgery,
220114 Minsk, Belarus

Abstract. This paper deals with detection of speech changes due to amyotrophic lateral sclerosis (ALS) – fatal neurological disease with no cure. The detection process is based on analysis of running speech test. However, in contrast to conventional frame-based classification (in which whole signal is analysed) we proposed to use selected vowels extracted from the test signal. It is shown that similarity of spectral envelopes of different vowels and formant frequencies are crucial features for bulbar ALS detection. Applying the proposed features to classifier base on linear discriminant analysis (LDA) the detection accuracy of 84.8% is achieved.

Keywords: Amyotrophic lateral sclerosis · ALS bulbar dysfunction · ALS detection · Voice pathology identification

1 Introduction

Amyotrophic Lateral Sclerosis (ALS) is an incurable, neurodegenerative disease with a fast progressing course. Motor neuron deterioration (due to ALS) leads to decreasing muscle function and resulting in problems with movement, breathing, speech and swallowing [5]. The disease is referred to as limb (or spinal) ALS when the first symptoms appear in the arms or legs. The other type is bulbar ALS when first symptoms are changes in voice, speech and problems with swallowing. At the time of diagnosis, up to 30% of patients with ALS present with bulbar symptoms [5]. Also difficulty with speech is the first symptoms in approximately 30% of persons with ALS [16]. This difficulty with speech is referred to as dysarthria. Dysarthria is motor disorder of speech characterized by abnormalities of the articulation and intelligibility of speech, phonation and rate of facial movements can also be affected. However, symptoms of dysarthria may not be evident until about 80% of motor neurons are lost [17].

Despite the fact that bulbar symptoms significantly impact the quality of life no standardized bulbar ALS-specific test exists, besides the part of ALSFRSR for speech and swallowing. The detection of the ALS bulbar dysfunctions provokes numerous problems especially on early ALS stages.

© Springer Nature Switzerland AG 2019
S. V. Ablameyko et al. (Eds.): PRIP 2019, CCIS 1055, pp. 192–204, 2019.
https://doi.org/10.1007/978-3-030-35430-5_16

Thus objective bulbar and speech motor assessment tools are needed for improving early disease detection [17, 18]. Such tools can also be used for monitoring disease progression, and optimizing the efficacy of ALS drug trials [8, 12].

In previous studies different approaches are used for ALS detection. One of them is to determine the type of dysarthria and then make the decision about presents ALS-bulbar changes. There are five main types of dysarthrias: Flaccid dysarthria (FD), Spastic dysarthria (SD), Ataxic dysarthria (AD), Hypokinetic dysarthria (HP) and Hyperkinetic dysarthria (HPD). It is known that ALS dysarthria is a combination of FD and SD [17]. In [2] dysarthria classifier designed based on neural network self-organizing maps is achieved an accuracy of 85.8%. The drawback of this approach is that it incorporates subjective measures that require perceptual ratings by an expert diagnostician. One more problem is to collect a representative dataset for all types of dysarthrias. Another approach to ALS detection is to use specific databased containing ALS and normal speech samples. In this case, different acoustic features are extracted from speech that is used for classification by support vector machine (SVM) [9, 12] or deep neural network (DNN) [9]. Typically, clinical assessment requires the reading of specially-designed passages to elicit dysarthria. Such a *running* (or continuous) speech test often used for automatic ALS [12] or other voice pathology detection [3]. For classification the speech is separated by frames and feature vector calculated for each frame. Initial classification is performed for each frame. To get a robust decision from classifier, the predicted class decisions from all extracted feature vectors are combined using majority voting to obtain one decision for given test recording [12]. This approach is referred to as frame-based classification [3]. In this work we proposed another approach to detect ALS bulbar changes based only on the part of running speech test containing vowels. Using vowels extracted from the continuous speech results in a good accuracy of 84.8% using linear classifier based on linear discriminant analysis (LDA) with only one feature. Also our research reveals important changes in formant structure of ALS speech.

2 Speech Analysis

2.1 Running Speech Test

According to the idea of this research for detection of bulbar motor changes only part of running speech test containing vowels can be used. In [18] an analysis and selection of suitable vowels have been made. It has been shown that vowels /i/ and /æ/ are the most appropriate choice for ALS dysarthria detection since their pronouncing requires a considerable efforts of tongue muscles.

In our experiments we use speech records with counting from 1 to 3 (in Russian). For the analysis we have selected close in time fragments of speech signal containing the vowels /æ/ and /i/, (sounds were selected from the sentence "ædin, dvæ, tri".

2.2 Dynamic Time Warping (DTW)

For automatic marking (and selection) of the needed vowels from speech test recording the dynamic time warping (DTW) algorithm was used [6,14]. The DTW algorithm performs the "alignment" of two time sequences through a timeline transformation based on the similarity between the elements of two sequences. This means that, having the marked boundaries of vowels in one reference (or etalon) signal, and having performed the alignment with analysed signal, it is possible to obtain the boundaries of vowels in the analysed signal.

The reference and input signals are divided into frames following with short-time Fourier transform (STFT) calculation. Thus, the input for the DTW algorithm are two sequences of vectors: $S = (\mathbf{s}_1, \mathbf{s}_2, \ldots, \mathbf{s}_n)$ and $T = (\mathbf{t}_1, \mathbf{t}_2, \ldots, \mathbf{t}_m)$, where each vector is the STFT of corresponding frame. In general, the lengths of the sequences are not equal, since each speaker pronounces a test phrase with a different rate. At the first stage, local distances between the elements of two sequences are calculated:

$$D_{i,j} = \sum_{k=1}^{P} |\mathbf{s}_{i,k} - \mathbf{t}_{j,k}|, \quad i = 1, \ldots, n, \ j = 1, \ldots, m, \tag{1}$$

where P – number of the points in frequency domain.

At the second stage, the global distance matrix is calculated based on the relation:

$$Q_{i,j} = D_{i,j} + \min(Q_{i-1,j}, \ Q_{i-1,j-1}, \ Q_{i,j-1}). \tag{2}$$

An example of global distance matrix is given in Fig. 1. Etalon signal S and analysed signal T are presented in the form of spectrograms. The global distance matrix is graphically presented in the centre of the figure. Blue colour means small distances between signal frames, and red one means a long distance.

At the third stage, the optimal deformation path is constructed [13], which minimizes the distance between S and T establishes the correspondence between them (see Fig. 1).

As a result of the algorithm, two signals are matched due to which we can get the boundaries of vowels /i/ and /æ/ in the input signal. Practical experiments with described algorithms reveals that to be more robust in vowels selection two practical tricks can be helpful:

- the sex of speaker in etalon record should be the same as in analysed signal (therefore there are two etalon signals (male and female) need to be prepared);
- a regularization term need to be add to Eq. (2):

$$Q_{i,j} = D_{i,j} + \min(Q_{i-1,j}, \ Q_{i-1,j-1}, \ Q_{i,j-1}) + \lambda \left| i - j\frac{n}{m} \right|, \tag{3}$$

where λ – regularization parameter, n – length of the sequence S, m – length of the sequence T. In our experiments we have used $\lambda = 0.075$.

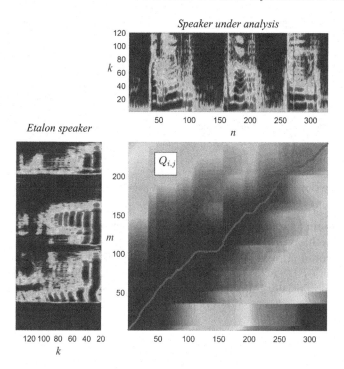

Fig. 1. Matrix of global distance $Q_{i,j}$ and optimal deformation path (red line) (color figure online)

3   Feature Extraction

When vowels are extracted from running speech test they passed to feature extraction stage.

In [18] distance between spectral envelopes of the vowels /i/ and /æ/ has been used as highly informative feature:

$$d_1(E_i, E_a) = \sum_{k=1}^{P} |E_i(k) - E_a(k)|, \tag{4}$$

where $E_i(k)$ is envelope of the vowel /i/, $E_a(k)$ – envelope of the vowel /æ/, P – the number of points in frequency domain. The rationale of using (4) is that dysarthria in ALS (as stated in [17]) is characterized by "abnormal vowel production", "distorted vowels" and "monoloudness". Thus it can be expected that $d_1(E_i, E_a)$ measure would be greater for healthy voices and smaller for pathological voices. Examples of envelopes with a high degree of similarity is given in Fig. 2b, example of vowels from healthy individual are shown in Fig. 2a.

We also use information about formant structure of the speech. In [8] it has been shown that reduced second formant trajectory is characteristic for ALS speech. In [18] has been shown that mutual location of the formants of vowels /i/

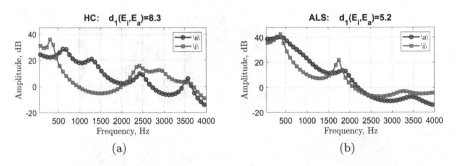

Fig. 2. Envelopes of vowels /æ/ and /i/: (a) healthy speaker; (b) ALS patient

and /æ/ contains important information for detection of bulbar motor changes in speech. In this work we decide to consider separately location 1st and 2nd formants of vowel /i/ and /æ/ as a feature for pathology detection. The location of the formants $F1_a$, $F2_a$, $F1_i$ and $F2_i$ is done using LPC analysis [1].

Another potentially informative feature for pathology detection is formant convergence for vowels /i/ and /æ/ [11]. In this work we consider two following parameters:

$$F1_{conv} = |F1_i - F1_a|, \tag{5}$$

$$F2_{conv} = |F2_i - F2_a|. \tag{6}$$

We also used voice quality parameter – breathiness that is estimated as difference between the amplitude of the first harmonic ($h1$) and the third formant ($a3$) [7]:

$$h1a3 = h1 - a3. \tag{7}$$

Parameter $h1a3$ is calculated for both vowels /æ/ and /i/.

4   Classification

4.1   Linear Discriminant Analysis

For classification normal and pathological cases, we use linear discriminant analysis (LDA) [15]. Classification function for LDA is

$$f(\mathbf{x}) = \mathrm{sgn}(\langle \mathbf{w}, \mathbf{x} \rangle + b), \tag{8}$$

where $\mathbf{x}$ – feature vector, $\langle \cdot \rangle$ – dot product, b is a bias and $\mathbf{w}$ – weight vector, that is chosen according to Fisher criterion to maximize the quotient

$$J(\mathbf{w}) = \frac{(\mu_{\mathbf{w}}^+ - \mu_{\mathbf{w}}^-)^2}{(\sigma_{\mathbf{w}}^+)^2 + (\sigma_{\mathbf{w}}^-)^2}, \tag{9}$$

where $\mu_{\mathbf{w}}^+$ and $\mu_{\mathbf{w}}^-$ are the mean of the projections of the positive and negative samples onto direction $\mathbf{w}$, $\sigma_{\mathbf{w}}^+$ and $\sigma_{\mathbf{w}}^-$ are the corresponding standard deviations. Thus Fisher criterion minimizes the within-class variance and maximizes the between-class variance. Practical guidance for calculating $\mathbf{w}$ and b using eigenvalue decomposition can be found in [15].

4.2   Classifier Validation

The goal of validation is to estimate of the generalization performance of the classification based on the selected set of features, when presented new (previously unseen) data. Most studies uses cross-validation to achieve this goal [3,9,12].

To determine the accuracy of the proposed ALS detector we used k-fold cross validation method [10], with k equal to 5. At the beginning, the training set was randomly mixed, then the training procedure was performed based on 80% of the data, the remaining 20% were used for testing. This procedure was repeated 40 times, then the mean value and the standard deviation were calculated for the accuracy parameters.

The obtained ALS detectors were compared using parameters such as overall accuracy (Acc), sensitivity (Sens), specificity (Spec):

$$Acc = \frac{TP + TN}{TP + FP + FN + TN}$$
$$Sens = \frac{TP}{TP + FN}$$
$$Spec = \frac{TN}{TN + FP}$$

where TP, TN, FP, FN – the number of true positive, true negative, false positive and false negative results of classification, respectively. In this case, positive means a prediction that the voice sample is produced by a speaker with ALS.

Receiver operating characteristic (ROC) curves were also used to represent graphically the performance of the proposed classifiers [4]. The ROC curve reveals the diagnostic accuracy expressed in terms of sensitivity and 1-specificity. Also the area under the ROC curve (AUC) was calculated, representing the ability of a classifier to rank a randomly chosen positive test example higher than a negative one. In this respect, this is equivalent to Wilcoxon's Rank Sum test (also known as the Mann-Whitney U test).

5   Experiments

Verification of the proposed ALS detection algorithm was performed using real world clinical samples. Speech recording of Russian speaking patients with ALS was carried out in Republican Research and Clinical Center of Neurology and Neurosurgery (Minsk, Belarus). Our previous work on ALS detection [18] used a dataset that contains the non-age-matched healthy controls, which may introduce a bias in classification performance. In this study we have recorded 30 speakers, with 15 healthy (7 males, 8 females) and 15 ALS patients (9 males, 6 females). The average age in the healthy group was 53.8 years (SD 9.2, Min 33, Max 64) and the average age in the ALS group was 54.1 years (SD 9.3, Min 33,

Max 66). The samples recorded at 44.1 kHz using smartphone with a standard headset and stored as 16 bit uncompressed PCM files.

To characterize the speech of ALS patients and healthy speakers we extract features (described above) and study their statistics. Box plot and kernel density function (the estimation of probability density function) for $d_1(E_i, E_a)$ is shown in Fig. 3. It can be seen that d_1 performs well making good separation between classes.

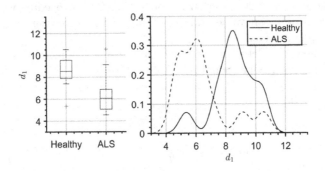

Fig. 3. Distance between envelopes $d_1(E_i, E_a)$: box plot and kernel density function

In Figs. 4 and 5 statistics of formants for the vowel /æ/ are given. The separation between classes is not so good as in previous case, however we can observed, that the variance of formant location for ALS patients is smaller than in healthy group.

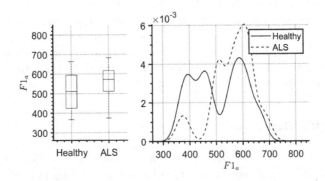

Fig. 4. First formant of the vowel /æ/: box plot and kernel density function

Figures 6 and 7 characterizes statistics of the formant for vowel /i/. First formant in both groups shows almost the same distribution. However, the second formant shows a good separation between classes.

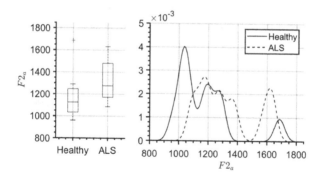

Fig. 5. Second formant of the vowel /æ/: box plot and kernel density function

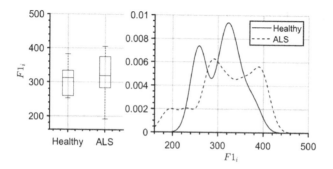

Fig. 6. First formant of the vowel /i/: box plot and kernel density function

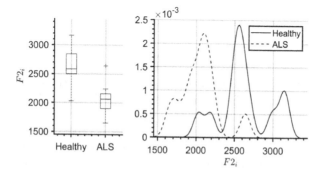

Fig. 7. Second formant of the vowel /i/: box plot and kernel density function

Figures 8 and 9 characterizes statistics of the formants convergence. There is no significant information in feature $F1_{conv}$. But $F2_{conv}$ shows significant difference between healthy and ALS groups. Partly it is due to $F2_{conv}$ contains information about $F2_i$.

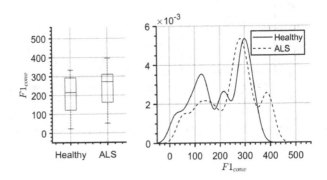

Fig. 8. First formants convergence: box plot and kernel density function

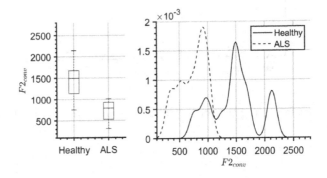

Fig. 9. Second formants convergence: box plot and kernel density function

In Figs. 10 and 11 statistics of $h1a3$ feature are given. It can be seen that $h1a3_i$ gives better separation between the ALS and healthy controls. There is no significant information in feature $h1a3_a$.

In order to find feature set that gives the best classification results we have performed exhaustive search of all feature subsets. It is possible since total number of features is $n = 9$ and therefore the number of possible combination is $2^n = 512$. In Table 1 ten best results is given. It can be seen that highest accuracy is obtained using only one feature $F2_i$. However, using additional features (rows 2 and 3 in Table 1) helps to get classifiers with highest sensitivity and specificity.

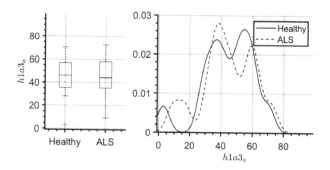

Fig. 10. Breathiness estimation ($h1a3$), vowel /æ/: box plot and kernel density function

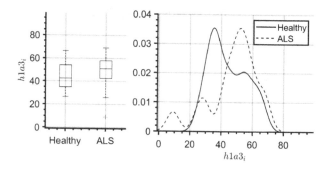

Fig. 11. Breathiness estimation ($h1a3$), vowel /i/: box plot and kernel density function

Table 1. Classification results

Feature vector	Accuracy, %	Sensitivity, %	Specificity, %
$[F2_i]$	**84.8 ± 3.5**	88.3 ± 5.8	81.2 ± 3.0
$[d_1\ F2_i]$	83.1 ± 3.7	**89.3 ± 5.0**	76.9 ± 4.8
$[d_1\ F2_{conv}]$	82.8 ± 3.6	75.2 ± 5.6	**90.3 ± 5.2**
$[d_1\ F1_{conv}\ F2_{conv}]$	82.5 ± 3.6	78.5 ± 5.9	86.5 ± 3.8
$[F1_i\ F2_i]$	82.5 ± 3.7	84.2 ± 7.3	80.8 ± 2.7
$[F1_a\ F2_i]$	82.4 ± 3.8	86.7 ± 6.0	78.2 ± 3.7
$[d_1\ F2_i\ h1a3_a]$	82.3 ± 4.2	88.7 ± 5.7	76.0 ± 5.0
$[F2_i\ h1a3_a]$	81.9 ± 4.1	85.8 ± 7.1	78.0 ± 3.4
$[d_1\ F2_i\ h1a3_i]$	81.8 ± 4.7	82.8 ± 8.3	80.8 ± 6.3
$[d_1\ F1_a\ F2_i]$	81.7 ± 4.1	88.0 ± 6.1	75.5 ± 5.1

In Fig. 12 ROC curves for classifiers with highest accuracy, sensitivity and specificity are given. In is inserting that classifier with hist accuracy gives the lowest AUC.

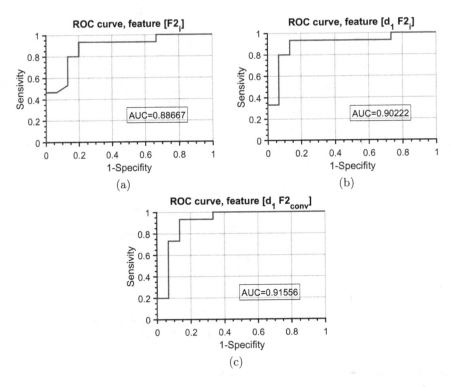

Fig. 12. ROC curves :(a) feature $[F2_i]$; (b) features $[d_1 \ F2_i]$; (c) $[d_1 \ F2_{conv}]$

6 Conclusion

The paper presented an approach to automatic detection of bulbar ALS changes using running speech signal analysis. In contrast to traditional frame-based method in which whole test signal is used for classification we proposed to use only vowels /i/ and /æ/ (extracted from the test signal). Automatic extraction of the vowels is done using DTW algorithm that aligned analysed input signal with marked reference signal. Spectral envelopes and formant frequencies locations of obtained vowels are used for feature calculation. It was found that distance between envelopes of vowels /i/ and /æ/, second formant of the vowel /i/ and second formants convergence of vowels /i/ and /æ/ are the most informative features for ALS bulbar changes detection. The classification between healthy and ALS groups is done on the based of linear discriminant analysis. The best accuracy 84.8% is achieved using only one feature (second formants of vowel /i/).

References

1. Atal, B.S., Hanauer, S.L.: Speech analysis and synthesis by linear prediction of the speech wave. J. Acousti. Soc. Am. **50**(2B), 637–655 (1971). https://doi.org/10.1121/1.1912679
2. Castillo Guerra, E., Lovey, D.F.: A modern approach to dysarthria classification. In: Proceedings of the 25th Annual International Conference of the IEEE Engineering in Medicine and Biology Society (IEMBS). vol. 3, pp. 2257–2260 (2003). https://doi.org/10.1109/IEMBS.2003.1280248
3. Cordeiro, H., Meneses, C.: Low band continuous speech system for voice pathologies identification. In: Proceedings of the Signal Processing: Algorithms, Architectures, Arrangements, and Applications (SPA), pp. 315–320 (2018). https://doi.org/10.23919/SPA.2018.8563393
4. Flach, P.: Machine Learning: The Art and Science of Algorithms that make Sense of Data. Cambridge University Press, United Kingdom (2012)
5. Green, J.R., Yunusova, Y., Kuruvilla, M.S., Wang, J., Pattee, G.L., Synhorst, L., Zinman, L., Berry, J.D.: Bulbar and speech motor assessment in ALS: challenges and future directions. Amyotroph. Lateral Scler. Frontotemporal Degener. **14**(7–8), 494–500 (2013). https://doi.org/10.3109/21678421.2013.817585
6. Gvozdovich, A., Rushkevich, Y., Vashkevich, M.: Detection of bulbar amyotrophic lateral sclerosis based on speech analysis. Doklady BGUIR **116**(6), 52–58 (2018)
7. Hanson, M.: Glottal characteristics of female speakers. Ph.D. thesis, Dept. Division Appl. Sci., Harvard University, Cambridge, MA, USA (1995)
8. Horwitz-Martin, R.L., et al.: Relation of automatically extracted formant trajectories with intelligibility loss and speaking rate decline in amyotrophic lateral sclerosis. In: Proceedings of Interspeech 2016, pp. 1215–1219 (2016). https://doi.org/10.21437/Interspeech.2016-403
9. Illa, A., et al.: Comparison of speech tasks for automatic classification of patients with amyotrophic lateral sclerosis and healthy subjects. In: Proceedings of IEEE International Conference on Acoustics, Speech and Signal Processing (ICASSP), pp. 6014–6018 (2018). https://doi.org/10.1109/ICASSP.2018.8461836
10. Kohavi, R.: A study of cross-validation and bootstrap for accuracy estimation and model selection. In: Proceedings of International Joint Conference on Artificial Intelligence, pp. 1137–1143 (1995)
11. Lee, J., Littlejohn, M.A., Simmons, Z.: Acoustic and tongue kinematic vowel space in speakers with and without dysarthria. Int. J. Speech-Lang. Pathol. **19**(2), 195–204 (2017). https://doi.org/10.1080/17549507.2016.1193899
12. Norel, R., Pietrowicz, M., Agurto, C., Rishoni, S., Cecchi, G.: Detection of amyotrophic lateral sclerosis (ALS) via acoustic analysis. In: Proceedings of Interspeech, pp. 377–381 (2018). https://doi.org/10.21437/Interspeech.2018-2389
13. Rabiner, L., Juang, B.H.: Fundamentals of Speech Recognition. Prentice Hall signal processing series. Prentice-Hall, Upper Saddle River (1993)
14. Rafałko, J.: Marking the allophones boundaries based on the dtw algorithm. In: Proceedings of the Signal Processing: Algorithms, Architectures, Arrangements, and Applications (SPA), pp. 245–249 (2018). https://doi.org/10.23919/SPA.2018.8563359
15. Shawe-Taylor, J., Cristianini, N.: Kernel Methods for Pattern Analysis. Cambridge University Press, New York (2004)

16. Spangler, T., Vinodchandran, N.V., Samal, A., Green, J.R.: Fractal features for automatic detection of dysarthria. In: Proceedings of IEEE EMBS International Conference on Biomedical Health Informatics (BHI), pp. 437–440 (2017). https://doi.org/10.1109/BHI.2017.7897299
17. Tomik, B., Guiloff, R.J.: Dysarthria in amyotrophic lateral sclerosis: a review. Amyotrophic Lateral Sclerosis **11**(1–2), 4–15 (2010). https://doi.org/10.3109/17482960802379004
18. Vashkevich, M., Azarov, E., Petrovsky, A., Rushkevich, Y.: Features extraction for the automatic detection of ALS disease from acoustic speech signals. In: Proceedings of Signal Processing: Algorithms, Architectures, Arrangements, and Applications (SPA), pp. 321–326 (2018). https://doi.org/10.23919/SPA.2018.8563414

Fuzzy Morphological Filters for Processing of Printed Circuit Board Images

Alexander Inyutin[✉] and Alexander Doudkin

United Institute of Informatics Problems, Surganov st., 6, 220012 Minsk, Belarus
avin@lsi.bas-net.by, doudkin@newman.bas-net.by

Abstract. The paper describes evaluation of effectiveness of morphological filters for removal of noise on images of layers of printed circuit boards by criteria of the minimum noise and computing complexity of filters and the minimum layout distortions. For assessment, the filters are applied with different parameters to a set of images on which a search and classification of defects of layout are carried out further.

Keywords: Mathematical morphology · Noise reduction · Printed circuit board · PCB · Layout · Image

1 Introduction

During optical inspection of printed circuit board (PCB) layout, the main stask of image processing are search and classification of defects, after which a decision about its quality is made. To improve the quality of inspection it is important to remove image noises caused by processes taking place in the matrix of CCD sensor, as well as dust and other impurities. Filters for noise reduction can be [28]:

- based on frequency domain Fourier or Wavelet transformations,
- semantic,
- based on scanning the image with window masks (median, morphological, etc).

Using morphological filters that have such options as size and shape of structures element, allows more flexibility in the process of removing noise from the image in comparison with another ones [29].

The paper is organized as follows. Section 1 reviews the general approach of mathematical morphology: basic definitions and soft and fuzzy modifications. Section 2 presents the main contribution on the paper - new fuzzy morphology operators. An evaluation of the effectiveness of morphological filters is studied in Sect. 3 in according to the criterion of minimal noise, the criterion of minimal noise considering computing complexity of the filter and the criterion of minimal layout distortion. Finally, an integrated filter efficiency criterion is proposed in this section. The last section presents a conclusion.

© Springer Nature Switzerland AG 2019
S. V. Ablameyko et al. (Eds.): PRIP 2019, CCIS 1055, pp. 205–215, 2019.
https://doi.org/10.1007/978-3-030-35430-5_17

The basic operators of classical mathematical morphology – erosion and dilation [10, 19, 30], are expressed as

$$\text{Dilate}(A, B) = \cup \{A + b : b \in B\} \tag{1}$$

$$\text{Erode}(A, B) = \cap \{A - b : b \in B\} \tag{2}$$

where A – an original image, b – a pixel of a structuring element B.

Filters based on the open and close operations are a sequence of erosion and dilation

$$\text{Open}(A, B) = \text{Dilate}(\text{Erode}(A, B), B) \tag{3}$$

$$\text{Close}(A, B) = \text{Erode}(\text{Dilate}(A, -B), -B) \tag{4}$$

There were offered soft morphological operators – soft erosion and dilation of the signal $f \colon \mathbb{Z}^m \to \mathbb{R}$ by structuring systems $[B_1, B_2, k]$ and filters based on them [11, 12]:

$$f \ominus [B_1, B_2, k] \, (x) = k \text{ - th smallest value of multiset}$$

$$\{k \langle\rangle f(b_2) : b_2 \in B_2(x)\} \cup \{f(b_1) : b_1 \in (B_1(x))\} \text{for all } x \in \mathbb{Z}^m, \tag{5}$$

$$f \oplus [B_1, B_2, k] \, (x) = k - \text{ th biggest value of multiset}$$

$$\{k \langle\rangle f(b_2) : b_2 \in B_2(x)\} \cup \{f(b_1) : b_1 \in (B_1(x))\} \text{ for all } x \in \mathbb{Z}^m. \tag{6}$$

The structuring system $[B1, B2, k]$ consists of three parameters: the finite sets B_1 and B_2, $B_2 \in B_1$, wherein $B_1, B_2 \in \mathbb{Z}^m$, positive integer k satisfies $1 \leq k \leq \text{Card}(B_1)$. Set $B = B_1 \cup B_2$, $B_1 \cap B_2 = \varnothing$ is called structuring set, B_1 – a center, B_2 – an abroad, k – ordinal index of the center (parameter of repeatability).

The following definition of operators of binary soft morphology is proposed in [18, 20]:

$$A \ominus [B_1, B_2, k] \, (x) = \{x \in A | \, (k \times \text{Card}\left[A \cap (B_1)_x\right] + \text{Card}\left[A \cap (B_2)_x\right] \geq$$

$$\geq k \times \text{Card}[B_1] + \text{Card}[B_2] - k + 1\} \tag{7}$$

$$A \oplus [B_1, B_2, k](x) = \{x \in A|$$

$$|\, (k \times \text{Card}\left[A \cap (B_1^S)_x\right] + \text{Card}\left[A \cap (B_2^S)_x\right] \geq k \tag{8}$$

where k – an ordinal index, which determines how many times the kernel elements are recorded in the final result. If $k = 1$ or $B = B_1$ ($B_2 = \varnothing$), the operators of the soft morphology turn to standard mathematical morphology operators.

The operators of mathematical morphology based on the fuzzy sets are proposed in [31]. To date, there is no single approach to determine the fuzzy erosion and dilation.

Different definitions of basic operations of fuzzy morphology are given in [2–6, 14–17, 21, 25, 32, 33]. Fuzzy membership function is typically defined as a function of the brightness of the pixels of the image $\mu\widetilde{A}(x) = f_A(x)$.

For example, according to [21], the operators of fuzzy erosion and dilation can be written by a fuzzy structuring element as follows (in terms of membership functions):

$$\mu_{A\ominus B}(x) = \min_{y\in B}[\min[1,\, 1 + \mu_A(x+y) - \mu_B(y)]]$$

$$= \min[1, \min_{y\in B}[1 + \mu_A(x+y) - \mu_B(y)]] \tag{9}$$

$$\mu_{A\oplus B}(x) = \max_{y\in B}[\min[0,\, \mu_A(x-y) + \mu_B(y) - 1]]$$

$$= \max[0, \max_{y\in B}[\mu_A(x-y) + \mu_B(y) - 1]] \tag{10}$$

where $x, y \in \mathbb{Z}^2$ – spatial coordinates, μ_A and μ_B – membership functions of the image and the structuring element respectively.

The approach combining a soft and fuzzy morphology is described in [1, 8, 9]. Fuzzy soft erosion and dilation can be expressed as follows (the definition of fuzzy morphology was used according to [21]):

$$\mu_{A\ominus[B1,\,B2,\,k]}(x) =$$

$$= \min[1, \underset{y\in B1, z\in B2}{\overset{(k)}{\min}}(\{k\langle\rangle\,(\mu_A(x+y) -$$

$$-\mu_{B1}(y) + 1)\} \cup \{\mu_A(x+z) - \mu_{B2}(z) + 1\})] \tag{11}$$

$$\mu_{A\oplus[B1,\,B2,k]}(x) =$$

$$= max[0, \underset{(x-y)\in B1, (x-z)\in B2}{\overset{(k)}{\min}}(\{k\langle\rangle(\mu_A(x-y) +$$

$$+ \mu_{B1}(y) - 1)\} \cup \{\mu_A(x-z) + \mu_{B2}(z) - 1\})] \tag{12}$$

where $x, y, z \in \mathbb{Z}^2$ – spatial coordinates, μ_A, μ_{B1} and μ_{B2} – membership function of image A, a core B_1 and soft boundary B_2 of structuring element respectively. If a fuzzy structuring element is satisfied the conditions $B \in \mathbb{Z}^2$: $B = B_1 \cup B_2$, $B_1 \cap B_2 = \varnothing$. If $k = 1$, the operators of the fuzzy soft morphology turn to standard mathematical morphology operators.

It should be noted that the publications in modern literature confirm the actuality of soft [13, 23, 24, 26] and fuzzy [7, 15, 22, 27] morphology for image processing.

2 New Fuzzy Morphology Operators

As fuzzy membership functions we offer to use ratio of cardinalities of sets n_{fit} and n_{unfit}

$$\mu_{\tilde{\tilde{A}}}(x) = |n_{fit}| / |n_{unfit}|, \forall x \in \tilde{\tilde{A}} \tag{13}$$

where $n_{fit} = \{\overline{a_i \wedge b_i}\}$ – the set non-zero pixels $a \in A$ on an image A within the boundaries of structuring element matched by value with nonzero pixels $b \in B$ of structuring element B, $n_{unfit} = \{a_i \wedge b_i\}$ – the set of pixels on the image within the boundaries of structuring element, the value of which has not coincided with the value of the corresponding pixels of structuring element.

The operators of fuzzy morphology are defined as follows

$$FuzzyErode(A, B, t) = \left\{ \begin{array}{l} |n_{fit}| + t \leq |n_{unfit}| \rightarrow a = 0 \\ |n_{fit}| + t > |n_{unfit}| \rightarrow a = 1 \end{array}, a \in A \right\}, \tag{14}$$

$$FuzzyDilate(A, B, t) = \left\{ \begin{array}{l} |n_{fit}| + t \leq |n_{unfit}| \rightarrow a = 1 \\ |n_{fit}| + t > |n_{unfit}| \rightarrow a = 0 \end{array}, a \in A \right\}, \tag{15}$$

where t is the similarity threshold, A is the binary image, B is the structuring element. The fuzziness of these operators is determined by the fuzzy degree of similarity of the structuring element to the image.

A fuzzification is performed at the stage of calculating the membership function as the ratio of cardinalities of sets n_{fit} and n_{unfit}. A defuzzification is performed in the stage of determining the value of a pixel based on the value of its membership function. The fuzzy open and close operators, based on formulas (14)–(15), are not idempotent, so they can be re-used with the same structuring element many times. It is proposed to use this property for the construction of fuzzy morphological filters.

In the classical binary, grayscale and fuzzy mathematical morphology, each pixel value may be defined multiple times in a single pass of the operator depending on the values of the pixels in the source image. To provide high spatial resolution, operators (14) and (15) determine the value of each pixel in the image only once, based on calculations in the mask element structures. Use the similarity threshold allows varying the degree of influence on the result of the smallest structures element.

3 An Evaluation of the Effectiveness of Morphological Filters with Different Parameters

Fuzzy mathematical morphology has the ability to adjust the noise removal process by selecting filter parameters. It is proposed to evaluate the effectiveness of morphological filters with different parameters using the integral quality criterion estimated by the coefficient Q (described in Sect. 3.4). To calculate the coefficient, a set of filters with different parameters can be applied to a set of test images (described in Sects. 3.1–3.3). Then it is necessary to calculate the area with remaining noise, and finally to search and to classify the layout defects.

The assessment of filters efficiency was investigated for 168 various parameters:

- morphological Open, Close, consecutive OpenClose and CloseOpen filters with the structuring elements in the form of a square and a rhombus with size from 2 × 2 to 5 × 5 pixels;

- similar operations of fuzzy morphology and also a fuzzy erosion and dilatation which at certain parameters can delete noise of the image without distortion of the sizes. The value of a threshold of the filter was from one to a half of number of pixels of the structuring element, the number of iterations of the filter – from one to three.

The test data is the set of three PCB images ranging in size from 640 × 480 to 1280 × 960 pixels with different minimum track width and synthesized noise. All images had breaks and short circuits of various sizes (the size of the minimum defect width is from one to three pixels). The noise that is added to the image leads to the formation of defects such as pinhole, mouse bite, spur and spurious copper. An example of the original image is shown in Fig. 1.

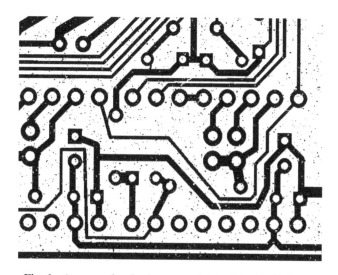

Fig. 1. An example of a fragment of the original PCB image

After filtering, a search for defects was done by comparison PCB image with its ideal image (without noises) and the defects were classified into six classes: pinhole, mousebite, spur, spurious copper, break and short.

3.1   The Criterion of Minimal Noise

The first variant of assessment of filtration is based on criterion of the minimum quantity of noise, which remains on the image after filtration. Therefore, for assessment it is required to calculate the average ratio of the noise area S_{noise} after filtration to the image area S_{img} for all set of test images:

$$Q1 = \frac{1}{n} \sum_{j=1}^{n} \frac{Snoise_j}{Simg_j}, \tag{16}$$

where n is the amount of test images. Than the value of $Q1$ is less, so much the filter removes noise better. The coefficients $Q1$ for all tested filters are shown in Fig. 2, which illustrates that the results can differ by more than 60 times.

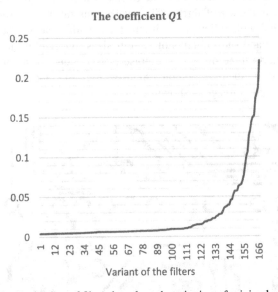

Fig. 2. Evaluation of filters based on the criterion of minimal noise

The best filter on this criterion is a double-applied FuzzyOpenClose operation with a 3×3-pixels diamond-shaped structuring element and a filtering threshold equal to one.

3.2   The Criterion of Minimal Noise Considering Computing Complexity of the Filter

The criterion of minimum noise with taking into account computing complexity of the filter Q2 is required in addition to increase noise reduction and can be used if a high-speed filter operations:

$$Q2 = i \times Cplx \times Q1 \tag{17}$$

where i is the number of filter iterations; $Cplx$ - its conditional computing complexity that equals to a multiplication of height and width of the structuring element (or their sum for the square structuring elements in operations of classical mathematical morphology). The value of Q2 is the lower, the filter removes the better.

The coefficient Q2 for all tested filters is shown in Fig. 3.

The coefficient *Q2*

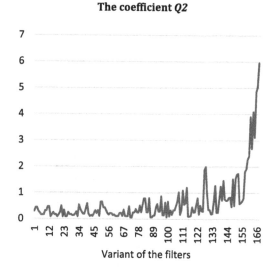

Fig. 3. Evaluation of filters, taking into account their conditional computational complexity

The best filter results, taking into account the its conditional computational complexity, have one-time operation of fuzzy erosion or dilation by square structuring element with size 3×3 pixels and threshold equals to 4. Operation of fuzzy erosion and dilation with this threshold value can remove noise from an image in one pass with minimal changes to the form. Double application of these operations reduces the noise on the image till 1.6 times.

3.3 The Criterion of Minimal Layout Distortion

Application of areal filters can lead to the formation of short circuits and breaks in the layout image. The coefficients $Q1$ and $Q2$ do not take into account the distortions of the layout that the filter introduces. To estimate the filtering of topological images, it is proposed to use the criterion of minimum distortion of layout, which, for example, can be calculated by the formula

$$Q3 = Q2 + Nerr \tag{18}$$

where *Nerr* is the number of short circuits and breaks introduced in the process of removing noise. The value of Q3 is the smaller, the filter removes noise from images with minimal distortion the better.

The coefficient Q3 is shown in Fig. 4 for all tested filters. The figure illustrates that the total amount of distortion can reach hundreds, that it was unacceptable for the inspection of the layout. In other words, incorrectly chosen filtering parameters worsen the result of the inspection.

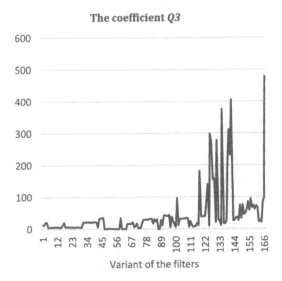

Fig. 4. Evaluation of filters based on the amount of layout distortion

3.4 Integrated Filter Efficiency Criterion

It is proposed to use the integrated filter efficiency criterion Q for more accurate selection of the filtering settings, which has the following form:

$$Q = k1 \times Q1 + k2 \times Q2 + k3 \times Nerr \tag{19}$$

where $k1$, $k2$ and $k3$ are weight coefficients for the criteria of the minimum noise and computing complexity of filters and the minimum layout distortions, respectively.

The value of Q is the smaller the filter removes noise with minimum work time and induced layout distortion.

For example, to select an effective filter that does not introduce distortions in the image layout and its operation speed does not matter, $Qwrk$ can determine as

$$Qwrk = Q1 + 0.1Q2 + Nerr \tag{20}$$

The values of the integral coefficient $Qwrk$ determined by (20) for all tested filters shown in Fig. 5.

The optimal filter based on $Qwrk$ is a single pass of FuzzyErode with 3×3-pixel diamond-shaped structuring element and a filtering threshold equals to two. The example of the operation of this filter is shown in Fig. 6.

In Fig. 6 you can see that after filtration to the image remains a lot of impulse noise, but using area filters for removing it would break links between tracks, which is unacceptable for the inspections of PCB layout.

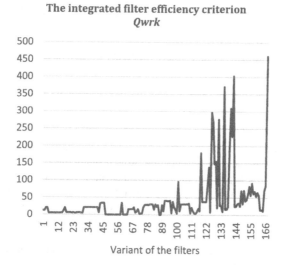

Fig. 5. The value of the integrated filter efficiency criterion $Qwrk$

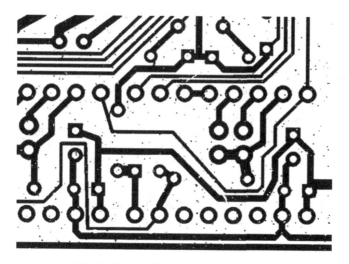

Fig. 6. The result of the optimal filtering

4   Conclusion

The new fuzzy morphology operators were proposed. They were applied for filtering of noise on PCB layout images. Effectiveness of the morphological filters was evaluated by criteria of the minimum noise and computing complexity of filters and the minimum layout distortions. The evaluation allows to choose the optimal filter settings based on noise removal requirements and to formulate the integrated filter efficiency criterion. In a whole, application of fuzzy morphology operators, which have more parameters for filtering, gives the better result for noise removing from images with little details of PCB or when they are placed relative close to each other.

Acknowledgement. The work was partially supported by Belarusian Republican Foundation for FundamentalResearch (project No. Ф19МС-032).

References

1. Vardavoulia, M.I., et al.: Binary, gray-scale and vector soft mathematical morphology: extensions, algorithms, and implementations. Adv. Imaging Electron Phys. **119**, 1–53 (2001)
2. Bloch, I.: Duality vs. adjunction for fuzzy mathematical morphology and general form of fuzzy erosions and dilations. Fuzzy Sets Syst. **160**(13), 1858–1867 (2009)
3. Bloch, I.: Fuzzy and pattern morphology. Pattern Recognit. Lett. **14**(6), 483–488 (1993)
4. Bloch, I., Maitre, H.: Fuzzy mathematical morphologies: A comparative. Pattern Recognit. **28**(9), 1341–1387 (1995)
5. Bloch, I.: Lattices of the fuzzy sets and bipolar fuzzy sets, and the morphology. Inf. Sci. **181**(10), 2002–2015 (2011)
6. Bloch, I.: Spatial reasoning under imprecision using the theory of morphology. Int. J. Approx. Reason. **41**(2), 77–95 (2006)
7. Fatichah, C., et al.: Interest-based ordering for chickening Fatichah. J. Adv. Comput. Intell. Intell. Inform. **16**(1), 76–86 (2012)
8. Gasteratos, A., Andreadis, I.: Non-linear image processing in hardware. Pattern Recognit. **33**(6), 1013–1021 (2000)
9. Gasteratos, A., Andreadis, I.: Soft mathematical morphology: extensions, algorithms and implementations invited contributions. Adv. Imaging Electron Phys. **110**, 63–99 (1999)
10. Giardina, C.R., Dougherty, E.R.: Morphological Method in Image and Signal Processing. Prentice Hall, New Jersey (1988)
11. Koskinen, L., et al.: Soft morphological filters. In: Proceeings of the SPIE Image Algebra and Morphological Image Processing II, vol. 1568, pp. 262–270 (1991)
12. Kuosmanen, P., Astola, J.: Soft morphological filtering. J. Math. Imaging Vis. **5**(3), 231–262 (1995)
13. Liu, T., Li, X.: Infrared small targets detection and tracking based on soft morphology Top-Hat and SPRT-PMHT. In: Proceedings of the IEEE Congress on Image Processing and Signal Processing (CISP), Shanghai, vol. 2, pp. 968–972 (2010)
14. Maccarone, M.C.: Fuzzy mathematical morphology: concepts and applications. Vistas Astron. **40**(4), 469–477 (1996)
15. Nachtegael, M., et al.: A study of interval-valued fuzzy morphology based on the minimum-operator. In: Proceedings of SPIE 7546 - Proceedings of Second International Conference on Digital Image Processing, 26 February 2010, Singapore SPIE, vol. 7546, pp. 75463H-1–75463H-7 (2010)
16. Kerre, E.E., Nachtegael, M.: Classical and fuzzy approaches to morphology fuzzy techniques in image processing. In: Kerre, E.E., Nachtegael, M. (eds.) fuzzy techniques in image processing. Studies in Fuzziness and Soft Computing, vol. 52, pp. 3–57. Springer, Heidelberg (2000). https://doi.org/10.1007/978-3-7908-1847-5_1
17. Kerre, E.E., Nachtegael, M.: Connections between binary, gray-scale and fuzzy mathematical morphologies. Fuzzy Sets Syst. **124**(1), 73–85 (2001)
18. Pu, C.C., Shih, F.Y.: Threshold decomposition of gray-scale soft morphology into binary soft morphology. CVGIP – Graph. Models Image Process. **57**(6), 522–526 (1995)

19. Serra, J.: Image analysis and Mathematical Morphology, 610 p. Academic Press (1982)
20. Shih, F.Y., Pu, C.C.: Analysis of the properties of soft morphological filtering using the threshold decomposition. IEEE Trans. Signal Process. **43**(2), 539–544 (1995)
21. Sinha, D., Dougherty, E.R.: Fuzzy mathematical morphology. J. Vis. Commun. Image Represent. **3**(3), 286–302 (1992)
22. Sussner, P., Valle, M.E.: Classification of fuzzy mathematical morphologies based on concepts of inclusion measure and duality. J. Math. Imaging Vis. **32**(2), 139–159 (2008)
23. Tickle, A.J., et al.: Upgrading to a soft multifunctional image processor. In: Proceedings of SPIE Optical Design and Engineering III. SPIE, vol. 7100, pp. 71002H-1–71002H-12 (2008)
24. Tian, Y., Zhao, C.: Optimization of the soft morphological filters with parallel annealing-genetic strategy. In: Proceedings of the International Conference on Pervasive Computing Signal Processing and Applications (PCSPA), Harbin, China, 17–19 September 2010, pp. 576–581 (2010)
25. Wu, M.: Fuzzy morphology and image analysis. In: Proceedings of the 9th ICPR, Rome, 14–17 November 1988, pp. 453–455 (1988)
26. Yan, X., Wang, Y.: Edge detection for feather and down image via BEMD and soft morphology. In: Proceedings of International Conference on Computer Science and Network Technology (ICCSNT), Harbin, China, 24–26 December 2011, vol. 3, pp. 1603–1607 (2011)
27. Yang, X.: Fuzzy morphology based feature identification fuzzy information and engineering. In: Cao, B., Wang, G., Guo, S., Chen, S. (eds.) Fuzzy Information and Engineering 2010. Advances in Intelligent and Soft Computing, vol. 78, pp. 607–615. Springer, Heidelberg (2010). https://doi.org/10.1007/978-3-642-14880-4_67
28. Gonzalez, R., Woods, R.: The World of Digital Processing. Digital image processing Technosphere, p. 660 (2005)
29. Song, J., Delp, E.J.: A study of the generalized morphological filter. Circuits Syst. Signal Process. **11**(1), 229–252 (1992)
30. Materon, G.: Random sets and integral geometry, Mir., 318 (1978)
31. Zadeh, L.: Fuzzy sets. Inf. Control **8**(3), 338–353 (1965)
32. De Baets, B., Kerre, E.E., Gupta, M.M.: The fundamentals of fuzzy mathematical morphology: part 1. Int. J. Gen Syst **23**, 155–171 (1995)
33. Kitainik, L.: Fuzzy Decision Procedures with Binary Relations, p. 255. Kluwer Academic Publishers, Boston (1993)

FPGA Based Arbiter Physical Unclonable Function Implementation with Reduced Hardware Overhead

Alexander A. Ivaniuk[ID] and Siarhei S. Zalivaka[✉][ID]

Belarusian State University of Informatics and Radioelectronics,
220013 Minsk, Belarus
{ivaniuk,zalivako}@bsuir.by

Abstract. The existing implementations of the arbiter physical unclonable function (PUF) are based on synthesis of configurable symmetric paths, each link of which is a pair of two-input multiplexers providing two configurations of test signal translation: straight and exchange. To build a single link on FPGA, it is necessary to use two built-in LUT blocks, providing the implementation of two multiplexers, and the hardware resources of the LUT blocks are not fully utilized. The paper presents a new architecture of symmetric paths of the arbiter PUF, providing efficient use of the hardware resources of LUT blocks for various Xilinx Artix-7 FPGA family.

Keywords: Physical Unclonable Function · Arbiter · FPGA · LUT · Symmetrical path

1 Introduction

Protection of digital devices against unauthorized use, copying and modification can be achieved by various methods, algorithms and technical means (e.g. encryption, watermarking and fingerprinting, active and passive metering, formal verification, etc.). Relatively novel scientific area named physical cryptography can be highlighted among many mentioned above methods. This direction is mainly based on so called Physical Unclonable Functions (PUFs) [1]. The main idea of PUFs is in extraction of unique physical characteristics from a fabricated digital device. Manufacturing process variations of integrated circuits bring a lot of random, unpredictable changes to its structure. Therefore, each instance of a manufactured integrated circuit becomes unique and irreproducible with unpredictable physical characteristics. These unique changes can be extracted by designing special digital circuits which can produce unique digital responses as a result of applying specific digital challenges to the device. In general, circuit implementation of a PUF can be represented as a block with n digital inputs getting n-bit challenge C from all possible 2^n combinations and producing one single-bit output value R (Response). The behaviour of such circuit

S. V. Ablameyko et al. (Eds.): PRIP 2019, CCIS 1055, pp. 216–227, 2019.
https://doi.org/10.1007/978-3-030-35430-5_18

can be represented as a boolean function mapping $\{0,1\}^n \rightarrow \{0,1\}$. The randomness of this function can be explained by the fact that the exact mapping of the set of challenges to the set of responses is unknown until the device is fabricated. This property also depends on uncontrollable variations of all manufacturing stages. Thus, the set of all possible challenge-response pairs of a PUF $CR_\alpha = \{c_0 r_0, c_1 r_1, \ldots, c_{2^n-1} r_{2^n-1}\}$ determines the uniqueness of an instance α of the digital device and $r_i = \mathrm{PUF}_\alpha(c_i)$, $i = \{0, 1, \ldots, 2^{n-1}\}$ determines unique dependency between a response r_i and a challenge c_i.

PUF should meet the following criteria to be utilized in physical cryptography [1,2].

1. Hardware overhead for PUF implementation should not exceed the hardware cost of a protected device.
2. Collection, storage and analysis of the set CR_α should be physically infeasible using modern equipment within reasonable time. The PUF, which matches this criterion, is called a strong PUF for parameter $n \geq 64$. To store the whole set of R_α, the 16 exabyte memory device is required. At the same time, collection of all possible values of R_α takes approximately 580 years if the response time of a memory device is 1 ns.
3. Knowing information about the challenge-response pair $c_i r_i$ for a particular instance of a device α it is impossible to calculate, simulate or design a mathematical model to predict value of a pair $c_j r_j$, $i \neq j$, or any other subset of such pairs. If a PUF satisfies mentioned condition, it can be considered *random* and *unpredictable*.
4. For a particular device α the set of responses R_α^*, $|R_\alpha^*| < |R_\alpha|$, can be extracted many times with a high degree of reliability by applying corresponding set of challenges C_α^*, $|C_\alpha^*| < |C_\alpha|$ to the inputs of a PUF. The PUF which has this property can be considered stable (*reliable*).
5. The set $D = \{\alpha_0, \alpha_1, \ldots, \alpha_{m-1}\}$, $|D| = m$, for different instances of a digital device with embedded PUF circuit and fabricated using the same technology, should match the following condition $CR_{\alpha_0} \neq CR_{\alpha_1} \neq \ldots \neq CR_{\alpha_{m-1}}$. This condition can be strengthened by additional condition $R_{\alpha_0}^* \neq R_{\alpha_1}^* \neq \ldots \neq R_{\alpha_{m-1}}^*$ for a corresponding set of challenges $C_{\alpha_0} = C_{\alpha_0} = \ldots = C_{\alpha_{m-1}}$, $|C_{\alpha_0}| = |C_{\alpha_1}| = \ldots = |C_{\alpha_{m-1}}| = \lceil log_2 m \rceil$. The PUF which has this property can be considered *unique*.

The PUF design which matches criteria described above can be efficiently used as a cryptographic primitive for following tasks.

- unclonable identification of digital devices;
- reliable authentication of digital devices;
- irreproducible random number sequences generation;
- hardware implementation of hash functions;
- hardware implementation of watermarks and fingerprints;
- protection digital devices against illegal cloning and modifying.

There are many circuit implementation of PUFs for digital device [1,2]: arbiter PUF, ring oscillator PUF, butterfly PUF, memory based PUFs, etc.

Almost all of mentioned PUF designs are based on measuring delay differences between signals propagated by symmetrical paths formed by a set of sequentially connected digital elements.

One of the most widely used methods of a PUF implementation for digital devices based on measuring delay differences is called Arbiter PUF (A-PUF) [3–6]. In contrast to the other mentioned PUFs, this type can be classified as a strong PUF and involves acceptable hardware overhead. However, practical implementation of this PUF has some disadvantages, which are under investigation of many developers and researchers in physical cryptography area. One main issue of A-PUF design is its low reliability of challenge-response pairs set and a vulnerability to an accurate modeling using known subset of pairs CR_α^*, $|CR_\alpha^*| \ll |CR_\alpha|$ as circuit structure has linear dependency between challenge and response values.

2   Classical Arbiter PUF Design

Classical Arbiter PUF (A-PUF) implementation usually contains three blocks, namely Test Pulse Generator (TPG), Symmetrical Paths Block (SPB) and Arbiter Block (AB). This structure is shown in Fig. 1.

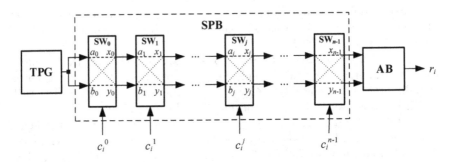

Fig. 1. Classical Arbiter PUF block level design.

SPB usually embeds n paths switching blocks (SW$_j$) controlled by external signals $c_i^j \in \{0,1\}$, $j = \{0,1,2,\ldots,n-1\}$, which correspond to the input challenge bits. Each switch SW$_j$ has two inputs a_j, b_j and two outputs x_j, y_j. If $c_i^j = 0$ paths are configured in a straight mode, i.e. signal goes from input a_j to output x_j and from b_j to y_j, correspondingly. Otherwise ($c_i^j = 1$), switch SW$_j$ has an exchanging configuration, so input a_j is now connected to y_j and b_j to x_j. Thus, n switching blocks provide 2^n possible path configurations for propagation of two test pulses generated by TPG block. Arbiter block determines which of two signals arrives earlier, i.e. if signal from output x_{n-1} came faster than the one from output y_{n-1} AB produces response value $r_i = 1$. Otherwise, it outputs $r_i = 0$.

AB of classical A-PUF design usually triggered by rising edge of a test pulse produced by TPG. Therefore, synchronous D Flip-Flop (DFF) is used for response generation. Signal from x_{n-1} is propagated to the clock input of DFF and y_{n-1} – to the data input. One main problem of this circuit is metastability state of the DFF, which degrade overall stability of the A-PUF design. This issue can be resolved by implementing AB as latches (e.g. RS latch) or multiple flip-flops [4].

Major hardware overhead in A-PUF design with $n \geq 8$ switches is located in SPB. Consider a detailed implementation of SW components. Basic approach to implement one switching block usually utilizes a two-multiplexers circuit shown in Fig. 2a.

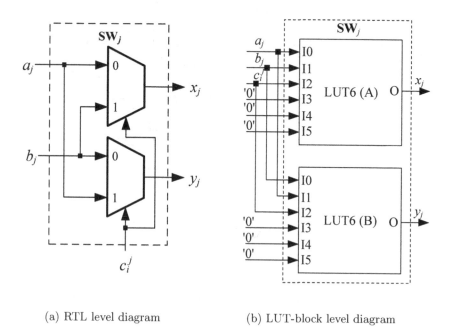

(a) RTL level diagram   (b) LUT-block level diagram

Fig. 2. Circuit implementation of SW block.

The circuit in Fig. 2a can be synthesized as two LUT6 blocks as shown in Fig. 2b, which correspond to the combinational circuit of 6-input multiplexer and configurable memory. Input signals a_j and b_j are fed into the corresponding input ports I0 and I1 of the upper LUT6 (A) block and to the I1 and I0 ports of the bottom LUT6 (B) block, respectively. The challenge signal c_i^j is passed to the I2 input ports of both LUT6 blocks. The other input ports (I3, I4, I5) are not utilized if the standard synthesis configuration is used. The output signals x_j and y_j correspond to the output port O of the LUT6 block.

FPGA chips fabricated by Xilinx usually have 4- to 6-input LUT blocks. The number of inputs in hardware blocks depends on the FPGA architecture [7]. LUT block contains a configuration memory and a set of multiplexers for translation values stored in this memory. Address for the memory is formed by signals from multiplexer select inputs. Redundant inputs are usually fed with constant '0' value.

There are four types of LUT6 blocks in Xilinx Artix-7 FPGA, LUT6 (general output), LUT6_D (general and local output), LUT6_L (local output), LUT6_2 (two outputs). Figure 3 shows the structure of LUT6_L block which is configured as a multiplexer x_j from block SW_j (see Fig. 2). As shown in Fig. 3, only 12.5% of LUT6 block resources are utilized. Therefore, if number of switches is significant, it will lead to a substantial LUT overhead to implement A-PUF circuit.

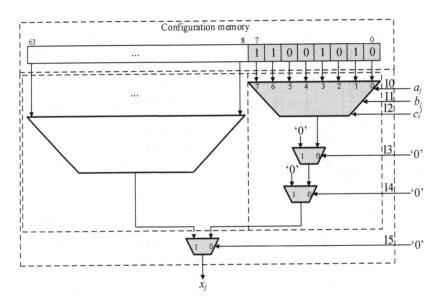

Fig. 3. Circuit implementation of a multiplexer using LUT6_L.

For example, for $n = 128$ implementation of the SPB requires 256 LUT blocks of Xilinx Artix-7 FPGA, which is around 1% of all resources available in XC7A100T chip [7].

3   Proposed Symmetrical Path Design

Classical implementation of A-PUF in FPGA provides SPB with unique parameters, e.g. delays of internal multiplexers providing translation of a chosen signal to an output port [8].

Assume time required for rising edge of a test signal to reach output x_j from input a_j ($c_i^j = 0$) be denoted as $\delta(x_j, a_j)$ and as $\delta(x_j, b_j)$ for input b_j, output x_j ($c_i^j = 1$), respectively. Similarly denote these characteristics for a second multiplexer, $\delta(y_j, a_j)$ ($c_i^j = 1$) and $\delta(y_j, b_j)$ ($c_i^j = 0$). To estimate these parameters the post place-route modeling of SW_j has been performed for

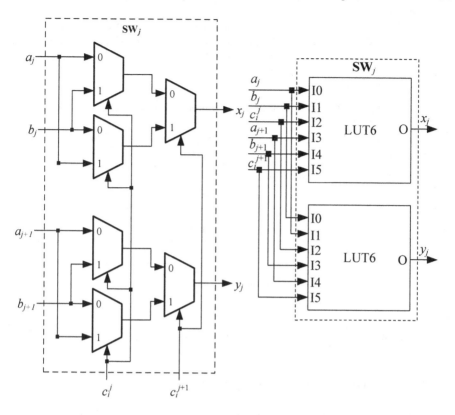

(a) RTL level diagram   (b) LUT-block level diagram

Fig. 4. Circuit implementation of SW block based on full utilization of LUT6 FPGA block.

XC7A100T FPGA platform. As a result, following values for SW_0 block have been obtained, $\delta(x_0, a_0) = 0.809\,\text{ns}$, $\delta(x_0, b_0) = 0.309\,\text{ns}$, $\delta(y_0, a_0) = 1.022\,\text{ns}$, $\delta(y_0, b_0) = 1.022\,\text{ns}$. For the neighbour block SW_1 these values differ significantly, $\delta(x_1, a_1) = 0.719\,\text{ns}$, $\delta(x_1, b_1) = 0.506\,\text{ns}$, $\delta(y_1, a_1) = 0.296\,\text{ns}$, $\delta(y_1, b_1) = 0.083\,\text{ns}$. These results can be explained by uniqueness of utilized LUT blocks and asymmetrical configuration of its connections. Unique values of the delays prove that the second copy of the switching block can be implemented using unutilized resources of a LUT block. Therefore, all unused inputs (I3, I4 and I5) can be reconfigured for an additional switching block. Figure 4 shows both, circuit implementation of the block containing SW_j (see Fig. 4a) and the synthesized scheme on LUT6 blocks (see Fig. 4b).

This circuit provides four configurations of inputs a_j, b_j, a_{j+1}, b_{j+1} to outputs x_j, y_j: two straight connections when $c_i^j = 0, c_i^{j+1} = 0$ and $c_i^j = 1, c_i^{j+1} = 1$, and two exchanging connections when $c_i^j = 1, c_i^{j+1} = 0$ and $c_i^j = 0, c_i^{j+1} = 1$.

Table 1 presents the rising edge delays for test signal for different combinations of inputs and outputs depending on c_i^j, c_i^{j+1}. These values have been obtained using post place-route modeling for $n = 16$ A-PUF implemented in Xilinx Artix-7 XC7A100T FPGA.

Table 1. Delay values for two different switching blocks.

Challenge bits $c_i^j c_i^{j+1}$	Delay type	Delay value for SW_1 block, ns
00	$\delta(x_j, a_j)$	0.443
	$\delta(y_j, b_j)$	0.481
01	$\delta(x_j, a_{j+1})$	0.392
	$\delta(y_j, b_{j+1})$	0.497
10	$\delta(x_j, a_j)$	0.609
	$\delta(y_j, b_j)$	0.654
11	$\delta(x_j, a_{j+1})$	0.660
	$\delta(y_j, b_{j+1})$	0.565

Shown results proves the high potential of using proposed design as A-PUF implemented in FPGA.

4   Hardware Overhead Analysis

As shown above, proposed structure of an SPB fully fits the LUT6 architecture. This approach provides significant reduction of hardware resources in FPGA chip. TPG and AB blocks bring negligible hardware overhead to the overall design comparing to the SPB. Implementation of the TPG block usually requires three LUT blocks and three flip-flops, AB uses only one flip-flop if implemented as in [4]. The major hardware resources are required for SPB. Proposed architecture requires double less LUT blocks comparing to the classical A-PUF design.

Table 2 presents a comparison for two implementations of A-PUF in XC7A100T FPGA, namely classical A-PUF (G_0) and a proposed one (G_1). As shown in table, proposed A-PUF switching blocks architecture requires double less hardware for its implementation. This design can be implemented in FPGA based on LUT blocks with more than 6 inputs [7].

Table 2. Hardware overhead for A-PUF implementation in Xilinx-7 FPGA ($n = 128$).

FPGA resource	# Utilized blocks		Total # of blocks	% of hardware overhead	
	G_0	G_1		G_0	G_1
Slices	131	69	15,850	0.83	0.44
Flip-Flops	4	4	126,800	0.0003	0.0003
LUT6	259	131	15,850	1.63	0.83

5   Arbiter PUF Figures of Merit Analysis

The modeling of two approaches for A-PUF implementation for XC7A100T FPGA have been conducted using Xilinx ISE 14.7 CAD [9]. These approaches have been post place-route simulated as 16-bit A-PUFs. AB has been implemented as synchronous D Flip-Flop (technological component FDC).

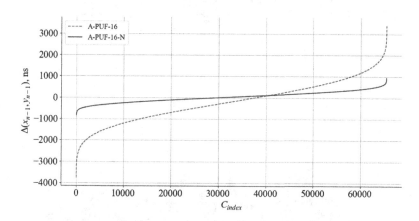

Fig. 5. Graph of $\Delta(x_{n-1}, y_{n-1})$ for two different A-PUF implementations.

A-PUF design and testbenches have been designed using Verilog. Testbenches provide feeding of all possible 2^n challenges to the inputs, generation of a test signal and response values analysis. Furthermore, testbenches have been designed in order to analyse delay difference $\Delta(x_{n-1}, y_{n-1})$ between rising edges of two copies of a test signal, propagated from the outputs x_{n-1} and y_{n-1} to the inputs of AB.

As shown in Fig. 5, the curve of $\Delta(x_{n-1}, y_{n-1})$ values for A-PUF-16-N (proposed design) is much more symmetric in both axes. Furthermore, nonlinear dependency between coordinates makes challenge-response relation much more complicated comparing to the classical A-PUF design. Asymmetry in A-PUF-16 (classical design) graph implies that the set of challenge-response pairs is unbalanced, i.e. probability of zero response bit is much bigger than the probability of one.

Furthermore, the range of delay values $\Delta(x_{n-1}, y_{n-1})$ has shrunken. As a result, the range for classical A-PUF design is $[-3772; 3396]$ ns and for the proposed architecture with the same n, this range has become much more narrow $[-832; 943]$ ns. This fact can be explained by decreasing length for symmetric paths as number of LUT blocks is also decreased. Inter-chip uniqueness has been estimated for both, A-PUF-16 and A-PUF-16-N circuits.

To calculate this metric eight identical components of A-PUF on each chip have been simulated and compared on the same set of challenges. This metric is estimated as 0.489 for A-PUF-16 and 0.473 for A-PUF-16-N, respectively.

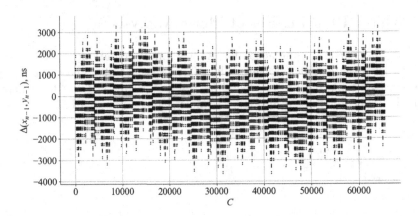

Fig. 6. Graph of $\Delta(x_{n-1}, y_{n-1})$ depending on challenge values for A-PUF-16 design.

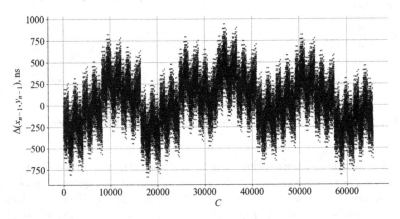

Fig. 7. Graph of $\Delta(x_{n-1}, y_{n-1})$ depending on challenge values for A-PUF-16-N design.

The ideal value for uniqueness figure of merit is 0.5. Real values of reliability and uniqueness strongly depend on parameter n, AB implementation and can be actually measured only on real hardware [10] by feeding the same challenges multiple times.

Figures 6 and 7 show functional dependency of values $\Delta(x_{n-1}, y_{n-1})$ on challenge values, sorted in ascending order by the value of C for A-PUF-16 and A-PUF-16-N circuits, respectively.

As shown in figures, circuit A-PUF-16-N has better randomness and values of $\Delta(x_{n-1}, y_{n-1})$ are less correlated to the challenge values C. This fact can increase the complexity of the machine learning modeling for an attacker [3].

6   Future Works

The proposed design still utilizes two LUT6 for implementation of SW_j block. Alternatively, this block can be synthesized based on two-output LUTs (LUT6_2 or CFGLUT5 in Xilinx 7 Series FPGAs [11]). Both of these LUT blocks utilize one of the inputs to configure the outputs, i.e. if the passed value is '0' then both outputs produce the same value, otherwise the output values are different. Since one of the inputs has to be used in order to provide two distinct outputs, 6 input values for SW_j and SW_{j+1} cannot be fit to 5 available inputs. Therefore, it is more promising to use CFGLUT5 block for a single-LUT SW_j block implementation as it also provides dynamically reconfigurable memory. This feature of the CFGLUT5 makes PUF reconfigurable and increases its uniqueness and security [12].

The circuit implementation of the SW_j block is shown in Fig. 8.

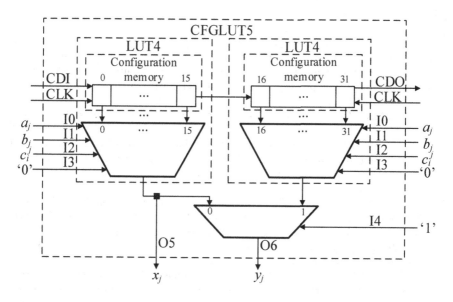

Fig. 8. Circuit implementation of SW block using CFGLUT5.

The input values a_j, b_j and c_i^j are mapped to the inputs I0, I1 and I2, respectively. The input I3 is fed with '0' as it is not utilized for switching block implementation. The input I4 gets the value of '1' as LUT block should have two different outputs O5 and O6 which are mapped to the output values x_j and y_j. The CFGLUT5 can be also dynamically reconfigured using serial port CDI and reconfiguration clock CLK. Thus, switch block can be reconfigured to different paths increasing uniqueness and decreasing the vulnerability to machine learning attacks.

7   Conclusion

This paper presents a new architecture for symmetrical paths block in arbiter based physical unclonable function for efficient implementation in FPGA. Proposed approach utilizes the internal configuration of embedded LUT blocks and saves valuable hardware resources as well as enhances uniqueness and randomness of a classical A-PUF design.

All experimental data described in this paper has been obtained using CAD Xilinx ISE 14.7 [9] and Verilog hardware description language. The results are to be verified on a real hardware implementation to compute true values of interchip uniqueness and randomness. The proposed design has to be also verified on vulnerabilities related to machine learning based modeling attacks. The circuit is also highly configurable and can be used to design a logically reconfigurable PUFs.

References

1. Zalivaka, S.S., Zhang, L., Klybik, V.P., Ivaniuk, A.A., Chang, C.-H.: Design and implementation of high-quality physical unclonable functions for hardware-oriented cryptography. In: Chang, C.-H., Potkonjak, M. (eds.) Secure System Design and Trustable Computing, pp. 39–81. Springer, Cham (2016). https://doi.org/10.1007/978-3-319-14971-4_2
2. Ivaniuk, A.A.: The design of embedded digital devices and systems, 337 p. Bestprint, Minsk (2012). (in Russian)
3. Zalivaka, S.S., Ivaniuk, A.A., Chang, C.-H.: Reliable and modeling attack resistant authentication of arbiter PUF in FPGA implementation with trinary quadruple response. IEEE Trans. Inf. Forensics Secur. **14**(4), 1109–1123 (2018). https://doi.org/10.1109/TIFS.2018.2870835
4. Zalivaka, S.S., Puchkov, A.V., Klybik, V.P., Ivaniuk, A.A., Chang, C.-H.: Multi-valued arbiters for quality enhancement of PUF responses on FPGA implementation. In: Proceedings Asia and South Pacific Design Automation Conference (ASP-DAC 2016), Macau, China, January 2016, pp. 533–538 (2016). (Invited paper). https://doi.org/10.1109/ASPDAC.2016.7428066
5. Hori, Y., Yoshida, T., Katashita, T., Satoh, A.: Quantitative and statistical performance evaluation of arbiter physical unclonable functions on FPGAs. In: Proceedings International Conference "Reconfigurable Computing and FPGAs", Mexico, pp. 298–303 (2010). https://doi.org/10.1109/ReConFig.2010.24
6. Becker, G.T.: On the pitfalls of using Arbiter-PUFs as building blocks. IEEE Trans. Comput.-Aided Des. Integr. Circuits Syst. **34**(8), 1295–1307 (2015). https://doi.org/10.1109/TCAD.2015.2427259
7. Series FPGAs Data Sheet: Overview. https://www.xilinx.com/support/documentation/data_sheets/ds180_7Series_Overview.pdf. Accessed 13 Feb 2019
8. Morozov, S., Maiti, A., Schaumont, P.: An analysis of delay based PUF implementations on FPGA. In: Sirisuk, P., Morgan, F., El-Ghazawi, T., Amano, H. (eds.) ARC 2010. LNCS, vol. 5992, pp. 382–387. Springer, Heidelberg (2010). https://doi.org/10.1007/978-3-642-12133-3_37
9. ISE Design Suite. https://www.xilinx.com/products/design-tools/ise-design-suite.html. Accessed 20 Feb 2019
10. Nexys 4 Artix-7 FPGA Trainer Board: https://store.digilentinc.com/nexys-4-artix-7-fpga-trainer-board-limited-time-see-nexys4-ddr. Accessed 20 Feb 2019
11. Xilinx 7 Series FPGA Libraries Guide for Schematic Designs: https://www.xilinx.com/support/documentation/sw_manuals/xilinx13_2/7series_scm.pdf. Accessed 05 Sept 2019

12. Katzenbeisser, S., et al.: Recyclable PUFs: logically reconfigurable PUFs. In: Preneel, B., Takagi, T. (eds.) CHES 2011. LNCS, vol. 6917, pp. 374–389. Springer, Heidelberg (2011). https://doi.org/10.1007/978-3-642-23951-9_25

Automatic Analysis of Moving Particles by Total Internal Reflection Fluorescence Microscopy

Olga Nedzved[1,2], Luhong Jin[3], Alexander Nedzved[1,4(✉)],
Wanni Lin[3], Sergey Ablameyko[1,4], and Yingke Xu[3]

[1] Belarusian State University, Minsk, Belarus
olga_nedzved@tut.by
[2] Belarusian State Medical University, Minsk, Belarus
[3] Department of Biomedical Engineering, MOE Key Laboratory of Biomedical
Engineering of Ministry of Education, Zhejiang University, Hangzhou, China
[4] United Institute of Informatics Problems, Minsk, Belarus

Abstract. Using of TIRF microscopy videosequences allows to study the propagation of intracellular protein vesicles to the cell surface upon insulin stimulation with high spatio-temporal resolution. Traditional tracking algorithms make mistakes for overlapping points at the intersection trajectories. Therefore, a particle registration algorithm based on background correction has shown optimal results for detecting moving particles or particles of variable size. In this paper we test traditional tracking methods and check performance for tracking protein particle in cell from video sequence TIRFM microscopy. We test four algorithms for detection vesicles location: Laplacian of Gaussian (LoG), Difference of Gaussian (DoG), Determinant of Hessian and algorithm on base continues brightness analysis. In our opinion for determination of position of protein vesicles the best algorithm is based on continues brightness analysis. There are many algorithms for tracking single objects and multitracking algorithms based on them. We used a function that takes a tracker type as input and creates a tracker object. We analyzed seven different multitracking algorithms with realization in OpenCV (BOOSTING, MIL, KCF, TLD, MEDIANFLOW, MOSSE, CSRT) and additional tracker on base of optical flow. In such tests, MEDIANFLOW tracker gives best results for predictable motion and small displacements. This tracker gives an error message in case of incorrect tracking, unlike other trackers that continue to work even the tracking failed.

Keywords: Particles tracking · TIRFM · Super resolution microscopy

1 Introduction

Many vital life activities occur in the cell level, such as cell signaling transduction or protein transport. Tracking and analyzing of subcellular structures are very important for biochemical and cell biology research.

One of the problems of cell biochemistry is propagation of intracellular GLUT4 storage vesicles to the cell surface upon insulin stimulation. GLUT4 is facilitative

© Springer Nature Switzerland AG 2019
S. V. Ablameyko et al. (Eds.): PRIP 2019, CCIS 1055, pp. 228–239, 2019.
https://doi.org/10.1007/978-3-030-35430-5_19

insulin-regulated glucose transporter protein that is located in adipose tissue and skeletal and cardiac muscle tissues in the absence of insulin. The insulin influence on spatiotemporal regulation of GLUT4 vesicle transport is important for understanding of the pathogenesis of type 2 diabetes in human [1].

Insulin involved in spatiotemporal regulation of GLUT4 vesicle exocytosis. For understanding of insulin influence on intracellular transport of GLUT4 it is necessary to solve next tasks: to determine protein vesicles density in near-membrane area; to construct vesicles trajectories; to find speed of vesicles. For solution of these tasks, we use video sequences obtained with help of ultra-high resolution microscopy.

Total internal reflection fluorescence microscopy (TIRFM) is one of types of ultra-high resolution microscopy. It allows to observe complex dynamic processes in living cells with big temporal and spatial resolution and capture a large number of real-time series image [2].

This microscopic method based on the physical phenomenon of total internal reflection. When the angle of incidence corresponds to the angle of total internal reflection, the electromagnetic field of the reflected light still spreads into the second medium along the z-axis and decays exponentially. This evanescent field penetrates to a depth of several hundred nanometers and causes fluorescence of individual molecules in a thin layer near the cell membrane. The small depth of penetration of the evanescent wave is the main advantage of TIRF-microscopy compared with traditional fluorescence microscopy. Electromagnetic wave is excited only in the fluorophore molecules, located very close to the membrane, creating very thin optical layer. Outside this layer, the fluorescence is minimal, which allows to obtain images with very high contrast.

Since the super-resolution microscopy imaging technology has made such a great progress, researchers have a chance quantitatively analyze the dynamic information for molecules in living cell.

2 Single Particle Tracking

Single particle tracking (SPT) technology is a key technology for processing series images and quantitatively analyzing particle dynamic processes. It has been used for descriptive studies of plasma membrane protein [3] and lipid diffusion [4]. Traditional SPT algorithms can be subdivided into two categories based on whether they use a probabilistic model. The key of the algorithms using probabilistic models is that they require prior knowledge about objects, such as the direction, speed and tendency of particles movement. This prior knowledge used to design filters for selecting candidate points for each trajectory. Therefore, the algorithms using a probabilistic model are more suitable for scenarios where the trend of particle motion can be estimated. While the non-probability algorithms based on image features without the constraints of prior knowledge, are more suitable for scenes with random motion.

However, traditional tracking algorithms have a common problem. They often make mistakes at the intersection trajectories. It can be attributed to two main reasons. Firstly, there is no point compensation method for overlapping points at the intersecting trajectories. Therefore, only one point can be detected in the overlapping positions according to the optimal rule in the tracking algorithm. Meanwhile, the remaining particles will have broken trajectories at this frame because there are no points that can be connected. Secondly, they usually lack effective motion prediction models. That is, in the case where there are multiple particles gathering at close positions, they are likely to make error connection as the tracker uses inefficient motion feature filters for each particles. In other words, the motion prediction model is not appropriate, resulting in a trajectory line matching error. Although several tracking methods have took the terrible effect of point overlapping into consideration, they adopt post-processing to refine the trajectory after the auto-tracking procedure with the help of human observation. For example, [5] asks user to input the gap-closing parameters such as the maximum distance and the maximum frame gap between two trajectories. These strategies are obviously too time-consuming and inefficient for an automatic particle tracking application.

3   Properties of Video Sequence

Video sequence represents the motion of protein containing vesicles inside the cell almost in real time. The acquisition frequency is 30 frames per second (fps). Motion of vesicles has three-dimensional space representation with horizontal and vertical coordinates in the frame correspond to the movement of vesicles in the imaging plane. The changing of the vesicle brightness corresponds to the change in the axial localization of the vesicle. The image from video sequence is represented on Fig. 1.

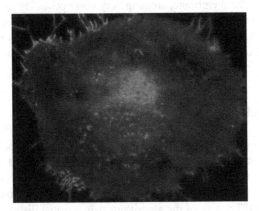

Fig. 1. Cell image from video sequence of TIRF microscopy.

Protein particles look like blobs with Gaussian shape of brightness surface:

$$PSP_{Gaussian} = K \cdot \exp\left(-\frac{(x - x_0)^2 + (y - y_0)^2}{r^2}\right),$$

where x_0, y_0 are coordinates of the center and r is radius of the blob.

Blobs look like bright regions on the dark background in video sequence. This feature can be used to extraction of particles.

4 Extraction of Protein Vesicles

4.1 Determination of Blobs Position

For tracking of vesicles, it is necessary to determine their location starting from the first frame of the video sequence before the tracking. We test four algorithms for detection such blobs: Laplacian of Gaussian (LoG) [6], Difference of Gaussian (DoG) [6, 7], Determinant of Hessian (DoH) [8] and algorithm on base continues brightness analysis.

In general, the LoG is the most accurate but slowest approach (Fig. 2). It computes the Laplacian of Gaussian images with successively increasing standard deviation and stacks them up in temporary image. Blobs are local maxima in this stack image. In this case, only constant bright blobs on dark backgrounds are detected.

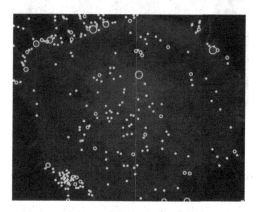

Fig. 2. Result of blobs extraction by Laplacian of Gaussian (LoG) (200 objects).

The DoG algorithm is a faster approximation of LoG approach (Fig. 3).

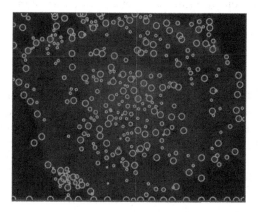

Fig. 3. Result of blobs extraction by difference of Gaussian (DoG) (250 objects).

In this case, the image is blurred with increasing standard deviations. Than the difference between two blurred images are stacked up in a temporary image. This method is more useful for detecting larger blobs.

The DoH is the fastest approach. It detects blobs by finding maxima in the matrix of the Determinant of Hessian of the image (Fig. 4). Bright on dark as well as dark on bright blobs are detected. This algorithm cannot accurately detect small blobs with area less than three pixels. The detection speed is independent of the blobs size.

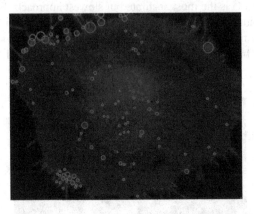

Fig. 4. Result of blobs extraction by determinant of Hessian (DoH) (110 objects).

Testing of the described algorithms showed high variability of the number of particles images and their sizes. Therefore, a particle registration algorithm based on background correction has shown optimal results for detecting moving particles or particles of variable size.

The registration of particles appearance performs on binary images obtained after the segmentation based on the background analysis. The algorithm of segmentation creates a mask of moving objects based on the difference with the background. This background segmentation algorithm based on a Gaussian set of pixel brightness values in the video sequence of images [9]. The weights in this set correspond to components of the normal distribution of brightness over time:

$$w_k^{n+1} = (1 - \alpha)w_k^n + \alpha p(\omega_k | x_{n+1}),$$

where ω_k is the kth Gaussian component, $1/\alpha$ defines the time constant which determines change, p is probability that a certain pixel has a value of x_n at time n.

Obtained distributions are ordered by the number of component k on the base of control relationships w_k/σ_k, then the background model is estimated as:

$$B = \arg\min_b \left(\sum_{j=1}^{b} w_j > T \right).$$

In this case, the brightness threshold for the binarization of images of particles T is the minimum value for the model. This is the minimum a priori probability of the background presence in the selected area. The threshold is determined at a distance of more than 2.5 standard deviations from the maximum of distribution B.

This method processes several frames to get a mask of moving objects on the frame. In our case, processing of 500 frames performs to form a background in the cell field. Identification of the particles motion performs for each selected binary object by the detection of the center coordinates. Accuracy of this algorithm based on Gaussian shape of blobs depends on maximum value of sigma-distribution and threshold for the amplitude of the distribution.

The algorithm based on continues brightness analysis performs a set of thresholding binarization for different levels of brightness. Removal of big size object performed for each binary result. Finally, all results are combined into common binary image with objects correspond to blobs (Fig. 5).

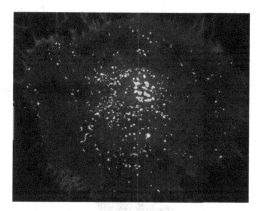

Fig. 5. Result of blobs extraction by algorithm based on continues brightness analysis (280 objects).

This algorithm has long processing time, but allows to extract all small particles. After blob extraction, it is necessary to remove all objects outside cell region detected by simple thresholding. As result there are from 200 to 500 protein vesicles extracted for one cell.

4.2   Creation of Region of Interest

Object detection algorithm detects not only moving particles, but also cell membrane motion, what complicates the analysis of tracking results. Correction of zone of interest allows to exclude false objects from tracking.

The first step before tracking is determination of cell region. The mean value of pixels at the image border is interpreted as background value. The simple brightness thresholding by this value allows to extract body of cell (Fig. 6).

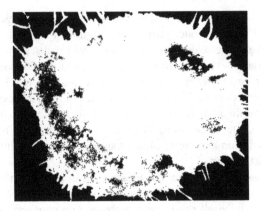

Fig. 6. Image of cell body after thresholding.

The hole filling operation allows to determine a region of cell (Fig. 7a). Excessive number of blobs in near-membrane area of the cell corrected by decreasing the region of interest with an extension of a structure element with a size greater than 20 pixels.

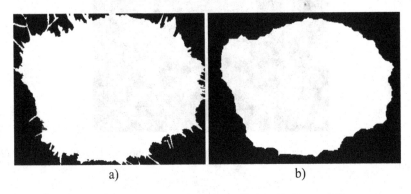

a)   b)

Fig. 7. Regions of cells body (a) and region of interest (b).

5 Multitracking of Protein Vesicles

Tracking of protein vesicles is difficult for two reasons: it is necessary to process many objects at the same time and track trajectories of particle of interest. The complexity of the task increases with increasing number of monitored objects. Using of the multi-tracking algorithms allows to solve this problem.

Choice of the proper algorithm depends not only on the algorithm principle, but also on its implementation. Programming language, compiler and manual optimization can significantly affect the performance and robustness of the algorithm. For this reason, we decided to carry out an analysis of pre-implemented tracking algorithms available in OpenCV library and simplify objects data set for tracking.

5.1 Simplification of Tracker

Information about cells structure used for simplification of tracker algorithm. Cytoskeleton formed from tubulin provides structure and shape of the cell. This stable structure also provides protein transport logistics. It allows to use integral optical flow to describe position of microtubular structure in cell.

Considering computation of optical flows for several consecutive frames, we can obtain integral optical flow $IOF_t^{itv}(p)$ for any pixel $I_t(p)$ as a vector field that records accumulated displacement information in time period of itv frames for all pixels in selected sequence:

$$IOF_t^{itv}(p) = \sum_{i=0}^{itv-1} OF_{t+i}(p_{t+i}),$$

where itv is the frame interval parameter used to compute integral optical flow [10, 11], p_{t+i} is the coordinate in I_{t+i} of pixel $I_t(p)$. In other words, if $I_t(p)$ stays in the video scene, $I_t(p_t)$, $I_{t+1}(p_{t+1})$,$\cdots$,$I_{t+itv-1}(p_{t+itv-1})$ are the same pixel in different frames.

Optical flow indicates the speed of protein vesicles motion in direction of the cell membranes according to the morphology of microtubules. Binarization allows taking binary image of protein particles trajectories (Fig. 8).

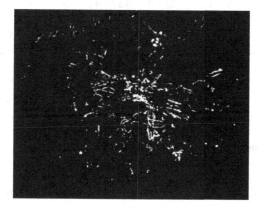

Fig. 8. Ways of protein particle in cell.

The motion is represented in optical flow. Integral optical flow is accumulation of motion. It is like as particle track. As result it is possible apply it as motion filter. After conjunction this image (Fig. 8) with image contained protein vesicles (Fig. 3) only moving objects remain (Fig. 9). Such operation allows to remove all errors that based on fluctuations and distortions on video without movable vesicles.

The use of the integral optical flow allows to reduce the number of the analyzed objects twice.

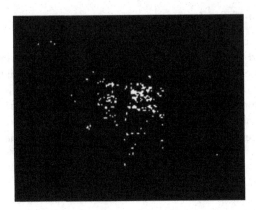

Fig. 9. Image with particle that have actual motion (97 objects).

5.2   Determining the Best Tracking Algorithm

There are many algorithms for tracking single objects and multitracking algorithms based on them. We used a function that takes a tracker type as input and creates a tracker object. We analyzed seven different trackers with realization in OpenCV (BOOSTING, MIL, KCF, TLD, MEDIANFLOW, MOSSE, CSRT) and additional tracker on base of optical flow.

BOOSTING tracker [12, 13] based on an AdaBoost algorithm that use the HAAR cascade detector. This classifier needs training at runtime with positive and negative object examples. The initial bounding box supplied by the blobs position is taken as the positive sample for the object, and many image patches outside the bounding box are treated as the background. The classifier runs on every pixel in the neighborhood of the previous location and the score of the classifier is recorded. The classifier is updated with additional data when number of frames increases.

MIL (Multiple Instance Learning) tracker [14] is similar to the BOOSTING tracker. The difference is that instead of considering only the current location of the object as a positive example, it examines a neighborhood around the current location to generate several potential positive samples. Even if the current location of the tracked object is not accurate, when samples from the neighborhood of the current location put in the positive examples set there is a good chance that this set contains at least one image in which the object is properly centered and detection of object is more stable.

KCF (Kernelized Correlation Filters) tracker [14] based on fact that the multiple positive samples used in the MIL tracker have large overlapping regions. Mathematical processing of this overlapping data allows to KCF tracker to increase speed and accuracy of tracking at the same time.

TLD (Tracking, learning and detection) tracker [15, 16] decomposes the tracking task into three components—(short term) tracking, learning, and detection. The detector localizes all objects appearances that have been observed so far and corrects the tracker. The learning estimates detector's errors and updates it.

MEDIANFLOW tracker [17] tracks the object in both forward and backward directions in time and measures the discrepancies between these two trajectories.

Minimizing this ForwardBackward error enables them to reliably detect tracking failures and select reliable trajectories in video sequences.

MOSSE (Minimum Output Sum of Squared Error) tracker [18] uses adaptive Fourier correlation for object tracking which produces stable correlation filters when initialized using a single frame. MOSSE tracker is robust to variations in lighting, scale, pose, and non-rigid deformations.

CSRT tracker [19] uses the Discriminative Correlation Filter with Channel and Spatial Reliability (DCF-CSR). It constructs the spatial reliability map for adjusting the filter support to the part of the selected region from the frame for tracking. This provides enlarging and localization of the selected region and improved tracking of the non-rectangular regions or objects.

Optical flow [19] is the pattern of apparent motion of image objects between two consecutive frames caused by the camera or object motion. This tracker uses an optical flow estimation technique to determine the motion vectors in each frame of the video sequence. By thresholding the motion vectors, it creates binary feature image containing blobs of moving objects. The tracker locates blobs in each binary feature image. Results window tracks the number of blobs in the region of interest.

All trackers tested on a set of 18 video sequences of cell monitoring. We used computer with Intel Core i7 6700HQ for tests. Results of testing are represented at the Table 1.

Table 1. Characteristics of trackers for cell monitoring.

Tracker	Mean accuracy	Mean frame rate, fps		
		1 object	5 objects	50 objects
BOOSTING	86%	60	19	2
MIL	58%	16	3.7	0.36
KCF	67%	120	96	50
TLD	10%	11	4	0.18
MEDIANFLOW	89%	92	55	10
MOSSE	93%	170	140	110
CSRT	93%	35	10	0.97
Optical flow	90%	60	19	2

In such tests, MEDIANFLOW tracker gives best results for predictable motion and small displacements. This tracker gives an error message in case of incorrect tracking, unlike other trackers that continue to work even the tracking failed.

The MOSSE based on a blob convolution method therefore it has great capabilities for tracking blobs. The binding to the shape of blobs and removing unnecessary parts can significantly optimize this algorithm. It also has good speed characteristics.

The tracker on base of optical flow does not depend on the number of objects and characterised by quality results. Only this tracker works without memory errors if the number of objects is more than 100. Other algorithms lead to either poor results or too long runtime.

6   Conclusion

Determination quantity and direction of propagation of intracellular protein vesicles upon insulin stimulation allows to solve important biochemical problem. In this work we compared different algorithms for protein blobs tracking at the TIRF microscopy videosequences. We also benchmark tracking algorithms and determine attributes especially difficult for current trackers. Inaccuracy in tracking algorithms are associated with overlapping points on intersection paths. Thus, common process of cell analysis from TIRF videosequence consist of two basic parts: blobs detection and multitracking. Tracking algorithm based on background correction has shown optimal results for the detection of protein vesicles.

Before tracking positions of protein particles detected by image segmentation. We test five algorithms for detection blobs on videosequences: Laplacian of Gaussian (LoG), Difference of Gaussian (DoG), Determinant of Hessian (DoH) and algorithm on base continues brightness analysis. In our opinion for determination of position of protein vesicles the best algorithm is based on continues brightness analysis. It allows to extract almost all protein particles and optical flow is very effective method for their tracking.

Also, we test seven multitracking algorithms with realization in OpenCV (BOOSTING, MIL, KCF, TLD, MEDIANFLOW, MOSSE, CSRT) and additional tracker on base of optical flow. In such tests, MEDIANFLOW tracker gives best results for predictable motion and small displacements. This tracker gives an error message in case of incorrect tracking, unlike other trackers that continue to work even the tracking failed. MOSSE algorithm based on a blob convolution method has great capabilities for tracking blobs. The binding to the shape of blobs and removing unnecessary parts can significantly optimize this algorithm.

Acknowledgments. This research was supported by projects of BRFFI F18R-218 "Development and experimental research of descriptive methods for automatization of biomedical imagesanalysis" and BRFFI F18KI-015 "Living cells properties computing by tracking active component on images", and by the National Natural Science Foundation of China (31811530055 and31571480) and the Fundamental Research Funds for the Central Universities (2019FZJD005,2019XZZX003-15 and 2019XZZX003-06).

References

1. Zhou, X., Shentu, P., Xu, Y.: Spatiotemporal regulators for insulin-stimulated GLUT4 vesicle exocytosis. J. Diabetes Res. 1–9 (2017), https://doi.org/10.1155/2017/1683678. Accessed 20 Aug 2019
2. Toomre, D., Manstein, D.J.: Lighting up the cell surface with evanescent wave microscopy. Trends Cell Biol. 11(7), 298–303 (2001)
3. De, B.M., Geuens, G., Nuydens, R., Moeremans, M., De, M.J.: Probing microtubule-dependent intracellular motility with nanometre particle video ultramicroscopy (nanovid ultramicroscopy). Cytobios 43(174), 273–283 (1985)

4. Zhang, F., et al.: Lateral diffusion of membrane-spanning and glycosylphosphatidy linositol-linked proteins: toward establishing rules governing the lateral mobility of membrane proteins. J. Cell Biol. **115**(1), 75–84 (1991)
5. Tinevez, J.Y., et al.: TrackMate: an open and extensible platform for single-particle tracking. Methods **115** (2016). https://doi.org/10.1016/j.ymeth.2016.09.016. Accessed 20 Aug 2019
6. Haralick, R., Shapiro, L.: Computer and Robot Vision, vol. 1, pp. 346–351. Addison-Wesley, Boston (1992)
7. Mikolajczyk, K., et al.: A comparison of affine region detectors. Int. J. Comput. Vis. **65**(1/2), 43–72 (2005)
8. Chen, Ch., Ye, Sh, Nedzvedz, O.V., Ablameyko, S.V.: Integral optical flow and its application for monitoring dynamic objects from a video sequence. J. Appl. Spectrosc. **84**(1), 120–128 (2017)
9. Nedzvedz, O., Ablameyko, S., Chen, H.: Application of the integral optical flow for identification of the cell population motion in the microscopic images. Cent. Eur. Res. J. **3** (2), 80–88 (2017)
10. Kim, T., Woodley, T., Stenger, B., Stenger, B., Cipolla, R.: Online multiple classifier boosting for object tracking. In: IEEE Computer Society Conference on Computer Vision and Pattern Recognition 1–6 (2010)
11. Grabner, H., Bischof, H.: On-line boosting and vision. In: Proceedings IEEE Conference on Computer Vision and Pattern Recognition (CVPR), vol. 1, pp. 260–267 (2006)
12. Babenko, B., Yang, M.-H., Belongie, S.: Robust object tracking with online multiple instance learning. IEEE Trans. Pattern Anal. Mach. Intell. **33**(8), 1619–1632 (2011)
13. Henriques, J.F., Caseirio, R., Martins, P., Batista, J.: High-speed tracking with kernelized correlation filters. IEEE Trans. Pattern Anal. Mach. Intell. **37**(3), 583–596 (2015)
14. Kalal, Z., Mikolajczyk, K., Matas, J.: Tracking-learning-detection. IEEE Trans. Pattern Anal. Mach. Intell. **34**(7), 1409–1422 (2012)
15. Kalal, Z., Mikolajczyk, Z., Matas, J.: Forward-backward error: automatic detection of tracking failures. In: 20th International Conference on Pattern Recognition, Istanbul, pp. 2756–2759 (2010)
16. Bolme, D.S., Beveridge, J.R., Draper, B.A., Yui Man, L.: Visual object tracking using adaptive correlation filters. In: IEEE Computer Society Conference on Computer Vision and Pattern Recognition, San Francisco, CA, pp. 2544–2550 (2010)
17. Lukežič, A., Vojíř, T., Čehovin, L., Zajc, J., Matas, M.K.: Discriminative correlation filter with channel and spatial reliability. Int. J. Comput. Vis. **126**(8), 671–688 (2018)
18. Ma, Y.: An object tracking algorithm based on optical flow and temporal–spatial context. Cluster Computing. 1–9 (2017), https://doi.org/10.1007/s10586-017-1487-y. Accessed 20 Aug 2019

Equipment Condition Identification Based on Telemetry Signal Clustering

Alexander Eroma[1,2], Andrei Dukhounik[1,2], Oleg Aksenov[1,2],
and Yauheni Marushko[3(✉)]

[1] Octonion Technology, 25-203 Yanki Kupaly Street, 220030 Minsk, Belarus
{aeroma, adukhounik, oaksenov}@octonion.by
[2] Belarusian State University of Informatics and Radioelectronics,
6 P. Brovki Street, 220013 Minsk, Belarus
[3] United Institute of Informatics Problems, National Academy of Sciences
of Belarus, St. Surganova 6, 220012 Minsk, Belarus
marushkoee@gmail.com

Abstract. This paper deals with the problem of pattern detection in telemetry data, in particular, the approach of automatic machine state detection based on the vibration signal proposed. The approach based on the analysis of the signal via clustering. The paper provides basic information about telemetry data analysis, vibration data analysis, and machine condition monitoring. Also, an overview of cluster analysis methods provided. The proposed approach based on clustering of objects represented with feature set extracted from vibration signals. Given the explanation of the technique and illustrative example of the application of the proposed approach applied to vibration data provided by SmartEdge Agile device for industrial electric motor considered.

Keywords: Signal processing · Vibration signals · Clustering · Unsupervised learning · Predictive maintenance

1 Introduction

In general, telemetry is information on the values of measured parameters (voltage, current, pressure, temperature, acceleration, etc.) of controlled objects. Telemetry signal analysis widely used in different areas. One of the possible telemetry measures is the acceleration and its derivative the vibration. In this case, telemetry signal can be considered as a discrete time series and time series analysis and signal processing techniques can be applied.

Signal processing techniques can be broadly classified as time domain and frequency domain. Generally, studies use both methods in applications that include the detection of wear or breakage of the instrument and the determination of the integrity of the surface.

Time Domain. Various time domain based metrics suggested by different researches, let's consider some of them:

© Springer Nature Switzerland AG 2019
S. V. Ablameyko et al. (Eds.): PRIP 2019, CCIS 1055, pp. 240–253, 2019.
https://doi.org/10.1007/978-3-030-35430-5_20

- mean is the most common feature of the time domain;
- standard deviation is also one of the generally used statistical methods for time domain feature extraction, which characterizes the spread of a data set's individual values about its mean;
- skewness is a measure of asymmetry of a signal distribution or measure of distribution's third central moment;
- kurtosis is a measure of peakedness of probability distribution or measure of the fourth central moment.

Frequency Domain. Frequency domain analysis or so-called spectral analysis considers not only the amplitudes of the signal but also its frequency characteristics. So while the time series is a graph in the time domain, the spectrum is a graph in the frequency domain. The initial step of the spectral analysis is a transformation of the signal from the time domain into the frequency domain. Usually, Fourier transform used as an appropriate tool to perform the translation between time and frequency domain. Spectral representation of signal can be used for analysis of specific frequencies or frequency ranges. Figures 1 and 2 illustrate an example of signal spectral representation.

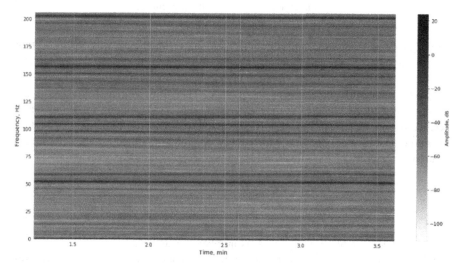

Fig. 1. Example of signal spectrogram

Nowadays various telemetry data are widely used in different industries and agriculture. The special place occupied here by vibration data. Vibration is a physical phenomenon produced by oscillation of any physical body. Vibration itself is an acceleration of the object, produced by periodic oscillation. The vibration of an object is characterized by changes in amplitude, frequency, and intensity. The vibration of industrial machines and engines is of great interest, as enables a range of approaches for machine condition monitoring and failure prediction. The primary target group for vibration analysis is machines which produce a constant level of vibration, which in

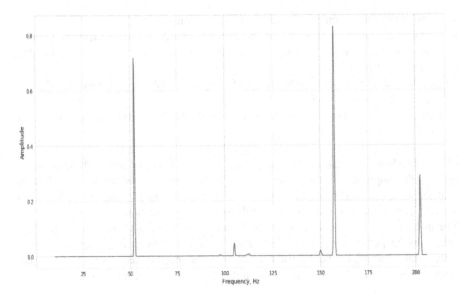

Fig. 2. Example of signal spectrum

theory can be decomposed in vibration harmonics. Machines with reciprocating engines is another group, but their analysis can differ from machines with rotational motion because of non-constant vibration component. Vibration changes may indicate breakdowns or identify breakdowns in advance. Therefore, vibration analysis is the process of monitoring changes in the vibration system and searching for anomalies.

Generally, the root mean square or RMS value is the most useful metric in vibration analysis because it naturally tied with energy of vibration signal which determinate destructive capability of the vibration [3]:

$$RMS = \sqrt{\frac{\sum_{i=1}^{N} x_i^2}{N}} \tag{1}$$

where x_i is the i-th sample of signal, N is number of samples.

Major instrument for vibration measurements is an accelerometer. It measures proper acceleration, which means, that place, where the accelerometer is placed affects measured data. An important note is, that even if there is no any source of vibration, the accelerometer can still measure some small vibrations. This caused by two reasons, first of all, absolute rest state is unattainable, and another one is, that accelerometer has its own small vibration.

Both time domain and frequency domain features used in vibration analysis in order to solve the following problems:

- hidden defects detection;
- quick faults detection;
- prescriptive faults detection.

For the acceleration measurements SmartEdge Agile device [1], which provides 3-axis inertial accelerometer sensor [2], used in this research (Fig. 3):

Fig. 3. Smart Edge Agile device

Vibration analysis is one of the basic tools for so-called predictive maintenance (PdM) [4, 5], which is a dynamically growing vector of researches in the last decade. Historically happened, that PdM is Expert Driven approach, this means, that special person measured data for one engine, analyze it, found some thresholds and then uses this as rules. Nowadays, when the Internet of Thing (IoT) ecosystem grows rapidly, it is important to utilize advantages given by IoT for PdM purposes. This gives an opportunity to develop a Data Driven approach based on analyzing measured data and doesn't require special people for analyzing every machine [6]. The following is an example of popular PdM applications based on vibration data analysis:

- novelty detection or anomaly detection in terms of machine learning. Novelty detection requires founding unusual states of the machine [7];
- state monitoring. Can be considered as clustering or classification in terms of machine learning. This is very close to anomaly detection, as newly detected states can be treated as a novelty [7];

– fault prediction and trends forecasting yet another important task as it allows to identify time frame when the machine will require maintenance. In terms of machine learning, this can be called as a regression task or pure forecasting of time series or trend extraction [8, 9].

Considering the above the definition of the machine condition identification problem can be formulated as follows: by given set of observations $X = \{x_1, \ldots, x_n\}$ of telemetry signal build the partition $P = \{A^1, \ldots, A^c\}$ where $x_i, i = 1 \ldots n$ is a i-th telemetry sample of n samples with the known value of similarity $\mu_j(x_i), i = 1, \ldots, n, j = 1, \ldots, c$ to a $A^j - j$-th signal pattern of c patterns.

2 Analysis of Existing Approaches

In this paper state monitoring (or states identification) technique is proposed and compared with some existing approaches. Commonly [7–11] vibration analysis built on top of the following steps:

1. Identify the vibration machine. It can be any engine or motor performing rotating motions: water-pump, washing machine, industrial motor, etc.
2. Place accelerometer on installation and measure of big enough amount of data, normally this is raw vibration - acceleration from one or several axes.
3. Analyze data for different purposes: novelty detection, fault prediction, etc.

Analyzing part consist of supervised machine learning algorithms for classification or clustering for states identification or novelty detection, and regression for forecasting and fault prediction.

This leads to creating models which can work only on particular machines with particular accelerometer with special parameters, which were set during data collection. In addition, the sensor should be placed in the exact place, where it was placed during data collection. A disadvantage of such models is that they are not able to scale and not adaptive. Parameters affecting the operation of the model:

1. accelerometer and accelerometer parameters;
2. machine characteristics;
3. accelerometer sensor fixation method;
4. accelerometer sample rate.

Some of these issues can be solved by proper data normalization and extraction of features, which are not affected by these parameters, but this manipulation makes models poorer. Another specific point is, that usually researchers consider supervised models.

One more constraint is data should be properly collected and labeled. Both tasks can be challenging, especially when considering low power devices with a limited amount of computational resources like ROM, RAM, and CPU. Once a dataset has been collected, it requires labeling procedure, which may not always be possible in case of long-term observations or observations of normal machine states only. Due to these disadvantages, it turns out, that such approach is still very similar to the Expert Driven approach.

3 Cluster Analysis

Among the variety of approaches to solving classification problems, a special place is occupied by automatic classification, also called unsupervised pattern recognition, numerical taxonomy or cluster analysis [12, 13]. At the substantive level, the task of classifying objects in the absence of classified training samples is to divide the analyzed set of objects into a certain, previously known or unknown number of homogeneous in a certain sense, groups, called classes, clusters, images or taxons, so that the objects of one group are as much as possible similar to each other, and the groups themselves differed from each other as much as possible [12].

Let's consider the ways of representation of source data in the classification problem in the absence of a training sample. Let $X = \{x_i, \ldots, x_n\}$ - is a set of n objects so each object can be described with m-features. In that case, source data can be represented with the following matrix:

$$X_{m*n} = \left(x_1^1 \cdots x_n^1 \vdots \cdots \vdots x_1^m \cdots x_n^m \right) \tag{2}$$

where x_i^t represents value of t-th feature of i-th object. Also referred to as object-feature matrix [12, p. 143]. So the i-th column $X_i = \left(x_i^1, x_i^2, \ldots, x_i^m \right)$ of matrix (2) fully characterize the object x_i and interpreted as point in m-dimensional space $I^m(X)$.

In some cases, mutual distances between objects of the X set can be known. In that case source data can be represented as a matrix of mutual distances of objects $x_i, \ldots, x_n$:

$$d_{n*n} = \left(d_{11} \cdots d_{1n} \vdots \cdots \vdots d_{n1} \cdots d_{nn} \right) \tag{3}$$

where d_{ij} represents distance between x_i and x_j objects. It's obvious that the more similar the x_i and x_j objects, the closer corresponding points located in a feature space.

Considering the above, in general, the problem of classification of objects in the absence of a training sample consists is to divide into a previously known or unknown number of homogeneous classes of the entire initial set of objects $X = \{x_1, \ldots, x_n\}$ which are represented in the form of an "object-feature" matrix or "object-object" matrix.

Mainly cluster analysis algorithms can be divided into the heuristical, hierarchical, optimization and approximation approaches [13, p. 15–16].

4 Proposed Approach

Given research based on analysis of vibration of the industrial electrical motor. Motor rotating frequency is 52 Hz, all measurements were performed with these parameters. The aim is to find an algorithm, which allows identifying different states of the machine and in the future can be extended to be running on the device and analyze data in real time. Measurements were done with 208 Hz and 416 Hz sample rate. Based on

Nyquist–Shannon–Kotelnikov sampling theorem [14], at least 2 times more than machine main rotating frequency sample rate required.

Below is the outline of the analysis approach:

1. Measure raw vibration using accelerometer on device and store it on flash for further offline analysis;
2. Split all data into time windows, each window is 0.5 s. It means 104 measurements for 208 Hz or 208 measurements to 416 Hz. The same experiments have also been performed for 1.0 s windows and gave similar results;
3. Calculate statistical and descriptive features on this window, e.g. mean, std, skewness, kurtosis, etc.

The approach above can be represented as following execution pipeline (Fig. 4):

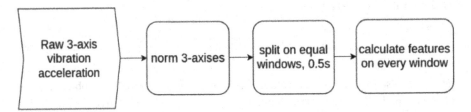

Fig. 4. Features acquisition

5   Experiment Description

Fixed-mount electric motor with possibility of rotation mode variation have been used for measurements. Nine rotation modes have been observed.

There is an illustrative example of measured data on Figs. 5, 6, 7 and 8, which covers approximately 500 s of measurements. Given example describes nine regimes of machine work, let us consider them as $0, 1, \ldots, 8$. It's easy to separate all these states with human eyes, but it may be challenging for automatic detection approach because of the nature of vibration data.

Visualization of standard deviation of vibration acceleration feature given in Fig. 9, calculated on the same timeframe as for Figs. 5, 6, 7 and 8. On this graph it is even easier to separate states with human eyes.

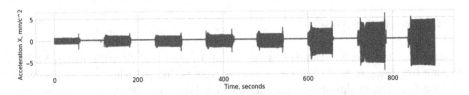

Fig. 5. Raw data at X axis

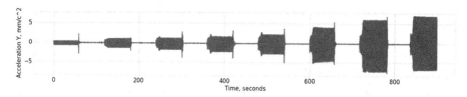

Fig. 6. Raw data at Y axis

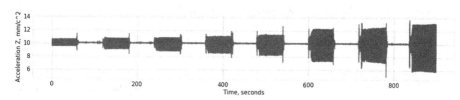

Fig. 7. Raw data at Z axis

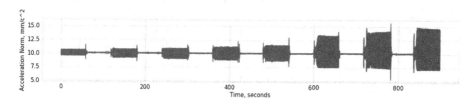

Fig. 8. Raw data module

For the next steps features described above used as input of models. Dealing with such features introducing big compression of the data, what is key point enabling possibility to execute such data analysis pipeline using low end devices.

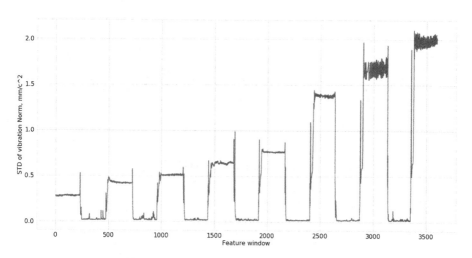

Fig. 9. Acceleration module standard deviation

From the graphs it's clear, that there are several types of intervals, we can identify via vibration:

– stationary states [15];
– dynamic states (transitions) [15].

From statistical point of view, dynamic states are very similar to structural shifts [16] and stationary states are very similar to intervals, which can be approximated by a line parallel to X axis.

The goal is to find appropriate analysis pipeline to be running on a device and working in online mode, so only pattern recognition with unsupervised methods considered. Several commonly used clustering algorithms like k-means, BIRCH, DBSCAN, etc., have been validated.

First lets apply BIRCH, DBSCAN and k-means and other clustering algorithms to source dataset using multiple features: mean, std, rms, peak-to-peak and using single feature only: std.

Result of BIRCH clustering with multiple features illustrated on Fig. 10 and with single feature on Fig. 11. For lack of space results of DBSCAN and k-means algorithms presented for single feature case only on Figs. 12 and 13.

As shown on Figs. 10 and 11 both clustering methods with multiple features and single std feature produce similar results. For BIRCH algorithm some objects from multiple clusters are combined into single cluster in multi-feature case, at the same time these objects are correctly extracted into different clusters in single-feature case.

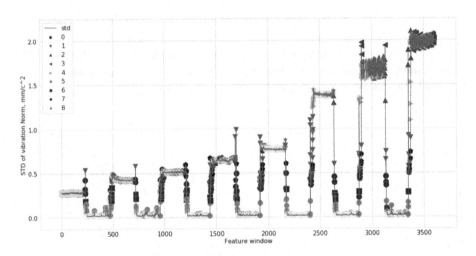

Fig. 10. BIRCH clustering with multiple features

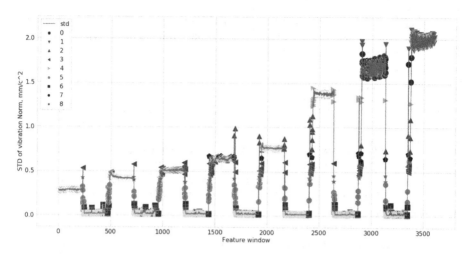

Fig. 11. BIRCH one feature

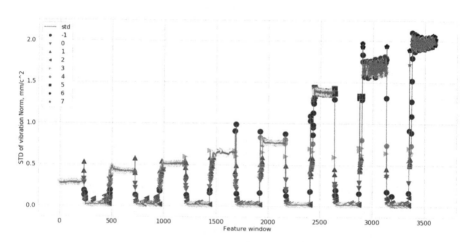

Fig. 12. DBSCAN one feature

Let's introduce numerical measure in order to evaluate clustering quality. Source dataset must be supplied with appropriate clusters labels and following algorithms must take place:

1. Given y_labels, y_pred (arrays of integers). Where y_labels are labels for every record in the dataset, labels are cluster ids (including -1 as a unclustered records); y_preds are predicted labels by any clustering algorithm.
2. Set $unique\_clusters := unique(y\_labels)$; $seen\_predicted\_clusters := \{\}$ (empty set); $total\_score := []$ (empty array)
3. Take the first $cluster\_id$ from $unique\_clusters$.
4. Set $cluster\_array\_ids := []$ (empty list) and then put all ids from the array y_labels where $value == cluster\_id$ into $cluster\_array\_ids$.

5. Set *most_frequent_predicted_cluster* := *y_preds*[*cluster_array_ids*].*mode*(), it means: find the most frequent predicted cluster id from values with ids from *cluster_array_ids* (−1 values should be ignored).

6. Set *score_for_cluster* := 0.

7. Following condition is checked:

   if *most_frequent_predicted_cluster* in *seen_predicted_clusters*, then go to step 11, else go to step 8;

8. Set *count_of_matches* := *len*(*y_preds* == *most_frequent_predicted_cluster*), it means: find count of values in *y_preds* equal to *most_frequent_predicted_cluster*.

9. Set *score_for_cluster* := *max*(1., *count_of_matches*/*len*(*cluster_array_ids*).

10. Add *most_frequent_predicted_cluster* into *seen_predicted_clusters*.

11. Add *score_for_cluster* into *total_score*.

12. Perform steps 4..11 for all others *cluster_id* from *unique_clusters*.

13. Evaluate result as *average*(*total_score*) and stop.

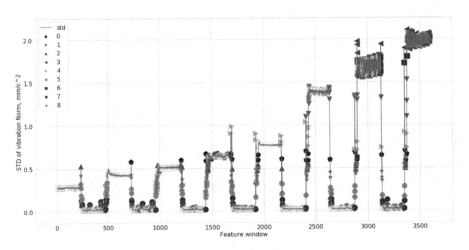

Fig. 13. K-means one feature

Proposed measure should be represented in the following way: minimal possible value is 0, maximum is 1. The higher numeric value of measure means the higher clustering quality.

Intuition under the steps 7, 8, 9: score for the particular cluster is literally "how many records labelled by this cluster id are in the observed indices and labeled by the same id". This value is limited by 1. Because this cluster can cover more records, which could be: unclustered or belong to others cluster in the initial labeling. Case, when these records belong to others clusters, should be handled in special way. That is why unique *most_frequent_predicted_cluster* should be observed only once, so if for some *cluster_id* it covers more records (case when *max*(1., *count_of_matches*/ *len*(*cluster_array_ids*) returns 1.) for some other clusters *score_for_cluster* will be less than 1.

Following Table 1 illustrates results of clustering quality measure for different clustering algorithms using multiple and single features and proves the assumption that desired clustering quality can be achieved with clustering single feature only.

Table 1. Clustering quality measure evaluation

Clustering method	Quality measure (multi-feature)	Quality measure (single-feature)
K-means	0.824	0.982
Birch	0.834	0.981
DBSCAN	0.935	0.841
MiniBatchKMeans	0.977	0.982
GaussianMixture	0.843	0.971

As shown in Table 1 above best clustering quality achieved with k-means algorithms with single clustering feature. Let's analyze clustering structure obtained from the k-means clustering. For that purpose center of cluster as average value of clustering feature and radius of cluster as standard deviation of clustering feature are extracted (Table 2).

Table 2. Centrums and radiuses of clusters

Index of pattern	Cluster centrum	Cluster radius
1	0.0232	0.0098
2	0.2828	0.0088
3	0.427	0.0151
4	0.5111	0.0114
5	0.6392	0.0158
6	0.7673	0.0082
7	1.383	0.0143
8	1.6516	0.0206
9	1.9773	0.0436

Table 2 data indicates that there is a dependency between clusters centers and clusters radiuses: the higher value of cluster center, the higher value of cluster radius obtained. This dependency illustrated on Fig. 14 as well.

Taking into account the nature of source data, following can be concluded: the more vibration level observed, the more clustering metric variation takes place.

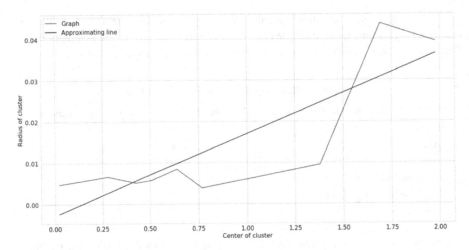

Fig. 14. Dependency between centrum and radius of cluster

6   Conclusions

The data acquisition pipeline was proposed and the technique for machine condition monitoring was shown. Proposed method based on unsupervised learning and in particular BIRCH, DBSCAN and k-means and other clustering for vibration signal processing. The illustrative example with clustering of the signal based on standard deviation feature was shown. The proposed technique allows automatically identifying different states by using a small amount of features extracted from the telemetry signal. The values of the membership function obtained as a result of the clustering procedure can be used for continuous monitoring of the state of the machine, as well as the detection of equipment degradation.

Clustering quality measure have been proposed. High level of clustering quality can be achieved with using single clustering feature only. Proportional dependency between vibration level and characteristics of obtained clustering structure have found.

Results of given research can be used to extend the proposed technique to enable online telemetry signal analysis and machine condition monitoring executed on end devices.

The work was sponsored by Octonion Technology and partially supported by Belarusian Republican Foundation for Fundamental Research (project No. Ф18В-005) and the State Committee on Science and Technology of the Republic of Belarus (project no Ф18ПЛШГ-008П).

References

1. Your AI journey with Brainium and SmartEdge Agile https://www.avnet.com/wps/portal/us/solutions/iot/building-blocks/smartedge-agile/. Accessed 25 Feb 2019
2. LSM6DSL official documentation. https://www.st.com/resource/en/datasheet/lsm6dsl.pdf. Accessed 21 Feb 2019
3. Vibration Analysis: FFT, PSD, and Spectrogram Basics. https://blog.mide.com/vibration-analysis-fft-psd-and-spectrogram. Accessed 25 Feb 2019
4. Jung, D., Zhang, Z., Winslett, M.: Vibration analysis for IoT enabled predictive maintenance. In: 2017 IEEE 33rd International Conference on Data Engineering (ICDE) (2017). https://doi.org/10.1109/icde.2017.170
5. Selcuk, S.: Predictive maintenance, its implementation and latest trends. Proc. Inst. Mech. Eng. Part B: J. Eng. Manuf. **231**(9), 1670–1679 (2016). https://doi.org/10.1177/0954405415601640
6. Schwabacher, M.: A Survey of Data-Driven Prognostics. Infotech@Aerospace (2005). https://doi.org/10.2514/6.2005-7002
7. Miljković, D.: Novelty detection in machine vibration data based on cluster intraset distance (2016)
8. Mosallam, A., Medjaher, K., Zerhouni, N.: Time series trending for condition assessment and prognostics. J. Manuf. Technol. Manag. **25**(4), 550–567 (2014). https://doi.org/10.1108/jmtm-04-2013-0037
9. Amruthnath, N., Gupta, T.: Fault class prediction in unsupervised learning using model-based clustering approach. In: 2018 International Conference on Information and Computer Technologies (ICICT) (2018). https://doi.org/10.1109/infoct.2018.8356831
10. Betta, G., Liguori, C., Paolillo, A., Pietrosanto, A.: A DSP-based FFT-analyzer for the fault diagnosis of rotating machine based on vibration analysis. IEEE Trans. Instrum. Meas. **51**(6), 1316–1322 (2002). https://doi.org/10.1109/tim.2002.807987
11. Al-Badour, F., Sunar, M., Cheded, L.: Vibration analysis of rotating machinery using time–frequency analysis and wavelet techniques. Mech. Syst. Signal Process. **25**(6), 2083–2101 (2011). https://doi.org/10.1016/j.ymssp.2011.01.017
12. Ayvazyan, S.A., Buchstaber, V.M., Enyukov, I.S., Meshalkin, L.D.: Applied statistics: classification and dimension reduction. In: Ayvazian, S.A. (ed.) Finance and Statistics, 607 p. (1989)
13. Viatchenin, D.A.: Fuzzy methods of automatic classification, 219 p. Technoprint, Minsk (2004)
14. Kotel'nikov, V.A.: On the carrying capacity of the "ether" and wire in telecommunications. In: Material for the First All-Union Conference on Questions of Communication. Izd. Red. Upr. Svyazi RKKA, Moscow, Russian (1933)
15. Smirnova, V. (ed.): Basis of vibration measurement. According to the materials of the company DLI. http://www.vibration.ru/osn_vibracii.shtml. Accessed 21 Feb 2019
16. Pasinetti, L.L.: Structural Change and Economic Growth, Chap. 11. Cambridge University Press, Cambridge

Temporal Convolutional and Recurrent Networks for Image Captioning

Natalia Iskra[1($\boxtimes$)] and Vitaly Iskra[2]

[1] Belarusian State University of Informatics and Radioelectronics,
Minsk, Republic of Belarus
niskra@bsuir.by
[2] Omnigon Communications LLC, New York, NY, USA
vitaly.iskra@omnigon.com

Abstract. Recently temporal convolutional networks have shown excellent qualities in sequence modeling tasks [1]. Taking this fact into account, in this paper we investigate the possibilities of replacing recurrent networks in architectures targeted specifically at image captioning. We evaluate the solution on Visual Genome dataset [2], which provides extensive set of labels and descriptions that thoroughly grounds visual concepts to natural language.

Keywords: Image captioning · Convolutional neural networks · Recurrent neural networks · Visual Genome · Dilated convolution · Weight normalization · Dropout · Adam optimization

1 Introduction

Recent thorough study [1] has shown the advantages of convolutional neural networks (CNN) over recurrent neural networks (RNN) in tasks that include modeling of various sequences. Among other synthetic stress tests, such as adding sequences or copying big chunks of data, relatively simple convolutional structures (e.g. TCN) outperform canonical recurrent architectures (e.g. LSTM, GRU) on sequential handwritten symbols classification, audio sequences modeling, character-level and word-level language processing. Although in general CNN structures have additional memory requirements for data storage during evaluation and domain transfer, as opposed to RNN structures, the following advantages are prevalent:

- convolutions during training and evaluation can be performed in parallel;
- CNNs have better control of the model capacity due to flexible receptive fields configuration;
- unlike RNNs, CNNs are devoid of exploding gradients;
- CNNs can share filters across layers thus there is no need to store partial results when processing long input sequences;
- by sliding 1-D kernels along the input sequence, CNN can manage variable length data just like RNN.

Since convolutional approach proved to be effective for language modeling tasks, it is of the highest interest to examine its benefits for tasks, which include sentence

© Springer Nature Switzerland AG 2019
S. V. Ablameyko et al. (Eds.): PRIP 2019, CCIS 1055, pp. 254–266, 2019.
https://doi.org/10.1007/978-3-030-35430-5_21

modeling, such as machine translation, text summarization or image annotation. In this paper we investigate image captioning task, as the architectures of traditional solutions often include hybrid CNN + RNN approach, where CNNs are used mainly to process the image and RNNs – to produce the language description. We are particularly interested in dense captioning task [3] as it generalizes object detection and image captioning in convolutional part of the model and it appears beneficial to aim towards further generalization over the language modeling part, i.e. caption generation.

2 RNN in Image Captioning

The goal of image captioning is to generate a syntactically and semantically correct natural language description for a given image. Intermediate steps of the task, as a rule, include object detection, object attributes estimation, relations between objects establishing and corresponding natural language sequences producing.

In Fig. 1 the simple ontology-based solution [4] is shown.

(street, traffic)

"the person rides the motorbike"

"the person walks the dog"

"the person stands near the bicycle"

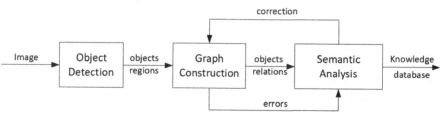

Fig. 1. Ontology-based image captioning. Source image from MS COCO dataset [5]

First, the object detection task is performed. Based on the objects and regions initial closeness graph is built. Graph construction unit specifies the relations. Semantic analysis unit determines the context (street, traffic) using ontology and detects possible errors. Errors can be corrected either by re-detecting the object on regions with errors, or using knowledge, stored in the knowledge base. According to the adjusted model, taking into account the subject-object language relationships and replacing the relations designation with appropriate language constructs (in this case, verbs) semantic descriptions can be constructed.

Although traditionally template-based [6] and retrieval-based [7] methods can be used for simple captions generation and, as a reverse task, for image retrieval based on its description, the so-called "novel" methods, that extensively use deep learning techniques, are rapidly developing currently [8].

The majority of applied architectures (e.g. encoder-decoder architecture shown in Fig. 2) typically use convolutional neural networks for image processing (objects and attributes detection) and recurrent neural networks (prevalently LSTM) for language modeling (text generation, quality ranking and evaluation).

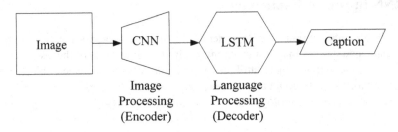

Fig. 2. Encoder-decoder architecture for image captioning

Different ways to connect CNN output to RNN have been applied. The straight-forward approach is to directly feed the output of the CNN (visual features) to the RNN. Another idea is to use so-called visual attention mechanism. The input to RNN is a sequence of encoded words; each word is enriched by a surrounding context [9]. Based on a current word, RNN (Fig. 3, right side graph) defines the probability of the next word in the sequence.

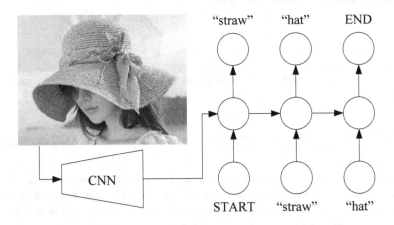

Fig. 3. Multimodal RNN model as described in [9]

The main disadvantages of using RNN-based models are:

– the model allows only sequential calculation and therefore does not support parallel computing;
– for long sentences data can be "forgotten" due to high memory demand.

To avoid the latter problem tree structures were proposed [10], however they also cannot be parallelized easily and may not be the best choice for image captioning task.

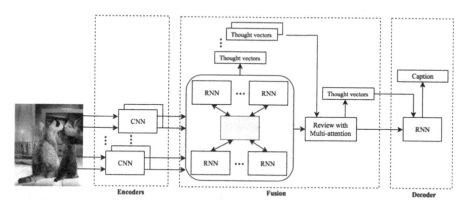

Fig. 4. Recurrent fusion network for image captioning [11]

Recent work on improving encoder-decoder framework for image captioning advances along the two orthogonal directions:

1. The usage of multiple encoders to obtain complementary information during the fusion process as proposed in [11]. The fusion process consists of two additional steps. Each step can be regarded as special RNN thus adding more reccurency into the model (Fig. 4).
   However, the results show high performance and the solution appears to better comprehend semantic meaning of the input image as opposed to single CNN as an encoder.
2. The employment of only convolution networks for both encoding (vision) and decoding (language) as proposed in [12] (Fig. 5).

The model can be trained in parallel and due to hierarchical structure can learn image concepts in a meaningful way. It has been also shown that increasing the kernel width in language model CNN is more effective than stacking additional layers.

In this work we are particularly interested in the second idea, as the use of only convolutional networks, especially the ones of lesser depth, can sufficiently compress the model size thus enabling the application on even mobile devices.

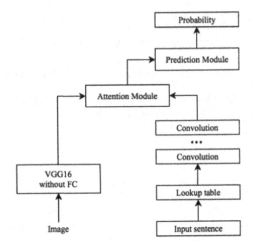

Fig. 5. Convolutional decoders for image captioning [12]

3   Experimental Setup

As a base model for experimental setup we have chosen Dense Captioning architecture [3]. This model jointly addresses localization and description tasks by deploying fully convolutional localization network architecture that processes an image with a single efficient pass and also allows for further optimization.

The base model overview is shown in Fig. 6.

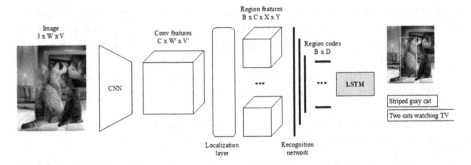

Fig. 6. Base dense captioning model as described in [3]

The input image is first processed by CNN VGG-16 architecture, which encodes the image as a set of uniformly sampled locations. The localization layer based on samples proposes regions similar to Faster R-CNN approach [13] but with bilinear interpolation instead of RoI pooling to enable gradient backwards propagation. The regions are processed with fully connected network. However, we use convolutional architecture shown in Fig. 7 as a language model instead of RNN (LSTM in Fig. 6). The whole model can be trained with gradient descent end-to-end.

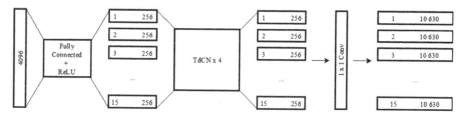

Fig. 7. Convolutional language model

The core of the model is a multilayer temporal convolutional network employing dilated convolutions (TCN or TdCN in Fig. 7).

The model is trained to map feature vectors, produced by the fully connected layer at the output of the region recognition network, to the sequence of words.

To prepare feature vectors to be processed by the TCN we first transform them by another fully connected layer followed by the ReLU non-linearity. The result is organized as a series of 1-D vectors that are fed to the sequence (4 blocks in total) of TCN-blocks. Each block contains several convolutions with weight normalization [14], ReLU activation and a dropout.

The scheme for one TCN-block with 3 convolutions is shown in Fig. 8.

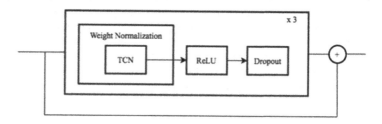

Fig. 8. Temporal dilated convolutional network structure

Following [1] we use dilation of 2 in temporal convolution layers in order to increase effective receptive field of the output. We also pad the input of each convolutional layer at the beginning with zeroes to achieve the same number of data frames in the output of each layer.

Three successive convolutions are joined into a block (TCN-block) surrounded by a residual connection [15]. Four successive TCN-blocks produce a number of 1-D vectors that are regarded as a sequence of word-vectors produced by the language model. Then the final 1×1 convolution followed by SoftMax is applied to these word-vectors to convert them into the probability vectors of widths equal to the vocabulary size (including special END and NULL tokens).

The resulting caption is constructed of words with highest probabilities until the END token is encountered.

4 Results

We test 2 approaches to train the language model:

1. Use feature maps from the pre-trained DenseCap model and train only the TCN language model.
2. Embed TCN language model into DenseCap and train the whole architecture end-to-end.

When training only the language model we split the features produced by the DenseCap detector into mini-batches of size 1024. We then use Adam [16] to train the language model.

The learning rate is 0.002, $\beta1 = 0.9$, $\beta2 = 0.999$.

We train 3 TCN-based models with convolutional layers of depths 8, 16 and 256 (as shown in Fig. 8) on Visual Genome dataset [2].

One mini-batch for the largest (256) model takes approximately 3 s on NVIDIA Tesla K80 GPU. The model converges after approximately 6,000–7,000 batches (6,000,000–7,000,000 samples), which takes around 6 h.

To compare, it took 2 days on NVIDIA Tesla P100 GPU to train LSTM-based model.

DenseCap produces around 8,500,000 samples on the whole Visual Genome training set, so in practice not even 1 full epoch is needed for the model to converge.

We calculate METEOR metric [17] for 4 language models: original DenseCap with LSTM and our 3 TCN-based models. The results are shown in Table 1.

Table 1. Experimental results.

Language model	METEOR
LSTM	0.150
TCN, 8	0.128
TCN, 16	0.135
TCN, 256	0.149

5 Analysis and Discussion

An example of an actual image captioning results is shown in Fig. 9.

Further, we would like to address the problem of image captioning results evaluation.

Unlike detection and recognition tasks, where the results can be evaluated directly, it is quite not trivial to establish whether the caption is correct or not. The evaluation concerns factual (correct objects and attributes), syntactical (correct structure of phrases) and semantical (correct relations and meaning) aspects [18].

Fig. 9. Image captioning results. Source image from Visual Genome dataset [2]

The most common approach is to use metrics, that numerically evaluate the closeness of the candidate solution for image captioning to the reference, where candidates and references can be presented either as sentences, or as graphs. Visual Genome provides both sentences and graphs. But as for now we are evaluating the sequence modeling abilities of TCN, the sentences will be used.

We use METEOR metric as it is quite simple to calculate and the original paper [3] provides results for comparison.

The METEOR (metric for evaluation of translation with explicit ordering) [17] algorithm performs word-to-word matching between candidate (the caption generated by the model) and reference (the sentence or set of sentences provided for each image for training and/or evaluation). It additionally considers stems of words and synonyms.

The following notions are used in the equation:

- *unigram* – a single word;
- *alignment* – mapping between unigrams such that each unigram in candidate maps to 0 or 1 unigram in reference and to 0 unigrams in candidate;
- *chunk* – the longest possible sequence of unigrams in adjacent positions, that create an alignment.

The METEOR score is computed as follows:

$$M = F(1 - p) \tag{1}$$

where M – final score for a candidate, F – harmonic mean, p – penalty.

$$p = 0.5 \left(\frac{c}{m} \right)^3 \tag{2}$$

where c – number of chunks, m – number of mapped unigrams.

The equation for harmonic mean, which combines unigram precision and recall is:

$$F = \frac{10PR}{R+9P} \qquad (3)$$

where P – unigram precision (ratio of mapped unigrams m, to the number of unigrams in a candidate w_t), R – unigram recall (ratio of mapped unigrams m, to the number of unigrams in a reference w_r).

It should be noted, that prevalently rather small (<0.2) values of METEOR for image captioning task are usually reached [5].

Although in original paper [3] the highest METEOR score of 0.305 on ground truth boxes is reported, we evaluate full cycle, including boxes detection and don't use additional techniques to try to improve the score.

As shown in Table 1, the performance of our TCN language model grows with the depth of convolutional layers and almost reaches that of the original LSTM of 0.15.

The analysis of the actual resulting captions shows, that TCN is biased towards words with high occurrence in the ground truth vocabulary such as articles "a", "the", prepositions "on", "of", etc. (Figure 10).

Ground truth:
"a round and white plate on a table"

LSTM: *"white on table"*

TCN: *"a white on on"*

Fig. 10. TCN is biased towards words with high occurrence in the ground truth vocabulary. Source image from Visual Genome dataset [2]

The captions produced by convolutional language model are also less intelligible, as the model is not trained to correlate the data (Fig. 11).

The result in Fig. 11 produced by LSTM-based model also shows, that the resulting caption can contain cycles ("<smth.> of a <smth.> of a <smth.>") which is common in recurrent models. TCN-based model is devoid of such occurrences.

It should be noted, that although TCN-based model doesn't take into account correlation between terms, it can be trained using n-grams (mainly 2- or 3-grams) that include common relations between objects in the vocabulary (e.g. "plate on table" instead of separate terms "plate", "on" and "table").

Ground truth:
"a basket full of fruits"

LSTM:
"basket of a fruit of a fruit"

TCN:
"a green on bananas"

Fig. 11. TCN can produce less intelligible results than LSTM. Source image from Visual Genome dataset [2] (Color figure online)

While analyzing the sentences produced by image captioning models it is also appropriate to address the so-called "human judgment" evaluation. It is important that results can be considered as "natural" by human peers.

There are quite a few satisfactory results, that exceed those produced by LSTM model, according to human judgment (Fig. 12).

Ground truth:
"white clouds in the sky"

LSTM:
"the sky is blue in color"

TCN:
"white clouds in blue sky"

Fig. 12. The case of TCN producing better results than LSTM. Source image from Visual Genome dataset [2]

It is evident that the convolutional language model requires considerably less resources and is amenable to optimization over a wide range of hyper parameters. The loss functions shown in Fig. 13 illustrate smooth model convergence.

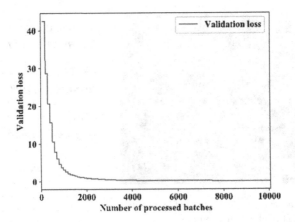

Fig. 13. Loss function over time for TCN, 256 with batches of 256

Further investigation of resources employed by the model shows, that the major part of the model is comprised of feature vectors (of size 4096) mapping, which is stipulated by the original DenseCap architecture. Therefore, for other encoder-decoder architectures the TCN-based language model can be further compressed.

6 Further Work

Further, we want to address the problems encountered by the TCN-based language model for image captioning and the ways to solve some of them:

- the problem of the vocabulary can be solved by penalizing frequent words, such as "a", "the", "this", etc.;
- adding the frequent relations (as provided by Visual Genome dataset) can teach the model to generate more intelligible sequences;
- the initial architecture can also be further modified to minimize memory consumption.

The intuition behind dealing with words that frequently occur in ground truth vocabulary is presented in consensus-based image evaluation method also known as CIDEr [19].

Given the sentence is represented using the set of *n*-grams – a set of 1 (unigram) or more ordered words. The measure of consensus encodes how often candidate *n*-grams are presented in the reference. Correspondingly n-grams not presented in the reference should not occur in the candidate. And finally, n-grams that commonly occur across all the references are likely to be less significant. Method CIDEr uses term frequency metric while calculating cosine similarity between candidate and references.

Similarly, we use term frequency weighing of the auxiliary terms (articles and prepositions) across the training vocabulary, resulting in better captions, e.g. for the cases, described above: "white plate" (Fig. 10), "green banana" (Fig. 11). Moreover, such candidates yield higher evaluation scores, as these 2-grams are presented in the reference.

7 Conclusion

To sum up, we have shown that to some extent convolutional language model, that deploys state-of-the-art elements, such as dilated convolutions, residual connections, dropout, weight normalization, Adam optimization, can be used for image captioning. It shows smooth convergence, consumes significantly less resources (time and memory), however, undoubtedly needs additional techniques to produce more natural results.

In our future work we plan to use additional techniques described above to catch up with the performance of the language model.

We also plan to apply TCN-based model to several other top-performing architectures developed recently, not limited to only encoder-decoder architectures.

References

1. Bai, S., Colter, J.Z., Coltun, V.: An empirical evaluation of generic convolutional and recurrent networks for sequence modeling. arXiv preprint arXiv:1803.01271 (2018)
2. Krishna, R., Zhu, Y., Groth, O., et al.: Visual genome: connecting language and vision using crowdsourced dense image annotations. Int. J. Comput. Vis. 1(123), 32–73 (2017)
3. Johnson, J., Karpathy, A., Fei-Fei, L.: DenseCap: fully convolutional localization networks for dense captioning. In: Proceedings of the IEEE Conference on Computer Vision and Pattern Recognition, pp. 4565–4574 (2016)
4. Iskra, N., Iskra, V., Lukashevich M.: Neural network based image understanding with ontological approach. In: Open Semantic Technologies for Intelligent Systems (OSTIS-2019), pp. 113–122 (2019)
5. Lin, T.-Y., et al.: Microsoft COCO: common objects in context. In: Fleet, D., Pajdla, T., Schiele, B., Tuytelaars, T. (eds.) ECCV 2014. LNCS, vol. 8693, pp. 740–755. Springer, Cham (2014). https://doi.org/10.1007/978-3-319-10602-1_48
6. Kulkarni, G., et al.: Baby talk: understanding and generating image descriptions. In: Proceedings of the 24th Conference on Computer Vision and Pattern Recognition (2011)
7. Sun, C., Gan, C., Nevatia, R.: Automatic concept discovery from parallel text and visual corpora. In: Proceedings of the IEEE International Conference on Computer Vision, pp. 2596–2604 (2015)
8. Hossain, M.D., Sohel, F., Shiratuddin, M.F., Laga, H.: A comprehensive survey of deep learning for image captioning. ACM Comput. Surv. (CSUR) 6(51), 118 (2019)
9. Karpathy, A., Fei-Fei, L.: Deep visual-semantic alignments for generating image descriptions. In: Proceedings of the IEEE Conference on Computer Vision and Pattern Recognition, pp. 3128–3137 (2015)
10. Liu, D., Hanwang, Zh., Zheng-Jun, Zh., Feng, W.: Explainability by parsing: neural module tree networks for natural language visual grounding. arXiv preprint, arXiv:1812.03299 (2018)
11. Jiang, W., Ma, L., Jiang, Y.-G., Liu, W., Zhang, T.: Recurrent fusion network for image captioning. In: Ferrari, V., Hebert, M., Sminchisescu, C., Weiss, Y. (eds.) ECCV 2018. LNCS, vol. 11206, pp. 510–526. Springer, Cham (2018). https://doi.org/10.1007/978-3-030-01216-8_31
12. Wang, Q., Chan, A.B.: CNN + CNN: Convolutional decoders for image captioning. arXiv preprint, arXiv:1805.09019 (2018)

13. Ren, S., He, K., Girshick, R., Sun, J.: Faster R-CNN: towards real-time object detection with region proposal networks. In: Advances in Neural Information Processing Systems, pp. 91–99 (2015)
14. Salimans, T., Kingma, D.: Weight normalization: a simple reparameterization to accelerate training of deep neural networks. In: Advances in Neural Information Processing Systems, pp. 901–909 (2016)
15. He, K., Zhang, X., Ren, S., Sun, J.: Deep residual learning for image recognition. In: Proceedings of the IEEE Conference on Computer Vision and Pattern Recognition, pp. 770–778 (2016)
16. Kingma, D., Ba., J.: Adam: a method for stochastic optimization. arXiv preprint, arXiv:1412.6980 (2014)
17. Banerjee, S., Lavie, A.: METEOR: an automatic metric for MT evaluation with improved correlation with human judgments. In: Proceedings of the ACL Workshop on Intrinsic and Extrinsic Evaluation Measures for Machine Translation and/or Summarization (2005)
18. Iskra, N., Shunkevich, D.: Ontological approach to image captioning evaluation. In: Proceedings of Pattern Recognition and Information Processing, pp. 219–223 (2019)
19. Vedantam, R., Zitnick, C.L., Parikh, D.: Cider: consensus-based image description evaluation. In: Proceedings of the IEEE Conference on Computer Vision and Pattern Recognition, pp. 4566–4575 (2015)

Modeling of Intelligent Systems Architecture Based on the Brain Topology

Oleg Baranovski, Viktor Krasnoproshin,
and Alexander Valvachev(✉)

Belarusian State University, Nezavisimosti Avenue 4,
Minsk, Republic of Belarus
lbov@mail.ru, krasnoproshin@bsu.by,
vanaisoftbgu@gmail.com

Abstract. The article presents the results of the unification of the architecture of computer intelligent systems based on the topology of the functional systems of the human brain intelligence. A pragmatic conceptual framework is proposed that eliminates the polysemy characteristic of this area, a set of models and algorithms is developed that unifies and standardizes the decision-making process. As part of the multi-agent approach, a special unified system architecture and the corresponding program library were developed and implemented. The effectiveness of the approach is demonstrated by an example of solving an applied problem.

Keywords: Intelligent systems · Ultra large scale systems · Decision making · Monitoring systems · Program agents

1 Introduction

As a result of globalization and informatization of the world community, the demand for intelligent systems (IS) has sharply increased, which solve some intellectual problems and predict the consequences of decisions faster and better than people [1]. Especially rapidly ISs are being developed in the fields of computer games, voice assistants, text translators, autonomous aircrafts and cars; diagnosis of diseases based on DNA and medical images; monitoring of the environment and agricultural land. But there are new areas of application for ISs. One of the most promising is the monitoring of new types of organizational and technical systems, which include: associations of computerized states, economic clusters, IT-giants, mega-shops, international corporations, banking associations, smart towns, smart grids, etc. [2, 3]. In the literature, such systems are defined in different ways: as hypersystems (K. Ivanov), extra-large systems (A.I. Berg), large-scale systems (J. Casti), large systems (G.I. Burkov), complex adaptive systems (M. Gell-Mann), ultra large scale systems (L. Northrop), etc. In this work, we use the last option - ULSS - as the most pragmatic [4].

ULSS includes a large number of geographically distributed components that are linked by common strategic objectives. Achieving goals depends on the performance of each component, therefore, the most important task is to determine the state of the components in real time and eliminate critical situations at an early stage of their

S. V. Ablameyko et al. (Eds.): PRIP 2019, CCIS 1055, pp. 267–279, 2019.
https://doi.org/10.1007/978-3-030-35430-5_22

development. For this, ISs performing online component monitoring (Intelligent Monitoring Systems - IMSs) are required. Systems should be simple to develop, deploy and operate. This is a necessary requirement, as many ULSS monitoring projects are experimental and have a minimal budget. In this case, monitoring is understood in a broad sense - as a system for monitoring an object, assessing its condition and making appropriate management decisions.

Currently, the monitoring systems sphere is dominated by the SCADA IS group [5]. They focus on a specific type of an object or process, a specific task, monogenic data and have a rigid original architecture. Unfortunately, such systems are difficult to modify, prone to hacker attacks and are quite expensive. Therefore, they are used to monitor stationary or mobile objects with constant processes in metallurgy, energy, oil and gas industry, transport and pharmaceutical companies.

The indicated features of these systems do not allow their use for monitoring ULSS, especially for pilot projects. Therefore, of great scientific and practical interest are methods of constructing easy-to-develop, easily modifiable and affordable IMS. Obviously, they must overcome the shortcomings of the SCADA group systems and facilitate a common view and understanding of ULSS and IMS. To do this, it is necessary to resolve the following problems:

- "The polysemy problem". The basic definitions and ontological models used to describe ULSS and IMS are often contradictory and more philosophical than pragmatic. A unified pragmatic conceptual basis is needed, clearly understood by customers, designers, programmers and users;
- "The problem of architecture unification". Existing IMSs were built according to original designs and original architectures, which led to a high cost of the result, non-interoperability of software modules and a narrow circle of their users. To reduce costs, it is necessary to develop a unified architecture sufficient to monitor ULSS;
- "The problem of data heterogeneity". The objects of observation in ULSS are people, processes, technical devices, etc. Therefore, the input data are of various types, including "int, byte, double, string, boolean", etc. The heterogeneity of data makes it difficult to develop unified algorithms for processing [2]. The way out of this situation is to develop a common ULSS and IMS mechanism for converting all input data to a type convenient for processing;
- "The problem of decision coherence". Decisions made at the entity level may conflict with the goals and limitations of the upper layers of ULSS. For example, deliveries of goods that are advantageous for an individual company may be contrary to the interests of the country as a whole. Therefore, decisions based on "hot" data often lead to strategic losses. To exclude such cases, a mechanism is needed to coordinate operational decisions of an object with its own knowledge base, as well as with the goals and limitations of higher levels;
- "The problem of knowledge losing". When streaming tasks, the database accumulates a gigantic array of potentially useful information, which is often accumulated over the years or erased. For more efficient use of information, it is necessary to develop a mechanism for periodically extracting knowledge and cleaning up databases.

Reducing the cost of IMS can be achieved in the traditional way - by unifying the processes of developing software systems on a single scientific and technological basis. The fundamental basis for this, as shown in the well-known works of J. von Neumann, N. Wiener, W. McCulloch, W. Pitts, A. Turing, Y. Bengio, P.K. Anokhin, G. Hinton, Y. Lecun and others, can serve the human brain intelligence models. Therefore, in this work, as a basis for the unification of the IMS architecture, some results of studies by neuroscientists were selected.

2 Conceptual Basis

As a basis for constructing a conceptual framework, the works of Berg [6], Klir [7], Anokhin [8], Burkov [9] are taken.

To construct a conceptual framework describing ULSS, it is proposed to use the definition of the academician Berg, because it is invariant to the IMS type and can be adapted to modern conditions: "ULSS is a collection of large systems interconnected "by induction" method" [6].

We formulate the conceptual framework in the form of the following provisions.

1. The modern information society consists of a set of ULSS.
2. ULSS consist of three types of entities: control mechanisms (*A*), heterogeneous subsystems of any nesting level (*B*) and objects (*C*), united by common strategic goals and global communications (*com*).
3. The activities of entities *A*, *B*, *C* are characterized by the parameters <*X*>, the values of which are formed in the sources *K* and measured by sensors (*dt*).
4. Entities a, b, c are controlled by people (ni) and intelligent systems (ai) of various types, including monitoring systems (IMS).
5. Based on the values of *X*, the IMS can determine the state (*V*) of entities *A*, *B*, *C* and make appropriate control decisions (*U*).

Next, we clarify the most important concepts: the task, data, information, knowledge on the basis of which we will unify the concept, composition and architecture of IMS [2].

Task is a verbal description of a situation requiring resolution for a specific purpose. Each task has priority, depending on the importance of the object of observation for homeostasis.

Scene is natural and artificial participants in solving a problem (actors), interconnected by communications.

Data is a set of parameter values that characterize the situation.

Information is filtered and structured data that have undergone primary processing, sufficient for the synthesis of knowledge.

Knowledge is the result of processing consolidated information sufficient to effectively solve a problem with a forecast of the impact of the result on the future.

An intelligent system is a self-learning hardware and software system that provides the collection of data and its transformation into information and knowledge to solve intellectual problems faster and more economically than people do.

These definitions impose serious restrictions on the structure of IMS, but give complete freedom of choice of methods for implementing each element of the structure.

3 Problem Statement

Let there be ULSS represented by a hierarchy of three types of entities: administration A, subsystems B, and objects C. Activities A, B, C are managed by niA, niB, niC to achieve the goals of GA, GB, GC within the framework of $ResA$, $ResB$, $ResC$ and restrictions $LimA$, $LimB$, $LimC$. ULSS entities are characterized by parameters XA, XB, XC whose heterogeneous values come from sources Z and are detected by dt sensors. Depending on the values of X, entities A, B, C can be in one of the possible states $V1, \ldots, Vk$, each of which corresponds to a control solution $U1, \ldots, Uk$.

It is required to develop methods and software for creating IMS, including:

- Unified decision-making scheme;
- Unified architecture of IMS, invariant to the nature of A, B, C;
- Method for normalizing heterogeneous values of X;
- Synthesis algorithm of a consistent solution, taking into account common goals, resources and constraints;
- Software for IMS building.

The decision must be open, i.e. the number of subsystems B can be any.

4 Decision

4.1 Unified Decision Making Scheme

According to the chosen approach, the ULSS monitoring scheme should correspond to certain brain functionality. To construct the scheme, we briefly consider the results of studies of neuroscientists, on which we will rely [10–13].

Evolutionarily, the brain has formed as three inextricably linked components:

- the ancient part of R (reptilian brain), receives and processes X signals (stimulus) from internal and external sources and ensures the survival of the object in the natural environment. The differentiability of the solutions is minimal. It has the highest priority, because provides biological homeostasis of the object;
- the middle part M (mammalian brain), receives the results of work from the ancient part and ensures survival in the group of mammals. The differentiability of solutions is increasing.
- the young part H (homo sapiens brain), receives results from the ancient and middle parts, ensures survival in human society (social environment). The differentiability of solutions is unlimited.

Each part included:

- Sensors that receive signals (stimuli) from internal and external heterogeneous sources;

- Functional for working with data (*fRdm, fMd, fHd*), information (*fRinf, fMinf, fHinf*), knowledge (*fRkn, fMkn, fHkn*);
- Short-term memory (*mRs, mMs, mHs*);
- Long-term memory (*mRl, mMl, mHl*).

The content of the ancient part of *R* is formed by evolution and is minimally subject to change for adaptation to the environment. Content *M* is more flexible in communication and food production. Content *H* is phenomenally flexible and changes in the learning process from birth to death. The memory is represented by neural networks "living actually" for various periods of time - from one hour to tens of years.

The decision-making process of the brain is as follows, given the above definitions:

- *X* signals from the medium are detected by *dt* sensors and enter *R*;
- *R* processes and analyzes *X*, formulated the task, its purpose and priority, selects the executor (*R, R-M, R-M-H*) to whom the task is transferred for the solution;
- The performer forms a scene, looks for a solution of *V, U* in long-term memory or forms a new one;
- The result *V, U* is coordinated (*fAgr*) with each part (with the veto right *R*) and a general decision *V, U* is formed;
- The result of *V, U* is transmitted to motor networks (*fMot*) for execution.

In fact, any solution is an agreed product that takes into account the interests of three parts.

When the volume of *X* signals decreases (for example, during sleep), the so-called default mode (*fDef*) is activated [12]. In the process of its work, information from short-term memory is processed into knowledge (training) and recorded in long-term memory. Information that is distinguished by the emotional power of the signal, novelty, discrepancy between real and expected situations, or a large number of repetitions of the situation is transferred to the "knowledge" class. Thus, the brain solves an endless stream of tasks, using the accumulated knowledge and acquiring a new one.

To build a unified ULSS structure and IMS architecture based on the described process, it is enough to compare:

- part R with entity A (ULSS manual);
- part M with entity B (subsystem ULSS);
- part H with entity C (ULSS objects);
- short-term memory - with a database of "hot" data (Hot Base);
- long-term memory - with a corporate knowledge base (Knowledge Base).

The input for *X* must be changed from *A* to *C*, because in ULSS, the bulk of the source data comes from the most active and volatile entity *C*. Entities *A* and *B* also receive data, but they are usually used to correct goals, limitations, and resources. To build the data processing functions *fCd, fBd, fAd*, there are many methods and libraries for recognizing text, digital, graphic, audio and video data types. For the functions of analysis and synthesis of information *fCinf, fBinf, fAinf*, methods of the Data Mining group [14] are used. For the knowledge extraction functions *fCkn, fBkn, fAkn*, the methods of the Knowledge Discovery group [14] are used, including the well-known

Deep Learning and Hierarchical Temporal Memory algorithms. The agreed result is implemented in motor skills or sent to ni- and ai-actors. In general, the described processes are presented in Fig. 1.

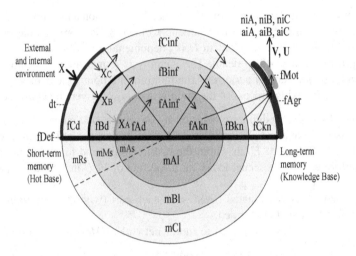

Fig. 1. Decision making scheme in ULSS

In general, this scheme is similar to the well-known Swanson scheme [11], but it details the structure of elements and opens up unlimited possibilities for the implementation of each of its elements inside a common rigid frame.

4.2   Multi-agents IMS Architecture

To build an IMS architecture based on this scheme, it is advisable to use a multi-agent approach [2, 3], because it is initially focused on the application in distributed systems.

An agent is an autonomous program of a unified structure that participates in solving a problem together with other agents. A group of agents sufficient to solve is called a multi-agent system (*MAS*) [2, 15].

As a result of applying the agent approach, in many cases it is possible to standardize the structure of program modules and the architecture of systems of a certain class [2]. The use of agents with a standard structure for a specific class of tasks significantly saves time for writing, debugging, and modifying programs. Agents are very effective in developing of systems for environmental monitoring, analysis of the social networks content, remote monitoring of people with disabilities.

The main problem in the use of agents is the diversity of their structure and the difficulty of choosing the most suitable one for solving the task.

To build a multi-agent IMS structure, it is enough to display the functionality of each level in Fig. 1 in *MAS* with its own Hot Base and Knowledge Base. As a result, we obtain the architecture shown in Fig. 2.

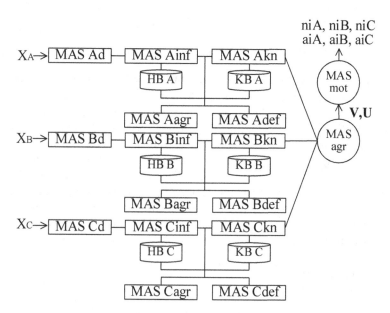

Fig. 2. Unified multi-agent IMS architecture

This model has several advantages:

- each ULSS participant solves his tasks taking into account the goals and limitations common to ULSS, which minimizes the threat of crisis in ULSS;
- participants of levels *A, B* observe and control the performance of lower levels and can undertake operational measures to improve their performance;
- in the event of a threat, each participant can quickly use the resources of higher levels, which also reduces the likelihood of a ULSS crisis as a whole;
- with the proper level of development of artificial intelligence, this scheme can function with minimal participation of people.

4.3   Agent Structure

The main way to reduce the development cost of *MAS* IMS is to unify the structure of its constituent agents. Within the framework of the chosen approach, it is proposed to use an agent model [2], similar to the well-known McCulloch-Pitts neuron model, as the basis for the standard structure:

$$ag = (sens, proc, eff, mem) \tag{1}$$

where: *sens* - input signal fixing devices; *proc* - solution synthesis algorithms; *eff* - execution of the decision; *mem* - the memory.

To adapt to IMS, we supplement (1) with five fields:

$$agIMS = (sens, proc, eff, mem, adr, links, pow, t, k) \tag{2}$$

where: adr - the address of the agent in the MAS to access the agent from other MAS; $links$ - addresses of other MAS agents to which the result of the agent's work is sent when solving a common problem; pow - input signal power (used to form short-term memory according to the "long-lasting potentiation" principle (T. Lomo) based on the emotional power of input signals; t - agent activation time (used to form short-term memory according to the "summation" principle (E. Kandel) based on a large number of repetitions of weak input signals; k - the number of agent activations (used in agent ranking mechanisms in order to minimize access time to the most popular ones).

This version of the agent structure is more universal, because allows you to separate in space the processes of working with data, information, knowledge and, if necessary, improve them individually.

4.4   Data Type Unification

In the brain, the initial data (signals from the sensors) are represented by two types - chemical and electrical. In ULSS, the data characterizing the entities A, B, C is represented by many types: *int*, *char*, *string*, *boolean*, which are quite difficult to process using mathematical methods. Obviously, it is best to reduce them to one type - *double*. To implement this idea, we use the fuzzy sets theory proposed by Zadeh [16]. The implementation includes three stages:

- Construction of a unified X-ranked scale E [0.00–1.00];
- Construction for each parameter $X1, \ldots, Xn$ of membership functions $f1, \ldots, fn$ to map them to the set E;
- Mapping with the help $f1, \ldots, fn$ of each input value of X to the range 0.00–1.00 and mathematical processing of the result.

This approach is quite simple to implement when developing sensors, each of which can be identified by an address in ULSS and by type of model (for a person, device, process, etc.). Regardless of the sensor type, the controller will produce a *double* type value that is convenient for mathematical processing.

4.5   Decision Making Algorithm

The decision-making process in ULSS, which consists of millions of objects in the face of growing global uncertainty, is quite complicated, so the methods for automating it are far from perfect. In the framework of the scheme shown in Fig. 2, this process becomes more regulated, because its participants are known, their roles, information flows and stages of their processing by analogy with the human brain intelligence. Accordingly, the decision-making algorithm should be similar. The following option is proposed.

In the description we will use the symbolism:

HB - hot base
KB - knowledge base
sat (to what) - the operator of "compliance"
agr (<who>, <that>) - the "agree" operator
snd (<to>, <what> - the "send" operator
do (to whom, what) - the "execute" operator
def (ai) - operator "default mode"

Step 01. // system deployment
  A, niA, aiA, GA, ResA, LimA, <>, <B, C>, XA, EA
  B, niB, aiB, GB, ResB, LimB, <A>, <C>, XB, EB
  C, niC, aiC, GC, ResC, LimC, <A, B>, <>, XC, EC

Step 02. // start *aiA, aiB, aiC*

Step 03. *XC =* **read** *(dt) HBC* // read object parameter values

Step 04. *VC = fCd / fDinf (XC, EC)* // object state assessment

Step 05. *UC = fCkn (VC, EC)* // make a decision

Step 06. **agr** *(<KB>, <VC, UC>)* // coordinate the solution with the knowledge base

Step 06. **snd** *(<aiB, aiA>, <XC, VC, UC>)* // send the decision for approval *B, A)*

Step 07. **arg** *(<aiA, aiB, aiC>, <XC, VC, UC>)* // matching

Step 08. // agree on goals
  if ((GC (UC) ⌐sat GB) or (GC (UC) ⌐sat GA))
  then VC, UC = arg (<aiA, aiB, aiC, niA, niB, niC>, <XC, VC, UC>)
  else VC, UC = VC, UC

Step 09. // negotiation of restrictions
  if ((LimC (UC) ⌐sat LimB) or (LimC (UC) ⌐sat LimA))
  then VC, UC = arg (<aiA, aiB, aiC, niA, niB, niC>, <VC, UC>)
  else VC, UC = VC, UC

Step 10. **snd** *(<aiC>, <VC, UC>)* // send the solution to the object

Step 11. **do** *(aiC, UC)* // execute the solution

Step 12. // evaluation the subsystem *B*
  XB = VC, UC
  VB = fDB / dDMDM (XB, EB)
  UB = KD (VB, EC)

Step 13. // evaluation the ULSS *A*
  XA = VB, UB
  VA = D / DM (XA, EA)
  UA = KD (VA, EA)

Step 14. **def** *(aiA (HBA, KBA), aiB (HBB, KBB), aiC (HBC, KBC))* // default mode

Step 15. goto Step 03

Advantages of the algorithm:

- decisions are made taking into account both hot data and experience gained at all levels of ULSS, which increases the likelihood of their correctness;
- the decision is made taking into account the interests of all levels of the ULSS hierarchy, which reduces the likelihood of conflicts and conflicts;

- the knowledge base is replenished only by agreed decisions;
- default mode provides continuous training *aiC*, *aiB*, *aiA* and cleansing databases from information garbage;
- decision-making at levels *B*, *C* that contradicts the general goals of ULSS is excluded, which ensures its homeostasis.

The disadvantage of the algorithm can be considered the individual subjectivity of the expert when loading the parameters *G*, *Res*, *Lim* during the deployment of IMS.

The algorithm was originally designed for collaboration between a person and *IMS*, because the final decision is made by the person. If *ai*-systems reach the level of human intelligence, then the participation of the latter in monitoring will be limited by the deployment of the system and the elimination of emergency situations.

Based on architecture, models and algorithms, an *aiBMS* ecosystem of software agents has been developed, focused on applications in the banking sector. It includes an agent for deploying a monitoring system and agents for working with a client, manager and top manager.

5 Usage Example

As an example of using aiBMS, let us consider one of the most important tasks of financial companies - monitoring the issuance of loans [17].

Let there be a bank that expands its activities into five new regions. It is required to develop a system that automates the decision-making process on granting loans or rejecting them.

Let us compare the topology and functionality of the human brain intelligence with the distributed structure and operations of the bank when issuing loans. Accordingly, the oldest, most conservative part will be represented by the top manager of the bank (*A*), the middle part by the regional managers (B), the youngest, newly created part by the clients of the regional branches (*C*). Information about *A*, *B*, *C* is in the databases and knowledge located in pre-prepared *xls*-files. The application of each client should be agreed on the basis of knowledge bases of each level. Depending on the result of the agreement, the application may be rejected or granted.

The solution to the problem involves two steps: system deployment and system operation.

The deployment of the system includes starting the bootloader and entering parameters from pre-created databases and knowledge that characterizes the scene participants and their main parameters. This process is performed by a bank expert using a deployment agent (Fig. 3).

In this case, the expert chose the integral indicator (*X01*) to evaluate the client, depending on the value of which the loan is issued or rejected. He also identified two possible client states (good, bad), their respective ranges (0.00–0.55, 0.56–1.00) and control decisions (to issue a loan, not to give a loan).

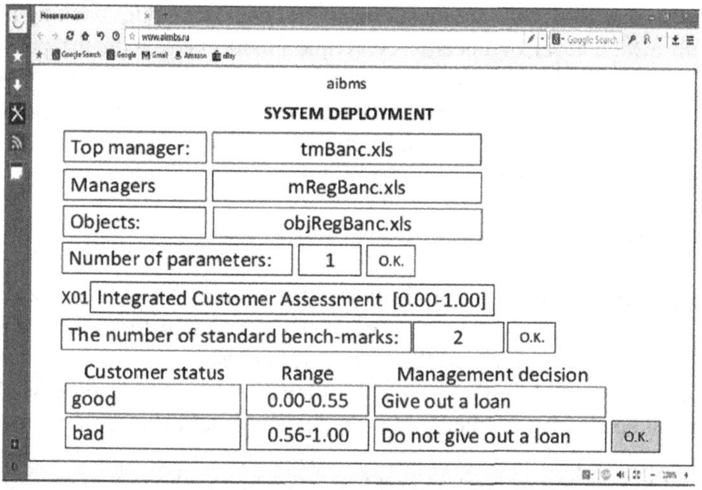

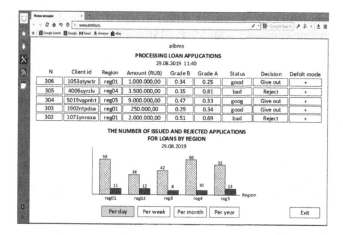

Fig. 3. System deployment

During the operation phase, the client enters data on himself and the requested loan amount in a dialogue with *MAS*. After entering the *MAS* data, *Cd*m and *Ckd* look for contradictions in them using *KB C* and transmit the result to *MAS Bd*. *MAS Bdm* and *Bkd* evaluate the client on the basis of *KB B* knowledge bases and transfer the result to level *A*, where the client is also evaluated on the basis of *KB A* knowledge bases. Then *MAS agr* aggregates and agrees results *C*, *B*, *A* according to the principle "the worst is chosen", makes the appropriate decision, visualizes it and passes the *MAS mot* for execution. After issuing a loan, knowledge about the client is formed and recorded in the knowledge base at all levels. The described processes are displayed in the interface of the top manager, which evaluates the work of regional managers for the day, week, month and year in real time (Fig. 4).

Fig. 4. Result of processing applications in the top manager interface

Systems similar to aiBMS are most effective in deploying pilot banking projects in regions with a high level of uncertainty. Triple credit check with the possible connection of own and external knowledge bases significantly reduces the number of bad loans. The constant increase in the volume of knowledge bases allows one to quickly identify unreliable customers when they appear in different regions.

6   Conclusion

The article presents the results of unification of the architecture of computer intelligent systems based on the topology of the functional systems of the brain. A pragmatic conceptual framework is proposed that eliminates polysemy in the given subject area and a set of models and algorithms that unifies the decision-making process. As part of the multi-agent approach, a unified system architecture and the corresponding program library were developed and implemented. The effectiveness of the approach is demonstrated by solving an applied problem related to bank lending processes.

As a result of testing the hypothesis about the possibility of standardizing the IS/IMS architecture based on the topology of the basic functional areas of the brain, the following conclusions can be drawn:

- The IS/IMS architecture can be reduced to six parts: three decision blocks, a block for coordinating decisions, a block for implementing a general decision, and a block for discovering and storing new knowledge. With an increase in the number of hierarchy levels, the general decision-making principle is not changed;
- Each decision block consists of functional modules for data input, synthesis of information and knowledge, database (short-term memory) and knowledge base (long-term memory);
- The structure of the program module is reduced to the structure of a neuron adapted to its use in the framework of a multi-agent approach;
- Unified architecture accelerates the development of IMS, in particular, monitoring systems for organizational and technical systems.

An important advantage of systems similar to aiBMS is the ability to deploy them over previously implemented CRM, MRP, SIM and others.

Unfortunately, the important problem of making operational decisions using the operations of "summation", "long-term potentiation" and "Papez circuit scheme" for dangerous situations without using long-term memory has remained unexplored.

References

1. Pascual, D.: Artificial Intelligence Tools: Decision Support Systems in Condition Monitoring and Diagnosis. CRC Press, Boca Raton (2015)
2. Vissia, H., Krasnoproshin, V., Valvachev, A.: Decision making in the information society. Lan, St. Petersburg (2018). (in Russian)

3. Krasnoproshin, V.V., Kuzmich, A.I., Valvachev, A.N.: Adaptive control system for mobile heterogeneous objects. In: Proceedings of International Congress on Computer Science: Information Systems and Technologies CSIST 2013, Minsk, Belarus, pp. 468–472 (2013)
4. Hissman, S.: Ultra-Large-Scale Systems: Socio-adaptive Systems. CMU, Pittsburgh (2016)
5. The 2018-2023 World Outlook for Transmission and Distribution (T&D) Supervisory Control and Data Acquisition (SCADA) Devices. ICON Group International (2017)
6. Berg, A.I.: Management, Information, Intelligence. Mysl, Moscow (1976). (in Russian)
7. Klir, J., Elias, D.: Architecture of Systems Problem Solving. Springer, Berlin (2012)
8. Anokhin, P.K.: Cybernetics of Functional Systems: Selected Works. Medicine, Moscow (1998). (in Russian)
9. Burkov, V., Goubko, M., Kondrat'ev, V., Korgin, N., Novikov, D.: Mechanism Design and Management: Mathematical Methods for Smart Organizations. Nova Publishers, New York (2013)
10. Schneider, G.: Brain Structure and Its Origins: in Development and in Evolution of Behavior and the Mind. The MIT Press, Cambridge (2014)
11. Swanson, L.: Brain Architecture: Understanding the Basic Plan. Oxford University Press, Oxford (2011)
12. Buckner, R.L., Andrews-Hanna, J.R., Schacter, D.L.: The brain's default network: anatomy, function, and relevance to disease. Ann. N. Y. Acad. Sci. **1124**(1), 1–38 (2008)
13. Kandel, E.: In Search of Memory: The Emergence of a New Science of Mind. W.W. Norton & Company, New York (2007)
14. Zyt, J., Klosgen, W., Zytkow, M.: Handbook of Data Mining and Knowledge Discovery. Oxford University Press, Oxford (2002)
15. Baranovski, O., Valvachev, A.: The standardized architecture of intelligent systems based on the brain topology. In: Proceedings of 14th International Conference on Pattern Recognition and Information Processing PRIP 2019, Minsk, Belarus, pp. 324–327 (2019)
16. Zadeh, L., Klir, G., Yuan, B.: Fuzzy Sets, Fuzzy Logic, and Fuzzy Systems. World Scientific Publishing, Singapore (1996)
17. Butenko, E.D.: Artificial intelligence in banks today: experience and perspectives. Finance Credit **24**(3), 143–153 (2018). (in Russian)

Performance of Sequential Tests for Random Data Monitoring Under Distortion

Alexey Kharin[✉]

Belarusian State University, Independence Av. 4, 220030 Minsk, Belarus
KharinAY@bsu.by

Abstract. Performance characteristics (error probabilities and expected sample sizes) of the sequential statistical tests are studied. Three models of data are considered in details. The results give a possibility to analyze robustness of the sequential algorithms of random data flow monitoring under contamination.

Keywords: Sequential test · Error probability · Expected number of observations · Performance characteristics · Markov chain · Distortion

1 Introduction

Sequential tests [1] applied in information processing [2] can significantly reduce the number of observations [3] used to provide the requested accuracy (small levels of error probabilities). The performance characteristics of the sequential tests are complicated for calculation in analytic way, and therefore, for the analysis of robustness [4, 5] even for quite simple models of data under distortions.

In practice, the observed random data flows do not follow exactly the hypothetical models, the hypothetical models are often distorted [6–8]. In this situation the sequential tests can lose their optimality, and the robustness analysis becomes an important part of the problem solution. If the result shows that the sequential test can not guarantee the requested accuracy, then the robust sequential test construction problem appears.

In this paper we develop the approach based on the works [9, 11] to construct the methodology of performance characteristics evaluation in monitoring of data from different models. This methodology enables robustness analysis and robust sequential test construction with the minimax risk (or the total error probability) criterion.

2 Case of Independent Observations with Special Probability Distributions

Denote by $\mathbf{N}, \mathbf{Z}, \mathbf{Z}_+, \mathbf{Q}, \mathbf{R}$ the sets of natural, integer, nonnegative integer, rational and real numbers respectively. Let on a probability space (Ω, F, P) random variables $x_t \in U = \{u_1, \ldots, u_M\}$, $t \in \mathbf{N}$, be observed, independent and identically distributed.

© Springer Nature Switzerland AG 2019
S. V. Ablameyko et al. (Eds.): PRIP 2019, CCIS 1055, pp. 280–288, 2019.
https://doi.org/10.1007/978-3-030-35430-5_23

The probability distribution of each random variable is discrete, depends on parameter $\theta \in \Theta = \{\theta_0, \theta_1\}$, $\theta_0, \theta_1 \in \mathbf{R}$, $\theta_0 \neq \theta_1$, and has the form

$$P(u; \theta) = P_\theta\{x_t = u\} = a^{-J(u;\theta)}, \ t \in \mathbf{N}, \ u \in U, \tag{1}$$

where $a \in \mathbf{Q}$, $a > 1$; $J(u; \theta): U \times \Theta \to \mathbf{Z}_+$ is a function satisfying the condition

$$\sum_{u \in U} a^{-J(u;\theta)} = 1. \tag{2}$$

Consider two simple hypotheses concerning the parameter value θ in (1):

$$H_0 : \ \theta = \theta_0, \ H_1 : \ \theta = \theta_1. \tag{3}$$

In information processing, this model is often used to distinguish between two alternative situations.

Denote the accumulated log-likelihood:

$$\Lambda_n = \Lambda_n(x_1, \ldots, x_n) = \sum_{t=1}^{n} \lambda_t, \tag{4}$$

where $\lambda_t = \log_a(P(x_t; \theta_1)/P(x_t; \theta_0)) = J(x_t; \theta_0) - J(x_t; \theta_1) \in \mathbf{Z}$ is calculated by observation x_t. From independence of x_t and (4) it follows that Λ_n, $n \in \mathbf{N}$, is a discrete time homogeneous Markov chain.

According to the sequential probability ratio test (SPRT) proposed by Wald [1] to distinguish between hypotheses (3) by n observations ($n = 1, 2, \ldots$) the decision is

$$d_\lambda = d_\lambda(n) = \mathbf{1}_{[C_+, +\infty)}(\Lambda_n) + 2 \cdot \mathbf{1}_{(C_-, C_+)}(\Lambda_n), \tag{5}$$

where $\mathbf{1}_D(\cdot)$ is used for the indicator function of a set D. Decisions $d_\lambda = 0$ and $d_\lambda = 1$ correspond to observation process termination and acceptance of H_0 (with $d_\lambda = 0$) or H_1 (with $d_\lambda = 1$) after n observations; $d_\lambda = 2$ means that the $(n + 1)$-th observation is required. In (5) $C_-, C_+ \in \mathbf{Z}$, $C_- < C_+$ are parameters of the test called the thresholds that are usually calculated according to [1]:

$$C_- = [\log_a(\beta_0/(1 - \alpha_0))], \ C_+ = [\log_a((1 - \beta_0)/\alpha_0)], \tag{6}$$

where α_0, β_0 are the admissible levels of error type I and II probabilities; $[\cdot]$ is used for the integer part of an argument.

With the thresholds (6) the factual values of error probabilities of type I and II may differ from the assigned levels α_0, β_0 [11], and the problem of the efficiency characteristics for the sequential test (4), (5) is important.

Introduce the notation: $\delta_{i,j}$ for the Kronecker delta; $\mathbf{I}_k$ for the identity matrix of order k; $\mathbf{0}_{m \times n}$ for the matrix of size ($m \times n$), with all elements equal 0; $\mathbf{1}(\cdot)$ for the unit step function; $\mathbf{1}_k$ for the k-vector column, with all components equal 1. Let $t^{(k)}$ be the expected value of the random number of observations (sample size) provided the hypothesis H_k, $k \in \{0, 1\}$ is true; α, β – the factual values of error type I and II probabilities for test (5); $N = C_+ - C_-$; $P^{(k)} = \left(p_{ij}^{(k)} \right) = \left(\begin{array}{ccc} I_2 & \vdots & 0_{2 \times N} \\ --- & \vdots & --- \\ R^{(k)} & \vdots & Q^{(k)} \end{array} \right) -$

the matrix of size $(N+2) \times (N+2)$, with blocks $R^{(k)}, Q^{(k)}$ defined by

$$p_{ij}^{(k)} = \begin{cases} \sum_{u \in U} \delta_{J(u;\theta_0)-J(u;\theta_1),j-i} P(u;\theta_k), i,j \in (C_-,C_+); \\ \sum_{u \in U} \mathbf{1}(C_- - i + J(u;\theta_1) - J(u;\theta_0)) P(u;\theta_k), i \in (C_-,C_+), j = C_-, \\ \sum_{u \in U} \mathbf{1}(J(u;\theta_0 - J(u;\theta_1)) + i - C_+) P(u;\theta_k), i \in (C_-,C_+), j = C_+; \end{cases}$$

$$\pi^{(k)} = \left(\pi_i^{(k)} \right), \quad \pi_i^{(k)} = \sum_{u \in U} \delta_{J(u;\theta_0)-J(u;\theta_1),i} P(u;\theta_k), \ i \in \{C_- + 1, \ldots, C_+ - 1\}$$

$$\pi_{C_+}^{(k)} = \sum_{i \geq C_+} \sum_{u \in U} \delta_{J(u;\theta_0)-J(u;\theta_1),i} P(u;\theta_k), \quad \pi_{C_-}^{(k)} = \sum_{i \leq C_-} \sum_{u \in U} \delta_{J(u;\theta_0)-J(u;\theta_1),i} P(u;\theta_k),$$

$$S^{(k)} = I_N - Q^{(k)}, \ B^{(k)} = \left(S^{(k)} \right)^{-1} R^{(k)}; \ W_{(i)} - \text{the } i\text{-th column of matrix } W.$$

Theorem 1. *If conditions (1)–(3) hold, and* $|S^{(k)}| \neq 0$, $k \in \{0,1\}$, *then the performance characteristics of sequential test (4), (5) are equal*

$$t^{(k)} = \left(\pi^{(k)} \right)' \left(S^{(k)} \right)^{-1} \mathbf{1}_N + 1,$$

$$\alpha = \left(\pi^{(0)} \right)' B_{(2)}^{(0)} + \pi_{C_+}^{(0)}, \ \beta = \left(\pi^{(1)} \right)' B_{(1)}^{(1)} + \pi_{C_-}^{(1)}.$$

Proof is based on the finite absorbing Markov chains theory [10]. The sequence

$$\zeta_n = C_- \cdot \mathbf{1}_{(-\infty, C_-]}(\Lambda_n) + C_+ \cdot \mathbf{1}_{[C_+, +\infty)}(\Lambda_n) + \Lambda_n \cdot \mathbf{1}_{(C_-, C_+)}(\Lambda_n)$$

is a homogeneous Markov chain with $N + 2$ states, and C_-, C_+ are the absorbing states. ■

Suppose the factual probability distribution of the observed random data is distorted w.r.t. the hypothetical probability distribution (1), (2), and it is described by the mixture of discrete probability distributions:

$$\bar{P}(u; \theta) = \bar{P}_\theta \{x_t = u\} = (1 - \varepsilon) P(u; \theta) + \varepsilon \tilde{P}(u; \theta), \ t \in \mathbf{N}, \ u \in U, \qquad (1')$$

where $\varepsilon \in [0, \frac{1}{2})$ is the probability of "contamination", the "contaminating" probability distribution has the form:

$$\tilde{P}(u; \theta) = a^{-\tilde{J}(u;\theta)}, \ u \in U, \ \theta \in \Theta, \qquad (1'')$$

where $\tilde{J}(u; \theta): U \times \Theta \to \mathbf{Z}_+$ is a function, different from $J(\cdot)$ and satisfying the condition

$$\sum_{u \in U} a^{-\tilde{J}(u;\theta)} = 1. \tag{2'}$$

To provide robustness of the sequential test w.r.t. distortions (1'), (1''), (2'), or, in other words, to get less sensitive performance characteristics under contamination, let us instead (4)–(6) consider the family of modified sequential tests:

$$d_n = 1_{[C_+, +\infty)}\left(\Lambda_n^g\right) + 2 \cdot 1_{(C_-, C_+)}\left(\Lambda_n^g\right),$$

$$\Lambda_n^g = \sum_{t=1}^{n} g(\lambda_t), \quad \lambda_t = J(x_t; \theta_0) - J(x_t; \theta_1),$$

$$g(z) = g_- \cdot 1_{(-\infty, g_-]}(z) + g_+ \cdot 1_{[g_+, +\infty)}(z) + z \cdot 1_{(g_-, g_+)}(z), \quad z \in \mathbf{R},$$

where $g_-, g_+ \in \mathbf{R}$ are the parameters of the test, $g_- < g_+$.

Using the methodology of Theorem 1, the performance characteristics can be calculated for any particular distortion for any test from the considered family of modified sequential tests. Then, solving the problem of minimization w.r.t. g_-, g_+ of the maximal value of the total error probability (w.r.t. the considered distortions), the minimax robust test is constructed.

3 Case of Arbitrary Distributions of Independent Observations

Let $\bar{P}_\theta$, $\theta \in \Theta$, be the factual probability distribution for each of the independent observations $x_1, x_2, \ldots \in U \subseteq \mathbf{R}$, that can differ from the hypothetical probability distribution P_θ due to distortions mentioned in the introduction.

Sequential test (4), (5) based on the function

$$\lambda(u) = \log \frac{p_{\theta_1}(u)}{p_{\theta_0}(u)}, \quad u \in U, \tag{7}$$

is denoted here by $\delta_\lambda = (\tau_\lambda, d_\lambda)$, where $\tau_\lambda = \inf\{n : d_\lambda(n) \in \{0, 1\}\}$ is the random stopping moment.

Let for this test

$$\alpha = \alpha(\delta_\lambda) = E_0\{\bar{P}_0\{d_\lambda = 1 | \tau_\lambda\}\}, \tag{8}$$

$$\beta = \beta(\delta_\lambda) = E_1\{\bar{P}_1\{d_\lambda = 0 | \tau_\lambda\}\}$$

be the factual values of the error type I and II probabilities correspondently, $p_{\theta_0}(u)$, $p_{\theta_1}(u)$ be the probability density functions w.r.t. some measure on U at the correspondent parameter value; $E_\theta\{\cdot\}$ be the mathematical expectation w.r.t. the probability distribution $\bar{P}_\theta$;

$$t^{(k)} = t^{(k)}(\delta_\lambda) = E_k\{\tau_\lambda\}, \; k \in \{0, 1\} \tag{9}$$

be the conditional mathematical expectation of the random sample size τ_λ under H_k being true.

Consider the set of the performance characteristics $\{\alpha(\delta_\lambda), \beta(\delta_\lambda), t_0(\delta_\lambda), t_1(\delta_\lambda)\}$ for the sequential test δ_λ. In theorem 1 exact expressions to calculate the performance characteristics (8), (9) are derived for test (4), (5) in case where the function $\lambda(\cdot)$ takes values in a discrete set, and distortions are absent ($\bar{P}_\theta \equiv P_\theta$). In the general case, for the test δ_λ denote ($k = 0, 1$):

$$Q^{(k)} = \left(q_{ij}^{(k)}\right), \; q_{ij}^{(k)} = \bar{P}_k\{\lambda(x_1) = j - i\}, \; i, j \in \{C_- + 1, \ldots, C_+ - 1\};$$

$$R^{(k)} = \left(r_{ij}^{(k)}\right), \; i \in \{C_- + 1, \ldots, C_+ - 1\}, \; j = C_-, C_+,$$

$$r_{iC_-}^{(k)} = \bar{P}_k\{\lambda(x_1) \le C_- - i\}, \; r_{iC_+}^{(k)} = \bar{P}_k\{\lambda(x_1) \ge C_+ - i\};$$

$$\pi^{(k)} = \left(\pi_i^{(k)}\right), \pi_i^{(k)} = \bar{P}_k\{\lambda(x_1) = i\}, \; i \in \{C_- + 1, \ldots, C_+ - 1\},$$

$$\pi_{C_-}^{(k)} = \bar{P}_k\{\lambda(x_1) \le C_-\}, \; \pi_{C_+}^{(k)} = \bar{P}_k\{\lambda(x_1) \ge C_+\}.$$

From the finite Markov chain theory [10], the condition $|S^{(k)}| \ne 0$ is equivalent to the finiteness of the test: $\bar{P}_\theta\{\tau_\lambda < \infty\} = 1$, $\theta \in \Theta$. This condition is satisfied for independent identically distributed observations except the case where $\bar{P}_\theta\{\lambda(x_1) = 0\} = 1$, meaning that the parameter values θ_0, θ_1 for the probability distribution $\bar{P}_\theta$ are not identifiable.

Let $\underline{\lambda}(x), \bar{\lambda}(x): U \to \mathbf{R}$ be some functions, $\delta_{\underline{\lambda}}, \delta_{\bar{\lambda}}$ – sequential tests (4), (5) based on these functions, $\underline{A}_n = \sum_{t=1}^n \underline{\lambda}(x_t)$, $\bar{A}_n = \sum_{t=1}^n \underline{\lambda}(x_t)$. Define Markov moments:

$$s_0 = \inf\{n : A_n \le C_-\}, \; s_1 = \inf\{n : A_n \ge C_+\}, \; \underline{s}_0 = \inf\{n : \underline{A}_n \le C_-\},$$

$$\underline{s}_1 = \inf\{n : \underline{A}_n \ge C_+\}; \; \bar{s}_0 = \inf\{n : \bar{A}_n \le C_-\}, \; \bar{s}_1 = \inf\{n : \bar{A}_n \ge C_+\}.$$

Denote:

$$\bar{\alpha} = \alpha(\delta_{\bar{\lambda}}), \; \bar{\beta} = \beta(\delta_{\bar{\lambda}}), \; \underline{\alpha} = \alpha(\delta_{\underline{\lambda}}), \; \underline{\beta} = \beta(\delta_{\underline{\lambda}});$$

$$Y = \{x \in U : \lambda(x) \in (C_- - C_+, C_+ - C_-)\}.$$

Theorem 2. *Let for the sequential test (4), (7), (5) functions $\underline{\lambda}(\cdot)$, $\overline{\lambda}(\cdot)$ satisfy the inequalities:*

$$\underline{\lambda}(x) \leq \lambda(x) \leq \overline{\lambda}(x), \ \forall x \in Y$$

and

$$t^{(k)} < \infty, \ t^{(k)}(\delta_{\overline{\lambda}}) < \infty, \ t^{(k)}(\delta_{\underline{\lambda}}) < \infty, \ K = 0, 1.$$

Then

$$\underline{\alpha} \leq \alpha \leq \overline{\alpha}, \ \overline{\beta} \leq \beta \leq \underline{\beta}; \tag{10}$$

and if $\overline{\alpha} - \underline{\alpha} \to 0$, $\underline{\beta} - \overline{\beta} \to 0$, then the following asymptotic expansions hold:

$$t_-^{(k)} \leq t^{(k)} \leq t_+^{(k)}, \ k = 0, 1; \ t_\pm^{(k)} = T_\pm^{(k)} + o(1),$$

where

$$T_-^{(0)} = \overline{\alpha} E_0\{\overline{s}_1 | \overline{s}_1 < \overline{s}_0\} + (1 - \underline{\alpha}) E_0\{\underline{s}_0 | \underline{s}_0 < \underline{s}_1\},$$

$$T_+^{(0)} = \underline{\alpha} E_0\{\underline{s}_1 | \underline{s}_1 < \underline{s}_0\} + (1 - \overline{\alpha}) E_0\{\overline{s}_0 | \overline{s}_0 < \overline{s}_1\};$$

$$T_+^{(1)} = \underline{\beta} E_1\{\underline{s}_0 | \underline{s}_0 < \underline{s}_1\} + (1 - \overline{\beta}) E_0\{\overline{s}_1 | \overline{s}_1 < \overline{s}_0\},$$

$$T_+^{(1)} = \overline{\beta} E_1\{\overline{s}_0 | \overline{s}_0 < \overline{s}_1\} + (1 - \underline{\beta}) E_1\{\underline{s}_1 | \underline{s}_1 < \underline{s}_0\}.$$

Proof consists in the analysis of relations between the defined Markov moments and the random events, related to these moments. The mathematical expectation properties are also used. ∎

As the result is obtained for any factual probability distribution of the observed random data, the methodology of robust sequential test construction described in Sect. 2 can be used also here.

4 Case of Observations with Markovian Dependence

Let a homogeneous Markov chain $x_1, x_2, \ldots$ be observed, taking values in a finite set $V = \{0, 1, \ldots, M - 1\}$, $2 \leq M < \infty$, with the initial probabilities vector $\pi = (\pi_i)$, $i \in V$, and the one-step transition probabilities matrix $P = (p_{ij})$, $i, j \in V$, correspondingly:

$$P\{x_1 = i\} = \pi_i, \ P\{x_n = j | x_{n-1} = i\} = p_{ij}, \ i, j \in V.$$

There are two simple hypotheses on the parameter values of the Markov chain:

$$H_0 : \ \pi = \pi^{(0)}, P = P^{(0)}, \ H_1 : \ \pi = \pi^{(1)}, P = P^{(1)}, \tag{11}$$

where $\pi^{(0)} = \left(\pi_i^{(0)}\right)$, $\pi^{(1)} = \left(\pi_i^{(1)}\right)$ are two given values for initial probabilities vector, $P^{(0)} = \left(p_{ij}^{(0)}\right) \neq P^{(1)} = \left(p_{ij}^{(1)}\right)$ are given matrices of one-step transition probabilities for the correspondent hypotheses.

Construct the sequential test similarly to (4), (5) for hypotheses H_0, H_1 from (11); according to it for given thresholds $C_-, C_+ \in \mathbf{R}$, $C_- < 0$, $C_+ > 0$, hypothesis H_0 is accepted by n observations, if $\Lambda_n \leq C_-$, hypothesis H_1 is accepted, if $\Lambda_n \geq C_+$, otherwise the test is proceeded, and the $(n + 1)$-th observation is taken. The sequence of random vectors $(\Lambda_n, x_n)'$, $n \in \mathbf{N}$, is a Markov chain:

$$P\{\Lambda_n, x_n | \Lambda_{n-1}, \Lambda_{n-2}, \ldots, \Lambda_1, x_{n-1}, x_{n-2}, \ldots, x_1\}$$
$$= P\{\Lambda_n, x_n | \Lambda_{n-1}, x_{n-1}\}.$$

Let $\pi^{(0)}, P^{(0)}, \pi^{(1)}, P^{(1)}$ be such that exist $a \in \mathbf{R}$, $m_i, m_{ij} \in \mathbf{Z}$, $i, j \in V$, to satisfy

$$\log \frac{\pi_i^{(1)}}{\pi_i^{(0)}} = m_i a, \ \log \frac{p_{ij}^{(1)}}{p_{ij}^{(0)}} = m_{ij} a,$$

Suppose for test (4), (5) the thresholds $C_-, C_+ \in \mathbf{Z}$, and introduce the notation: $t^{(k)}$ is the expected sample size till one of the hypotheses is accepted, provided H_k, $k \in \{0, 1\}$ is true;

$$W^{(k)} = \left(w_{ij}^{(k)}\right) = \left(\begin{array}{ccc} \mathbf{I}_2 & \vdots & \mathbf{0}_{2 \times MN} \\ --- & \vdots & --- \\ R^{(k)} & \vdots & Q^{(k)} \end{array} \right)$$

is the $(MN + 2)(MN + 2)$-matrix, with blocks $R^{(k)}, Q^{(k)}$ defined by elements $(s, t \in V)$:

$$w_{Mi+sMj+t}^{(k)} = \delta_{m_{st} j - i} p_{st}^{(k)}, i, j \in (C_-, C_+),$$

$$w_{Mi+sMj+t}^{(k)} = \begin{cases} \sum_{t \in V} \mathbf{1}(i + m_{st} - C_+), j = C_+, i \in (C_-, C_+), \\ \sum_{t \in V} \mathbf{1}(C_- - i - m_{st}), j = C_-, i \in (C_-, C_+); \end{cases} \tag{12}$$

$$S^{(k)} = \mathbf{I}_{MN} - Q^{(k)}, \ B^{(k)} = \left(S^{(k)}\right)^{-1} R^{(k)}, \ k \in \{0, 1\};$$

$$\omega^{(k)} = \left(\omega_i^{(k)}\right), \ i \in \{MC_- + 1, \ldots, MC_+ - 1\},$$

$$\omega_{Mi+s}^{(k)} = \delta_{m_s,i}\pi_s^{(k)}, i \in (C_-, C_+), \ s \in V \tag{13}$$

$$\omega_{MC_-}^{(k)} = \sum_{s \in V} \mathbf{1}(C_- - m_s)\pi_s^{(k)},$$

$$\omega_{MC_+}^{(k)} = \sum_{s \in V} \mathbf{1}(m_s - C_+)\pi_s^{(k)}. \tag{14}$$

Theorem 3. *If the described observation model takes place, and* $|S^{(k)}| \neq 0, k \in \{0, 1\}$, *then for the performance characteristics of sequential test* (4), (5) *the following expressions are valid:*

$$t^{(k)} = \left(\omega^{(k)}\right)' \left(S^{(k)}\right)^{-1} \mathbf{1}_{MN} + 1,$$

$$\alpha = \left(\omega^{(0)}\right)' B_{(2)}^{(0)} + \omega_{MC_+}^{(0)}, \ \beta = \left(\omega^{(1)}\right)' B_{(1)}^{(1)} + \omega_{MC_-}^{(1)}.$$

Proof is consisting in application of the absorbing Markov chains theory to the sequence

$$\xi_n = MC_- \cdot \mathbf{1}_{(-\infty, C_-]} \left(\frac{\Lambda_n}{a}\right) + MC_+ \cdot \mathbf{1}_{[C_+, +\infty)} \left(\frac{\Lambda_n}{a}\right) +$$

$$+ \left(\frac{\Lambda_n}{a} M + x_n\right) \cdot \mathbf{1}_{(C_-, C_+)} \left(\frac{\Lambda_n}{a}\right),$$

$n \in \mathbf{N}$, that is a homogeneous Markov chain with $MN + 2$ states; two states ($\xi_n = MC_-$ and $\xi_n = MC_+$) are absorbing. The one-step transition probabilities matrix is given by (12), and the initial states probabilities vector is given by (13), (14). ∎

Using the method similar to Theorem 2 in case of observations that are forming a Markov chain, the performance characteristics can be evaluated for the situation, where the assumption concerning the increments of the test statistic Λ_n is not satisfied.

The performance characteristics can be evaluated with the discussed approach also in the situation, where the data are contaminated.

5 Conclusion

In the paper the methodology developed by the author for calculation of performance characteristics for sequential tests is discussed in the context of different observed data models.

The theory is also extended to the case of inhomogeneous independent data [15].

The results can also be used for robustness analysis under distortions of the observations, and for the robust sequential test construction [12–14].

The developed methodology is also applicable for the complex hypotheses setting to calculate the performance characteristics of sequential statistical tests, and to derive the robust sequential procedures [9, 12].

References

1. Wald, A.: Sequential Analysis. Wiley, New York (1947)
2. Mukhopadhyay, N., Datta, S., Chattopadhyay, S.: Applied sequential Methodologies. Marcel Dekker, New York (2004)
3. Ghosh, B., Sen, P.K.: Handbook of Sequential Analysis. Marcel Dekker, New York (1991)
4. Lai, T.: Sequential analysis: Some classical problems and new challenges. Statistica Sinica **11**, 303–408 (2001)
5. Huber, P., Ronchetti, E.: Robust Statistics. Wiley, New York (2009)
6. Kharin, Yu.: Robustness in Statistical Forecasting. Springer, New York (2013)
7. Kharin, A.: Robust Bayesian prediction under distortions of prior and conditional distributions. J. Math. Sci. **126**(1), 992–997 (2005)
8. Kharin, A., Shlyk, P.: Robust multivariate Bayesian forecasting under functional distortions in the chi-square metric. J. Statist. Planning Infer. **139**, 3842–3846 (2009)
9. Kharin, A.Yu.: Robustness of sequential testing of hypotheses on parameters of M-valued random sequences. J. Math. Sci. **189**(6), 924–931 (2013)
10. Kemeny, J.G., Snell, J.L.: Finite Markov Chains. Springer, New York (1960)
11. Kharin, A.Y.: An approach to performance analysis of the sequential probability ratio test for the simple hypotheses testing. Proc. Belarus. State Univ. - Ser. Phys.-Math. Sci. **1**, 92–96 (2002)
12. Kharin, A.Yu.: Robustness of Bayesian and sequential statistical decision rules. BSU, Minsk (2013)
13. Kharin, A.Y.: Performance and robustness evaluation in sequential hypotheses testing. Commun. Stat. – Theory Methods **45**(6), 1663–1709 (2016)
14. Kharin, A.Y.: An approach to asymptotic robustness analysis of sequential tests for composite parametric hypotheses. J. Math. Sci. **227**(2), 196–203 (2017)
15. Kharin, A., Tu, T.T.: Performance and robustness analysis of sequential hypotheses testing for time series with trend. Austrian J. Stat. **46**(3&4), 23–36 (2017)

Robust Person Tracking Algorithm Based on Convolutional Neural Network for Indoor Video Surveillance Systems

Rykhard Bohush$^{(\boxtimes)}$ and Iryna Zakharava

Polotsk State University, Blokhina Street, 29, Novopolotsk, Republic of Belarus
bogushr@mail.ru, ira9992011@yandex.ru

Abstract. In this paper, we present an algorithm for multi person tracking in indoor surveillance systems based on tracking-by-detection approach. Convolutional Neural Networks (CNNs) for detection and tracking both are used. CNN Yolov3 has been utilized as detector. Person features extraction is performed based on modified CNN ResNet. Proposed architecture includes 29 convolutional and one fully connected layer. Hungarian algorithm is applied for objects association. After that object visibility in the frame is determined based on CNN and color features. For algorithm evaluation prepared videos that was labeled and tested using MOT evaluation metric. The proposed algorithm efficiency is illustrated and confirmed by our experimental results.

Keywords: Person · Tracking · Indoor · CNN · CUDA

1 Introduction

Object tracking task in indoor environments is far away from solving. Tracking algorithms have a variety of technical applications such as surveillance, autonomous driving systems, action recognition and etc. These practical applications claim robust object segmentation, identification and real-time processing. Multi person tracking is more challenging because of complicated background, multiple occlusions, fast object movements and dynamic background changing. Also in indoor environments there are limitations in camera position. It leads to object occlusions, person proportions disfeaturing and may complicate tracking.

MOT (Multi object Tracking) challenge analysis shows that the most common algorithm for tracking is tracking-by-detection approach [1]. MOT proposes evaluation metric for tracking algorithms and publishes evaluation results for them. A tracking-by-detection approaches use an ensemble of a detector and an assignment problem solver. For object detection can be used Haar cascades, Support Vector Machine (SVM) and CNNs. For assignment problem solving can be used object association based on "strong" and "weak" object features comparison. As "weak" features we denote the temporal shift, color and shape. As "strong" features can be used HOG, SIFT, SURF and CNN features. CNN approaches are stable to light variance, dynamic background changing and in case partial occlusions, but claim a lot of computational cost.

© Springer Nature Switzerland AG 2019
S. V. Ablameyko et al. (Eds.): PRIP 2019, CCIS 1055, pp. 289–300, 2019.
https://doi.org/10.1007/978-3-030-35430-5_24

2 Related Works

A tracking-by-detection approaches use a variety of techniques to solve detection and assignment. That is the reason why in this section not only algorithms dedicated to tracking but and approaches which are trying to solve the assignment problem, or person re-identification for human tracking are reviewed.

In [2], authors have proposed an algorithm, which uses MOG2 background extractor as person detector and Kalman filtering for object movement prediction. For tracking was utilized Lukas-Kannade optical flow. This approach cannot be applied for difficult indoor video due to errors in case multiple objects and dynamic background changing. Another one algorithm [3] was used cascade head detection. After that, the algorithm recalculates a human body location using stable percentage ratio. For assignment problem, solving was exploited bag of features approach. Presented approach performs better assignment than in [2] but it has limitation of the person positions that can be recognized by using only head detector. CNN based algorithms perform robust detection and assignment in case complicated articulation, light changing and etc. In [4] authors presented CNN architecture for re-identification Sia-meseNet which uses two identical architectures that share features due image processing. As input, this architecture has two images and as the output CNN performs binary classification two objects on these images contain one identity or not. Zhao et al. [5] use CNN PartNet that extracts features from the most distinguished part from an image. This approach for person re-identification performs good results but it leads to big computational cost. In application to tracking problem in [6] was tested SiameseNet and approach based on Faster CNN for feature extraction. Euclidean distance feature matching performs better results than SiameseNet even without training CNN for person re-identification task. In [7] authors perform object tracking using points based on the human body joints extraction using CNN. Distance between these points on two frames used for re-identification. More robust tracking performed in [8] that builds a graph consisted of spatial edges connecting the detections within a frame and temporal edges connecting detections of the same joint type over frames The body keypoints based algorithm shows more stable approach in case partial occlusions but these approaches useless in case low resolution and need a lot of computational cost.

In [9] proposed enhanced SORT [10] model which is called DeepSort. This approach is based on custom CNN architecture for "strong" feature extraction. Kalman filtering was used to predict object movements. DeepSort performs high-speed processing at 40fps but this value calculated only for tracking part. In [11] DeepSort approach with Yolov3 detector [12] and whole algorithm runs on 11.5 fps using NVIDIA GTX 1060. DeepSort shows the best result in MOT16 [13]. However, for the feature extraction it is better to use CNN architecture with residual connections that performs better results in deep architectures than fully convolutional models and helps to avoid overfitting during training [14].

We propose the person tracking algorithm for indoor video surveillance using CNNs. As person detector we decided to use Yolov3 that is has low percentage ratio of errors results and fast enough for real-time processing. The tracking was performed as an assignment problem solving and as main parameter was used similarity value.

This value contains "strong" and "weak" features. Modified ResNet34 architecture for "strong" feature extraction is used. In addition, we calculate "weak" features like the temporal shift, object width and height variation. To reduce computational time all CNN operations was performed on GPU with CUDA support.

3 Algorithm Description

The algorithm includes in four sub-tasks: object detection, assignment problem solving, tracklets update, tracklets post processing. The general scheme of our algorithm is presented in Fig. 1.

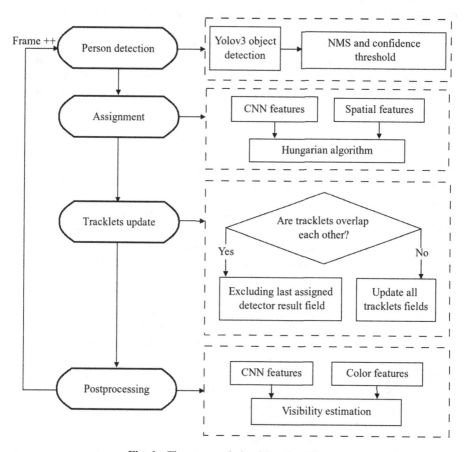

Fig. 1. The proposed algorithm flow-chart

Frames from the stationary video surveillance camera are input to the algorithm. First, people are detected in the frame. Then detected areas filtered out using Non-Maxima suppression and confidence threshold before assignment. For each pair of detections and trackers calculated similarity value that used as input for assignment algorithm decision making. According to the association results values in the tracklets fields update with the criterion for last detector result field. The last step is used to decide on the visibility of the object in the frame and tracking results correction.

Person detection task can be presented as function of the detector from an image as:

$$\{cl, l, p\} = Dt(im), \tag{1}$$

where Dt – detection approach; cl, l, p – detector output results as cl – object class, l – object location, p – confidence score.

YOLO v3 model was used for object detection. It has fully convolutional architecture for feature extraction Darknet-53 which is containing 53 convolutional layers, 23 residual connections and achieve 93.8% top-5 accuracy. For detector was chosen main parameters: input layer size [480 × 480], confidence threshold = 80%, NMS threshold = 0.7.

For assignment problem solving of person we store information about every identity in tracklet, which includes total information about individual object. Tracklet contains the name or current tracklet index, the image of last assigned detector result, the current object image, object coordinates on current and previous frame and the visibility value and is presented as:

$$tr = \{n, im_{dt}, im_{curr}, coor_{curr}, coor_{prev}, v\}, \tag{2}$$

where n – tracklet name; im_{dt} – image of last assigned detector result; im_{curr} –current object image; $corr_{curr}$ – object coordinates on current frame; $corr_{prev}$ – object coordinates on previous frame; v – visibility value.

Because our task is the indoor surveillance systems, the tracklet period of life is very important parameter. On the street surveillance systems object normally has one entry point and one exit point. In the indoor environments, this rule does not work and objects can have multiple input and output points. That is why in the indoor surveillance systems required longer period of life value for tracklet.

Tracklet life span increasing leads to some errors. Main of them is false positive results and wrong assignment to new object. To solve the first problem we calculate the visibility value using a last assigned detector result. The second one is solved by using the threshold values due to similarity matrix calculation. In addition, to prevent indexing errors after multiple occlusions image of last assigned detector result field in tracklets updates only when objects on current frame do not overlap each other.

The CNN architecture for feature extraction is presented in Fig. 2. This architecture based on ResNet-34 and constructed for person re-identification task solving. The input convolution layer [7 × 7] was replaced, because minimal sized convolutional layers performs better results in re-identification task [15]. The number of fully connected layer outputs was reduced from 1000 to 128 to transform feature map from the last convolutional layer to feature vector that describes input person image. Convolutional layers number was reduced to 29. This value was chosen during tests as minimal layers size with maximum accuracy.

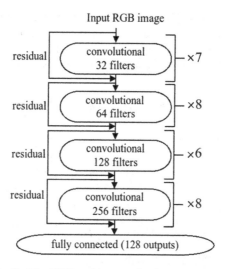

Fig. 2. The CNN architecture for feature extraction

Assignment is calculated based on similarity value as:

$$D = D_{cnn} + dx + dy + dw + dh, \tag{3}$$

where D_{cnn} – Euclidean distance between current and last aligned object CNN features; dx, dy, dw, dh – «weak» features – horizontal shift, vertical shift, width variance, height variance relatively.

A similarity matrix is formed after calculating all assignment values:

$$DD = \begin{pmatrix} D_{00} & \cdots & D_{0K} \\ \vdots & \ddots & \vdots \\ D_{L0} & \cdots & D_{LK} \end{pmatrix}, \tag{4}$$

where D_{KL} – similarity value, K – tracklets number, L – current frame person detector results number.

At the next step the association is based on Hungarian algorithm [16]:

$$a = \arg\min(tr_i, dt_{0..L}), \tag{5}$$

where t_i - tracklet; $dt_{0..L}$ – person detector results; a – assignment decision from (−1) to L. If a = (−1), then current tracklet not associated.

For robust assignment last aligned object image field in tracklet container updates only when objects do not overlap each other. To measure the overlapping value we calculate *IoU* (Intersection Over Union) as:

$$IoU = \frac{T_i \cap T_{i+1}}{T_i \cup T_{i+1}}, \tag{6}$$

where T_i and T_{i+1} are tracklet coordinates.

For visibility value "strong" and "weak" features calculation is performed. As "strong" features we use CNN features between the last aligned detector result and the object on current frame, as "weak" features was used H channel from HSV color space.

The similarity for histograms is computed as follows [17]:

$$if \left| H_i^{tr} - \overline{H^{tr}} \right| > \left| H_i^{dt} - \overline{H^{dt}} \right|, \quad R = \frac{1}{N^2} \sum_{i=0}^{N-1} \frac{(H_i^{dt} - \overline{H^{dt}})}{(H_i^{tr} - \overline{H^{tr}})},$$

(7)

$$else: \quad R = \frac{1}{N^2} \sum_{i=0}^{N-1} \frac{(H_i^{tr} - \overline{H^{tr}})}{(H_i^{dt} - \overline{H^{dt}})}.$$

where H^{tr} – current object color histograms; H^{dt} – last aligned object color histograms; N– number of histogram samples; $\overline{H^{tr}} = \frac{1}{N} \sum_{i=0}^{N-1} H_i^{tr}$;; $\overline{H^{dt}} = \frac{1}{N} \sum_{i=0}^{N-1} H_i^{dt}$.

The visibility value can be represented as:

$$v = \begin{cases} 0 & if \ D_{feat} < 0.3 \ and \ R > 0.2; \\ 1 & in \ other \ cases, \end{cases}$$

(8)

where D_{feat} – Euclidean distance between current and last aligned object CNN features.

If the visibility value is equal to 1, then object still present in the frame, other values mean that object is invisible.

4   Training

Proposed CNN for person re-identification was trained on custom database that used samples from the PRID [18] and the ILIDS-VID [19]. The PRID contain 749 identities. They are similar appearing on a simple background with luck of texture features. The custom database was escalated by the ILIDS-VID which is has more complicated examples but contain only 300 identities. They are has complicated background and wear. The database contains 1030 identities approximately 100 images for each of them. Also, due training was performed color jittering for database escalation. Some samples from the PRID and the ILIDS-VID shown in Fig. 3.

CNN for person re-idintification was trained on PC with CPU Intel Core i5-8600, 3.6 GHz, 16 Gb RAM, two GPU Nvidia GTX 1060. Main parameters for training: learning rate = 0.001, momentum = 0.9. Testing database contains 300 identities, about 100 photos for each of them. With pretrained CNN for person re-idintification we achieve 99.9% accuracy. Mean loss function in the end of training was $7.4 \cdot 10^{-6}$.

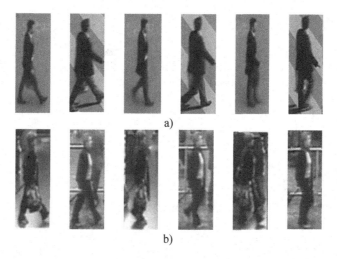

Fig. 3. Samples from person re-identification dataset: (a) shown moving object on simple background from PRID; (b) challenging images with different pose and complicated background from ILIDS-VID

5   Experimental Results

For the algorithm quality evaluation we prepare indoor video sequences with various shooting conditions. Five video sequences obtained using a stationary video camera in indoor environments with various light conditions, number persons in the frame and resolution was used for testing (Fig. 4). Description for test videos presented in Table 1.

Table 1. Description for test videos

Video sequence	Resolution	Description
1 (Figure 4a–c)	[1920 × 1080]	3 persons on the video; Multiple input points for one identity; Multiple occlusions by background; Width and height variation during occlusions;
2 (Figure 4d–f)	[1920 × 1080]	3 persons on the video; Multiple occlusions by background; Multiple inter object overlapping;
3 (Figure 4g–i)	[1280 × 960]	2 persons on the video; Multiple occlusions by background; Width and height variation during occlusions;
4 (Figure 4j–l)	[1920 × 1080]	3 persons on the video; Multiple input points for one identity; Multiple occlusions by background; Long term multiple inter object overlapping;
5 (Figure 4m–o)	[3840 × 2160]	2 persons on the video; Multiple inter object overlapping; Light variance

Fig. 4. Some scenes from test video sequences

For the algorithm evaluation is used MOT metric from. Therefore, we labeled these videos according to MOT requirements. This metric was developed for a multi object tracking algorithms evaluation and contain the following parameters [20]:

- The ratio of correctly identified detections over the average number of ground-truth and computed detections (IDF);
- Multiple Object Tracking Accuracy. This measure combines three error sources: false positives, missed targets and identity switches (MOTA);

- Multiple Object Tracking Precision. The misalignment between the annotated and the predicted bounding boxes (MOTP);
- The total number of false positives (FP);
- The total number of false negatives (missed targets) (FN);
- Processing speed n frames per second excluding the detector (Freq).

Our algorithm was implemented in C++ using OpenCV and dlib [21]. All CNN operations were performed on GPU with CUDA support. With our implementation was collected MOT evaluation results that shown in Table 2. For the video 1 and 5 MOTA values lower than the other, because of multiple inter objects occlusions with fast shape changing during it. For the other test videos where objects shape does not significantly change during occlusions MOTA values are higher.

Table 2. MOT experimental results for each test video sequences

Number of video sequences	IDF1	FP	FN	MOTA	MOTP
1	70	173	203	83.2	78.9
2	96.7	24	51	93.5	76.8
3	98.7	12	19	97.4	81
4	92.8	8	27	97.1	82.1
5	93	88	183	88.2	77.8

Processed frames parts are given in Fig. 5. Since our approach start indexing from 0, for DeepSort algorithm the first index there is 1. Due to processing we do not have to see indices larger than 0 in cases our algorithm (Fig. 5d–f) and 1 in case DeepSort (Fig. 5a–c) for one person in video. If we will see them it will show us errors like false positive detector results or poor assignment. DeepSort algorithm makes the new objects when one person is partially hidden from background (Fig. 5b), or cannot track it (Fig. 5c). Our algorithm processed one object with the same index without false negative results (Fig. 5d–f). The second example is presented for three object tracking in video (Fig. 5g–l). Figure 5g–i demonstrate that indices are bigger than 3 for DeepSort. Also it has a lot indices switching between different identities. Figure 5j–l show that indices stay on the tracked objects even with long time occlusions for proposed algorithm.

The MOT average values show algorithm effectiveness for all test videos. In Table 3 we show the final MOT metrics for Deep Sort and the proposed algorithm.

Table 3. Comparison MOT metrics for algorithms

Algorithm	MOTA	MOTP	FP	FN	IDF	Freq
DeepSort [10]	87.2	**81.1**	**113**	997	60.1	**60**
Proposed	**90.3**	79.1	305	**403**	**87.9**	**60**

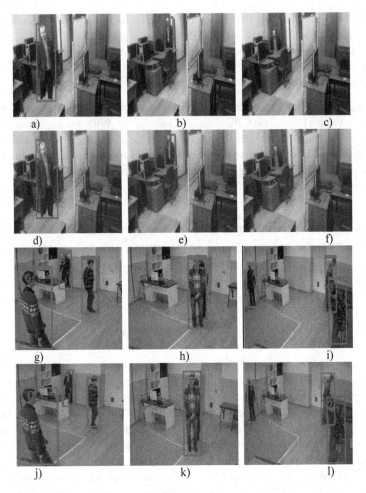

Fig. 5. Examples for person tracking: DeepSort (a,b,c,g,h,i) and proposed approach (d,e,f,j,k,l)

The data obtained (Table 3) show that our algorithm increases the value of correctly identified objects. Also the number of false negative results is reduced too. The false positive numbers is higher than in DeepSort because of higher life time for the tracklet which is help to track objects even if they are hidden behind the background or another object in small period of time. The value F_{req} is processing speed in MOT evaluation metrics detector part do not taken into account. Processing speed including detection task for our approach runs at 25 fps using NVIDIA GTX 1060.

6 Conclusion

Person tracking for indoor surveillance is challenging task. We have presented our real-time tracking-by-detection algorithm which is specified for indoor environments. Our algorithm contains following steps: person detection, assignment problem solving, tracklets formation, tracklets post processing. Object detection performed with CNN Yolov3. For assignment proposed CNN architecture based on ResNet-34 and pre-trained on person re-identification dataset. For the algorithm evaluation was prepared 5 test video that filmed in indoor environments with various light conditions, number persons in the frame and resolution. Experimental video was prepared and labeled according to MOT requirements. With our algorithm we achieve following results using MOT metric: MOTA = 90.3, MOTP = 79.1, FP = 305, FN = 403, IDF = 87.9. To reduce computational cost all CNN operations was performed on GPU with CUDA technology.

Consequently, proposed approach has perspectives in indoor surveillance systems. For the future work it is planned to apply our algorithm for multi camera tracking task.

References

1. MOTChallenge: The Multiple Object Tracking Benchmark. https://motchallenge.net. Accessed 14 Aug 2019
2. Miguel, M.D., Brunete, A., Hernando, M., Gambao, E.: Home camera-based fall detection system for the elderly. Sensors 17(12), 2864 (2017)
3. Kuplyakov, D., Shalnov, E., Konushin, A.: Markov chain Monte Carlo based video tracking algorithm. Program. Comput. Softw. 43(4), 224–229 (2017)
4. Tao, R., Gavves, E., Smeulders, A.W.: Siamese instance search for tracking. In: 2016 IEEE Conference on Computer Vision and Pattern Recognition (CVPR), pp. 1420–1429. IEEE, Las Vegas (2016)
5. Zhao, L., Li, X., Zhuang, Y., Wang, J.: Deeply-learned part-aligned representations for person re-identification. In: 2017 IEEE International Conference on Computer Vision (CVPR), pp. 3239–3248. IEEE, Venice (2017)
6. Chahyati, D., Fanany, M.I., Arymurthy, A.: Tracking people by detection using CNN features. Proc. Comput. Sci. 124, 167–172 (2017)
7. Insafutdinov, E., et al.: ArtTrack: articulated multi-person tracking in the wild. In: 2017 IEEE Conference on Computer Vision and Pattern Recognition (CVPR), pp. 1293–1301. IEEE, Honolulu (2016)
8. Iqbal, U., Milan, A., Gall, J.: PoseTrack: joint multi-person pose estimation and tracking. In: 2017 IEEE Conference on Computer Vision and Pattern Recognition (CVPR), pp. 4654–4663. Honolulu (2016)
9. Wojke, N., Bewley, A., Paulus, D.: Simple online and real time tracking with a deep association metric. In: IEEE International Conference on Image Processing (ICIP), pp. 3645–3649. IEEE, Beijing (2017)
10. Bewley, A., Ge, Z., Ott, L., Ramos, F.T., Upcroft, B.: Simple online and real time tracking. In: 2016 IEEE International Conference on Image Processing (ICIP), pp. 3464–3468. IEEE, Phoenix (2016)
11. Real-time Multi-person tracker using YOLO v3 and deep_sort with tensorflow. https://github.com/Qidian213/deep_sort_yolov3. Accessed 14 Aug 2019

12. YOLOv3: An Incremental Improvement. Source. https://arxiv.org/abs/1804.02767. Accessed 14 Aug 2019
13. MOT16 Results. https://motchallenge.net/results/MOT16. Accessed 14 Aug 2019
14. He, K., Zhang, X., Ren, S., Sun, J.: Deep residual learning for image recognition. In: IEEE Conference on Computer Vision and Pattern Recognition, pp. 770–778. IEEE, Las Vegas (2016)
15. Wu, L., Chunhua, S., Hengel, A.: PersonNet: person re-identification with deep convolutional neural networks. https://arxiv.org/pdf/1601.07255.pdf. Accessed 14 Aug 2019
16. Kuhn, H.W.: The Hungarian method for the assignment problem. Naval Res. Logistics Q. **2**, 83–97 (1995)
17. Bogush, R., Maltsev, S.: Minimax criterion of similarity for video information processing. In: Siberian Conference on Control and Communications, pp. 120–127. IEEE, Tomsk (2007)
18. Person Re-ID (PRID) Dataset. https://www.tugraz.at/institute/icg/research/team-bischof/lrs/downloads/prid11/. Accessed 14 Aug 2019
19. iLIDS Video re-IDentification (iLIDS-VID) Dataset. http://www.eecs.qmul.ac.uk/~xiatian/downloads_qmul_iLIDS-VID_ReID_dataset.html. Accessed 14 Aug 2019
20. Keni, B., Stiefelhagen, R.: Evaluating multiple object tracking performance: the CLEAR MOT metrics. EURASIP J. Image Video Process. **1**, 1–10 (2008)
21. King, D.W.: Dlib-ml. machine learning toolkit. J. Mach. Learn. Res. **10**, 1755–1758 (2009)

Influence of Control Parameters and the Size of Biomedical Image Datasets on the Success of Adversarial Attacks

Vassili Kovalev[1(✉)] and Dmitry Voynov[2]

[1] United Institute of Informatics Problems,
Surganova Street, 6, 220012 Minsk, Belarus
vassili.kovalev@gmail.com
[2] Belarus State University, Nezavisimosti Av, 4, 220030 Minsk, Belarus
voynovdd@gmail.com

Abstract. In this paper, we study dependence of the success rate of adversarial attacks to the Deep Neural Networks on the biomedical image type, control parameters, and image dataset size. With this work we are going to contribute towards accumulation of experimental results on adversarial attacks for the community dealing with biomedical images. The white-box Projected Gradient Descent attacks were examined based on 8 classification tasks and 13 image datasets containing a total of 605,080 chest X-ray and 317,000 histology images of malignant tumors. We concluded that: (1) An increase of the amplitude of perturbation in generating malicious adversarial images leads to a growth of the fraction of successful attacks for the majority of image types examined in this study. (2) Histology images tend to be less sensitive to the growth of amplitude of adversarial perturbations. (3) Percentage of successful attacks is growing with an increase of the number of iterations of the algorithm of generating adversarial perturbations with an asymptotic stabilization. (4) It was found that the success of attacks dropping dramatically when the original confidence of predicting image class exceeds 0.95. (5) The expected dependence of percentage of successful attacks on the size of image training set was not confirmed.

Keywords: Adversarial attacks · X-ray images · Histology images

1 Introduction

1.1 The Problem of Security of Computerized Diagnosis

It is well recognized that the security issues of computerized disease diagnosis are of paramount importance. Recently, the Deep Learning technologies gave the community well-grounded promises to become an effective tool in biomedical image analysis and computerized diagnosis [1, 2]. Currently, a large fraction of studies focused on the development of increasingly more accurate models while less attention has been given to the security and robustness of these models. Unfortunately, it was found that along with the high success, the Deep Learning brought some new security problems. This time the security worries arose from the vulnerability of methods capitalizing on Deep

© Springer Nature Switzerland AG 2019
S. V. Ablameyko et al. (Eds.): PRIP 2019, CCIS 1055, pp. 301–311, 2019.
https://doi.org/10.1007/978-3-030-35430-5_25

Neural Networks (DNN) to so-called adversarial attacks. The vulnerability to adversarial image examples was first noticed in [3] and more systematically discussed by researchers from Google in [4]. A bit later, in 2015-2016 a group of researchers has provided several examples of the vulnerability of DNNs to adversarial attacks [5]. It was experimentally proven that adversarial attacks may lead to failures in making correct classification decision. In the context of Computer Assisted Diagnosis (CAD) systems this corresponds to possible failures in correct disease diagnosis. Contrary to the "traditional" computer viruses, these attacks are performed with the help of so-called adversarial images which are nothing but specially crafted images that push DNNs to wrong classification decisions. More recently, there have been several works published on the problem of adversarial attacks, their types, and possible ways of defense (see, for example, surveys [6, 7] and paper [8]).

1.2   Basic Properties of Adversarial Attacks and the Purpose of This Study

In general, the problem of adversarial attack is not studied well as yet. Moreover, several key points that have been discovered recently are counter-intuitive. The basic properties of adversarial attacks were intensively studied in [3, 4, 8] and illustrated on large image datasets coming from computer vision applications. In our view, the most interesting facts and statements from papers [3, 4, 8] which are relevant to the present study are as follows:

- The state-of-the-art DNNs demonstrate good generalization performance on different image classification tasks with high variability of image objects and backgrounds. Thus, we can expect such networks should be robust to small perturbations of input images. However, it is shown that very tiny and even imperceptible non-random (i.e., intentional, malicious, adversarial) image modifications could totally change the network's prediction result.
- The adversarial images which were specially crafted to attack one specific DNN are statistically hard to correctly classify for other DNNs too. This holds true even under condition the other DNNs are of different architecture, trained with different parameters and even on different image subsets.
- A popular approach in computer vision is to use convolutional network features as space where Euclidean distance approximates perceptual distance. However, this resemblance is clearly flawed if images that have an immeasurably small perceptual distance correspond to completely different classes in the network's representation.

It should be noted, though, that the majority of activities on studying adversarial attacks and possible methods of defense are carried out in the field of computer vision but not in the biomedical imaging domain.

Thus, the purpose of this paper is to study dependence of the success rate of adversarial attacks on the image type, image dataset size, and control parameters. In a more general context, with this work we are going to contribute towards accumulation of experimental materials on adversarial attacks for the biomedical imaging community.

2 Original Image Data

For studying adversarial attacks, we have selected two different kinds of biomedical images. The first image type is represented by chest X-ray images which often used in a screening for detecting lung diseases, diseases of cardiovascular system, and skeletal abnormalities as well as for monitoring various treatment processes. The second image type was represented by color histological images which are continuously playing the role of a gold standard in cancer diagnosis. These two opposite image types were chosen for experimentation because chest X-rays holding certain anatomical shape with the relatively high role of spatial, "geometrical" structure whereas the histological images can be viewed as a "shape-free" color texture.

2.1 Chest X-Ray Images

Norm of Chest X-Ray (X-Norm-All). All X-ray image data used with this study were the natively-digital X-ray scans which were extracted from a PACS system. The PACS records contain information on the results of a periodic chest screening of the population of a two-million city conducted during the years 2001–2014. Thus, the reduced version of the database we used here contains a total of 1,908,926 records. Each record corresponds to a single digital chest X-ray image. All the records also included data on patients' age, gender, and textual radiological reports. The reports are written in a free-form native, non-English language. Each report was made by an experienced radiologist. In complicated cases these reports were resulted from a joint image reading by a small board of radiologists. All the radiologists were employed in the framework of a large-scale telemedicine screening system on a permanent basis.

Pathology of Chest X-Ray (X-Path-All). Similar to the Norm, labeling of abnormal lung cases was done using a keyword match in the textual descriptions. As a result, 22,355 cases were labeled as belonging to the class of pneumosclerosis, 9,285 items were recognized as emphysema, 19,844 images were categorized to the fibrosis, 5,718 images got labels of "pneumonia", 2,897 lungs were recognized as the ones with focal shadows, 821 subjects were classified to the class of having bronchitis, and 793 cases have received the label of "tuberculosis". It should be appropriately stressed that one single case may have several labels of abnormality simultaneously. Also, it should be remembered that here we are dealing with the screening data. This particularly means that the above lung disease labels are preliminary and are not confirmed clinically. In other words, we should admit the presence of certain bias which is caused by over-estimation of the probability of presence of pathological changes what is natural for the screening stage. Finally, as a result of the above selection procedure, we end up with a total of 46,882 X-ray scans presenting various lung abnormalities.

The radiological reports present information on possible lung diseases, diseases of cardiovascular system (heart and blood vessels), and information on possible skeletal abnormalities such as scoliosis, deformation of ribs, etc. The list of lung abnormalities included pneumosclerosis, emphysema, fibrosis, pneumonia, focal shadows, bronchitis, and lung tuberculosis. Technically, all the X-ray scans were represented by 1-channel

16-bit non-compressed images which were originally stored in DICOM format. The image resolution varied from rarely occurred small size of 520 × 576 pixels to relatively large fraction which was sized to 2800 × 2531 pixels. Since all the images were natively digital, there were no film scanning artifacts presented in the image data.

An image was categorized into the class of Norm if there were no visible signs of any type of abnormalities in mediastinum, skeleton and the lungs themselves. Normal cases were selected from the database by way of parsing of radiological reports with the help of a small set of a limited number of key phrases the radiologists typically use to label images with the absence of any visible abnormalities. Because the well sufficient amount of images of the Norm was available, the only strict matches of the report texts with one of the key phrases have been considered. A small fraction of technically unusable images was discarded by the same reason. Following this procedure, a total of 1,215,648 cases were stored to the basic image dataset referred to as X-Norm-All which was used as a repository of the chest X-Ray of Norm in this study.

2.2   Histology Images

Ovary and Thyroid Cancer (H-OV-TH). The test histology image dataset was acquired from 46 patients with confirmed diagnosis of Ovary cancer (23 patients) and Thyroid cancer (23 other patients). All the data were sub-sampled from a private database resulted from previous project on studying angiogenesis of malignant tumors. Tissue probes represented tumor regions and surrounding non-tumor tissue which is conditionally termed here as Norm. After biopsy the issue samples were immunohistochemically processed using D2–40 mesothelial marker for highlighting tumor angiogenesis. An intermediate image dataset consisting of 4000 images and representing 4 classes including Ovary Tumor (H-OV-T, 1000 images), Ovary Norm (H-OV-N, 1000 images), Thyroid Tumor (H-TH-T, 1000 images), and Thyroid Norm (H-TH-N) was acquired with the help of fully-digital Leica DMD108 optical microscope. Finally, to be used for benchmarking the adversarial attacks, the intermediate color images of 2048 × 1536 pixels in size were partitioned into 256 × 256 sections without overlap. This procedure resulted in the histology image dataset H-OV-TH consisting of a total of 192,000 images, 48,000 images in each of four of above abbreviated classes.

Breast Cancer (H-BR). Brest cancer histology images employed with this study were sampled from a dataset of 500 whole slide Hematoxylin-Eosin stained images used for benchmarking of methods of prediction of breast cancer proliferation score [9]. A total of 125,000 color images of 256 × 256 pixels in size representing malignant tumors (H-BR-N, 62,500 images) and areas not affected by tumors (H-BR-N, 62,500 images, conditionally referred here to as Norm) were arbitrary sampled from 500 whole slide images on the highest resolution level.

2.3   Study Groups

Adversarial attacks were examined with the help of dedicated study groups presented in Table 1 together with their key characteristics.

Table 1. Study groups and their characteristics

Image type	Acronym	Classification task	N img total	N img by classes	CLS score
X-ray, Norm	X-NR2	2 age groups: G1: 20-35 years G2 50-70 years	200,000	G1: 100,000 G2: 100,000	0.98
X-ray, Norm	X-NR3	2 age groups: G1: 17-24 years G2: 25-41 years G3: 42-80 years	550,080	G1: 183,360 G2: 183,360 G3: 183,360	0.83
X-ray, region of Aorta	X-AO	2 classes: C1: Aorta with anterior rotation C2: Norm	27,000	C1: 10,980 C2: 16,020	0.78
X-ray, Tuberculosis	X-TB	2 classes: C1: Tuberculosis C2: Norm	28,000	C1: 14,000 (1,369) C2: 14,000	0.82
Histology, Ovary cancer	H-OV	2 classes: C1: Tumor C2: Norm	96,000	C1: 48,000 C2: 48,000	0.92
Histology, Cancer of Thyroid gland	H-TH	2 classes: C1: Tumor C2: Norm	96,000	C1: 48,000 C2: 48,000	0.94
Histology, Ovary cancer and Cancer of Thyroid gland	H-OV-TH	4 classes: C1: Ovary Tumor C2: Ovary Norm C3: Thyroid Tumor C2: Thyroid Norm	192,000	C1: 48,000 C2: 48,000 C3: 48,000 C4: 48,000	0.91
Histology, Breast cancer	H-BR	2 classes: C1: Tumor C2: Norm	125,000	C1: 62,500 C2: 62,500	0.97

For brevity purposes the necessary explanations on creation of study groups provided below in an itemized style.

1. Groups X-NR2 and X-NR3 of chest images of Norm of subjects of different ages constitute good test bed for classification tasks due to known age-related changes. In both cases the main principles for selecting images from original dataset X-Norm-All containing 1,215,648 items was to preserve gender balance as well as equivalent population of classification sub-groups.
2. In the aorta classification tasks X-AO the areas containing anterior regions of aorta were extracted automatically from original X-ray images and final results were examined visually. Since original images were of different size, these regions re-scaled to 256×256 based on individual resolution.
3. Due to the lack of lung tuberculosis images, the available dataset of 1,369 images was inputted to a dedicated augmentation procedure to finally get 14,000 items. Note that this is *only the case* in this study where the augmentation procedure was used.
4. The last column of Table 1 presents the original classification accuracy.

In all the occasions except for classification tasks X-NR3 the images used for experimentation on adversarial attacks were 256×256 pixels in size. Examples of input images used in adversarial experiments are presented in Figs. 1 and 2.

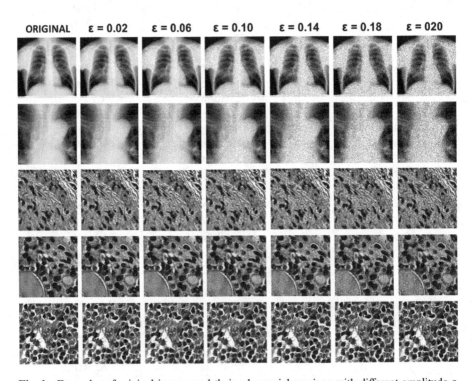

Fig. 1. Examples of original images and their adversarial versions with different amplitude ε.

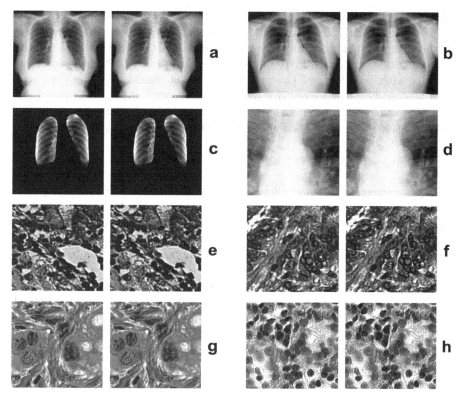

Fig. 2. Examples of successful attacks. Each image pair shows original image (left) and its adversarial version (on the right): (a) Aged person from the group 50–70 recognized as young one from the 20–35 group. (b) Young male subject from the group G1 aged 17–24 of classification task X-NR3 categorized to 42–80 group G3. (c) Tuberculosis patient misclassified to Norm. (d) Normal aorta misclassified as Pathology. (e) Normal Ovary tissue diagnosed as Cancerous. (f) Tissue of Thyroid Gland recognized as Ovary. (g) Breast cancer misclassified as Norm. (h) Fragment of image with normal tissue of breast was wrongly identified as being malignant.

3   Experimental Setup

The image data of each study group presented in Table 1 were split into the training and validation datasets in the proportion of 80/20 keeping same balance of class representatives. After that we trained several neural networks, one for each study group. The achieved classification scores are listed in last column of the Table 1. In order to reduce the variability of essential parameters, we used well known Inception V3 architecture as a single model and AdamOptimizer training optimizer.

As soon as the training was completed, we started to examine adversarial attacks. Usually generation of adversarial images is performed by applying specific intensity modifications to original images for producing their adversarial versions. Depending on what information are needed to generate adversarial examples the algorithms are categorized into the white-box and black-box attacks. For white-box methods architecture of network and trained weights should be available. Furthermore, in some cases loss function and training optimizer are also required. For black-box attacks the necessary information include the type of images that classified by DNN. In this paper we study the white-box Projected Gradient Descent (PGD) attacks algorithm. This algorithm is of gradient-based type. That means that the source of perturbations is a gradient of some function taken from DNN that can be calculated rapidly with the help of backpropagation technique. The formula of PGD attack is given by:

$$x_{k+1} = x_k - lr * \text{Clip}_{x,\varepsilon}\left(\nabla_x\left(y_p(x_k)\right)\right), k \in [0, max\_iter - 1] \tag{1}$$

In this equation the following three parameters are introduced: maximal amplitude of perturbation ε, number of executed iterations max_iter and the learning rate coefficient lr. In this work, we are focusing on examining the influence of ε and max_itert. The learning rate was not changed during the experiments and the same value of it was used for all classification tasks. Finally, we carry out the experiments in the following way:

(1) Define the set of values of ε which is going to be examined.

(2) For every value of ε and every image x in validation set of a classification task generate adversarial image x_k by formula (1), where k iterates from 1 to max_iter.

(3) Save probabilities that were predicted by DNN for adversarial images. We don't need to store the images themselves because saving logits is enough to perform further analysis.

4 Results

The experimentation pipeline described above was executed for all image datasets listed in Table 1. Values of the amplitude of perturbation ε were sampled evenly from the interval ranged from 0.02 to 0.20 with a step of 0.02 what is resulted in 10 repetitions of computational experiments. Examples of original images and their adversarial versions with different amplitude ε are given in Fig. 1. Eight illustrative examples of successful attacks are shown in Fig. 2. In all these attacks the adversarial image examples were created using amplitude $\varepsilon = 0.02$ and the number of iterations $N_I = 20$.

In order to assess the results of the attacks, we calculated the fraction of the images that have been misclassified. The "native" misclassifications made by DNN which are not related to attacks are not counted. We referred to this measure of success as the *Attack success rate*. At the first step we studied the dependency of the attack success rate on the perturbation amplitude ε. Motivation for looking onto this relation steams from the idea that permission to generate more perturbations with larger magnitude should lead to a higher attack rate. This is expected due to the nature of adversarial examples which is explained in [5]. Indeed, allowing the algorithm to search examples in a wider neighborhood gives it a greater chance to detect proper perturbations. The results summarized in form of corresponding plots of Fig. 3a suggest that the proposed idea is almost right: for 7 out of 8 datasets the expectation was confirmed.

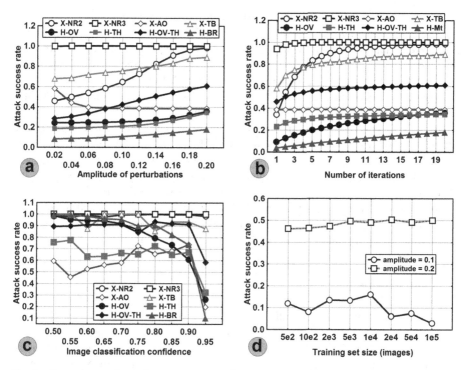

Fig. 3. Dependence of attack success rate on the amplitude of perturbations (a) the number of iterations (b) image classification confidence (c) and the size of image training set.

It should be noted that the nature of adversarial examples does not prove the statement in a formal way. As our algorithm moves in direction of gradient with fixed lr there is no warranty that heavier perturbations would not "overstep" the desired class. This could be the reason that the plot corresponding to the X-AO dataset demonstrates sort of descending behavior.

For better understanding of significance of the number of iterations, we have considered dependency of attack success rate on it. In general, the step-by-step modification of input images should gradually increase the rate and asymptotically become a constant when the amount of perturbation is high enough and almost every pixel lies on defined boundary. In this study such an assumption was confirmed what is evident from Fig. 3b.

As it can be seen from the figure, in 6 out of 8 datasets the limit seems to be reached while for 2 remaining the slope of plots appears to be sufficiently high.

During the experimentation it has been noticed that there is certain relation between the probability, i.e., confidence of categorization of the original, unperturbed image to a specific class and the result obtained on the subsequent step of its attack. In order to discover whether this phenomenon is regular, we have performed additional experiment which consists of the following steps:

(1) Bining the probability range of [0.5, 1.0] into 10 equal intervals (bins).

(2) Categorization of each image into one of 10 bins using its maximal probability produced by neural network. For instance, in case the output probabilities of two-class classification task predicted as [0.81, 0.19] it should be categorized into bin [0.80, 0.85].

(3) Calculate attack success rate separately for each histogram bin.

Figure 3c shows that the images failed to the bins which correspond to the highest probabilities are misclassified less often than the others. Furthermore, for image datasets H-OV and H-OV-TH this pattern is very prominent. Such a behavior could be caused by correlation between the image's probability and the size of class subspace. Namely, in case of high probability the classes' own neighborhoods should be larger.

Finally, we examined the links between the size of training image dataset and the attack success rate. To this end, we gradually increase the dataset size by way of sampling more and more images from H-BR, re-training the DNN, and attacking it again. However, results shown in Fig. 3d gives us no reason to support such a conclusion on our image datasets and conditions of experimentation.

5   Conclusions

Results reported with this study allow drawing the following conclusions.

(1) An increase of the amplitude of perturbation in generating malicious adversarial images leads to a growth of the fraction of successful attacks for the majority of image types examined in this study. The only exception was demonstrated by X-ray images of the aorta with anterior rotation which represent sort of "geometrical" kind of pathological changes.

(2) Histology images tend to be less sensitive to the growth of amplitude of adversarial perturbations.

(3) Percentage of successful attacks is growing with an increase of the number of iterations of the algorithm of generating adversarial perturbations with an asymptotic stabilization.

(4) It was found that the success of adversarial attacks dropping dramatically when the original confidence of predicting image class exceeds 0.95.

(5) Dependence of percentage of successful attacks on the size of image training set was not confirmed.

References

1. Litjens, G., Kooi, T., Bejnordi, B., Setio, A., Ciompi, F., Ghafoorian, M.: A survey on deep learning in medical image analysis. Med. Image Anal. **42**, 60–88 (2017)
2. Ker, J., Wang, L., Rao, J., Lim, T.: Deep learning applications in medical image analysis. IEEE Access **6**, 9375–9389 (2018)
3. Szegedy, C., et al.: Intriguing properties of neural networks. In: International Conference on Learning Representations (ICLR) 2014, pp. 1–10. Springer, Banff (2014)
4. Goodfellow, I., Shlens, J., Szegedy, C.: Explaining and harnessing adversarial examples (2015). arXiv preprint. arXiv:1412.6572v3

5. Papernot, N., McDaniel, P., Jhay, S., Fredriksonz, M., Celik, Z.B., Swamix, A.: The Limitations of Deep Learning in Adversarial Settings (2015). arXiv preprint arXiv:1511:07528v1
6. Akhtar, N., Mian, A.S.: Threat of adversarial attacks on deep learning in computer vision. IEEE Access **6**, 14410–14430 (2018)
7. Ozdag, M.: Adversarial attacks and defenses against deep neural networks: a survey. Procedia Comput. Sci. **140**, 152–161 (2018)
8. Madry, A., Makelov, A., Schmidt, L., Tsipras, D., Vladu, A.: Towards Deep Learning Models Resistant to Adversarial Attacks. arXiv preprint (2017). arXiv:1706.06083v3
9. Veta, M., Heng, Y.J., Stathonikos, N., et al.: Predicting breast tumor proliferation from whole-slide images. Med. Image Anal. **54**, 111–121 (2019)

Author Index